Washington, D.C.

- D.C., Inside the Diamond
- Northern Virginia
- Maryland: North by Northwest
- Maryland: East and South
- Originals, Oddballs and Outliers
- Kids' Rides

By Matt

Where to Bike LLC

Email: mail@wheretobikeguides.com
Tel: +61 2 4274 4884 - Fax: +61 2 4274 0988
www.wheretobikeguides.com

First published in the USA in 2011 by Where to Bike LLC.

Design and Layout - Justine Powell
Advertising - Phil Latz
Photography - All photos taken by Matt Wittmer unless otherwise specified
Mapping - Mapping Specialists Ltd
Printed in China by RR Donnelley

Cover: Photo by Matt Wittmer

Library of Congress Control Number: 2011923126
Author: Wittmer, Matt
Title: Where to Bike Washington, D.C.
ISBN: 978-0-9808755-2-2 (pbk.)
978-0-9808755-3-9 (box set)

The Cycling Kangaroo logo is a trademark of Lake Wangary Publishing Company Pty Ltd.

Where to Bike is a proud sponsor of World Bicycle Relief.

Where to Bike is a proud member of the Bikes Belong Coalition, organisers of the People for Bikes campaign.

peopleforbikes.org

Also in this series:

Where to Ride Melbourne
Where to Ride Adelaide
Where to Ride Perth
Where to Ride Sydney
Where to Ride Canberra
Where to Ride South East Queensland
Where to Ride Tasmania
Where to Ride Western & Northern Victoria
Where to Ride Eastern Victoria
Where to Ride Sydney MTB
Where to Ride London
Where to Bike Philadelphia

Coming Soon:

Where to Bike Los Angeles
Where to Bike San Francisco
Where to Bike New York City
Where to Ride Auckland
Where to Bike Portland
Where to Bike Orange County
Where to Bike Los Angeles MTB

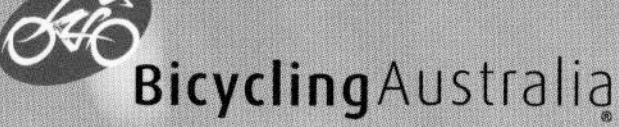

About us...

Cycling has many health and environmental benefits, but apart from these it's a fun leisure time activity for all ages. Most of our small team are active cyclists; we love to ride and hope that we can, through interesting, exciting and timely information, make your cycling experience more enjoyable.

Founded 20 years ago by Phil and Catie Latz, Lake Wangary Publishing Company began with a single black and white road cycling magazine. We now publish four cycling magazines as well as the growing series of Where to Ride guides in Australia, New Zealand, the UK and now Where to Bike in the United States.

We're committed to our vision of enhancing all aspects of cycling by providing information for all our customers. Whether through our magazines or books, we hope to make your riding experience as enjoyable as possible.

Look out for BA Press books and the 'cycling kangaroo' logos in newsstands and bookstores; it's your key to great cycling publications.

We have made every effort to ensure the accuracy of the content of this book, but please feel free to contact us at mail@wheretobikeguides.com to report any changes to routes or inconsistencies you may find.

For more information about *Where to Bike Washington, D.C.* and other books in this series, go to www.wheretobikeguides.com.

Washington, D.C.

Contents

D.C., Inside the Diamond

Northern Virginia

Kids' Rides

D.C. Diamond

Northern Virginia

Maryland: North by Northwest

Maryland: East and South

D.C. Originals

Author's Note

I wish I could say I rode 10,000 miles through the course of an entire year to place this book directly in your hands, but the truth of the matter is it was nearer nine thousand. Hard to believe, I know. And quite a boast, I realize. But I thought it a good idea to get any trust issues out in the open right up front. We're tethered now, and you should know straightaway that these pages come from a place of intense pride, and purpose.

While you've been doing what you do, I've been living what you're holding, and the care you take in your job is the care I took in mine. Though it did entail a considerable amount of the joyriding you might be imagining, producing this book was the hardest work I've ever done.

Instead of writing a book, in fact, I feel I've actually ridden one. The research was riding. The mapping was riding. The photography was riding. The text itself? Okay, written, but you get the point. My hope is the time spent shows. I took the turns you won't have to and dedicate these remaining 1289.3 miles to your riding pleasure.

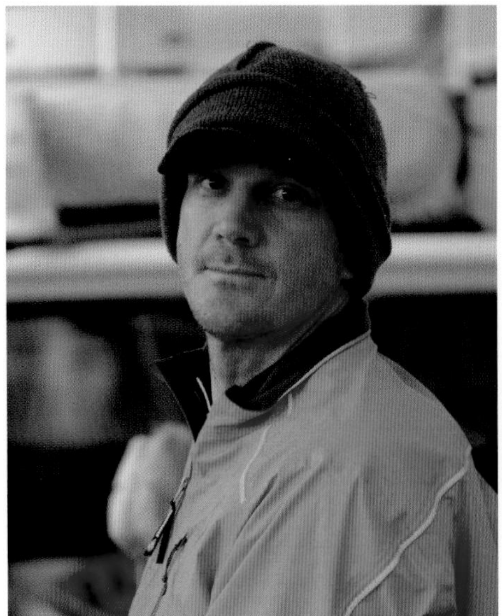

Photo by Elena Wigelsworth.

A project of this magnitude demands winnowing. Hundreds of pictures culled from thousands. Dozens of ride options reduced to a select few. Some chosen routes, such as Ride 18, include only a portion of what could be a much longer excursion. Most ride lengths, however, reflect the total miles possible, with the idea that given its neatly packaged entirety, you'd be free to make informed decisions for yourself. Ride 19 fits this mold.

In my estimation *Where to Bike Washington, D.C.* is best described as a travel guide for locals. Though you may journey around the world, in a region as large and varied as ours, you're a traveler here at home too. This book encourages, then, the cross-pollination of transplanted Marylanders with die-hard Virginians and the famous transients of D.C. with each of the former.

The capital region is a living organism, its people, its politics, its cement and steel, all continually in flux. Biking brings one closer than anything short of construction work to the bare dynamics of that change, and I've literally felt the area transform beneath my wheels throughout this endeavor. Scores of paths were added or refurbished. Bike lanes were laid by the tens of miles. Bikeshare came to town. D.C. now appears dead set on becoming a model for cycling throughout the country, and this book bears the marks of that commitment.

If you're still doubting my nine thousand, I recently met a rider who commutes over 30 miles per workday from near Fort Hunt, Virginia to the FBI Building downtown. The math I leave to you. Now that you're the proud owner of this book, your destiny is racking up the miles too. Which means you'll soon have some rides of your own. To share them, or voice any other comments, questions, or concerns, please connect by way of Facebook, Twitter, or at wheretobikewashingtondc.com.

Happy riding..!

Matt Wittmer
Author and photographer

About the Author

After a period of semi-retirement in his late 20s, Matt Wittmer chanced upon a second career in the world of bikes. A long ride to graduate school fed a love of the road and more adventure cycling followed. Writing about those trips followed in kind, photos too, and swiftly thereafter, cycling advocacy, and now authorship. An all-weather, all-continents bike rider, he divides his time between Washington, D.C. and wherever else affords him the privilege.

Acknowledgements

Heaps of thanks to the knowledgeable and gracious folks at Bicycling Australia, who gave me the freedom to have fun and the guidance to do what needed to get done. To Justine and Jody especially, though I've never heard your voices, your wise instruction rings through this book strong and true. And thanks be to the Mapping Specialists, D.C. Public Library's Washingtoniana Division, the Louis Stokes Health Sciences Library at Howard University, Bike and Roll D.C., and each and every one of the people (and parents of little people) who responded positively to my often frantic pleas for pictures. You all made my days.

"I tried to write poems like the songs they sang on Seventh Street," wrote Langston Hughes of his time in Washington, D.C., songs with "the pulse beat of the people who keep on going." This book is dedicated to those who keep on going, cyclists and otherwise, and to Mom and Elena, my champions.

Introduction

This book details 55 adult and 39 kids' rides centered upon the District of Columbia and spread within a radius approaching 50 miles from downtown D.C. throughout the greater metropolitan area. Many rides begin, pass, or finish within sight of the capital's famous monuments and memorials and have been designed with Metro trains in mind. Even more remain within easy reach of public transportation yet cover realms of serenity, natural beauty, and historic or contemporary import too often hidden from the everyday. Still others manage to slip the sometimes surly bonds of the city and suburbs altogether and break away into the great green spaces of Virginia horse country, along the shaded, blue waterways of Maryland, and into the rolling, tree-lined farmland of the mid-Atlantic.

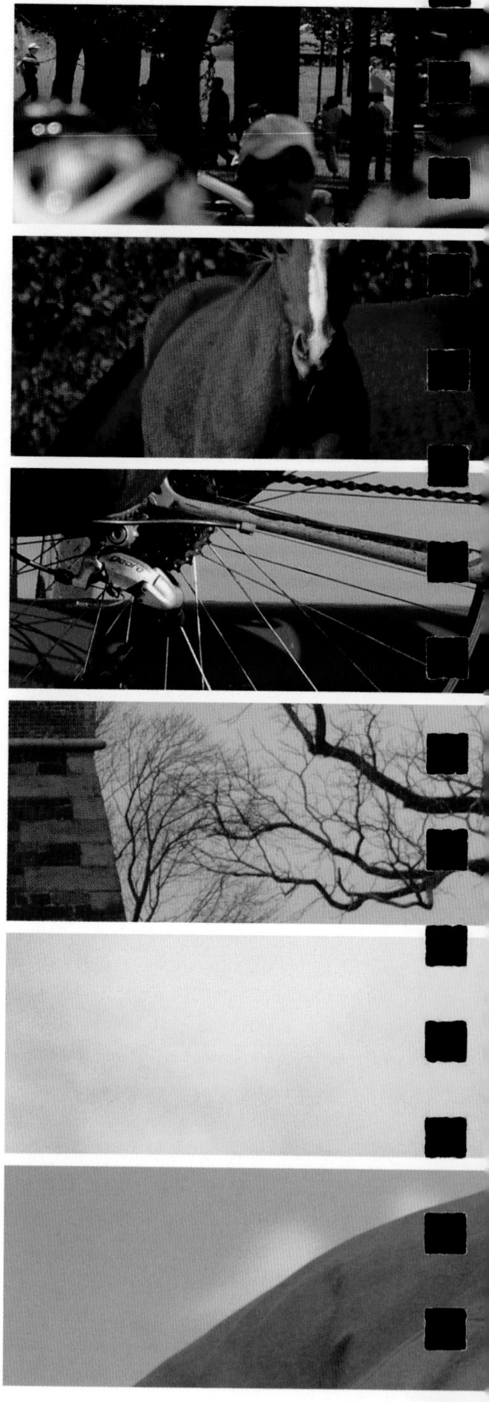

From short, safe paths directly down the street to challenging adventures bridging two states, from historic tours through revived neighborhoods, to brand-new stream valley trails on the area's outskirts, from established local classics to rides traversing freshly-minted bicycle lanes, from brushing the Potomac River, to skirting Chesapeake Bay, to skating the easternmost edge of the Blue Ridge Mountains, this truly comprehensive book plants its routes throughout the entire region.

Twelve core rides explore the thriving, historic spaces once included within the old boundaries of the District in a section called D.C., Inside the Diamond. Thirty-three others travel the variable landscapes of three distinct areas in groups of eleven each named Northern Virginia, Maryland: North by Northwest, and Maryland: East and South. And one section, entitled Originals, Oddballs, and Outliers, spans the others and extends region-wide, with the bonus of reaching beyond it.

Adult sections are designed in light of terrain, quality of cycling options, existing cycling infrastructure, and points of interest. And while all five employ varying ranges of difficulty, each offers an equally unique invitation to enjoy the D.C. area by bike and each aims to accommodate all riders, younger, older, hyper-fit, or those not quite there yet. With that in mind, a concluding kids' chapter presents a diverse array of safe, short, and fun family-centered rides for the learners ever among us.

Ride Overview

D.C., Inside the Diamond

Page	Ride	Ride Name	Terrain	Distance (miles)	WTB Rating	Kid Friendly
30	1	Iconic D.C.	Path On-Road	7.8	1	
34	2	Iconic D.C. Too	Path On-Road	13.9	2	
40	3	Lower Rock Creek	Path	9.0	1	
44	4	Upper Rock Creek	On-Road	8.1	1	partly
48	5	The National Arboretum	On-Road	5.0	1	
52	6	The KeyChain	Path On/Off-Road	14.2	3	partly
56	7	Arlington Trails	Path On-Road	17.1	2	partly
60	8	The Mount Vernon Trail North	Path On-Road	16.6	2	partly
64	9	Alexandria Old Towner	Path On-Road	9.8	1	
68	10	Capitol Hill and the Waterfront	Path On-Road	11.8	1	
72	11	Neighborhoods MidCity	Path On-Road	12.0	2	
76	12	Neighborhoods Northwest	On-Road	9.4	2	

Northern Virginia

Page	Ride	Ride Name	Terrain	Distance (miles)	WTB Rating	Kid Friendly
84	13	Purcellville North	Path On-Road	31.3	5	
88	14	Purcellville South	On-Road	35.2	5	
92	15	Middleburg	On-Road	24.8	4	
96	16	The Plains	On-Road	34.6	5	
100	17	Nokesville	On-Road	43.1	5	
104	18	The Cross County Trail	Path Off-Road	8.45	1	
108	19	The W&OD Rail Trail	Path	44.6	5	partly
112	20	The Mount Vernon Trail South	Path On-Road	20.6	3	partly
116	21	Mason Neck	Path On-Road	9.0	1	
120	22	Prince William Forest	Path On-Road	11.6	2	partly
124	23	Two Fairfax County Lakes	Path Off-Road	11.5	2	

Maryland: North by Northwest

Page	Ride	Ride Name	Terrain	Distance (miles)	WTB Rating	Kid Friendly
132	24	Sugarloaf Mountain	On-Road	34.3	5	
136	25	Rounding Triadelphia Reservoir	On-Road	53.0	5	
140	26	Magruder Branch–Damascus	Path	6.4	1	

144	27	The Rockville Millennium Trail	Path On-Road	13.35	2	partly
148	28	The Capital Crescent	Path On/Off-Road	23.5	3	partly
152	29	Poolesville	On-Road	26.1	3	
156	30	Rock Creek–Lake Needwood	Path	28.6	3	partly
160	31	Glen Echo–Potomac Loop	Path On-Road	13.55	2	partly
164	32	The Seneca Aqueduct Loop	On-Road	41.5	4	
168	33	The Matthew Henson Trail	Path	8.95	1	
172	34	Takoma Park–Sligo Creek	Path On-Road	18.3	2	partly

Maryland: East and South

Page	Ride	Ride Name	Terrain	Distance (miles)	WTB Rating	Kid Friendly
178	35	Anacostia Tributary Trails	Path On-Road	16.6	3	partly
182	36	National Harbor–Woodrow Wilson Bridge	Path Off-Road	6.5	1	
186	37	Merkle Wildlife Sanctuary	On-Road	23.0	3	
190	38	The WB&A Rail Trail	Path On-Road	11.4	1	
194	39	Henson Creek–Fort Washington	Path On-Road	35.0	4	
198	40	The BWI to the B&A and Back	Path	40.2	4	partly
202	41	Chesapeake Beach	On-Road	36.4	5	
206	42	BARC Loop	On-Road	17.7	2	
210	43	Smallwood	On-Road	21.6	3	
214	44	Around La Plata	On-Road	37.7	5	
218	45	The Indian Head Rail Trail	Path	26.0	2	partly

Originals, Oddballs and Outliers

Page	Ride	Ride Name	Terrain	Distance (miles)	WTB Rating	Kid Friendly
224	46	The Civil War Defenses of Washington	Path/MTB On/Off-Road	55.55	5	
230	47	WABA's 13 Colonies	On-Road	15.6	3	
234	48	WABA's 50 States	On-Road	65.5	5	
240	49	Booth's Flight	On-Road	51.1	5	
244	50	To Baltimore	Path On-Road	35.8	4	
248	51	The C&O Towpath to Great Falls	Path Off-Road	29.0	3	
252	52	White's Ferry–Point of Rocks	On/Off-Road	41.1	5	
256	53	To Annapolis	Path On-Road	28.0	4	
260	54	Lincoln's Commute	On-Road	8.0	1	
264	55	When the Cherries Blossom (Two Short Rides)	Path On-Road	6.45/4.1	1	

How to Use This Book

This book's rides are separated into six color-coded subdivisions named for either the territory they explore or their specialization. Five adult chapters form the bulk of the text and are followed by a final section of children's offerings which contains rides in each major adult region.

Every individual adult ride can be easily identified by spending a quick minute with its handy At a Glance section, where along with distance and total elevation data, you'll also find information specific to the type of terrain and amount of traffic each route encounters, the nitty-gritty of getting there, a particular selection's links to other rides, and options for food, drink, and interesting side trips while out along the course.

Each numbered route is also emblazoned with icons indicating the surface types traveled along its way. These include smooth bike path separated from roads, on-road segments including bicycle lanes, relatively wide and smooth dirt off-road trails, and more narrow and challenging natural mountain bike tracks. Finally, many rides are identified even further as being distinctly kid-friendly, park-like, urban, or rural in setting or character.

An About section follows each ride's At a Glance page and provides written detail concerning the history and contemporary relevance of the varying landscapes through which each route passes, along with any other notes of special interest. Highly-detailed GPS-generated maps and ride logs also accompany each selection, and riders are encouraged to navigate their way along each course using them both in conjunction.

As a final note, Where to Bike's signature gatefold flap acts as both an overall reference aid and, when used together with its bicycle-friendly binding, provides an efficient way to mark and save the specific pages you'll need while out exploring.

Ride Scale

To cement your preparation for each ride, all 55 adult selections are graded using the standardized Where to Bike rating scale (see chart below), whereby points are awarded based on a particular route's total distance, total elevation gain, and predominant surface.

Where to Bike Washington, D.C. exists to challenge all levels of enthusiasts, but recommends that those new to cycling or those resuming the sport after a period of inactivity begin with its least demanding rides, levels 1 and 2. Once initiated, the 5-stage beginner to experienced rating system encourages novices in their efforts at becoming fully-forged masters of the craft. Look for these symbols on the introductory page of each route to help you decide which ride is currently suitable for you and which rides the future holds in store:

	1 pt	2 pts	3 pts	4 pts	5 pts
Distance – Road (miles)	<12	12-19	19-25	25-37	>37
Distance – MTB (miles)	<6	6-9	9-16	16-25	>25
Climbing (feet)	<500	500 - 1,000	1,000 - 1,500	1,500 - 2,000	>2,000
Surface	Paved smooth	Paved rough	Unpaved smooth	Unpaved moderate	Unpaved rough

Accumulated Points	Riding Level/Grade	Suggested Suitability
3	1	Beginner
4-5	2	
6-7	3	Moderately fit
8-9	4	
10+	5	Experienced cyclist

Before You Go

If you're a novice rider or returning to your regimen after a lengthy lay-off, it's wise to consult a physician before resuming activity. It's also wise to ensure your bicycle and equipment are in good working order before heading out at any time. Here are some things to double-check:

- Inflate tires to suggested air pressure and inspect for damage/embedded debris
- Check brake pads and cables
- Check gear cables and shifters
- Clean and lubricate chain
- Give bike a thorough going-over to make sure all parts articulate and are rattle-free

Visit your favored local bike shop or ask an experienced cycling friend if you're unsure about any specifics concerning these points. And before you're out the door, make sure to let somebody know where you're planning to ride and how long you're likely to be away.

What to Take

Most of this book's rides keep you squarely within, or at least within easy reach, of civilization, but there are those few select offerings which bring you miles into the countryside. Regardless of where your route takes you, it makes good sense to keep this list of essential items forever at hand, and when the occasion calls, these ride-specific items on tap as well (along with any others you might deem necessary).

Essentials

- Appropriately-sized bicycle helmet with correctly adjusted chin straps
- Spare inner tubes, tire levers, and flat kit
- Portable air pump/ CO2 cartridges and inflator
- Multi-use tools, chain lubricant, and other tools specific to your bicycle
- Front and rear lights
- Water in the range of one quart per hour
- A sufficient number of high energy snacks
- Identification
- Cell phone/ phone card
- Portable first aid kit
- Enough money to get you home in case of emergency
- Detailed information concerning personal medical conditions

Though that might seem like a lot, it can all be carried either on your person or inside accessories fitted properly to your bicycle (including water bottle cages, baskets, front and back wheel racks, and bags of all shapes and sizes). The more serious your hobby becomes, the more certain you'll become of not only what 'essential' means to you, but how it's best carried as well.

Optional/ Ride-specific Items

- Bike bell
- Camera
- Sunglasses
- Sunscreen
- Strong lock
- Biking shoes, gloves and gear
- Rain poncho/ all-weather clothing
- Bike computer/ GPS unit
- Waterproof storage bags
- Wet wipes
- Binoculars

WORLD BICYCLE RELIEF
worldbicyclerelief.org

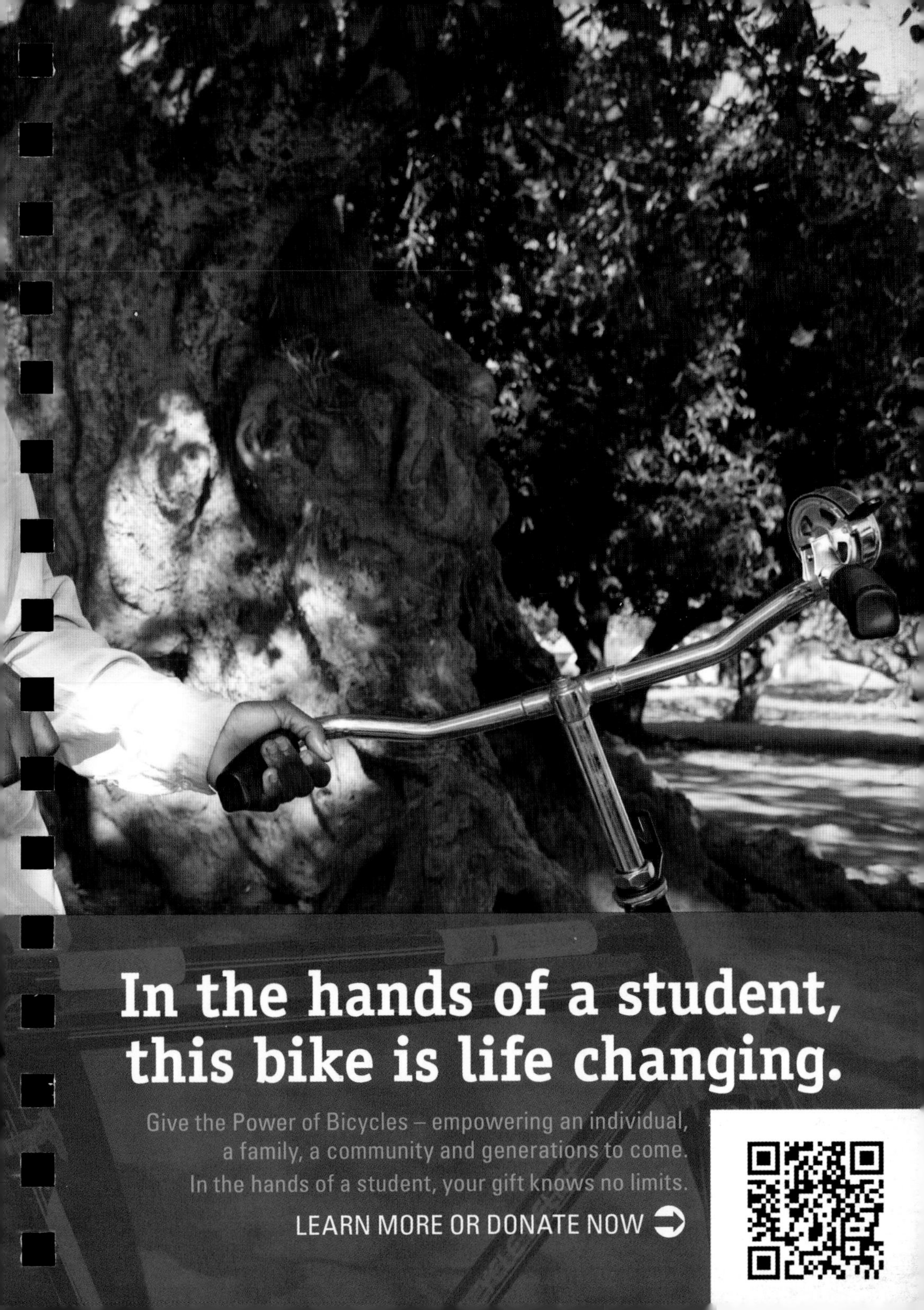
In the hands of a student,
this bike is life changing.
Give the Power of Bicycles – empowering an individual,
a family, a community and generations to come.
In the hands of a student, your gift knows no limits.
LEARN MORE OR DONATE NOW

On the Road/ On the Trail

Cycling fatalities and injuries occur each year on roads and trails through the greater Washington, D.C. area, and while this section's motive is not to scare you with cringe-worthy statistics, it does aim to make you aware that serious accidents do occur with some regularity and supply you with the tools to avoid them.

The helmet is the single most important piece of equipment in the prevention of life-threatening cycling injury. Wear it every time you ride, even on trails and seemingly benign pathways. Don't get complacent. It's unlikely anything of note will ever happen, but it can all too suddenly.

Heightened visibility also aids safety. Wear brightly colored clothes with reflective material and outfit your bicycle with head and tail lights.

Cyclists enjoy a freedom of movement other forms of transportation simply cannot match. We all appreciate the combination of speed, efficiency, and agility our bikes grant us, but we're wrong to think we can ride wherever and however we desire. Though it's easy to break the law, and hard sometimes to summon the patience and discipline not to, always remember that you are simply one among many moving objects along public roads and trails. Translated into a modest set of rules, this means, ride in the direction of traffic, stay in your lane, communicate your intentions, stop at red lights and stop signs, dismount when forced to the sidewalk, and respect those whose speeds may not match your own. Consideration helps us all.

Lastly, riding with ear plugs or headphones is not only dangerous and nature-defying, it makes communication amongst other road and trail users that much more difficult. If you must be plugged in, please keep one ear tuned to your surroundings.

Some Finer Points of Safe Riding:

- Stay right, and pass left.
- Alert other cyclists and pedestrians well in advance of passing by using a bell or vocal phrase such as, 'Passing on your left'.
- Move completely off paths, trails, and bike lanes when stopped.
- Stay single file when riding with others in crowded conditions.
- Make way for in-line skaters, fast riders, and horses.
- Yield to slower moving traffic including pedestrians, families out for a stroll, dog walkers, and young riders.
- Ride as if drivers do not see you and always attempt to make eye contact with drivers before maneuvering in the presence of vehicles.
- Watch for vehicles turning right and crossing your line of travel.
- Try to ride beyond a door's length from parked vehicles and beware of doors opening suddenly.
- Use a rearview cycling mirror.
- Use simple, straightforward hand signals when turning.
- Use turn lanes as you would when driving a vehicle.
- Use pedestrian crossings when traffic becomes overwhelming.

Given all the seeming defensive actions inherent in riding a bicycle, it's important to keep in mind that assertively claiming your place on the road or trail is equally important, especially in the city. Confident, decisive cyclists actually enhance their level of safety as well as those with which they share pathways. And it's important to remember that non-cyclists have the tendency to view all riders as one. Please ride responsibly, remembering whenever and wherever you cycle, you're the sole ambassador for all things bike.

A Few Tips for Better Biking in General:

Find a bike built for your size and riding style and get fitted by a professional.

Raise your seat. Too many riders lose power and tire quickly by sitting too low in the saddle. Seated correctly, the knee of the down-stroking leg should only be slightly bent when its respective peddle is nearest the ground.

Save those knees and increase your level of fitness by staying in easier gears and peddling more frequently than you may currently be accustomed. Somewhere between 70 and 90 revolutions per minute is recommended.

Finally, city riders should be certain to lock their bikes whenever leaving them, even for those minute-long shop stops. Use a solid steel U-lock and be sure to secure your bike to something immobile like a bike rack, street sign, parking meter, lamppost, or railing. You're best protected threading the lock through the frame and one wheel and using a second cable or U-lock to secure the opposite wheel. If your ride is equipped with a quick release seat, secure that as well. Finally, don't forget to take items with you which easily unclip, such as lights, pumps, bags, and water bottles. It may feel burdensome, but nearly every cyclist has had something stolen at one time or another and I would rather you not learn the hard way.

Ride assured the rewards of cycling greatly outnumber these scant few negatives, but in the event of bike theft, the due diligence of having taken a photo, noted your bike's frame number, and gotten it registered with the local police will go a long way toward recovery.

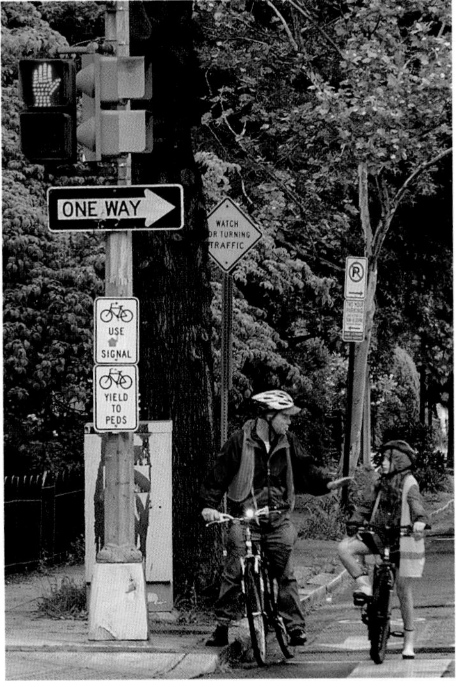

You, Your Bike and Transport in D.C.

The Washington, D.C. metropolitan region would be much less hospitable to bicycles without its extensive public transportation system, and *Where to Bike Washington, D.C.* would be less user-friendly and, perhaps, less wide-ranging, without its liberal use. Well over half this book's total rides can be easily accessed by trains or buses, and many of its adult offerings incorporate station-specific starts. When this book refers to the 'Metro' it invariably means the Washington Metropolitan Area Transit Authority's far-reaching, five-line train service, the fastest, most efficient, least-hassle-producing, and least expensive way to get you and your bike region-wide. Use its iconic map printed on the following pages and purchase a SmarTrip card for reduced fares.

WMATA oversees both the city's bus and rail service. Its **Metrotrains** allow standard-sized bicycles inside railcars all day Saturday and Sunday and weekdays at any time except 7-10 a.m. and 4-7 p.m. Bikes are free of charge, and cyclists are reminded to utilize each station's elevators and extra-wide fare gates. Currently, short rides of up to a few stops cost $1.85, and fares increase as distance traveled increases. Riders can expect to pay at or a little above $5.00 if traveling to and from stations located on opposite ends of the system.

Every **Metrobus** is also bike-accessible and equipped with a front rack capable of holding two bicycles. When using a rack, remember to remove your bike's storage containers and secure all loose items, and, as a deterrent to theft, consider locking one of your bike's wheels to its frame. Keep an eye on your bike while you ride, and let your driver know you'll be de-racking when you've reached your stop. Bikes are free of charge on buses as well, and current one-way trips cost $1.70. For complete train and bus policy, go to wmata.com and click on Getting Around to access its Bike 'N Ride information.

WMATA's **Circulator** buses also have racks. Its five lines run throughout D.C.'s core and over the Potomac River to Rosslyn, Virginia. Rides currently cost $1.00. Check dccirculator.com for route maps, hours of operation, and complete details.

And though this book won't give you reason to use the following rail services very often, if you find the need to head south or west into northern Virginia or north or west into Maryland, the following information might be of use:

VRE (Virginia Railway Express) is a commuter rail system which operates two lines out of Washington's D.C.'s Union Station. Its red line heads south to Fredericksburg and its blue southwest to Manassas. Currently, folding bicycles are permitted on all cars of all trains, while standard-size bicycles are only allowed on the last three northbound, the mid-day, any reverse-flow, and the last three southbound trains of each line. Check vre.org for more details.

MARC (Maryland Area Regional Commuter) operates a rail line running into western Maryland and two running between Baltimore and Washington, D.C.. Currently it allows for the transportation of folding bikes only. Access mta.maryland.gov/services/marc for further information.

Various public bus services also exist in greater D.C.'s suburban areas and work either in conjunction with Metro or help to extend its reach. Though it is far from impossible to access some of this book's outlying rides using these systems, it does require planning, and patience. Below are five, bike-friendly systems which could come in handy sometime down the road: Arlington Rapid Transit's ART buses; Fairfax County, Virginia's Connector fleet; Alexandria, Virginia's DASH system; Montgomery County, Maryland's Ride On routes; and the buses of the Potomac and Rappahannock Transportation Commission.

Renting a Bike

Capital Bikeshare is a self-service system with 1,100 bicycles located at 110 free-standing kiosks across Washington, D.C. and Arlington, Virginia. Its attractive, sturdy three-speeds are available 24 hours a day, 365 days a year and may be rented at any station and returned to any other. Day-long and five-day memberships, currently $5 and $15 respectively, may be purchased at any station kiosk while 30-day and annual memberships, currently $25 and $75 respectively, must be initiated using an on-line form. Subsequent to signing up, the first 30 minutes of each ride are free, and fees increase each additional half-hour. All members must be 16 years of age or older, 16 and 17 year olds must have the explicit permission of a parent or legal guardian, and all memberships require a valid credit card. Part of Capital Bikeshare's special appeal is the ease with which its portable bike stations can be relocated to reflect station use. For up-to-the-minute maps and specifics, visit capitalbikeshare.com.

Bike and Roll offers tours of D.C.'s monuments, memorials, and more, and rentals ranging from two-hours to half-days, full-days, and overnights. Its offices are located at Union Station, inside the Old Post Office Pavilion at 11th and Pennsylvania Avenue, NW, and along the waterfront in Old Town Alexandria, Virginia. Go to bikethesites.com for fees, hours, and complete details.

If these two services somehow leave you wanting, check local bike shops, as many of them rent bicycles by the day or hour as well.

Getting Your Own Bike to D.C.

For those planning on visiting the capital and bringing their own standard-size bicycles, long-distance planes, trains, and buses are all accommodating, but require additional fees, as well as partial disassembly and proper storage. Though most experienced bicycle tourists would recommend the purchase of a personal, hard-shell carrying case for bike transport, bike shops are often happy to give you one of their normally abundant cardboard shipping boxes free of charge. For detailed packaging instructions, go to adventurecycling.org and look for an article entitled 'Shipping a Bike' in its How-To Department. Ground shipping is also an option. Access bikeflights.com or shipbikes.com for rates and procedures.

Where to Bike recommends flying into Reagan National Airport when at all possible as it connects to Metrorail and makes for easier travel once on the ground. Northern Virginia's Dulles International Airport and Baltimore-Washington International Airport are also arrival options.

Though subject to change, Frontier Airlines currently leads the bikes-on-planes charge by having lowered them to only $20 with the purchase of a domestic economy ticket. At $50 per bicycle, Southwest and JetBlue are the next most accommodating airlines. Most major carriers tend to charge $100 or more per bicycle on domestic flights, and international trips are naturally almost always more expensive. The current fee for a checked bicycle on Amtrak is only $5, while interstate buses generally calculate fees based on weight and length of travel.

It should be noted that folding bicycles are quite popular in instances of long-distance travel and may be subject to different, often less involved, and less costly, shipping procedures than those outlined above.

Whichever bicycle you decide to bring to D.C. and however you choose to transport it, it's important to do two things before you set off. Always begin ironing out your travel logistics sooner than later and make sure you thoroughly follow the rules and regulations of your chosen mode. It's also a good idea to keep tools such as pedal wrenches, Allen wrenches, and packing tape on-hand for any last-minute pre-departure packaging and/or storage modifications which may arise.

System Map

Legend

- Red Line • Glenmont to Shady Grove
- Orange Line • New Carrollton to Vienna/Fairfax-GMU
- Blue Line • Franconia-Springfield to Largo Town Center
- Green Line • Branch Avenue to Greenbelt
- Yellow Line • Huntington to Fort Totten

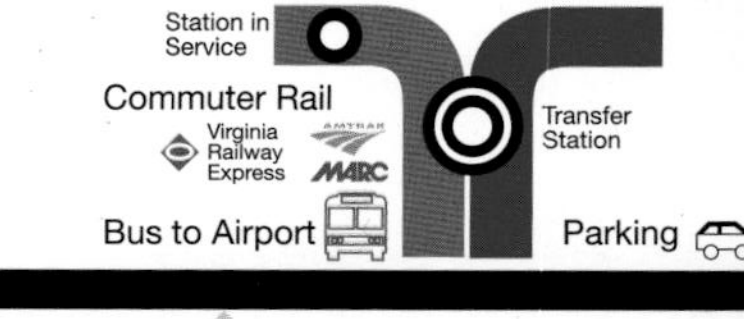

RED LINE

Shady Grove
Rockville
MARC
Twinbrook
White Flint
Grosvenor-Strathmore

Every other outbound Red Line train terminates at Grosvenor-Strathmore station Weekdays 7:00 to 9:30 a.m. and 4:00 to 6:30 p.m.

Medical Center
Bethesda
Friendship Heights
Tenleytown-AU
Van Ness-UDC
Cleveland Park
Woodley Park-Zoo/ Adams Morgan
Dupont Circle
Farragut North
Metro Center
Gallery Pl-Chinatown
Union Station
MARC
Fort Totten
Takoma
Silver Spring
MARC
Forest Glen
Wheaton
Glenmont

Capital Beltway

Montgomery County
District of Columbia
Prince George's County

Yellow Line service operates between Mt Vernon Sq/7th St-Convention Center and Fort Totten stations except Weekdays 5:00 to 9:30 a.m. and 3:00 to 7:00 p.m.

GREEN LINE

Greenbelt
B30 to BWI Thurgood Marshall Airport
MARC
College Park-U of Md
MARC
Prince George's Plaza
West Hyattsville
Georgia Ave-Petworth
Columbia Heights
U St/African-Amer Civil War Memorial/Cardozo
Shaw-Howard U
Mt Vernon Sq/7th St-Convention Center
Brookland-CUA
Rhode Island Ave-Brentwood
New York Ave-Florida Ave-Gallaudet U
McPherson Sq

New Carrollton
MARC
Landover
Cheverly
Deanwood
Minnesota Ave
...ing Road
...tol Heights

ORANGE LINE

Rosslyn
5A to Dulles Airport
Fairfax County
Arlington County
...gy Bottom-GWU
...ragut West
Ju...

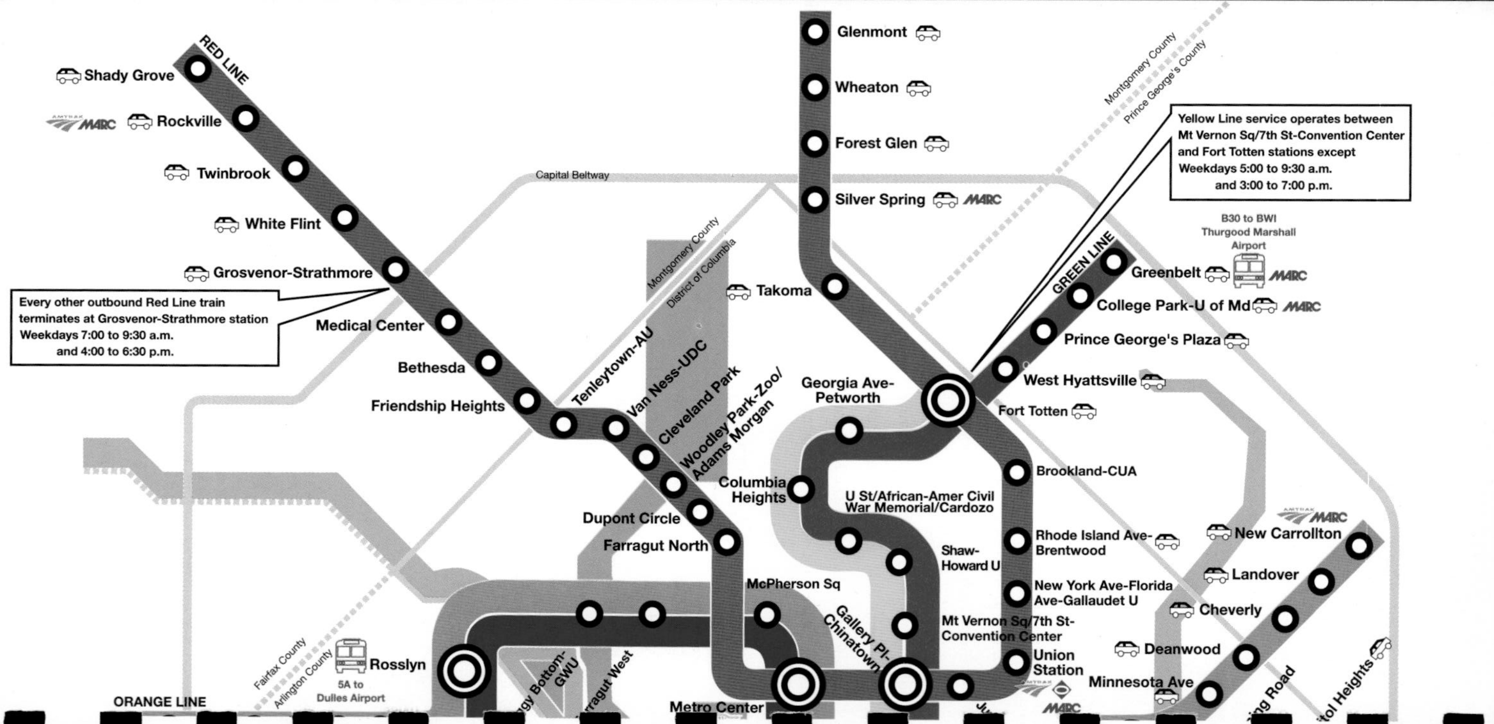

Washington, D.C.'s Metro System Map

ORANGE LINE

Vienna/Fairfax-GMU
Dunn Loring-Merrifield
West Falls Church-VT/UVA
East Falls Church
Ballston-MU
Virginia Sq-GMU
Clarendon
Court House
Rosslyn
5A to Dulles Airport
Fairfax C
Arlington Co
Foggy Botto
GWU
Farragut W
Metro Center
Federal Triangle
Smithsonian
Archives-Navy Mem'l-Penn Quarter
L'Enfant Plaza
Judiciary Sq
Station
MARC
Minnesota Ave
Benning Road
Capitol Heigh
Stadium-Armory
Potomac Ave
Eastern Market
Capitol South
Federal Center SW
Addison Road-Seat Pleasant
Morgan Boulevard
Largo Town Center
Potomac River
Arlington Cemetery
YELLOW LINE
Pentagon
Pentagon City
Crystal City
Waterfront-SEU
Navy Yard
Anacostia
Congress Heights
Southern Ave
Naylor Road
Suitland
Branch Ave
Anacostia River
Ronald Reagan Washington National Airport
Arlington County
Fairfax County
Alexandria
Van Dorn Street
Braddock Road
King Street
District of Columbia
Prince George's County
AMTRAK
BLUE LINE
Alexandria
Eisenhower Ave
Fairfax County
Capital Beltway
Huntington
Franconia-Springfield

N

Metro is accessible.

REV 09/08/08

No Smoking

No Eating or Drinking

No Animals (except service animals)

No Audio (without earphones)

No Litter or Spitting

No Dangerous or Flammable Items

Electra
Chérie
From A to Be.
© 2011 Electra Bicycle Company®, LLC.

BIKING ESSENTIALS

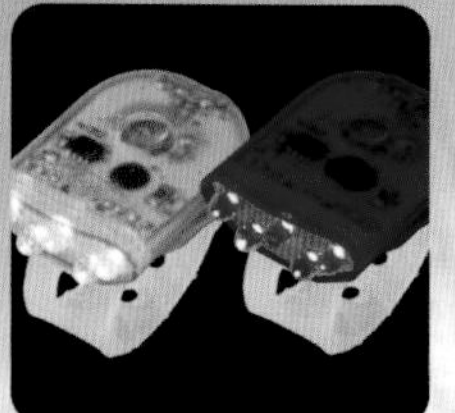

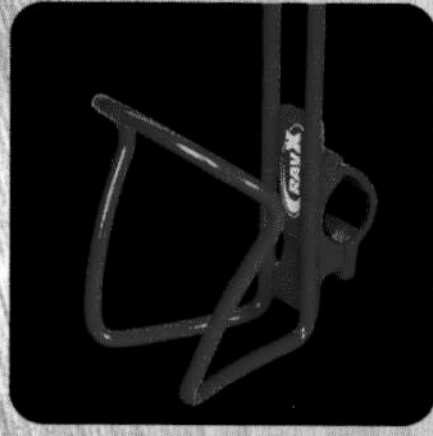

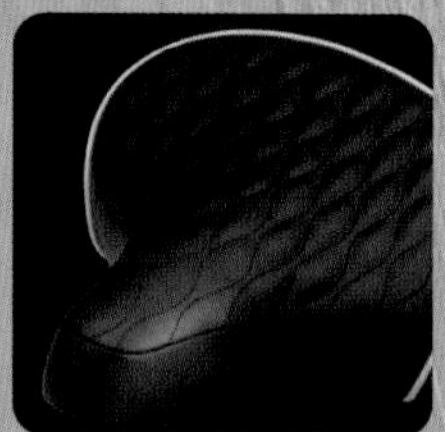
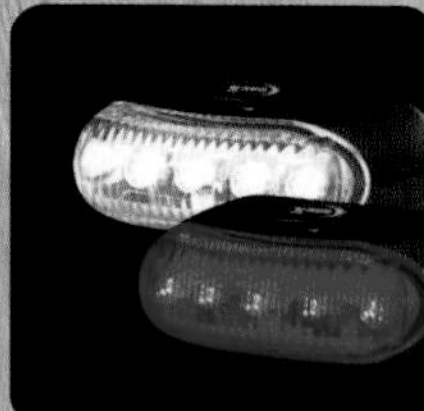
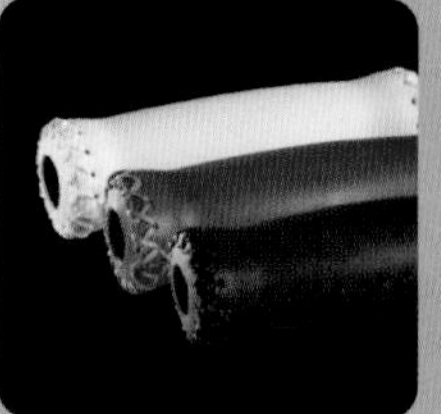

RIDE
D.C.
RIDE
GIANT.
GIANT
Whether you ride for fitness, fun, or the unique sense of freedom the cycling life offers, there's a Giant bike for every adventure. Let Giant be your trusted friend on every road, path or trail you ride.
Find your local Giant retailer at giant-bicycles.com
RIDE LIFE RIDE GIANT.

D.C. Inside the Diamond

Among other decidedly more precedent-shattering proclamations, the United States Constitution, in 1788, specified that a federal city no greater than 10 miles square be established as young America's new capital. A site agreeable to both northern and southern states was chosen, Maryland and Virginia were compelled to cede portions of their land to bring the project to fruition, Frenchman Pierre L'Enfant was placed in charge of its design, and a resulting diamond-shaped territory was oriented toward the four cardinal directions by the early 1790s. Christened the District of Columbia, this section's rides cover the area contained within its original boundaries.

Though Virginia took back its chunk of diamond years ago, its historic sites and cycling trails form such a seamless network with D.C.'s core it simply defied logic not to include them here. The entire area's landscape is hillier than a cursory visit downtown might suggest, with heights scattered both farther inland and along the Potomac and Anacostia rivers.

Long bastion of the free world, the District has now blossomed into an international cultural capital as well. L'Enfant's grand European-style avenues, increasingly striped for bikes, plus an ever-proliferating number of secure paths, each cut swaths through a core transportation grid that is more attuned to cyclists, and more pleasant, efficient, and safe for cycling than ever before.

Here, you'll meet the National Mall and all the major monuments and memorials (on both sides of the Potomac). You'll trace that river's banks, (both Yank and Dixie). You'll ride through D.C.'s largest park (and lose track of the fact you're still in the city). You'll get in-depth tours of Georgetown and Alexandria, two historic ports established long before the District twinkled in George Washington's eye. And you'll take door-to-door rides which introduce you to flesh-and-blood neighborhoods deep inside the capital's four quadrants.

Happy reading and riding (you'll notice the 'rithmetic's already done for you). And be sure to consult this book's 'Originals, Oddballs, and Outliers' for even more routes based inside the diamond.

Sunset at the Lincoln Memorial.

At a Glance

Distance 7.8 miles **Total Elevation** 215 feet

Terrain

Almost entirely flat aside from a stimulating climb up Capitol Hill.

Traffic

The majority of this ride traverses trails, plazas, crosswalks, sidewalks and bike lanes and is therefore set safely away from vehicles. Cyclists will have to negotiate space with walkers, joggers, and sightseers. On-road portions without bike lanes are minimal.

How to Get There

Riding Metro's Red Line to Union Station is easiest. Drivers should aim for the intersection of Massachusetts Avenue and North Capitol Street using the United States Capitol Building as a visual reference. Interstate 395, New York Avenue, and Constitution Avenue among many others, will bring you into downtown from points farther afield. If arriving by bus, check local schedules and aim to connect to the D.C. Circulator.

Food and Drink

The lower level of Union Station is packed with options, and snack and refreshment opportunities also exist in free-standing kiosks near the major monuments and memorials. Additionally, the Mitsitam Native Foods Café on the ground floor of the National Museum of the American Indian garners consistently positive reviews.

Side Trip

Choose among Smithsonians, historic buildings, houses of government, monuments, and memorials.

Links to 2 6 10 11 47 48 49 54 55

Where to Bike Rating 

About...

Here's knowledge worth passing along. D.C.'s better by bike. And a tour combining the National and Memorial malls with the Tidal Basin, the White House, Pennsylvania Avenue and the U.S. Capitol Building is especially better by bike. Walking them all simply takes too much time. Driving is out of the question. Only cycling grants you intimate connection and allows for unforeseen discovery within an appealing time-frame, and only this route links nearly all of Washington's world-renowned must-sees in such a grandly ambitious, yet easy-going way.

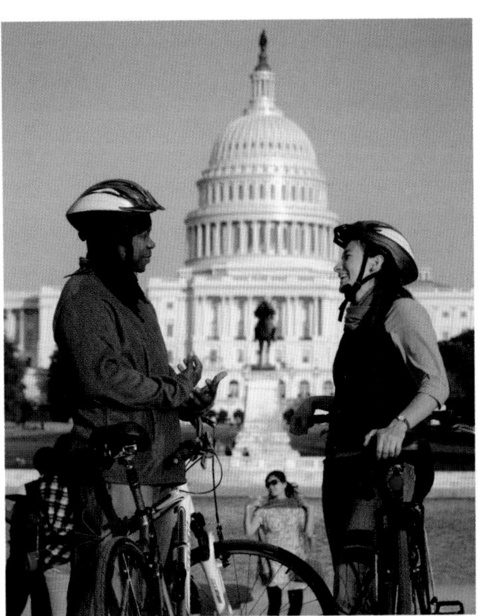

A light moment at the Capitol Reflecting Pool.

Just so you know, this route usually takes folks, on average, around two weeks to finish. Kidding, of course. It takes less than two hours. But it could take two weeks, easily. Here's the chance to fully investigate our nation's three houses of government, begin to assimilate the capital's overwhelming assortment of Smithsonian Museums, touch all the major presidential memorials, and be touched by memorials and monuments to war, peace, and historic American moments in between.

If this were a group tour, its leader would turn to you at least 40 times with the words, "Now, if you look to your…", but it's not, and all the better. Instead, your energy and curiosity set the agenda here. Using this route's guidance, you decide where you want to stop, and you choose what you want to see. Then do it all again, differently, when friends fly in, relatives visit, or that hot, new exhibit hits town.

The enormity of information encompassed along this route is impossible to encapsulate. Use this brief sketch, instead, to begin sharpening your own reference pencil before you ride.

Outside Union Station, D.C.'s best expression of the Beaux Arts, and beyond the Bikestation, its modern pod-like nod to the bicycle, expect a nice, gradual climb up Capitol Hill. This ride incorporates many curb cuts, and you'll begin to use them here.

Around the old iron dome sit the stunning Library of Congress, Supreme Court and its neoclassical columns, and the buttoned-down beauty of the Senate and House Office Buildings. A downhill brings you beside the U.S. Botanic Garden and onto the National Mall. Take your pick. There's art, history, science, air, and space, all free and at your toetips.

After heading due west toward the Washington Monument, turn left to the Tidal Basin and the cherry tree-ringed marble memorial to Jefferson. FDR's open-air, granite-walled rooms follow, and then come Martin Luther King, Lincoln, the inspirational reflecting pool, and the more inwardly reflective memorials to the States' great wars.

Now link to the president's house before swinging around to the 15th Street bikeway and down Pennsylvania Avenue (two of D.C.'s growing number of gifts to cyclists) all the way back to the Capitol Building. After Union Station, ride (and read) on.

Ride Log

0.0 Begin in front of Union Station Bikestation and head to junction of First St and Massachusetts to go left halfway around Columbus Circle.

0.15 Right onto Delaware.

0.25 Cross D St sliding right onto sidewalk.

0.45 Cross Constitution using sidewalk past guard stand, then enter Capitol plaza.

0.7 Dip right onto sidewalk to go downhill.

0.9 Enter roadway and swing halfway around Garfield Monument before going quickly right, then left onto upper sidewalk along Capitol Reflecting Pool.

1.05 Turn right in front of reflecting pool then left toward National Mall.

2.05 Turn left on sidewalk then right toward Washington Monument.

2.15 Cross 14th and 15th streets and go left along sidewalk.

2.45 Cross Maine Ave N and S to go left on sidewalk around Tidal Basin.

2.95 Enter road in front of Jefferson Memorial and continue straight.

3.1 Go right over bridge.

3.85 Cross Independence Ave toward Lincoln Memorial, then go right.

4.0 Go left into Lincoln Memorial plaza.

4.1 Now angle right through barricades and right again onto ramp to join paved path north of, and parallel to, reflecting pool.

4.55 Turn left onto path even with WWII Memorial's Atlantic Arch then angle right toward 17th and Constitution.

4.7 Cross 17th, then Constitution, to slide diagonally toward Ellipse path and White House.

5.0 Reach milestone marker with direct view of White House, then head back toward 17th by angling right at first opportunity and bearing left.

5.15 Right onto 17th St.

5.4 Right onto car-free Pennsylvania Ave.

5.7 Right onto 15th St bikeway.

5.9 Left into Pennsylvania Ave bike lane.

7.0 Jog right as lane ends to continue straight toward Capitol Building.

7.15 Circle part-way around Peace Monument to go left on First Ave.

7.35 Right onto Louisiana Ave.

7.65 Go left using sidewalks and crosswalks.

7.8 Finish.

P1 U.S. Capitol Building
P2 U.S. Supreme Court Building
P3 The Library of Congress
P4 U.S. Botanic Garden
P5 National Museum of the American Indian
P6 National Gallery of Art—East and West
P7 National Air and Space Museum
P8 Hirshhorn Museum and Sculpture Garden
P9 The Smithsonian Castle/ Arts and Industries
P10 National Museum of Natural History
P11 National Museum of American History
P12 Washington Monument
P13 U.S. Holocaust Museum
P14 Thomas Jefferson Memorial
P15 Lincoln Memorial
P16 Korean War Veterans Memorial
P17 Vietnam Veterans Memorial
P18 World War II Memorial
P19 The White House
P20 The Willard Hotel
P21 Old Post Office Pavilion

B1 BicycleSPACE, 459 I St, NW
BR1 Bike and Roll Union Station, 50 Massachusetts Ave, NE
BR2 Bike and Roll Washington, D.C., 1100 Pennsylvania Ave, NW

Iconic D.C.

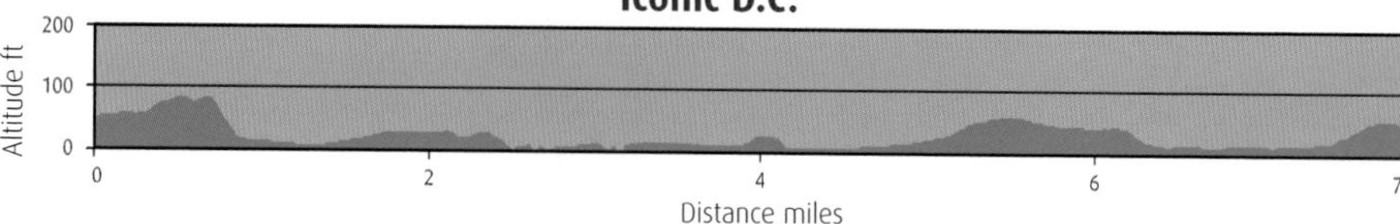

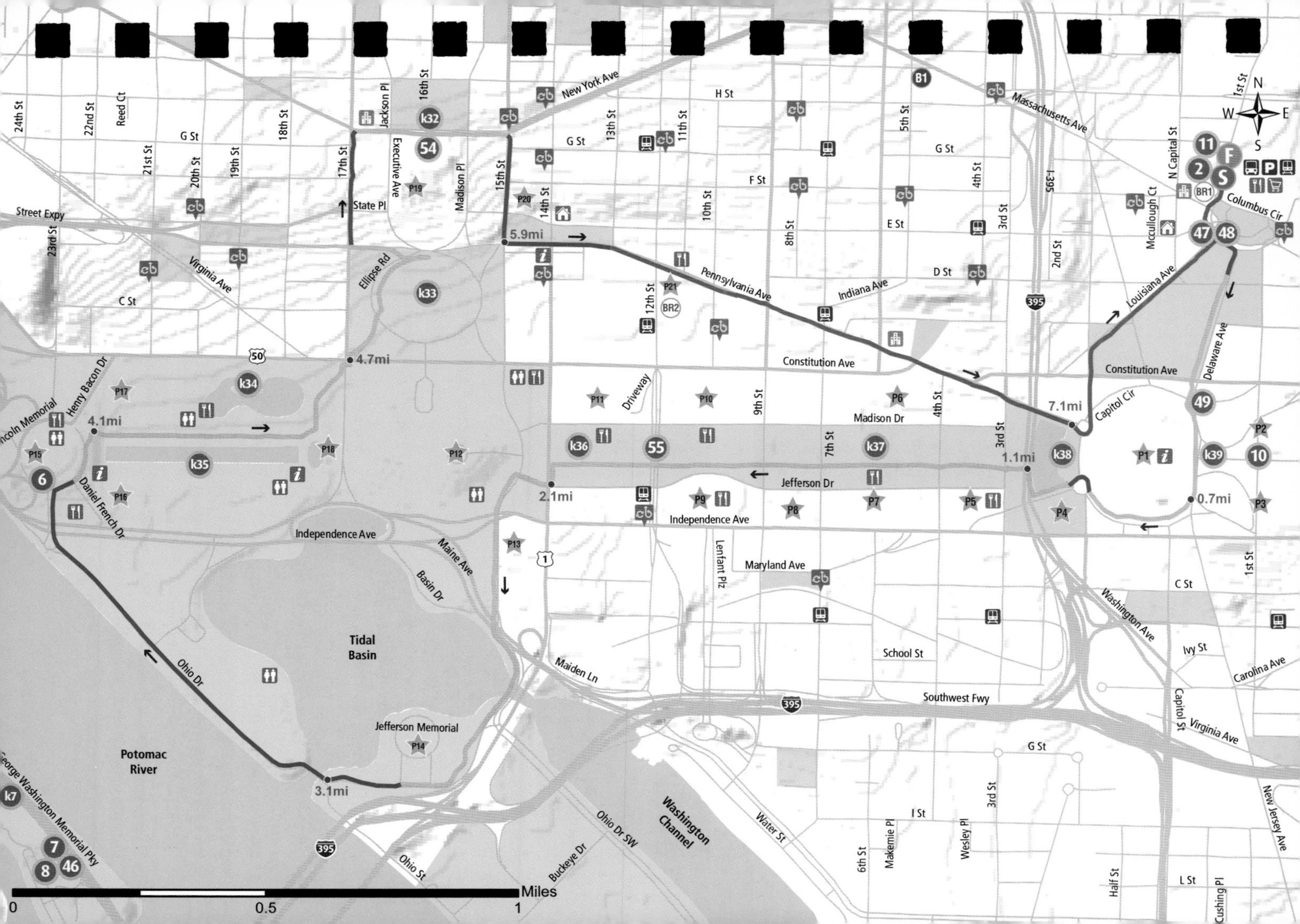

N
E
S
W
New York Ave
Massachusetts Ave
H St
G St
F St
E St
D St
C St
24th St
23rd St
22nd St
Reed Ct
21st St
20th St
19th St
18th St
17th St
Jackson Pl
16th St
Executive Ave
Madison Pl
15th St
14th St
13th St
12th St
11th St
10th St
9th St
8th St
7th St
5th St
4th St
3rd St
2nd St
I-395
N Capital St
Mccullough Ct
1st St
Columbus Cir
Street Expy
State Pl
Virginia Ave
Ellipse Rd
Pennsylvania Ave
Indiana Ave
Louisiana Ave
Delaware Ave
Constitution Ave
Capitol Cir
Driveway
Madison Dr
Jefferson Dr
Independence Ave
Maryland Ave
Lenfant Plz
Henry Bacon Dr
Lincoln Memorial
Daniel French Dr
Maine Ave
Basin Dr
Tidal Basin
Jefferson Memorial
Potomac River
Ohio Dr
Maiden Ln
Washington Channel
Ohio Dr SW
Ohio St
Buckeye Dr
Water St
Southwest Fwy
School St
Washington Ave
C St
Ivy St
Carolina Ave
Capitol St
Virginia Ave
G St
I St
Makemie Pl
Wesley Pl
6th St
Half St
L St
Cushing Pl
New Jersey Ave
George Washington Memorial Pky
5.9mi
4.7mi
4.1mi
3.1mi
2.1mi
1.1mi
7.1mi
0.7mi
Miles
0
0.5
1

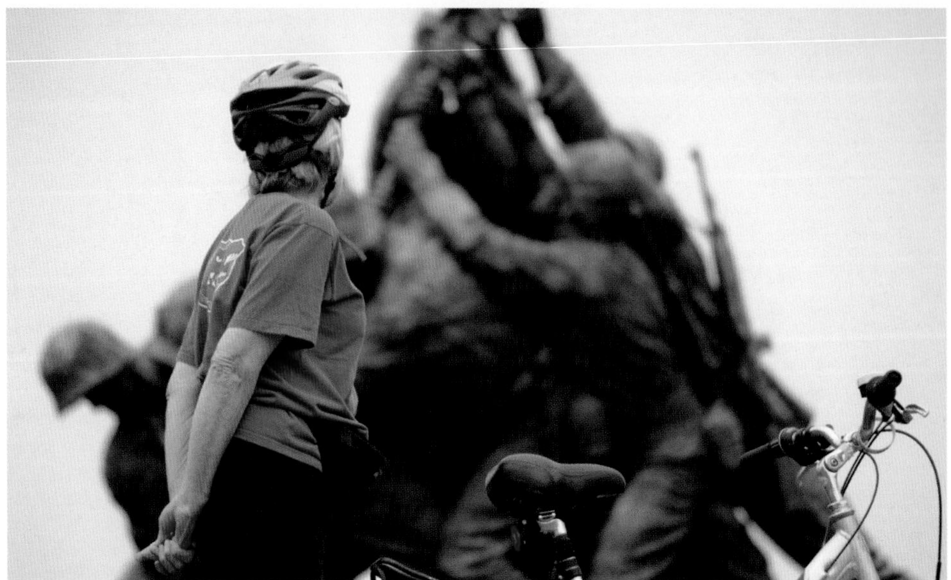
The Marine Corps War Memorial.

At a Glance

Distance 13.9 miles **Total Elevation** 515 feet

Terrain

Expect moderate ascents up Capitol Hill, toward the U.S. Marine Corps War Memorial (Iwo Jima), and along the access sidepath to the Teddy Roosevelt Bridge.

Traffic

The majority of this ride traverses sidewalks, crosswalks, plazas, bridge sidepaths, bike lanes, and trails, and is therefore set safely away from vehicles. Cyclists will have to negotiate space with walkers, joggers, and sightseers. On-road portions without bike lanes are minimal.

How to Get There

Riding Metro's Red Line to Union Station is easiest. Drivers should aim for the intersection of Massachusetts Avenue and North Capitol Street using the United States Capitol Building as a visual reference. Interstate 395, New York Avenue, and Constitution Avenue among many others, will bring you into downtown from points farther afield. If arriving by bus, check local schedules and aim to connect to the D.C. Circulator.

Food and Drink

The lower level of Union Station is packed with choices and further options exist along Louisiana Avenue and G Street. Refresh at stands near the sites as well. Additionally, the Old Ebbitt Grill offers a taste of historic D.C., and the Mitsitam Café at the the National Museum of the American Indian garners consistently positive reviews.

Side Trip

Shake your legs out on a walk through Arlington National Cemetery.

Links to 1 3 6 7 8 10 11 46 47 48 49 51 54 55

Where to Bike Rating 

About...

Designed as a companion piece to Ride 1, this tour also takes in Washington's best known monumental and memorial symbols and can be considered an extension of its sister selection. At nearly twice its length and with twice the climbing, but with additional stops new and old, famous and infamous, Iconic D.C. Too aims to satisfy both riders with a bit more stamina and experience as well as those craving the full extent of what the capital's core has to offer.

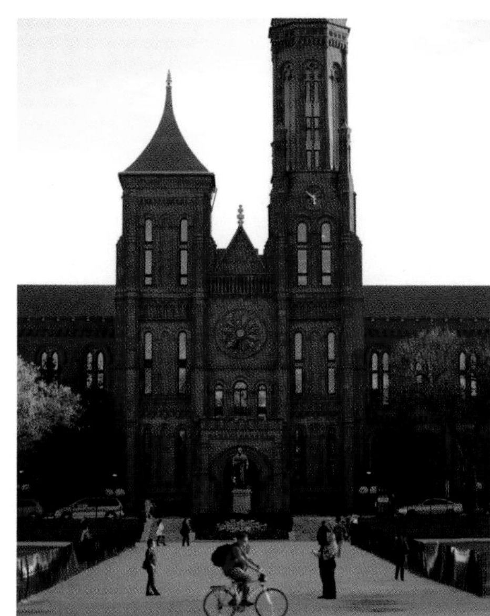

The Smithsonian Castle on the National Mall.

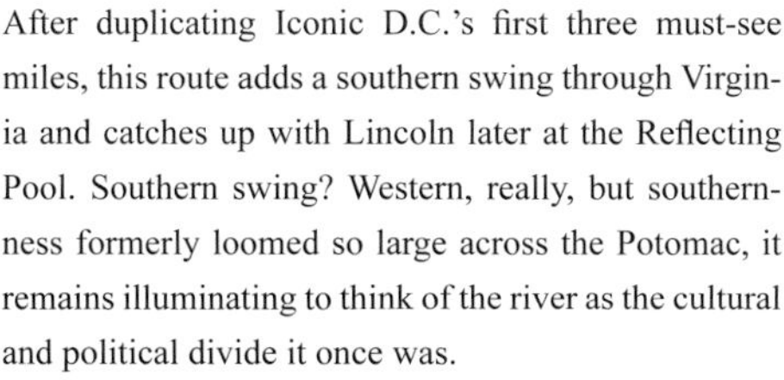

After duplicating Iconic D.C.'s first three must-see miles, this route adds a southern swing through Virginia and catches up with Lincoln later at the Reflecting Pool. Southern swing? Western, really, but southernness formerly loomed so large across the Potomac, it remains illuminating to think of the river as the cultural and political divide it once was.

Past the Jefferson Memorial, a gorgeous, occasionally wind-whipped cruise over the George Mason Bridge leads to a fine length of Mount Vernon Trail and the peace of Arlington National Cemetery. Eye the thick-columned structure high on the hill. Formerly home to Confederate General Robert E. Lee, Arlington House was confiscated from his possession as the Civil War began, and its surroundings converted to burial grounds. Once aimed toward the cemetery, turn right on a path leading to the powerfully affecting Marine Corps Memorial.

Back along the water, monumental D.C. sits directly to the right before a spin down a shaded boardwalk brings access to Theodore Roosevelt Island. Curl left instead to cross the bridge named in his honor. It's a little tight, but grants great views of Georgetown as well as the massive Kennedy Center for the Performing Arts and the neighboring Watergate Complex, all three of which offer prime examples of the capital's iconic living history.

A left takes you back riverside, and soon, behind Lincoln. Stay attuned to the cues here as you begin to stitch together a stretch of street crossings, sidewalks, curb cuts and paths while linking the war memorials to the White House. Then aim for the heart of downtown and turn off to Ford's Theater, another monument symbolic of the once-violent clash between American north and south. Shot here in April 1865, Lincoln was brought to the Petersen House across the street where he died the next morning.

At the FBI Building, turn onto Pennsylvania Avenue and head back toward the Capitol in the steps of the inaugural parade. Here numerous options exist for further investigation. View the country's most famous documents at the National Archives, take in the media-savvy Newseum, or pay your respects at the revealing Japanese American Memorial after rounding for home. Look for it left at the junction of Louisiana and New Jersey avenues.

Ride Log

"See up there where the stone changes color..."

0.0 Exit Union Station Metro elevator and curl right toward Massachusetts Ave exit. Once outside angle right through columns and begin ride in front of Bikestation front doors. Now merge right to the meeting of First St and Massachusetts and go left along Columbus Circle.

0.15 Right onto Delaware Ave.

0.25 Cross D St sliding right onto sidewalk.

0.45 Cross Constitution using sidewalk past guard stand.

0.5 Slide off sidewalk to enter Capitol plaza.

0.7 Before reaching guard stand, dip right onto sidewalk to go downhill.

0.9 Use sidewalk ramp to go right on First Ave. Go halfway around Garfield Monument to Maryland Ave.

1.0 Now turn right off street to go left on sidewalk along reflecting pool.

1.05 Turn right in front of reflecting pool then left toward wide pea gravel path on National Mall.

1.85 Pass Smithsonian Metro. Alternate beginning.

2.05 Turn left toward Jefferson on sidewalk then right toward Washington Monument.

2.15 After two road crossings (14th and 15th streets), go left along sidewalk.

2.45 After two road crossings (Maine Ave N and S), again go left along sidewalk.

2.95 Cross Ohio Dr to go right along path up to and over the 14th St (George Mason) Bridge.

3.55 Left to join Mt Vernon Trail.

4.5 Fork left to cross George Washington Pkwy once (then twice more).

5.1 Use crosswalk to cross road (Memorial Dr) right, jog ultra-briefly right and access path at left into Arlington Cemetery.

5.55 Turn right to go along roadway toward U.S. Marine Corps Memorial.

5.7 Bear right to circle memorial.

6.0 Turn right to join trail left toward the Netherlands Carillon.

6.15 Turn left to go along trail and soon to jog right

Ride Log continued...

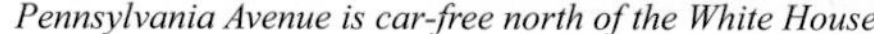

Pennsylvania Avenue is car-free north of the White House.

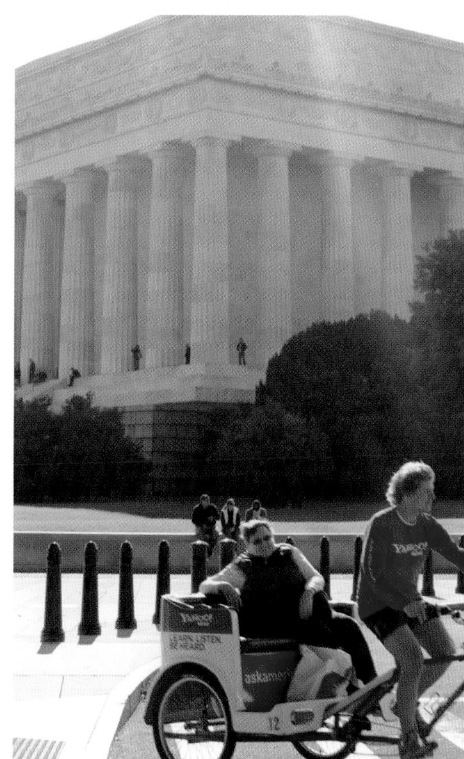

Pedi-cabs abound downtown.

doubling back on entry trail.

6.65 Turn left to jog right and cross roadway (Memorial Dr) soon to join opposite sidewalk.

6.95 Cross roadway to go right before two more road crossings toward Potomac River.

7.2 Go left along Mt Vernon Trail.

8.1 Turn left to curve up and over Theodore Roosevelt Memorial Bridge.

9.1 Turn left using crosswalks to go left on F St toward Potomac.

9.25 Go left to cross Rock Creek Pkwy and continue left along Potomac sidepath.

9.95 Cross roadway left to begin series of four road crossings toward front of Lincoln Memorial.

10.15 After fourth crossing continue safely straight and use ramp to access paved path running parallel to reflecting pool.

10.3 Bathrooms to left.

10.55 Turn left onto path even with WWII Memorial's Atlantic Arch then angle right toward corner of 17th and Constitution.

10.8 Cross 17th. Then cross Constitution. Now go right extremely briefly before sliding diagonally left toward White House Ellipse.

10.9 Cross road to continue left toward White House on Ellipse path.

11.1 Reach Milestone with direct view of White House. Circle and head back toward 17th by angling right at first opportunity. Then bear left.

11.2 Turn right onto 17th St.

Ride Log continued...

11.5 Turn right onto car-free Pennsylvania Ave.

11.8 Turn right onto 15th St to immediate left into G St bike lane.

12.2 Turn right onto 10th St.

12.5 Turn left into Pennsylvania Ave bike lane.

13.1 Jog right as lane ends to cross Third St straight toward Capitol Building. Beware left-turning traffic.

13.3 Begin circling part-way around Peace Monument to go left on First Ave.

13.5 Turn right onto Louisiana Ave.

13.8 Go left using sidewalks and crosswalks to return to Union Station Bikestation.

13.9 Finish.

The west building of the National Gallery of Art.

P1 National Postal Museum
P2 U.S. Capitol Building
P3 Department of Agriculture
P4 Bureau of Printing and Engraving
P5 Thomas Jefferson Memorial
P6 Arlington National Cemetery
P7 Marine Corps War Memorial
P8 Kennedy Center for the Performing Arts
P9 Watergate Complex
P10 Lincoln Memorial
P11 World War II Memorial
P12 The White House
P13 Corcoran Gallery of Art
P14 Eisenhower Executive Office Building
P15 Department of the Treasury
P16 Old Ebbitt Grill
P17 Ford's Theater
P18 FBI Building
P19 National Archives
P20 Newseum
P21 National Japanese American Memorial

B1 BicycleSPACE, 459 I St, NW
B2 District Hardware—The Bike Shop, 1108 24th St, NW
B3 Cycle Life USA, 3255 K St, NW
B4 Big Wheel Bikes, 1034 33rd St, NW
B5 Bicycle Pro Shop, 3403 M St, NW
B6 Revolution Cycles, 3411 M St, NW
BR1 Bike and Roll Union Station, 50 Massachusetts Ave, NE
BR2 Bike and Roll Washington, D.C., 1100 Pennsylvania Ave, NW
BR3 Thompson Boat Center, 2900 Virginia Ave, NW

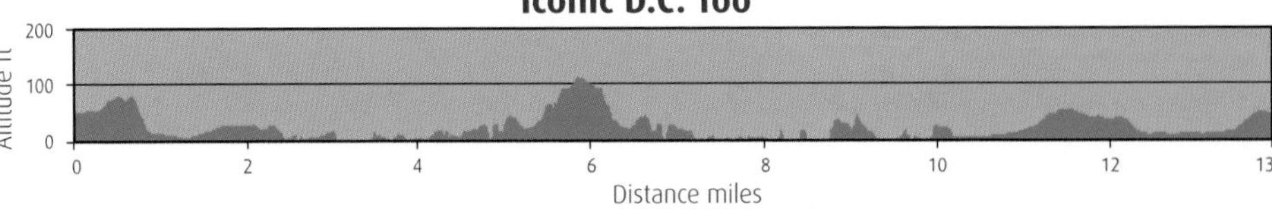

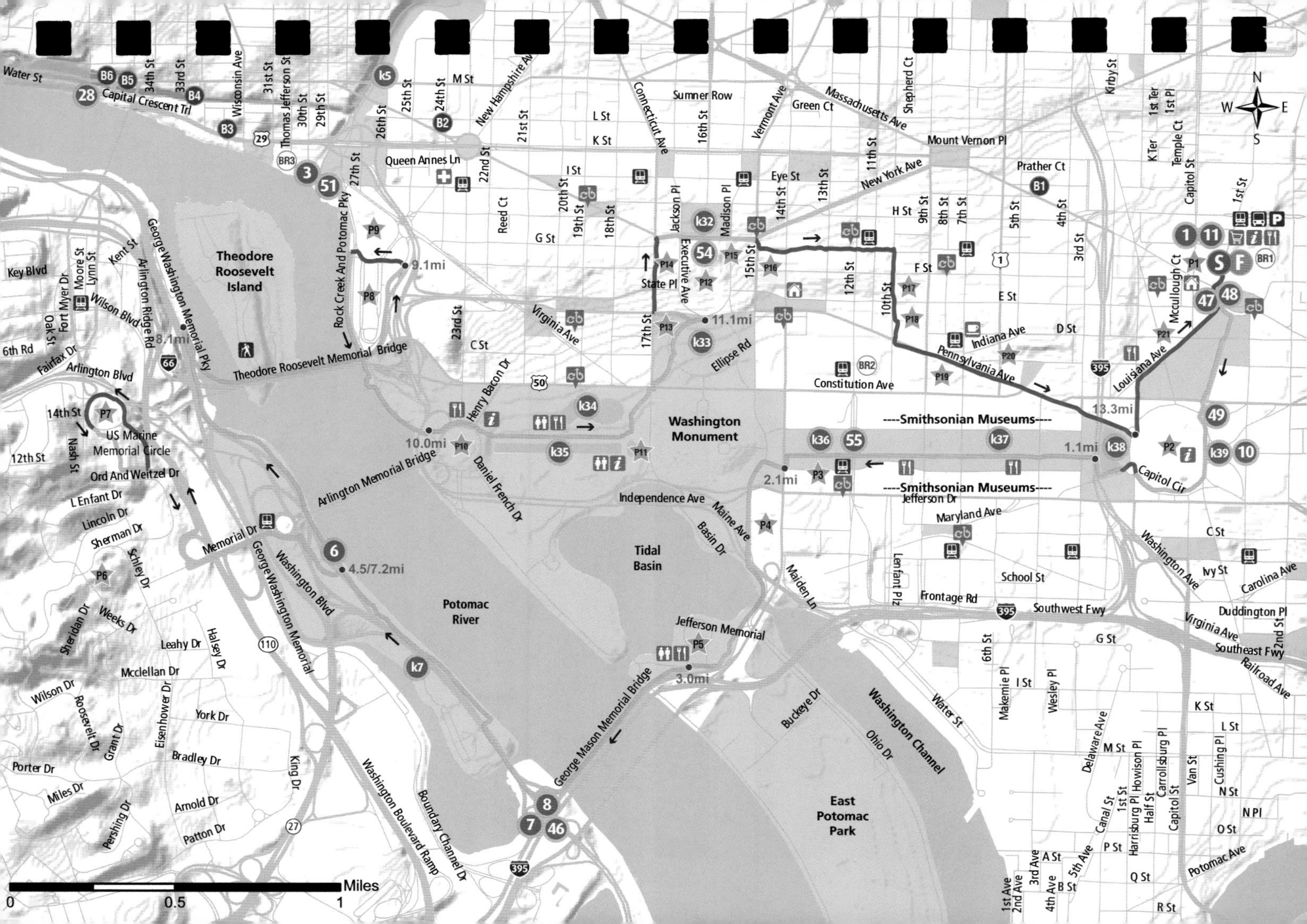

Theodore Roosevelt Island
Washington Monument
Smithsonian Museums
Tidal Basin
Potomac River
East Potomac Park
Washington Channel
Jefferson Memorial
Theodore Roosevelt Memorial Bridge
Arlington Memorial Bridge
George Mason Memorial Bridge
George Washington Memorial Pky
Rock Creek And Potomac Pky
US Marine Memorial Circle
Capital Crescent Trl
Pennsylvania Ave
Constitution Ave
Independence Ave
Virginia Ave
Louisiana Ave
Connecticut Ave
New Hampshire Ave
Massachusetts Ave
New York Ave
Vermont Ave
Wisconsin Ave
Maryland Ave
Indiana Ave
Washington Ave
Capitol Cir
Southwest Fwy
Southeast Fwy
Washington Blvd
Washington Boulevard Ramp
Boundary Channel Dr
Memorial Dr
Ohio Dr
Buckeye Dr
Maine Ave
Basin Dr
Maiden Ln
Ellipse Rd
Henry Bacon Dr
Daniel French Dr
Executive Ave
State Pl
Jefferson Dr
Frontage Rd
Water St
Lenfant Plz
Arlington Blvd
Wilson Blvd
Arlington Ridge Rd
Ord And Weitzel Dr
Queen Annes Ln
Mount Vernon Pl
Sumner Row
Green Ct
Potomac Ave
Railroad Ave
Delaware Ave
Canal St
Miles
0
0.5
1
13.3mi
11.1mi
10.0mi
9.1mi
8.1mi
4.5/7.2mi
3.0mi
2.1mi
1.1mi
N
E
S
W

This trail can take you places.

At a Glance

Distance 9.0 miles **Total Elevation** 355 feet

Terrain

Mostly well-paved bike path with a handful of bridge crossings and a few short uphill sections.

Traffic

No cars of course, but it can get crowded with runners, walkers, and bicyclists on weekends. Be mindful of your speed and be cautious at all road crossings.

How to Get There

Metro's closest station is the Orange/Blue Foggy Bottom stop. If arriving by bus, jump on the Circulator to Georgetown. Drivers should access the Rock Creek and Potomac Parkway. There's parking at Thompson Boat Center.

Food and Drink

Restaurants are located near ride's end and beginning around the Georgetown Waterfront Park or up around the junction of Calvert and Connecticut. There are no options directly along the trail.

Side Trip

Lock up and take in the National Zoo or go the way of the first President Roosevelt and scramble among Rock Creek Park's deep gorges.

Links to 2 4 6 12 48 51

Where to Bike Rating

About...

Look at a map of greater D.C., and you'll see how its grandest natural space splits the city down the middle, from Maryland near to the National Mall. This ride cuts you through that wedge of deep woods and rugged terrain, effectively covering the lower half of the park as it narrows nearing the Potomac. It's a well-trod, popular path that intimately winds over and around Rock Creek for much of its way. And, while you're at it, there's also infamous Watergate and a cruise right through the National Zoo.

Rock Creek demands a close-up.

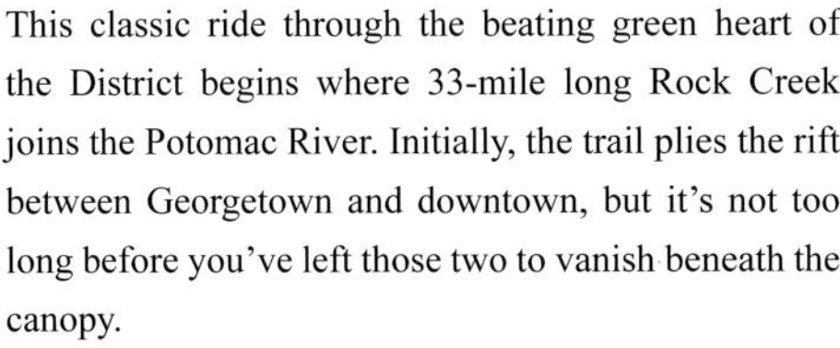

This classic ride through the beating green heart of the District begins where 33-mile long Rock Creek joins the Potomac River. Initially, the trail plies the rift between Georgetown and downtown, but it's not too long before you've left those two to vanish beneath the canopy.

A bridge is the first site worthy of notice. It is, in fact, one of three commanding bridges you'll twice encounter on this out-and-back affair. See if you can spot one of the four buffalo sculptures flanking the corners of the sandy-colored P Street Dumbarton span. You'll undoubtedly see its odd display of numerous carved Native American heads.

Now you'll begin to catch glimpses of, then cross, Rock Creek as Oak Hill Cemetery spills down beside you. Then, a few more crossings and a brief chugging uphill, brings you to a clearing from which Connecticut Avenue's Taft Bridge rises heroically.

Be cautious crossing an oftentimes busy Shoream Drive as it climbs to Woodley Park, then fork right under the Taft. The Duke Ellington Bridge, another magnificent span, quickly follows. Certainly now you've begun to feel the park's imposing depth and density.

At twice the size of New York's more famous Central Park, Rock Creek just may be two times as wild as well. Resembling a wilderness more than fulfilling the usual park-like vision of rolling lawns and strolling couples, this is definitely one of America's great urban expanses, and a true bastion for advocates of "the strenuous life".

Hardy President Theodore Roosevelt used to take his legendary scrambles here, and its status as an escape hatch from the bustle above is D.C. legend. Established in 1890, it is one of the oldest parks in the entire National Park Service, and a hero of sorts, all the more honorable for being so staunchly in the city and home to such a variety of diversions.

The National Zoo sits not far past the Ellington Bridge. In warmer months an open gate begs you continue along the creek. In colder, however, you may have to settle for a quick tunnel walk. Either way, the facility's main lower entrance sits not too far ahead, as does Pierce Mill, your retrace point.

Ride Log

Entering D.C.'s City of Trees.

0.0 Begin at the Thompson Boat Center entranceway sign off Rock Creek Parkway opposite Virginia Ave. With the Watergate Complex behind you, head away from downtown. Be cautious at road crossings!
0.2 Pass C&O Canal Historical Park at left.
1.05 Oak Hill Cemetery at left. Pass over bridge.
2.0 Stay right to cross road. Take trail's right fork to dip under bridge.
2.3 Trail angles left at tunnel.
2.55 Cross road to continue.
2.95 National Zoo entrance at left.
3.5 Cross wooden bridge to continue along creek.
3.8 Cross creek again and continue left.
4.25 Pass Pierce Mill.
4.5 Turn around at parking lot to retrace path.
5.2 Right over bridge.
6.75 Right away from tunnel.
7.0 Road crossing.
7.95 Bridge over creek.
9.0 Finish at Thompson Boat Center.

P
P1 Watergate Complex
P2 C&O Canal & Towpath
P3 Dumbarton Bridge
P4 Oak Hill Cemetery
P5 Taft Bridge
P6 National Zoo
P7 Pierce Mill

B
B1 District Hardware—The Bike Shop, 1108 24th St, NW
B2 Cycle Life USA, 3255 K St, NW
B3 Big Wheel Bikes, 1034 33rd St, NW
B4 Bicycle Pro Shop, 3403 M St, NW
B5 Revolution Cycles, 3411 M St, NW
B6 City Bikes, 2501 Champlain St, NW

BR
BR1 Thompson Boat Center

Lower Rock Creek

Altitude ft: 200, 100, 0
Distance miles: 0, 2, 4, 6, 8, 9.0

N
W
E
S
Broad Branch Rd
Ridge Rd
Colorado Ave
Blagden Ave
Argyle Ter
Webster St
Varnum St
Upshur St
Taylor St
Crestwood
Shepherd St
Arkansas Ave
4
4.5mi
Beach Dr
P7
Reno Rd
Sedgwick St
Wisconsin Ave
Rodman St
Quebec St
Ordway St
Park Rd
16th St
Piney Branch Pky
Cleveland Park
Porter St
Idaho Ave
Newark St
Macomb St
Lowell St
Klingle Rd
Mount Pleasant
Woodley Rd
Klingle Rd
Connecticut Ave
Park Rd
Mount Pleasant St
Kenyon St
Irving St
Driveway
Cathedral Ave
Garfield St
P6
3.0/6.0mi
Harvard St
Cleveland Ave
34th Pl
Fulton St
36th St
Woodley Park
Calvert St
Lanier Pl
Columbia Rd
B6
Euclid St
Biltmore St
Tunlaw Rd
Normanstone Dr
48
2.0/7.0mi
P5
Champlain St
Observatory Ln
Naval Observatory
Massachusetts Ave
k4
Wisconsin Ave
Rock Creek Pkwy
W St
Florida Ave
Kalorama Rd
37th St
Wyoming Ave
California St
Vernon St
Waterside Dr
Sheridan-Kalorama
19th St
T St
16th St
New Hampshire Ave
S St
P4
Decatur Pl
15th St
Reservoir Rd
R St
Corcoran St
35th St
34th St
12
Dupont Circle
Q St
Georgetown
P3
Church St
P St
0.8/8.2mi
17th St
k5
O St
Rock Creek And Potomac Pky
33rd St
28th St
Massachusetts Ave
Rhode Island Ave
Prospect St
Dumbarton Ave
N St
B5
B4
Canal Rd
25th St
24th St
23rd St
22nd St
21st St
20th St
M St
Connecticut Ave
Capital Crescent Trl
28
B3
31st St
30th St
29th St
26th St
29
P2
B1
L St
Vermont Ave
B2
K St
29
Potomac River
51
66
Pennsylvania Ave
18th St
I St
BR1
S
6
F
Virginia Ave
Foggy Bottom
H St
Jackson Pl
k32
Madison Pl
Theodore Roosevelt Island
P1
G St
7
8
46
2
Miles
0
0.25
0.5
1
White House

As fast as you please.

At a Glance

Distance 8.1 miles **Total Elevation** 405 feet

Terrain

Beach Drive is well-maintained and flat aside from one modest incline. The Daniel Road hill is a challenge, and Oregon is hilly and a touch bumpier. Glover is smooth with a little climbing and one long, twisting downhill to finish.

Traffic

This ride is best done on weekends when Beach Drive closes to cars 7am Saturday to 7pm Sunday. Oregon draws traffic but a sidepath beginning off Wise Road frees you from it if it proves to be intimidating. Weekdays on Beach are a different story as its two lanes are narrow, winding, and not nearly as bicycle friendly.

How to Get There

Take Metro's Red Line to Van Ness and make your way down into the park by way of Tilden Street. Or drive and park just south of this ride's beginning and ending near Blagden Road at the intersection of Beach Drive and Broad Branch Road.

Food and Drink

There is no opportunity for food along this route. Best bring your own. Restrooms pop up periodically and water can be found at the nature center just off the route at mile 6.5.

Side Trip

Use Tilden Street to Linnean Avenue to visit Hillwood Estate, Museum and Gardens.

Links to 

Where to Bike Rating 

About...

Closing Beach Drive to cars in upper Rock Creek Park on Saturdays, Sundays, and holidays was quite the forward-thinking idea in 1970's America. But what started as a National Park Service experiment quickly took off, and in no time became a D.C. institution. Its long-running success is simple. The creek up here is at its finest, the road at its most inviting, and the hordes who flock here at their happiest. Come join the party!

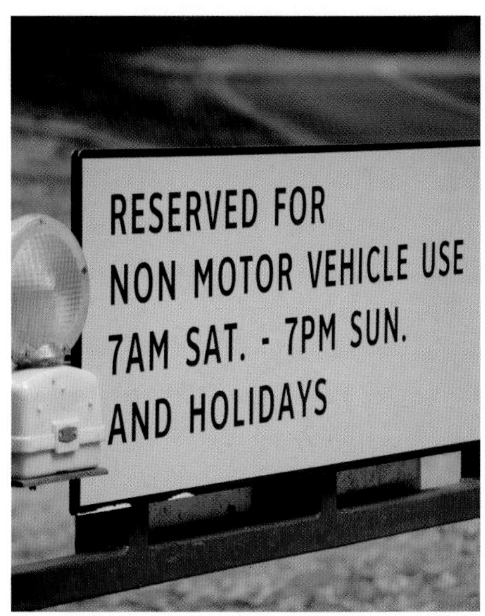

One of D.C.'s best ideas.

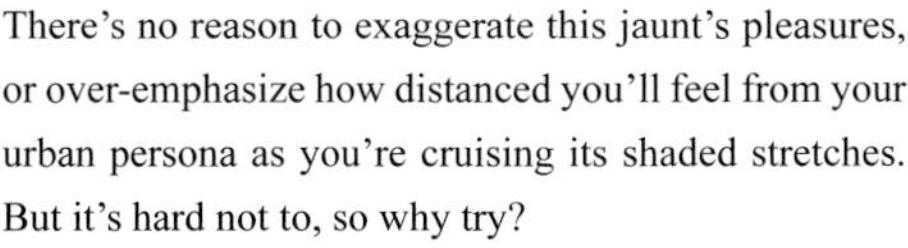

There's no reason to exaggerate this jaunt's pleasures, or over-emphasize how distanced you'll feel from your urban persona as you're cruising its shaded stretches. But it's hard not to, so why try?

With the creek playing its tricks with light and sound and the trees watching grandly overhead, it's easy to see why this is one ride to revisit each and every time you get the chance. No cars mean no noise, no broken sightlines, and nearly no worries. It's very nice being surrounded only by others of your particular genus and species, and, for a change, you've got the entire road all to yourselves.

Here's the deal. Wonderful weekend Beach runs car-free until its intersection with Wise Road at mile 3.5. Turn around there for a seven mile spin if you want to completely avoid all things motorized.

If you continue on, and you shouldn't feel threatened one bit doing so, the route will join trafficked Wise Road for a very brief downhill stretch before it doglegs right as you go left to connect to another sweet section of bikes-only Beach which continues until mile 4.25. Want 8.5 miles round-trip to be your day's total? Turn back now and retrace.

Otherwise, proceed ahead, then left, to attack the hills of Wyndale and Daniel roads before joining Oregon Avenue, Rock Creek Park's western edge. Though not car-free, it's a fun, rolling pedal.

Fort DeRussy, a D.C. Civil War era fortification which saw action in the Battle of Fort Stevens, is a short hike into the woods just before reaching Military Road. Bring your imagination as portions of its earthworks are its only remaining discernible feature.

Crossing straight at Military Road, you'll soon fork left passing the entrance road to both the Rock Creek Horse and Nature centers. Take a pit stop here too, if you wish. Either way, you're soon home via canopied Ridge Road and its long, winding descent back to Beach.

While Ride 4 has not been deemed kid-friendly in its entirety, it does include substantial sections which are entirely safe for family use.

Ride Log

A nice Sunday afternoon combo.

0.0 Begin at white distance marker across from parking lot near Beach Dr's intersection with Broad Branch Rd NW.

3.5 Wise Rd. Traffic possible.

3.6 Bear left to stay on Beach Dr.

4.25 Continue straight.

4.5 Left on Wyndale Rd to immediate left on Daniel Rd.

4.7 Straight onto Oregon Ave.

5.1 Continue straight on Oregon. Parallel trail available at left.

5.75 A left on Bingham Dr shortcuts you back to Beach.

6.4 Go straight across Military Rd. Oregon becomes Glover (then Ridge) Rd.

6.5 Bear left to pass Rock Creek Nature and Horse centers.

8.1 Return to white distance marker.

P1 Pulpit Rock
P2 Joaquin Miller Cabin
P3 Ft DeRussy
P4 The Rock Creek Nature Center and Planetarium
P5 Rock Creek Park Horse Center
P6 Hillwood Estate, Museum, and Gardens, 4155 Linnean Avenue, NW

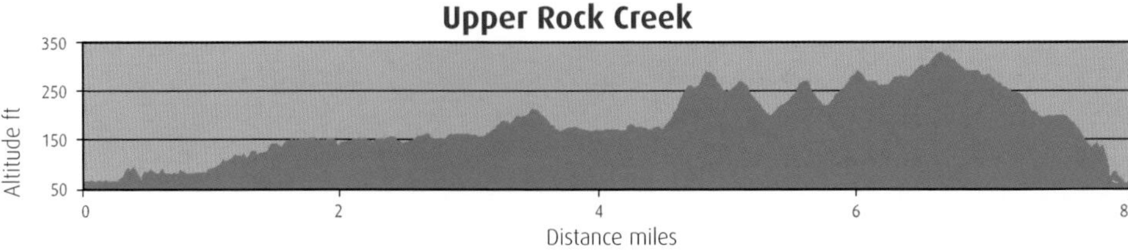

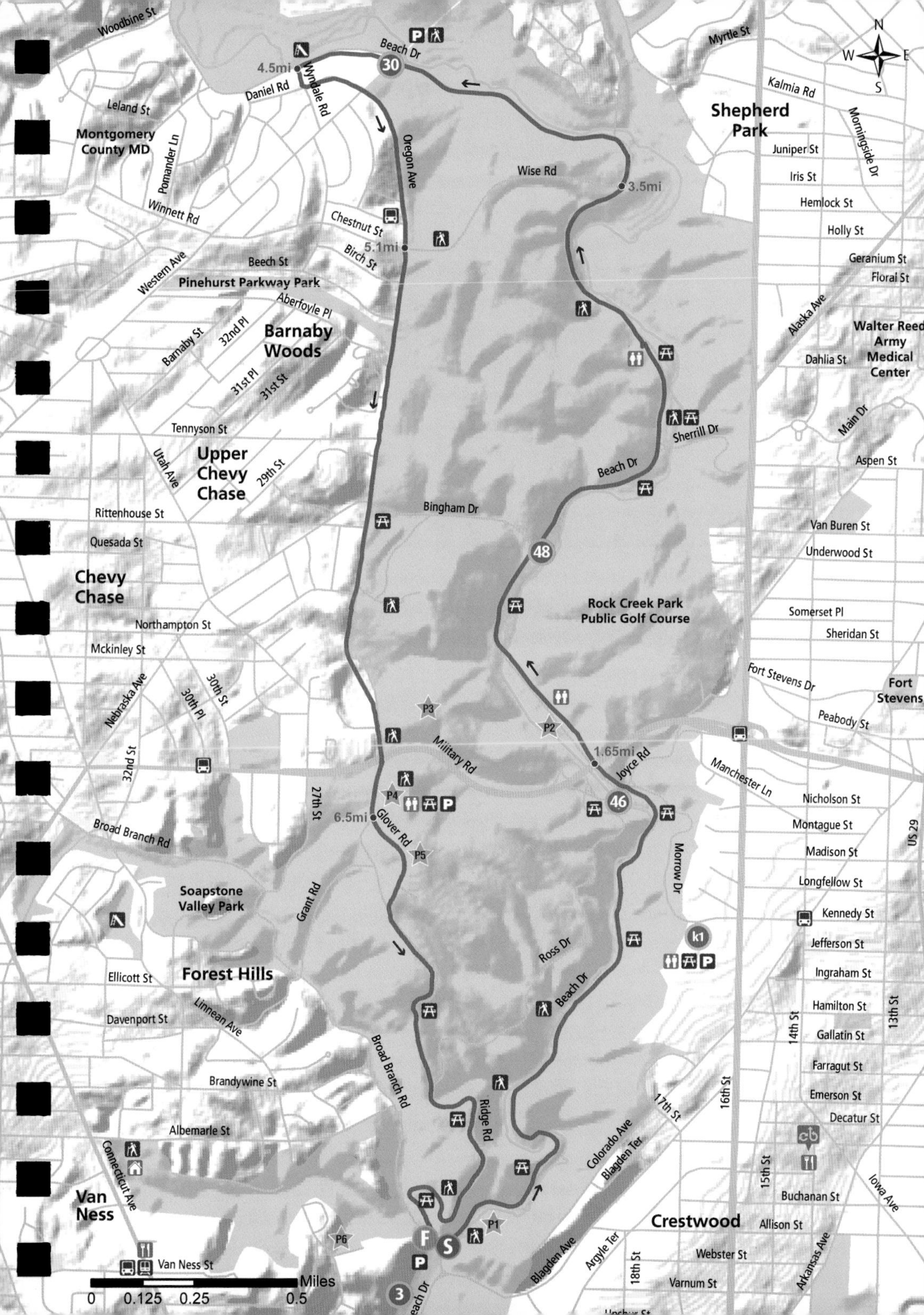

Woodbine St
Beach Dr
Myrtle St
N
W
E
S
Kalmia Rd
4.5mi
30
Wyndale Rd
Daniel Rd
Leland St
Montgomery County MD
Shepherd Park
Juniper St
Morningside Dr
Oregon Ave
Pomander Ln
Wise Rd
3.5mi
Iris St
Hemlock St
Winnett Rd
Chestnut St
Holly St
5.1mi
Birch St
Geranium St
Western Ave
Beech St
Floral St
Pinehurst Parkway Park
Aberfoyle Pl
Alaska Ave
Walter Reed Army Medical Center
Barnaby St
32nd Pl
Barnaby Woods
Dahlia St
31st Pl
31st St
Main Dr
Sherrill Dr
Tennyson St
Upper Chevy Chase
Utah Ave
29th St
Beach Dr
Aspen St
Rittenhouse St
Bingham Dr
Van Buren St
Quesada St
48
Underwood St
Chevy Chase
Rock Creek Park Public Golf Course
Somerset Pl
Northampton St
Sheridan St
Mckinley St
Fort Stevens Dr
Fort Stevens
Nebraska Ave
30th St
30th Pl
P3
P2
Peabody St
Military Rd
1.65mi
32nd St
Joyce Rd
Manchester Ln
27th St
P4
46
Nicholson St
6.5mi
Glover Rd
Montague St
Broad Branch Rd
P5
Madison St
Morrow Dr
US 29
Longfellow St
Grant Rd
Soapstone Valley Park
Kennedy St
k1
Ross Dr
Jefferson St
Forest Hills
Ellicott St
Ingraham St
Linnean Ave
Beach Dr
Davenport St
Hamilton St
14th St
13th St
Gallatin St
Broad Branch Rd
Brandywine St
Farragut St
Ridge Rd
16th St
Emerson St
17th St
Albemarle St
Decatur St
Colorado Ave
Blagden Ter
Connecticut Ave
15th St
Iowa Ave
Van Ness
Buchanan St
P1
Crestwood
Allison St
F
S
P6
Blagden Ave
Argyle Ter
18th St
Webster St
Arkansas Ave
Van Ness St
Varnum St
Miles
0
0.125
0.25
0.5
3

The iconic Capitol Columns.

At a Glance

Distance 5.0 miles **Total Elevation** 440 feet

Terrain

Excellent network of well-maintained and interconnected roads traversing rolling hills.

Traffic

Many people choose to walk the grounds, keeping traffic light. For those who do drive, a maximum speed limit of 20 mandates safety. Watch out though, your downhills just might break it!

How to Get There

The most difficult part of this ride is getting here. If you have the time and are so inclined, head to Stadium Armory on the Orange/Blue Lines and take bus B2 heading north up Bladensburg Road. Disembark across from Yellow Cab and go right down R Street. If you ride here, be forewarned, the going is grungy and more than a little difficult. Avoid New York Avenue altogether and use side streets whenever possible. If driving though, New York's probably your quickest ticket.

Food and Drink

Water fountains and minimal vending are located in or near the visitor's center and Arbor House.

Side Trip

This ride is open to multiple interpretations. Let your curiosity guide you. Within the fences and with regard for the rules, there's really no going wrong.

Links to 46

Where to Bike Rating

About...

This is a heavily interactive ride if you so choose, and although it's all about pleasure, you may go home with the suspicion you somehow managed to sneak in a workout along the way as well. Come here to savor the sights and sounds and smells of lovingly-tended nature, and to spend a leisurely time stimulating your body, mind, and spirit. No matter the season, this peaceful piece of D.C. heaven delivers.

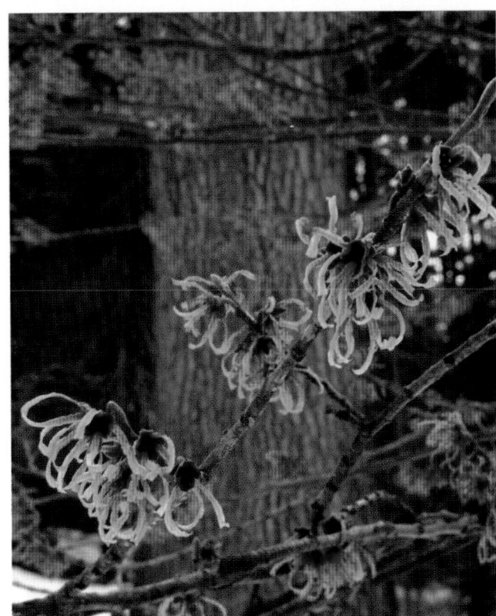

Winter color.

The National Arboretum is a glowing, green gem tucked away in a gritty, concrete corner of the District. Certainly off the traveler's radar, it somehow seems to perpetually remain off the locals' as well. Bicyclists should pay it some attention however, as beauty, safety, and accessibility combine to make it a highly enjoyable spin. Established in 1927, its 444-acres serve as one of the principle branches of the United States Agricultural Research Service. To discover what's blooming, pick up a map at the visitor's center before you start pedaling.

This isn't a difficult ride, but the area does mirror the ups and downs of greater D.C., so don't be surprised if the hills test you a bit. My chosen route is most definitely open to interpretation, yet I suggest completing the prescribed loop before doubling down to examine anything that really sparks your imagination.

After a healthy uphill to begin, a whizzing downhill brings you flying past the azaleas. A short flat section then proceeds to a breezy downhill before a second climb, this time toward the hills over the nearby Anacostia River.

Take a break and hike down toward its banks through the Asian Collections if you care to or take in the west-facing view off the top of Hickey Hill instead. Then cruise practically peddle-free past the conifers continuing downhill for a brief stretch along New York Avenue as it thunders beyond the fence-line. In not too long you're back at the visitor's center.

You probably saw the famous Capitol Columns on the last loop, but you'll get a close-up this time. Now take a quick spin through the Arboretum's mid-section, returning once again where you started. From here on out, you make the calls. Whatever you decide, don't miss the miniature masterpieces of the National Bonsai and Penjing Museum.

And, by the way, don't worry about getting lost out here. The roads are all connected and, way leading unto way, you'll find yourself back where you started without a worry in the world.

Ride Log

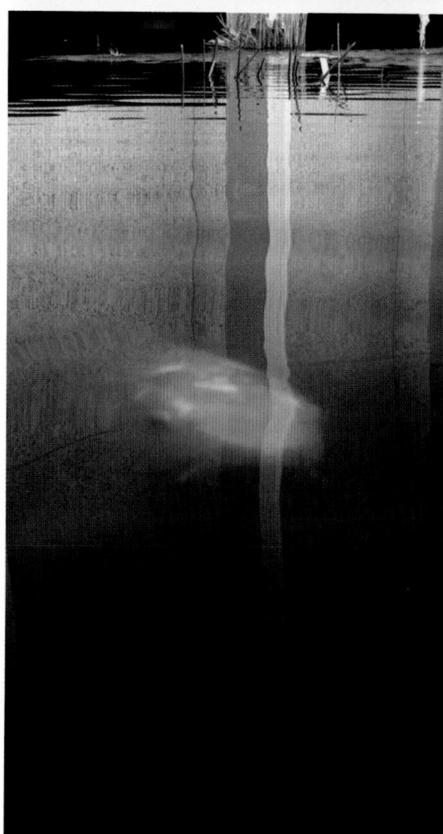

What you find here might surprise you.

P1 Arbor House and Friendship Garden
P2 Perennial and Boxwoods Collection
P3 Azalea Collections
P4 National Grove of State Trees
P5 National Youth Garden
P6 Fern Valley Native Plant Collection
P7 Holly Magnolia Collection
P8 Asian Collections
P9 Dogwood Collections
P10 Gotelli Dwarf and Slow Growing Conifer Collection
P11 National Herb Garden
P12 National Capitol Columns
P13 Research Fields
P14 National Bonsai and Penjing Museum

0.0 Begin by taking a right at stop sign nearest flag pole in visitor's center roundabout. Continue straight at second stop sign to climb to Boxwoods, Perennials, and Azaleas.

.45 View of U.S. Capitol and Washington Monument.

1.0 Continue straight. Capitol Columns soon to left.

1.55 Right onto Hickey Hill Rd toward Hollies, Magnolias, and Asian Collections.

2.0 Hickey Hill Overlook at left. Bathrooms soon to right.

2.15 Dip right toward Conifer Collection then follow road to left.

2.55 Continue straight. Bikes allowed.

2.9 Stay right after stop sign to continue toward visitor's center.

3.3 A left returns you to visitor center roundabout.

3.35 Go left this time at flag pole.

3.5 Veer right toward Capitol Columns and turn left opposite them.

3.95 Right onto Meadow Rd at stop sign.

4.2 Left onto Holly Spring Rd to another quick left onto Hickey Ln.

4.6 Left again at confluence onto Valley Rd to a quick right back onto Meadow.

5.0 Re-enter visitor's center roundabout and choose your next move.

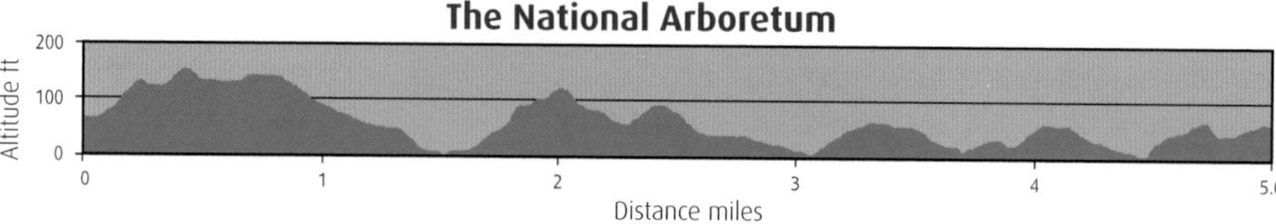

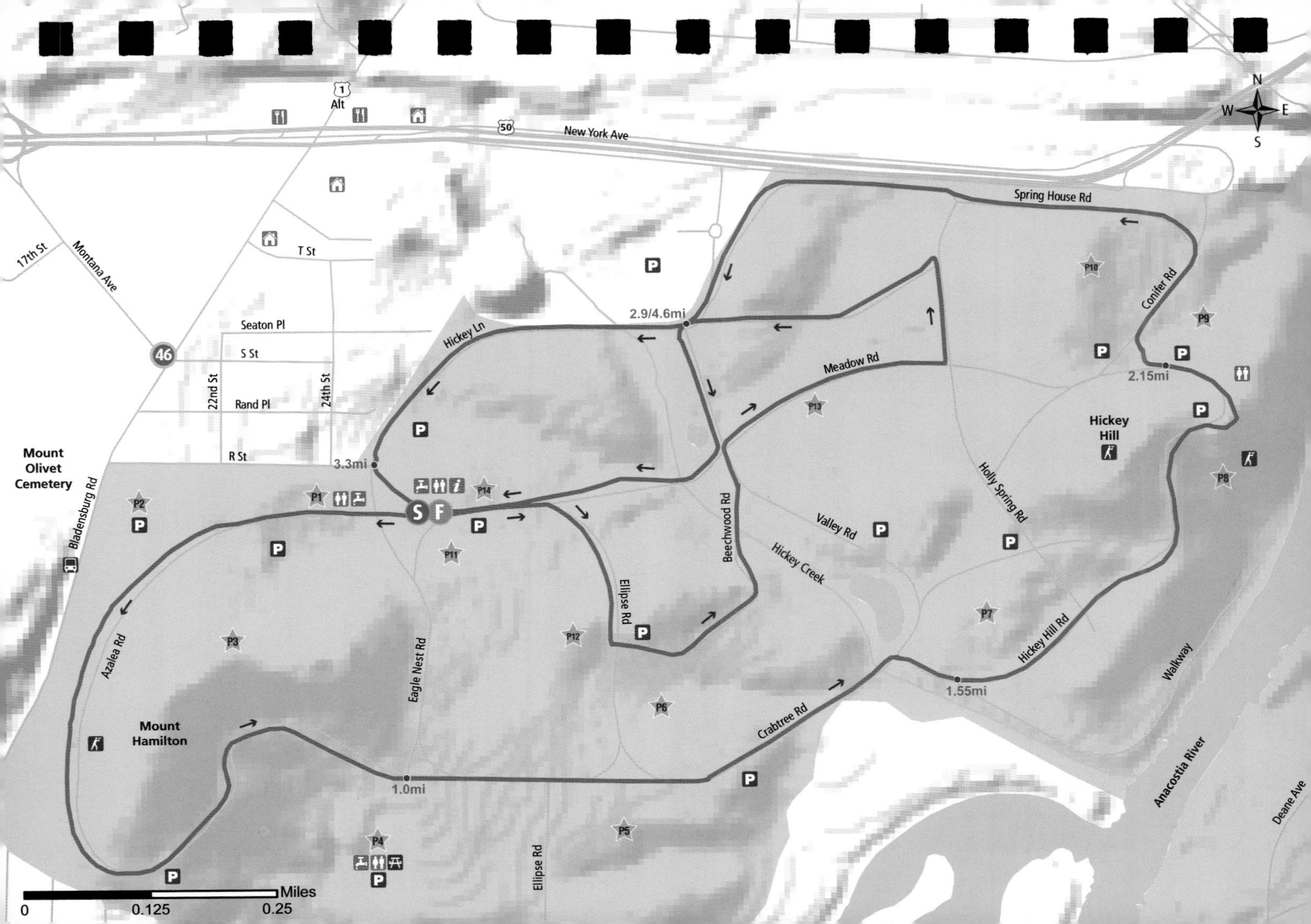

N
W
E
S
1
Alt
50
New York Ave
Spring House Rd
Conifer Rd
2.15mi
Hickey Hill
P10
P9
P8
17th St
Montana Ave
T St
46
Seaton Pl
S St
22nd St
Rand Pl
24th St
R St
Hickey Ln
2.9/4.6mi
Meadow Rd
P13
3.3mi
Mount Olivet Cemetery
Bladensburg Rd
P2
P1
S
F
P14
P11
Holly Spring Rd
Valley Rd
Beechwood Rd
Hickey Creek
Ellipse Rd
P12
P7
Hickey Hill Rd
Walkway
1.55mi
Azalea Rd
P3
Eagle Nest Rd
P6
Crabtree Rd
Mount Hamilton
1.0mi
Anacostia River
Deane Ave
P4
P5
Ellipse Rd
Miles
0
0.125
0.25

Monica on the C&O Towpath in Georgetown.

At a Glance

Distance 14.2 miles **Total Elevation** 855 feet

Terrain

This ride has a hilly first five miles before flattening. The C&O Canal Towpath is unpaved, natural, and a bit bumpy.

Traffic

Minimal. Nearly the entire ride consists of bicycle lanes and trails.

How to Get There

Take Metro's Orange/Blue Line to Rosslyn, Virginia. Drivers may utilize multiple routes toward one of this ride's three bridges, with eventual access to Theodore Roosevelt Island off the George Washington Parkway.

Food and Drink

Plentiful in and around Rosslyn Metro or in Georgetown.

Side Trip

Visit Roosevelt Island, Arlington National Cemetery, the National Mall, or the shops and restaurants of Georgetown, among many other options.

Links to 1 2 3 7 8 28 46 47 48 51

Where to Bike Rating

About...

This figure eight got its name for two reasons. It not only links the Key and Chain bridges, but positioned as it is at the core of D.C., and connecting as many local trails as it does, it's also a route from which you can hang a lot of other rides. Its way takes you over the heights of Arlington, down one of the country's most beloved cycling corridors, along one of the prettiest parts of the Potomac, and among some of our capital's most cherished public grounds.

The Star-Spangled Banner above Francis Scott Key Park.

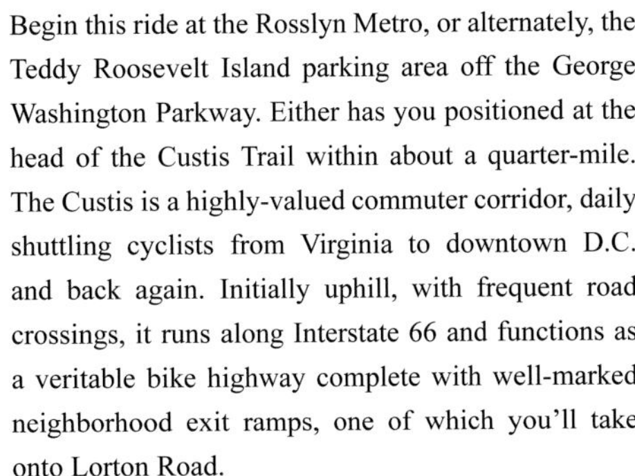

Begin this ride at the Rosslyn Metro, or alternately, the Teddy Roosevelt Island parking area off the George Washington Parkway. Either has you positioned at the head of the Custis Trail within about a quarter-mile. The Custis is a highly-valued commuter corridor, daily shuttling cyclists from Virginia to downtown D.C. and back again. Initially uphill, with frequent road crossings, it runs along Interstate 66 and functions as a veritable bike highway complete with well-marked neighborhood exit ramps, one of which you'll take onto Lorton Road.

Gear up for several big ups and downs in this ride's second section, pushing through what were once the deep, dark woods of North Arlington. A final crest at Old Glebe brings you above the Chain Bridge. As you sharply descend to river level, thank the sneaky 41st Street capillary for aligning you perfectly for a left-side bridge crossing. Now stop and take in the Potomac. It cuts a much more rugged, rock-strewn path here compared with its mellower, wider self farther below the fall line nearer D.C.

Soon it's on to the C&O Towpath and a straight shot back to the city. Though a touch bumpy, it's ultimately a beautiful, relaxed stretch of natural trail. (Read more about both the history of the Chesapeake and Ohio Canal and its modern incarnation as linear park and long-distance bike path in the About section of Ride 51.) Fletcher's Boathouse provides an opportunity to rest, picnic, fish, and boat in a picturesque setting.

Approaching Washington in this manner never ceases to be exciting. There's a simultaneous feeling of being amongst, yet safely sequestered from, the action. Feel the city energy begin to crackle, then join it, as you hop the canal, curl up through Francis Scott Key Park, and become one with the critical mass crossing Key Bridge. Then its left onto the Mount Vernon Trail for a spin down along the Potomac.

Expect great views as you cruise toward, and span, Arlington Bridge while passing some of D.C.'s most famous sites. After taking in the Lincoln Memorial, the Kennedy Center and the Watergate Complex, rejoin the first mile of the C&O Towpath slicing directly through Georgetown's high end shopping and restaurant district. Then cross Key Bridge a second time to finish.

While Ride 6 has not been deemed kid-friendly in its entirety, it does include substantial sections which are entirely safe for family use.

Ride Log

One of Georgetown's famous faces.

P1 Abner Cloud House—circa 1802
P2 Francis Scott Key Park
P3 Arlington House
P4 Lincoln Memorial
P5 Washington Monument
P6 Kennedy Center
P7 Watergate Complex

B1 Revolution Cycles, 3411 M St, NW
B2 Bicycle Pro Shop, 3403 M St, NW
B3 Big Wheel Bikes, 1034 33rd St, NW
B4 Cycle Life USA, 3255 K St, NW
B5 District Hardware—The Bike Shop, 1108 24th St, NW

BR1 Fletcher's Boathouse
BR2 Thompson Boat Center

0.0 Begin by going right out of the Orange/Blue Rosslyn Metro elevator. Take another immediate right to join N Moore St.

0.15 Slide right following sign for Custis Trail. Cross Lee Hwy N and S to take Custis left.

0.3 Continue straight until further notice.

1.05 Trail bears right. Follow Custis sign.

1.7 Left down ramp to bottom. Two more lefts bring you through Thrifton Hill Park.

1.9 Left onto Lorcom Ln.

2.25 Right onto Nelly Custis Dr.

4.45 Right onto Old Glebe followed by left on N Randolph St.

4.7 Right on 41st St N downhill toward Chain Bridge.

4.85 Join Chain Bridge sidepath.

5.2 Left onto downramp to join C&O Towpath.

8.55 Left up ramp to cross canal. Left at top of stairs. And left to cross Key Bridge.

9.05 Left to join Mt Vernon Trail. (Or straight, right, left to return to Rosslyn Metro.)

9.5 Pass footbridge to Roosevelt Island.

9.6 Jog left to continue on Mt Vernon Trail. (Continue straight to cross Roosevelt Bridge toward Kennedy Center.)

10.5 Right to cross GW Pkwy and curl toward Arlington Bridge.

11.3 Continue straight, then travel three-quarters of the way around the Lincoln Memorial.

11.7 Cross left, then continue right toward Potomac River.

12.0 Pass under Roosevelt Bridge.

12.5 Continue straight. (A left accesses Georgetown Waterfront Park.)

12.8 Turn left onto C&O Towpath.

13.5 Right up ramp. Left at top of stairs. Then left to cross Key Bridge.

14.0 Straight then right to cross Lee Hwy and Lynn St. Then slide left onto N Moore.

14.2 A left returns you to elevator.

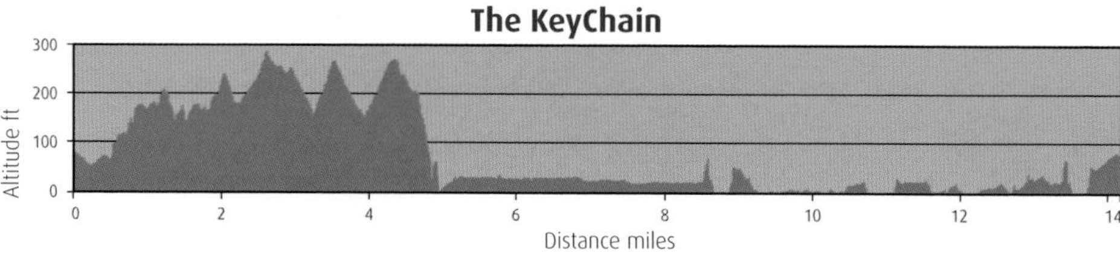

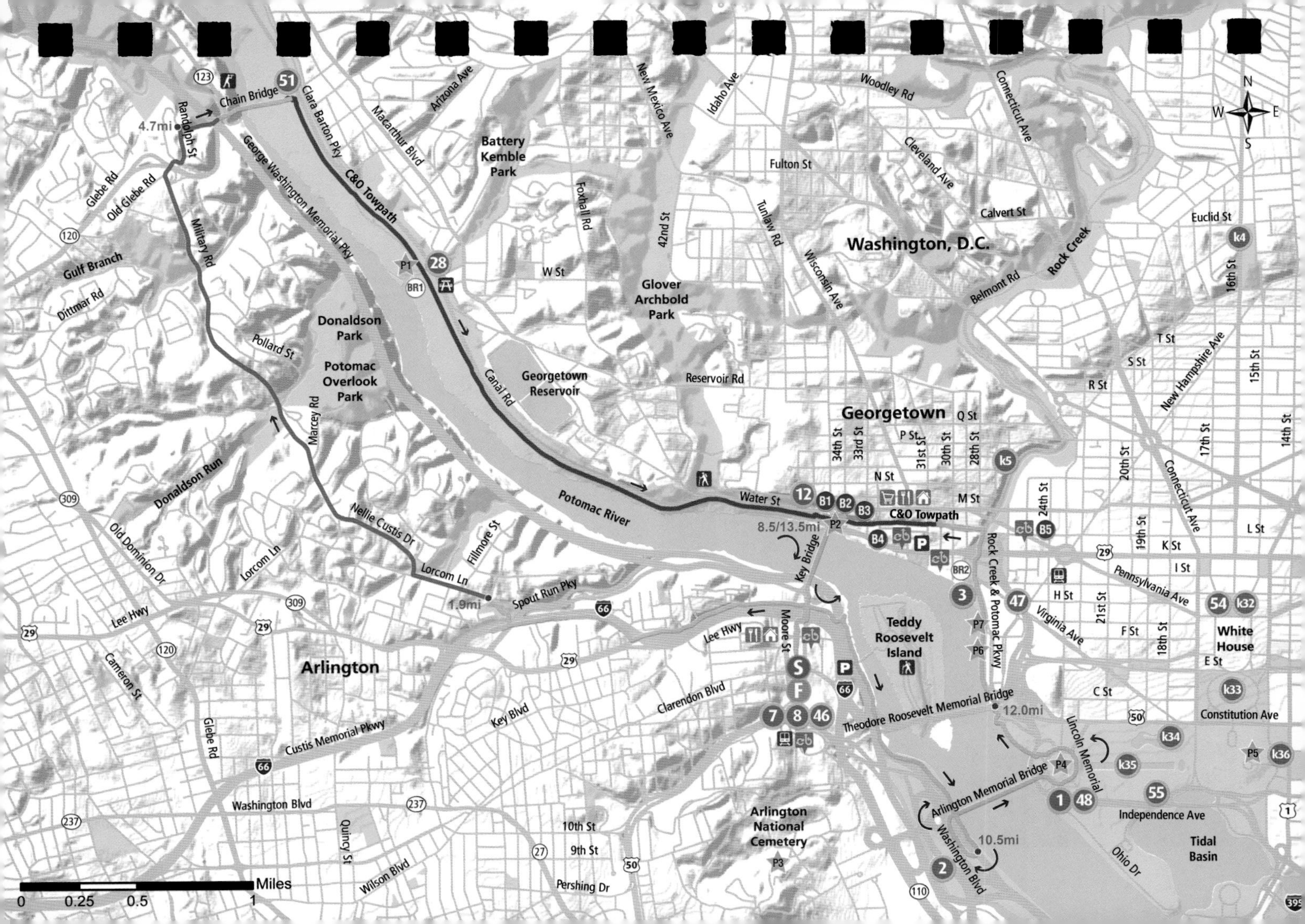
Washington, D.C.
Georgetown
Arlington
Potomac River
C&O Towpath
Chain Bridge
Clara Barton Pky
George Washington Memorial Pky
Battery Kemble Park
Glover Archbold Park
Georgetown Reservoir
Donaldson Park
Potomac Overlook Park
Gulf Branch
Donaldson Run
Rock Creek
Teddy Roosevelt Island
Arlington National Cemetery
White House
Tidal Basin
Lincoln Memorial
Key Bridge
Theodore Roosevelt Memorial Bridge
Arlington Memorial Bridge
Rock Creek & Potomac Pkwy
Randolph St
Military Rd
Glebe Rd
Old Glebe Rd
Dittmar Rd
Pollard St
Marcey Rd
Nellie Custis Dr
Lorcom Ln
Fillmore St
Spout Run Pky
Old Dominion Dr
Lee Hwy
Cameron St
Custis Memorial Pkwy
Washington Blvd
Quincy St
Wilson Blvd
10th St
9th St
Pershing Dr
Key Blvd
Clarendon Blvd
Moore St
Macarthur Blvd
Arizona Ave
Foxhall Rd
W St
42nd St
New Mexico Ave
Idaho Ave
Tunlaw Rd
Wisconsin Ave
Reservoir Rd
Fulton St
Woodley Rd
Cleveland Ave
Calvert St
Connecticut Ave
Belmont Rd
Euclid St
16th St
15th St
14th St
17th St
T St
S St
R St
New Hampshire Ave
Q St
P St
N St
M St
34th St
33rd St
31st St
30th St
28th St
Water St
Canal Rd
24th St
20th St
19th St
21st St
18th St
L St
K St
I St
H St
F St
E St
C St
Pennsylvania Ave
Virginia Ave
Constitution Ave
Independence Ave
Ohio Dr
Washington Blvd
4.7mi
1.9mi
8.5/13.5mi
12.0mi
10.5mi
51
28
12
3
47
54
1
48
55
2
7
8
46
S
F
P1
P2
P3
P4
P5
P6
P7
BR1
BR2
B1
B2
B3
B4
B5
k4
k5
k32
k33
k34
k35
k36
123
120
309
29
66
50
237
27
110
1
395
N
E
S
W
Miles
0
0.25
0.5
1

Practicing the art of relection along the Custis Trail.

At a Glance

Distance 17.1 miles **Total Elevation** 1000 feet

Terrain

There are some hills in this ride's opening miles, a couple of short, steep climbs on the Four Mile Run, and a series of gradual inclines passing National Airport. Everything else is flat to near-flat, and the way itself is smooth.

Traffic

No vehicular contact besides occasional street crossings, though riders must share the trail with walkers, joggers, and strollers.

How to Get There

Taking either Metro's Orange or Blue Line to Rosslyn is easiest. Drivers can park nearby at Teddy Roosevelt Island off the northbound lanes of the George Washington Memorial Parkway, reaching it by way of Interstates 66, 395, and numerous other roads and highways. If arriving by bus, check local schedules and aim to connect to the D.C. Circulator.

Food and Drink

Available around Rosslyn Metro or in Shirlington just past mile nine.

Side Trip

Save the 23-mile, county-sponsored Arlington History Ride for another day. But visit Arlington National Cemetery by turning left at mile 15.3, looping the Marine Corps Memorial, and continuing right uphill to enter Fort Meyer. Using its guarded back entrance into the graveyard, ask kindly if you can spin by Arlington House for the premier view of D.C., and then back downhill to this route, being sure to follow established guidelines all the while.

Links to   2 6 8 19 46

Where to Bike Rating 

About...

Home to such iconic D.C.-area sites as the Pentagon, the Marine Corps Memorial, and the nation's most famous cemetery, Arlington also plays a key role in U.S. government and is consistently ranked among the country's most prosperous, highly educated, and livable places. A friend to cyclists for years, this ride's trails are only a portion of the 50 miles of segregated path, 30 miles of lanes and sharrows, and nearly 80 miles of recommended routes currently incorporated into the county's progressive Bike Arlington program.

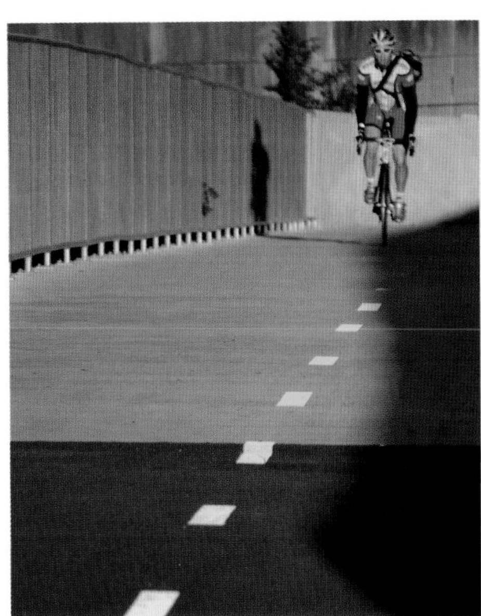

The Four Mile Run's seamless Shirlington Connector.

Along with a section of the City of Alexandria, the 26 square miles of Arlington County make up the missing piece of what used to be the diamond-shaped District of Columbia. Ceded to the U.S. government by the Commonwealth of Virginia to help form the capital in 1801, they were later reacquired in 1846 after a convoluted history combining politics, economics, law, and slavery.

John Smith met Algonquin-speaking natives here during his first trip up the Potomac in 1608, and the area was subsequently granted to a certain Lord Fairfax by England's King Charles II. Slower to develop than the ports of Georgetown and Alexandria, Arlington remained countryside well toward the Civil War, when a prized plantation belonging to the family of Confederate General Robert E. Lee was forcibly repossessed and reutilized as a burying ground.

These days, the county is a highly diverse, urban district ranking among the most bike-friendly jurisdictions in the nation, and one of only a select few eastern communities to earn silver-level status within the comprehensive rating system established by the League of American Bicyclists.

Today's ride begins with a stretch directly beside Highway 66 along the commuter-driven Custis Trail, so named for a family which played a prominent role in Arlington's early history. A positive outcome of the decades-long battle to build the interstate, its often hilly way is less aethetic than practical, but serves to shuttle you past residential neighborhoods and shopping complexes and benefits from numerous well-signed exits.

Be sure to stop and smell the roses as the route reaches the Four Mile Run Trail near the garden in Bon Air Park. Easily confused here with the W&OD Trail, the way you want tends to stay right of the run and incorporate more of nature. After a fabulous string of forested parks, the path pushes into the open toward the Shirlington Connector. Stay tight to the water now as it widens and becomes a tidal stream below the fall line and forms Arlington's border with Alexandria.

Spilling you onto the Mount Vernon Trail (detailed in Ride 8) just south of National Airport, the loop then carries you back north past some of D.C.'s best-known destinations on what could be the area's signature stretch of cycling.

While Ride 7 has not been deemed kid-friendly in its entirety, it does include substantial sections which are entirely safe for family use.

Ride Log

0.0 Exit right from Rosslyn Metro elevator to an immediate right onto N Moore St.

0.15 Slide right into bike lane then left to cross Lee Hwy North and South.

0.25 Take a left onto the Custis Trail.

1.05 Bear right.

2.5 Rest Stop. Water.

3.2 Left to continue over bridge.

4.55 Right.

4.7 Left onto the W&OD. Rest Stop. Water.

5.15 Slide right onto Four Mile Run Trail after underpass.

5.75 Bear left.

6.1 Bear right to curve uphill.

6.5 Bathrooms.

7.4 Continue right to slip along sidewalk.

7.7 Curl right to go up and over bridge then straight to continue.

8.55 Jog left then cross road to continue.

9.2 Shirlington restaurants to right.

9.25 Left along sidewalk then right to cross road and join Shirlington Connector.

9.85 Right to continue.

10.2 Dip right toward water.

11.2 Dip right.

11.6 Bear right to join Mt Vernon Trail.

15.3 Continue straight.

16.3 Turn right.

16.8 Cross at light, then turn left.

16.9 Turn right onto bike lane then left onto N Moore St.

17.1 Left to end at Rosslyn Metro elevator.

P1 Theodore Roosevelt Island
P2 Bon Air Park Rose Garden
P3 Ball-Sellers House
P4 Abingdon Estate
P5 Arlington Historical Museum
P6 Pentagon
P7 Pentagon Memorial
P8 Air Force Memorial
P9 Jefferson Memorial
P10 Washington Monument
P11 Lincoln Memorial
P12 Arlington House
P13 Marine Corps Memorial
P14 Kennedy Center

B1 Revolution Cycles, 3411 M St, NW
B2 Bicycle Pro Shop, 3403 M St, NW
B3 Big Wheel Bikes, 1034 33rd St, NW
B4 Cycle Life USA, 3255 K St, NW
B5 Big Wheel Bikes, 3119 N Lee Hwy
B6 Revolution Cycles, 2731 Wilson Blvd
B7 Eastern Mountain Sports, 2800 Clarendon Blvd
B8 Conte's, 3924 Wilson Blvd
B9 Phoenix Bikes, 4200 S Four Mile Run Dr
B10 Papillon Cycles, 2809 Columbia Pike
B11 Revolution Cycles, 220 20th St South
B12 Hudson Trail Outfitters Ltd, 1101 S Joyce St #B29

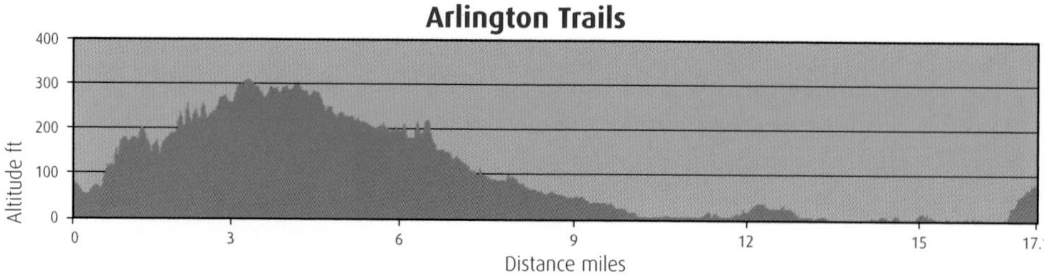

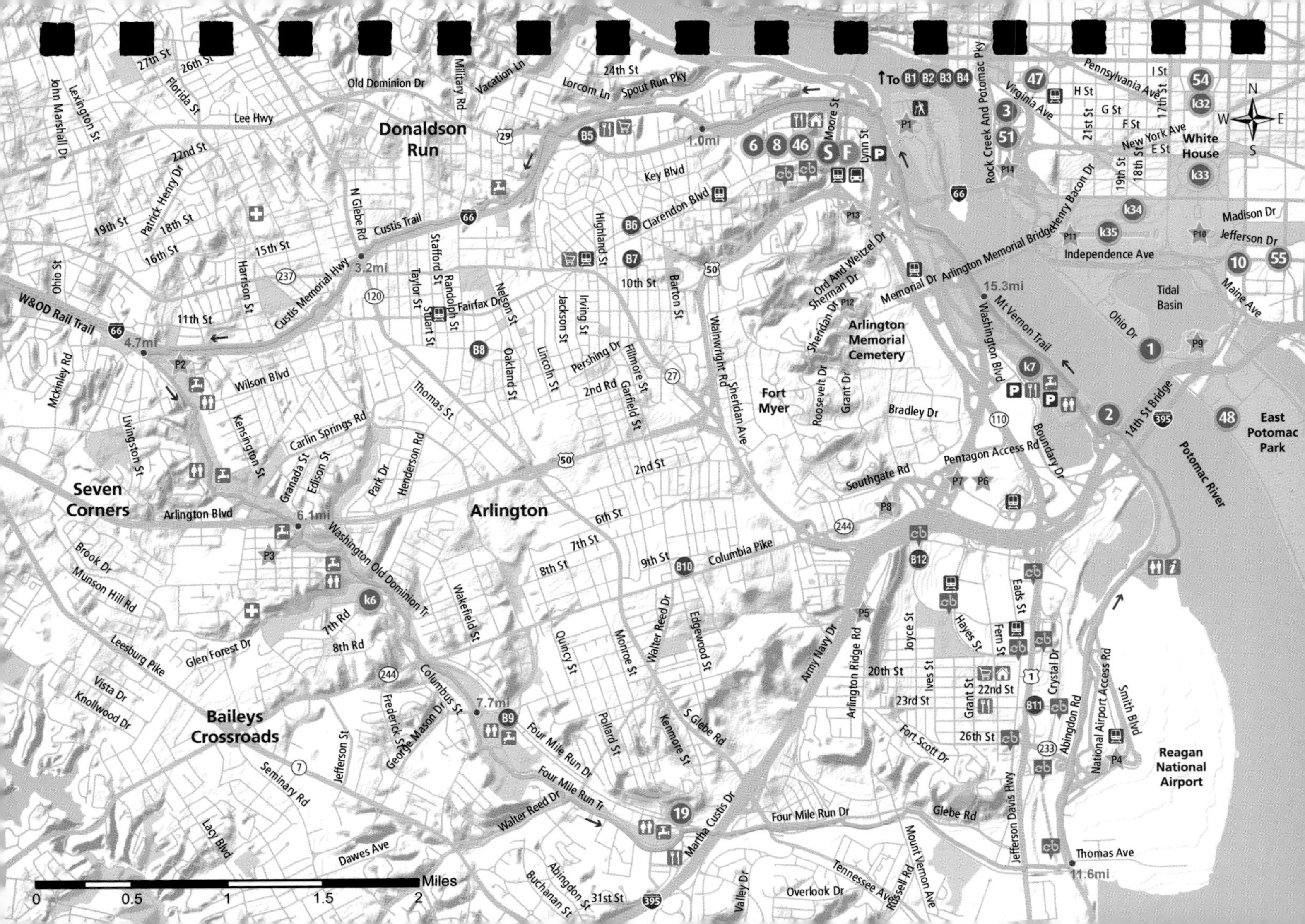

N
E
S
W
White House
East Potomac Park
Potomac River
Tidal Basin
Reagan National Airport
Arlington Memorial Cemetery
Fort Myer
Arlington
Donaldson Run
Seven Corners
Baileys Crossroads
Pennsylvania Ave
Virginia Ave
New York Ave
Independence Ave
Madison Dr
Jefferson Dr
Maine Ave
Ohio Dr
14th St Bridge
Rock Creek And Potomac Pky
Henry Bacon Dr
Arlington Memorial Bridge
Mt Vernon Trail
Washington Blvd
Boundary Dr
Pentagon Access Rd
Memorial Dr
Bradley Dr
Southgate Rd
Smith Blvd
National Airport Access Rd
Abingdon Rd
Crystal Dr
Eads St
Fern St
Hayes St
22nd St
Grant St
26th St
Jefferson Davis Hwy
Thomas Ave
Glebe Rd
Fort Scott Dr
Ives St
Joyce St
23rd St
20th St
Arlington Ridge Rd
Army Navy Dr
Mount Vernon Ave
Russell Rd
Tennessee Ave
Overlook Dr
Four Mile Run Dr
Valley Dr
Martha Custis Dr
Lynn St
Moore St
Ord And Weitzel Dr
Sherman Dr
Sheridan Dr
Grant Dr
Roosevelt Dr
Sheridan Ave
Wainwright Rd
Columbia Pike
Edgewood St
S Glebe Rd
Kenmore St
Walter Reed Dr
Monroe St
Pollard St
Quincy St
Four Mile Run Tr
Abingdon St
31st St
Buchanan St
Spout Run Pky
24th St
Lorcom Ln
Key Blvd
Clarendon Blvd
Barton St
10th St
Fillmore St
Garfield St
2nd St
9th St
6th St
7th St
8th St
Highland St
Irving St
Jackson St
Pershing Dr
2nd Rd
Lincoln St
Oakland St
Nelson St
Fairfax Dr
Randolph St
Stafford St
Stuart St
Taylor St
Thomas St
Wakefield St
Columbus St
George Mason Dr
Frederick St
Vacation Ln
Military Rd
Old Dominion Dr
Custis Trail
N Glebe Rd
Custis Memorial Hwy
Henderson Rd
Park Dr
Washington Old Dominion Tr
7th Rd
8th Rd
Jefferson St
Dawes Ave
Seminary Rd
Carlin Springs Rd
Edison St
Granada St
Wilson Blvd
15th St
Harrison St
Kensington St
Lee Hwy
Glen Forest Dr
Lacy Blvd
11th St
Arlington Blvd
26th St
27th St
Florida St
22nd St
Patrick Henry Dr
18th St
16th St
19th St
Livingston St
Lexington St
John Marshall Dr
Ohio St
Mckinley Rd
W&OD Rail Trail
Brook Dr
Munson Hill Rd
Leesburg Pike
Vista Dr
Knollwood Dr
To B1 B2 B3 B4
15.3mi
1.0mi
3.2mi
4.7mi
6.1mi
7.7mi
11.6mi
Miles
0
0.5
1
1.5
2

Racing to catch their flight out of Reagan National.

At a Glance

Distance 16.6 miles **Total Elevation** 540 feet

Terrain

Mostly flat trail with boardwalk sections, a string of modest hills near National Airport, and a short on-road stretch in Alexandria.

Traffic

The path can be busy. Be prepared to share with riders intent on speed as well as walkers, joggers, and sightseers.

How to Get There

Take either Metro's Orange or Blue Line to Rosslyn. Drivers can park nearby at Teddy Roosevelt Island off the northbound lanes of the George Washington Memorial Parkway. Reach it by way of Interstates 66 and 395, and numerous other roads and highways. If arriving by bus, check local schedules and aim to connect to the D.C. Circulator.

Food and Drink

Don't worry. This ride is well-fed. For quicker options stop near Rosslyn Metro, at the end of a short connector to Crystal City, at the café on Columbia Island, or near the turnaround in Alexandria. If you favor cloth napkin establishments, stick to Old Town or try Indigo Landing at the Washington Sailing Marina on Daingerfield Island.

Side Trip

Hike Teddy Roosevelt Island. Lock up and tour Arlington National Cemetery. Or use the Humpback Bridge underpass to access the Pentagon and Air Force memorials across the Boundary Channel beyond LBJ Memorial Grove.

Links to 

Where to Bike Rating 

About...

The Mount Vernon Trail follows the banks of the Potomac River and parallels the Washington Memorial Parkway from the Key Bridge all the way south to the doorstep of George Washington's estate and gardens. A flagship for multi-use paths throughout the country, *Where to Bike D.C.* includes two tours along its course. This particular jaunt, a true area classic since 1973, offers easy access to sacred national sites, unrivalled views of major monuments and memorials, and an introduction to Old Town Alexandria.

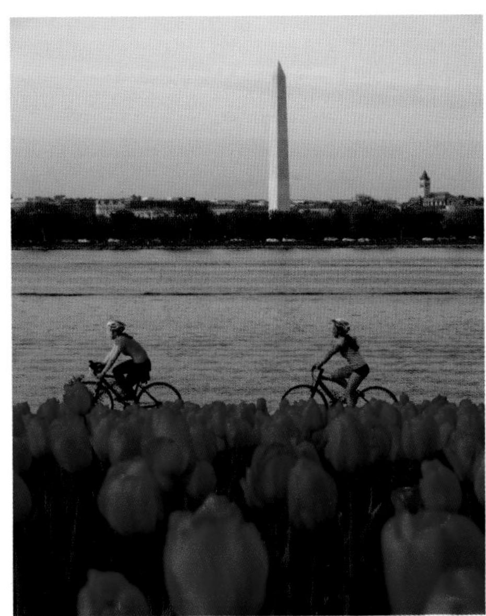

Two-wheeling through the tulips.

Only minutes off Metro and beyond an elevated boardwalk near undeveloped Teddy Roosevelt Island, this route hands you a royal view of the Lincoln Memorial and squeezes past multi-arched Arlington Memorial Bridge, symbol of north-south reunification after the Civil War.

Pathways here lead toward the National Mall and into Arlington National Cemetery, but today's focus steadies southward to the Navy-Merchant Marine Memorial. Look west near there off Humpback Bridge to the three silver contrails of the Air Force Memorial shooting above the Pentagon and over Columbia Island Marina.

The 14th Street Bridge offers more monumental connection but, again, your way continues straight, now toward breezy Gravelly Point. Nice days bring droves of folks out to enjoy the panorama of D.C. provided by this open space. Others recreate in its fields or planespot at its privileged location just north of National Airport. Be cautious as the path often crowds with strolling families and on-lookers.

After squeezing between runway 15 and the parkway, a touch of climbing brings left-leading airport access and a chance to check out former Abingdon Estate, home for a time to George Washington's stepson and step-granddaughter Nelly. The foundation of its plantation house remains, remarkably, due southeast between parking structures A and B.

Be cautious of cars curling along Aviation Circle up ahead, and once over Four Mile Run a modest ascent brings the route above the river before dropping it briefly beside the shoreline, past Washington Sailing Marina, and beyond a marsh-spanning boardwalk.

Now bear left to an open view across the Potomac, over more boardwalk, and briefly again uphill. Watch your speed moving forward as the path drops, winds through a caged walkway, and rises again, soon to curve past the first of two grassy riverside parks and edge into Alexandria.

Local activist Ellen Pickering fought to preserve the legacy of this historic city's shoreline and galvanized the push to construct this trail. Stories have her soliciting volunteers to spread its initial gravel sections from near here north to the 14th Street Bridge.

On-road now, two rail-track crossings signal intensifying action past Founders Park. Lock up and have a look around. Retrace when ready, or take the bike-friendly King Street Trolley to Metro and head back to Rosslyn from there.

While Ride 8 has not been deemed kid-friendly in its entirety, it does include substantial sections which are entirely safe for family use.

Ride Log

0.0 Exit right from Rosslyn Metro elevator to an immediate right onto N Moore St.

0.15 Slide right into bike lane then left to cross N Lynn St and Lee Hwy South following Mt Vernon Trail prompts.

0.25 Cross Lee Hwy North to turn right immediately onto Mt Vernon Trail.

0.65 Roosevelt Island. Parking. Alternate beginning.

0.75 Jog left to stay on Mt Vernon Trail. Straight takes you up on the Roosevelt Bridge toward the Kennedy Center.

1.7 Right to Arlington Memorial Bridge or Arlington National Cemetery.

2.7 Right to cross 14th St Bridge to Jefferson Memorial and East Potomac Park.

3.5 Gravelly Point. Bathrooms. Info.

4.4 Right to Crystal City. Metro access. Food. Revolution Cycles City Hub.

4.7 Left to National Airport. Abingdon.

5.0 Caution, merging traffic.

5.45 Stay right to continue along Mt Vernon Trail. Bear left to join Four Mile Run Trail.

6.3 Left to Daingerfield Island.

6.75 Bear left toward Potomac.

7.6 Cross tracks at an angle.

7.9 Left to join Pendleton St. Cross rail tracks.

8.35 End at King St, caddy-corner to Starbucks. Eat, shop, sightsee, people-watch and retrace as the feeling moves you.

8.8 Right to join trail.

9.1 Jog right across tracks to continue along trail.

10.3 Right to Daingerfield Island.

12.3 Left to Crystal City.

16.0 Roosevelt Island parking. Alternate ending.

16.4 Cross N Lynn St and cross Lee Hwy N & S before swinging right toward N Moore St.

16.6 Turn left to return to Rosslyn Metro elevator.

Taking it all in at Gravelly Point.

The Mount Vernon Trail North

Altitude ft: 200, 100, 0

0, 3, 6, 9, 12, 15, 16.6

Distance miles

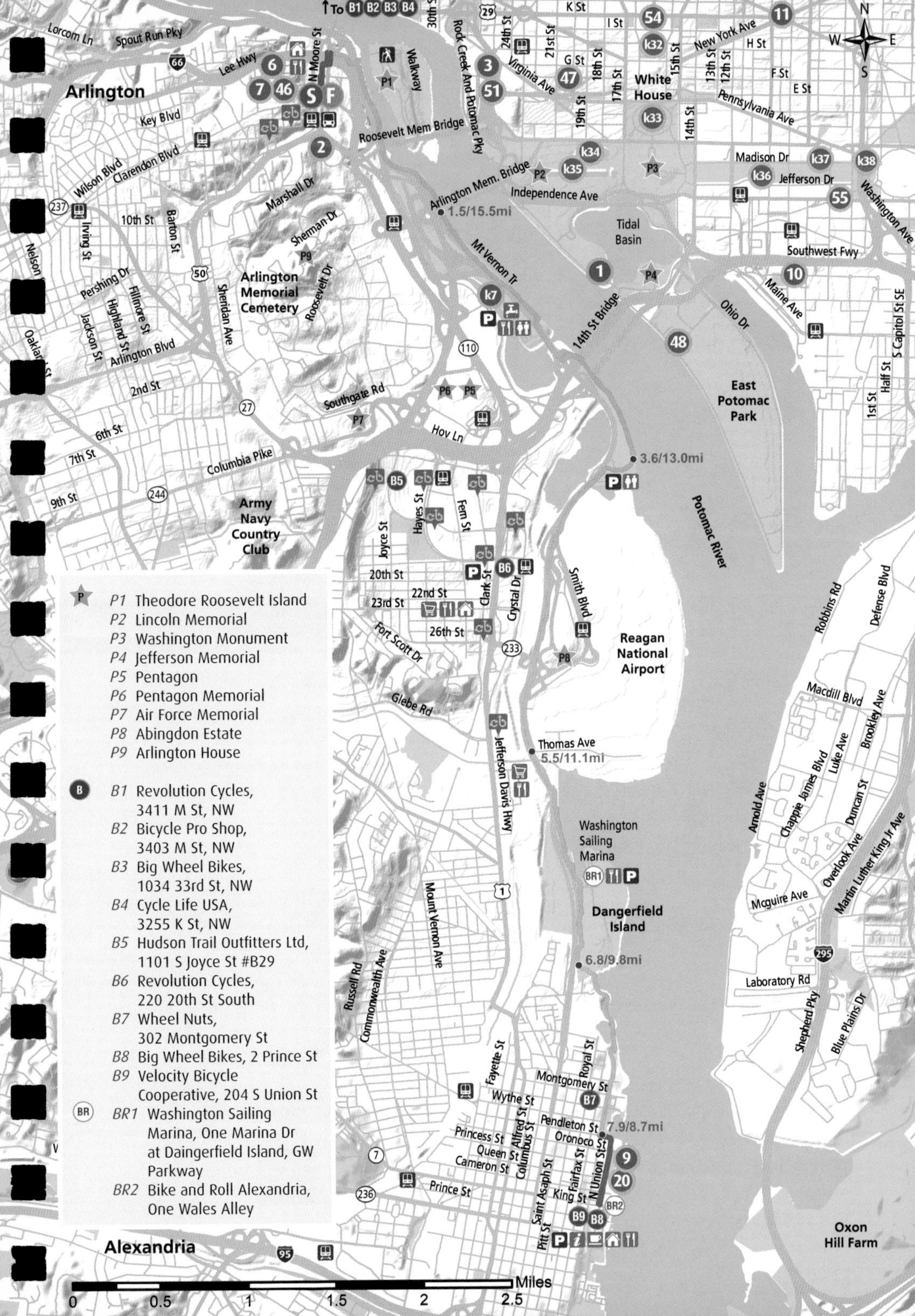

To B1 B2 B3 B4
Arlington
Alexandria
White House
Tidal Basin
Arlington Memorial Cemetery
East Potomac Park
Potomac River
Reagan National Airport
Army Navy Country Club
Washington Sailing Marina
Dangerfield Island
Oxon Hill Farm
Roosevelt Mem Bridge
Arlington Mem. Bridge
14th St Bridge
Independence Ave
Pennsylvania Ave
Constitution Ave
Southwest Fwy
Columbia Pike
Jefferson Davis Hwy
Mount Vernon Ave
Mt Vernon Tr
1.5/15.5mi
3.6/13.0mi
5.5/11.1mi
6.8/9.8mi
7.9/8.7mi
P1 Theodore Roosevelt Island
P2 Lincoln Memorial
P3 Washington Monument
P4 Jefferson Memorial
P5 Pentagon
P6 Pentagon Memorial
P7 Air Force Memorial
P8 Abingdon Estate
P9 Arlington House
B1 Revolution Cycles, 3411 M St, NW
B2 Bicycle Pro Shop, 3403 M St, NW
B3 Big Wheel Bikes, 1034 33rd St, NW
B4 Cycle Life USA, 3255 K St, NW
B5 Hudson Trail Outfitters Ltd, 1101 S Joyce St #B29
B6 Revolution Cycles, 220 20th St South
B7 Wheel Nuts, 302 Montgomery St
B8 Big Wheel Bikes, 2 Prince St
B9 Velocity Bicycle Cooperative, 204 S Union St
BR1 Washington Sailing Marina, One Marina Dr at Daingerfield Island, GW Parkway
BR2 Bike and Roll Alexandria, One Wales Alley
Miles
0
0.5
1
1.5
2
2.5

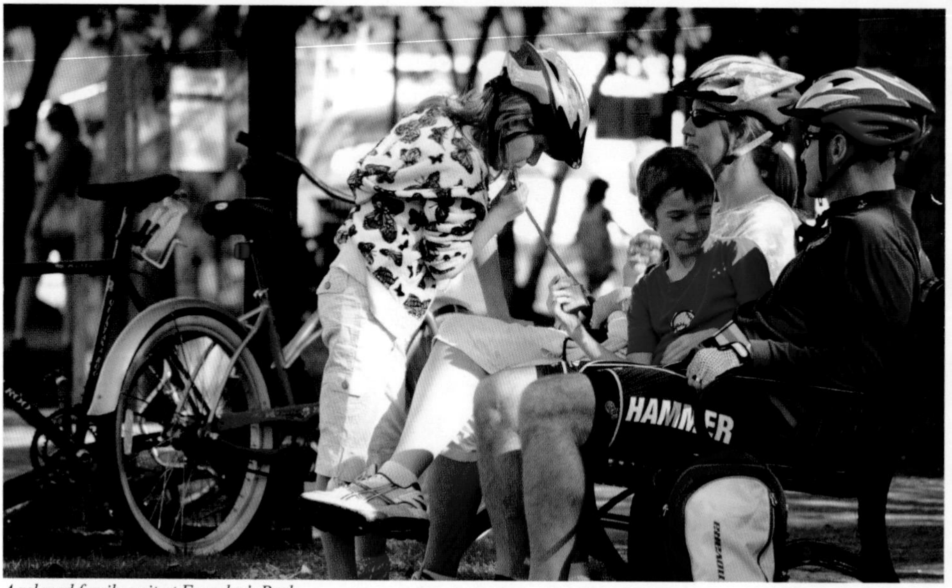

A relaxed family unit at Founder's Park.

At a Glance

Distance 9.8 miles **Total Elevation** 380 feet

Terrain

Besides a short section of trail near Jones Point Park, most of this route is on-road and nearly all flat. Expect one healthy climb up to the George Washington Masonic National Memorial.

Traffic

Busiest around the King Street Metro, take care in this ride's initial quarter mile, even walking if need be. Commonwealth and Mount Vernon are busy as well, but bike friendly. The remainder is mostly mild.

How to Get There

Using the Blue/Yellow King Street Metro is easiest. Otherwise, drive the Beltway to exit 176, Telegraph Road. Go right on Duke Street to a left on Callahan Drive looking to park along side streets, in Amtrak and Metro station lots, or, if planning a visit, perhaps up near the Masonic Memorial.

Food and Drink

Alexandria is brimming with options along King and Mount Vernon streets. Try Gadsby's in Old Town, a tavern frequented by Washington and Jefferson, or stop by The Dairy Godmother for frozen custard in Del Ray.

Side Trip

Shop Old Town's high-end boutiques. Or take Jamieson Avenue left within this ride's first half mile, turning left again on Holland Lane past the African American Heritage Park, then right down Eisenhower Avenue past its Metro and onto its sidepath next to Cameron Run. Then continue along the flat, scenic Holmes Run Trail.

Links to 8 20 36 46

Where to Bike Rating 

About...

Alexandria was established close to a century before the District of Columbia and remains the region's most well-preserved link to its past. An old colonial seaport saturated with history, its compact size, abundance of 18th and 19th century architecture, and tight cobblestone alleys make it a visitor's delight and one best experienced by walkers and cyclists. Lovely, intimate, and laced with class, this easy-going tour invites frequent stops and has one of the highest densities of sites per mile in all of *Where to Bike D.C.*

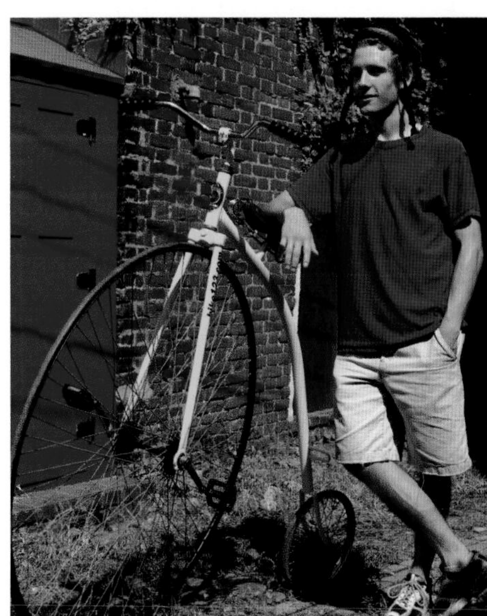

Old bike, old alley, Old Town.

This tour's first significant turn to Hooff's Run and past an old stone bridge brings you to a national cemetery commissioned before famous Arlington. Noteworthy burials include a group of Buffalo Soldiers as well as four men who drowned in pursuit of Lincoln's assassin. One of D.C.'s 40 original boundary stones sits in a yard at the left off South Payne. Placed in 1791 by surveyor Andrew Ellicott, it demarcates D.C.'s original southwestern border and is exactly one mile from the first marker placed at upcoming Jones Point.

Straight, quiet Wilkes then brings you through the old Orange & Alexandria railroad tunnel and onto the Mount Vernon Trail. Detailed in Ride 20, it dips to the Potomac, passes the southernmost stone at its home beside one of the oldest surviving inland lighthouses in the U.S., and scoots under massive Woodrow Wilson Bridge. Old Town now lies beyond a sign commemorating former riverside Civil War fort, Battery Rodgers, and colorfully-shuttered, flat-fronted neighborhood homes soon appear near Old Presbyterian Meeting House and its graveyard of early Alexandrians.

Turns thereafter begin to come faster and sites more frequent as the tour's core approaches a host of explorable options beyond the Lyceum on Prince Street and past a statue of a pensive Southern soldier. Initially settled in 1695, Alexandria grew into a significant colonial port. Home to an aspiring young Washington and a thriving slave market, Confederate-leaning yet Union-occupied, its complex history runs deep, and you'd be wise to stop by the Ramsay House for detailed information.

Now an artist's collective, the Torpedo Factory also houses the Alexandria Archaeology Museum. Braddock drew up French and Indian War plans in Carlyle House. City Hall sits beside one of the oldest continually operating marketplaces in the nation. The Stabler-Leadbeater Apothecary is frozen in time. Gadsby's Tavern served founding fathers and will still serve you. Christ Church predates the Revolutionary War. The Spite House is only seven feet wide. And Confederate General Lee grew up on Oronoco Street.

Beyond Braddock Road Metro a younger Alexandria emerges in the former streetcar suburbs of Del Ray and Rosemont. From there, climb up to, and perhaps up inside, the Washington Masonic Memorial for a route retrospective and a fantastic view of the region.

Ride Log

0.0 Curl right out of King St Metro elevator. Set odometer at gates and exit toward a right on King St, then immediately bear right onto Daingerfield.

0.25 Cross Duke to multi-use path beside Hooff's Run.

0.35 Cross Jamieson to join sidepath left. (National Cemetery).

0.5 Take successive right/left, right/left to join Wilkes St. (Boundary Stone).

0.85 Cross S Washington and continue straight on sidewalk connector.

1.2 Pass through Wilkes Tunnel.

1.4 Right onto S Union.

1.65 Dip left to join Mt Vernon Trail. Pass path to Jones Point Lighthouse.

2.4 Right under WW Bridge onto Royal St.

2.6 Right on Green then two blocks to a left on S Lee. (Battery Rodgers).

3.15 Left on Wolfe.

3.55 Right on Alfred.

3.7 Right on Prince St. (Friendship Firehouse).

4.15 Left onto S Lee. (Athenaeum). Right on King. Left on N Union. (Torpedo Factory).

4.45 Left on Queen St. Left on N Fairfax. (Carlyle House, City Hall, Market Square, Ramsay House. Apothecary).

4.7 Right on King. Left on N Royal. Left on Cameron. (Gadsby's Tavern).

5.0 Right on N Washington. (Christ Church). Right on Queen. Left on St Asaph. (Spite House).

5.3 Left on Oronoco. (Lee House).

5.5 Right on Alfred.

5.65 Left on Wythe.

- *P1* Alexandria National Cemetery
- *P2* One-mile boundary stone
- *P3* Wilkes Street train tunnel
- *P4* Lighthouse and southernmost D.C. boundary stone
- *P5* Battery Rodgers
- *P6* Old Presbyterian Meeting House
- *P7* Friendship Firehouse
- *P8* Lyceum
- *P9* Athenaeum
- *P10* Alexandria Archaeology Museum at Torpedo Factory Arts Center
- *P11* Carlyle House
- *P12* City Hall and Market Square
- *P13* Alexandria visitor center at Ramsay House
- *P14* Apothecary Museum
- *P15* Gadsby's Tavern
- *P16* Christ Church
- *P17* Spite House
- *P18* Lee House
- *P19* The Dairy Godmother
- *P20* The George Washington Masonic National Memorial

5.95 Jog left to merge onto Braddock Rd. (Metro).

6.15 Right on Mt Vernon.

7.35 Sharp left onto Commonwealth.

8.7 Right on W Walnut.

9.0 Use sidewalk briefly right to cross King to Upland. Then left on Hilltop Terrace and right on Carlisle to slip through fence left onto Masonic grounds. Follow driveway past parking around front and continue down drive to left on Callahan to immediate right to King St.

9.75 Slip right onto sidewalk before underpass to allow easier access to King St Metro.

9.8 Return to King St Metro elevator.

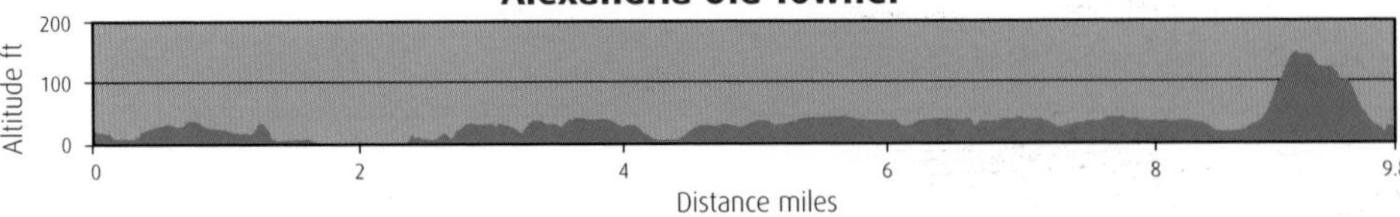

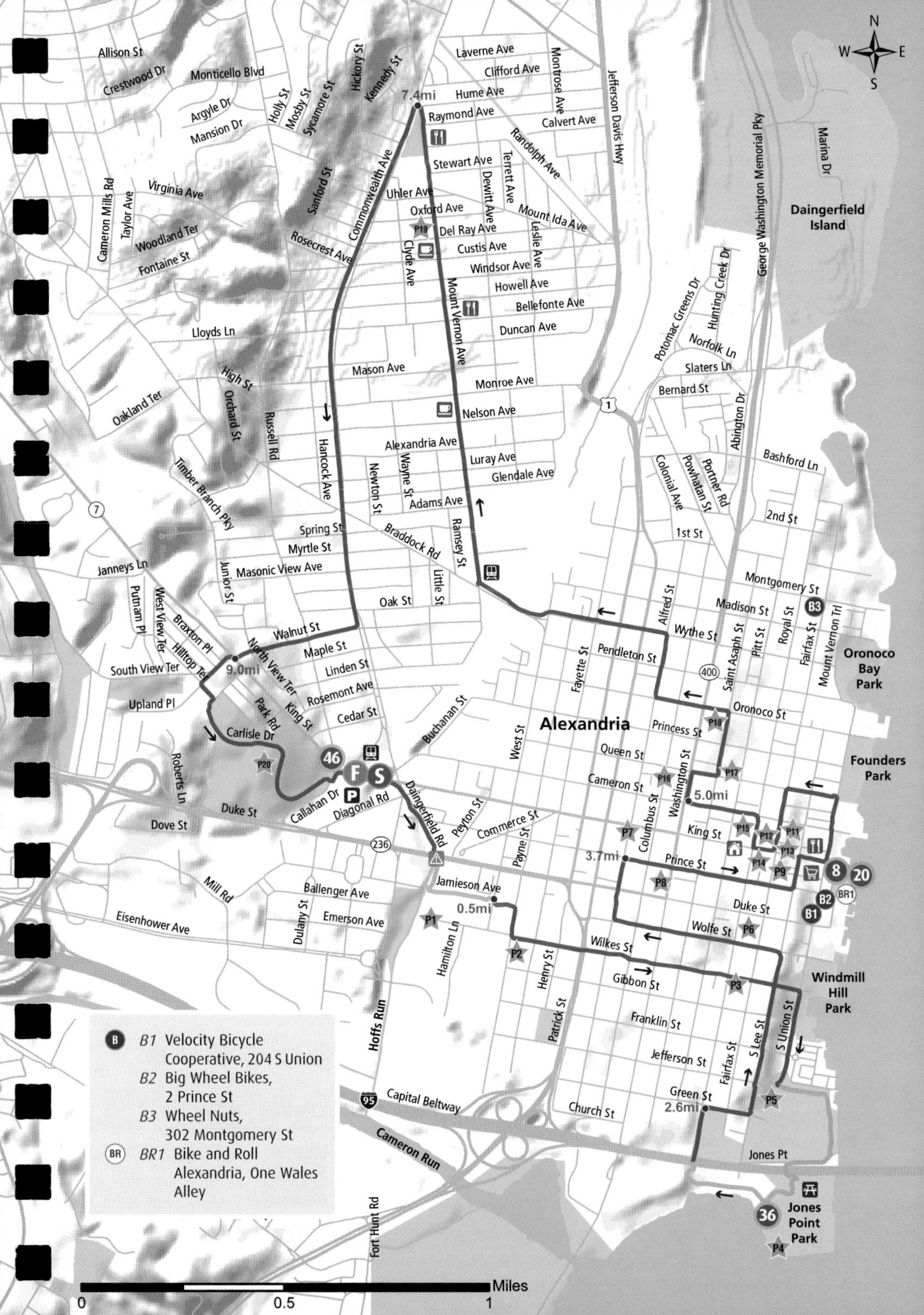

N
W
E
S
Allison St
Crestwood Dr
Monticello Blvd
Argyle Dr
Mansion Dr
Holly St
Mosby St
Sycamore St
Hickory St
Kennedy St
7.4mi
Laverne Ave
Clifford Ave
Hume Ave
Raymond Ave
Montrose Ave
Calvert Ave
Jefferson Davis Hwy
Randolph Ave
Stewart Ave
Terrett Ave
Dewitt Ave
Uhler Ave
Oxford Ave
Del Ray Ave
Mount Ida Ave
Leslie Ave
Custis Ave
Windsor Ave
Howell Ave
Bellefonte Ave
Duncan Ave
Clyde Ave
Mount Vernon Ave
Commonwealth Ave
Sanford St
Rosecrest Ave
Virginia Ave
Cameron Mills Rd
Taylor Ave
Woodland Ter
Fontaine St
Lloyds Ln
High St
Orchard St
Oakland Ter
Russell Rd
Mason Ave
Monroe Ave
Nelson Ave
Alexandria Ave
Luray Ave
Glendale Ave
Hancock Ave
Newton St
Wayne St
Adams Ave
Timber Branch Pky
Spring St
Myrtle St
Braddock Rd
Ramsey St
Masonic View Ave
Janneys Ln
Junior St
Little St
Oak St
Putnam Pl
West View Ter
Braxton Pl
Hilltop Ter
Walnut St
Maple St
North View Ter
Linden St
9.0mi
South View Ter
Upland Pl
Rosemont Ave
King St
Park Rd
Cedar St
Carlisle Dr
Roberts Ln
Buchanan St
Callahan Dr
Diagonal Rd
Daingerfield Rd
Duke St
Dove St
Peyton St
Commerce St
Payne St
West St
Mill Rd
Jamieson Ave
0.5mi
Ballenger Ave
Emerson Ave
Dulany St
Eisenhower Ave
Hamilton Ln
Henry St
Patrick St
Hoffs Run
Capital Beltway
Cameron Run
Fort Hunt Rd
Church St
Alexandria
Fayette St
Pendleton St
Alfred St
Wythe St
Madison St
Montgomery St
Princess St
Oronoco St
Queen St
Cameron St
Columbus St
Washington St
5.0mi
King St
3.7mi
Prince St
Duke St
Wolfe St
Wilkes St
Gibbon St
Franklin St
Jefferson St
Green St
2.6mi
Fairfax St
S Lee St
S Union St
Jones Pt
Saint Asaph St
Pitt St
Royal St
Fairfax St
Mount Vernon Trl
Potomac Greens Dr
Hunting Creek Dr
George Washington Memorial Pky
Norfolk Ln
Slaters Ln
Bernard St
Abingdon Dr
Colonial Ave
Powhatan St
Portner Rd
Bashford Ln
2nd St
1st St
Marina Dr
Daingerfield Island
Oronoco Bay Park
Founders Park
Windmill Hill Park
Jones Point Park
B1 Velocity Bicycle Cooperative, 204 S Union
B2 Big Wheel Bikes, 2 Prince St
B3 Wheel Nuts, 302 Montgomery St
BR1 Bike and Roll Alexandria, One Wales Alley
Miles
0
0.5
1

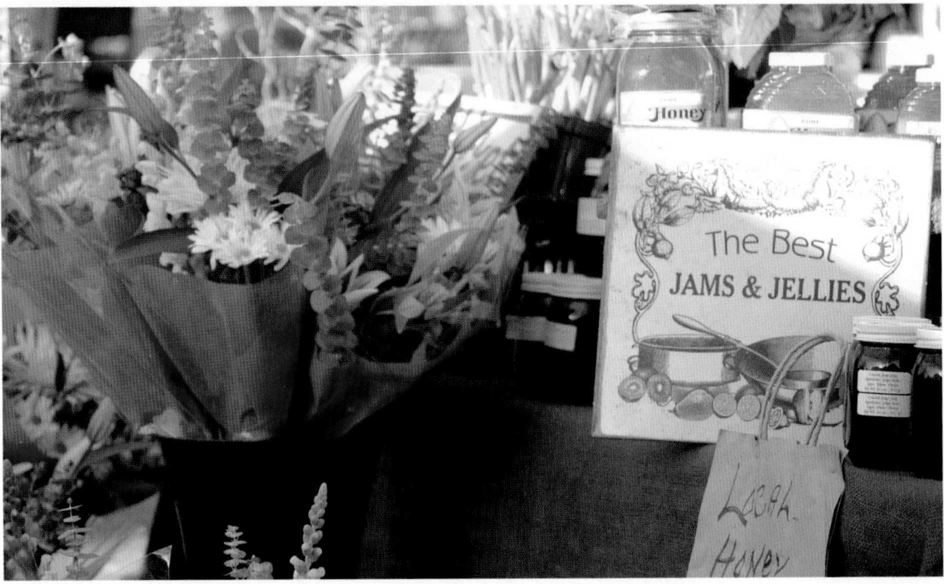

A pretty scene at Eastern Market.

At a Glance

Distance 11.8 miles **Total Elevation** 240 feet

Terrain

This flat course travels roads, two bridge sidepaths, riverside trail, and multiple bike lanes. Watch for debris on bridges.

Traffic

Aside from busy M Street, and sometimes P, you shouldn't have to tangle with many fast-moving vehicles here without the aid of a bike lane.

How to Get There

Take the Green Line Metro to the Navy Yard Station and use the Nationals Park exit (SE corner elevator to M and Half streets). If driving, use Interstates 295 and 395 to reach South Capitol Street and M Street SE. Look to park in a metered street space or nearby parking structure.

Food and Drink

Take this opportunity to eat fresh seafood at the Maine Avenue Fish Market. Or, if you're craving other fare, stop near Eastern Market in the Navy Yard, or along First Street SE.

Side Trip

Explore the entire eastern side of Anacostia's Riverwalk Trail. Swing through happening Barrack's Row on Eighth Street SW, south of Pennsylvania Avenue. Or continue cruising around the Capitol Hill neighborhood. It's blessed with a high percentage of bike lanes per square mile.

Links to 1 2 46 47 48 49 55

Where to Bike Rating

About...

This relaxed ride explores three interlocked, yet distinctive, D.C. neighborhoods. Beginning at Nationals Park, catalyst of the city's waterfront revival and anchor of the new Navy Yard, it tours the booming environs along the once-neglected Anacostia River, glides by the classy rowhouses of Capitol Hill's historic residential district, and tips its cap to a couple of cherished markets. Throw in two of democracy's most recognizable monuments and the largest library in the world, and you'll finish knowing the District's south has definitely risen again.

Join Neptune for a drink in front of the Library of Congress.

Former swampy Nacotchtank fishing grounds turned U.S. Naval shipyard, this route's first mile rolls past exciting urban renewal and briefly over the 11th Street Bridge to open space in Anacostia. Back over Sousa Bridge, peek left inside Congressional Cemetery, final resting place of a range of American notables. The tree-lined, west-side Anacostia Riverwalk Trail now eases you beyond Kingman Island before looping broadly around RFK Stadium to C Street and, soon, Capitol Hill. North Carolina Avenue jogs around two unique statues in Lincoln Park and continues to Eastern Market, city landmark since 1873 and home to fresh meats and produce as well as handmade arts and crafts. Capitol Hill developed as a neighborhood of local craftsmen and a boarding house community for members of Congress.

Now an emblematic stretch of D.C. riding brings you straight toward the U.S. Capitol and past Folger Shakespeare Library. The neoclassical Supreme Court Building sits immediately right, but the route heads left past the Library of Congress. No doubt you might be pulled in a few different directions here in the geographical center of the city. Simply explore what intrigues you. The Capitol's underground visitor center comes highly recommended but don't miss the Great Hall and Main Reading Room inside the LOC's Jefferson Building. They're two of Washington's most dazzling spaces.

Soon, New Jersey cuts you easily under Interstate 295 and I Street passes distinctive eras of southwest D.C. development on its way toward the floating barges of the Maine Avenue Fish Market. One of the few surviving open air seafood stands on the east coast, take the time to soak in the attention of vying vendors and sample the bounty of Chesapeake Bay.

Then, past the slips of Capitol Hill Yacht Club and the Maine Lobsterman Memorial peak left toward attractive Arena Stage before sliding onto a wide waterside path toward the Titanic Memorial. It pays homage to the ship's gentlemen who sacrificed scarce lifeboat seats to save the lives of women and children.

Be sure to look left down Washington Channel before leaving and glimpse "General's Row" on the grounds of Fort McNair, location of the National Defense University. Rounding home now, P Street carries you back to the ballfield and passes you to the safety of bike lanes, which lead, in turn, toward Metro.

Ride Log

P1 Nationals Park
P2 Yards Park
P3 Congressional Cemetery
P4 RFK Stadium
P5 Lincoln Park
P6 Eastern Market
P7 Folger Shakespeare Library
P8 U.S. Supreme Court Building
P9 U.S. Capitol Building
P10 Jefferson Building—Library of Congress
P11 Maine Avenue Fish Market
P12 Arena Stage
P13 Titanic Memorial
P14 Fort McNair
P15 Barrack's Row
P16 National Museum of the U.S Navy

B1 City Bikes-Capitol Hill, 709 8th St, SE
BR1 Bike and Roll Union Station, 50 Massachusetts Ave, NE

0.0 After exiting Metro's Navy Yard Station elevator, make your way down M St to a left on Half St. Set your odometer at Navy Yard Station's Ballpark exit and head directly toward the Centerfield Gate at Nationals Park.

0.1 Take a left onto N St.

0.3 Go straight/jog right to continue on N.

0.4 Turn right down Third St toward Yards Park then left toward Fourth St.

0.55 Left on Fourth.

0.75 Right on M St.

1.2 Right on 11th. Join path over bridge in one block.

1.8 Go right at ramp's bottom then right again along Anacostia Dr.

2.9 Go right on path as it curls up and over John Philip Sousa Bridge toward RFK Stadium.

3.3 Bear right at fork to cross road left and access Anacostia Riverwalk Trail.

5.0 Bear left under Metro tracks to go alongside Benning Rd.

5.2 Go left along Oklahoma Ave.

5.6 Go right onto C St.

5.95 Bear left to join North Carolina Ave.

6.15 Continue on N Carolina (rather than Constitution Ave bike lane).

6.55 Go right at Lincoln Park, left at 11th St, and right to rejoin North Carolina.

6.9 Pass Eastern Market at left.

7.05 Go right onto Sixth.

7.3 Go left onto East Capitol St.

7.5 Folger Shakespeare Library to left.

7.7 Take a left on First St then go straight across Constitution Ave to join sidewalk. Pass Library of Congress Jefferson Building.

8.15 Take a right on E to an immediate left on New Jersey.

8.45 Right on I St.

9.35 Left onto Seventh to cross Maine and go right on Water St.

9.75 Circle past Maine Street Fish Market.

10.4 Briefly enter parking lot to right before engaging riverwalk.

10.6 Continue left at Titanic Memorial to shortly join P St.

11.15 Cross S Capitol St to go right on sidewalk outside Nationals ballpark, then go left at Potomac Ave to join bike lane.

11.6 Left at Third to a right on Half.

11.8 Finish at Navy Yard Metro.

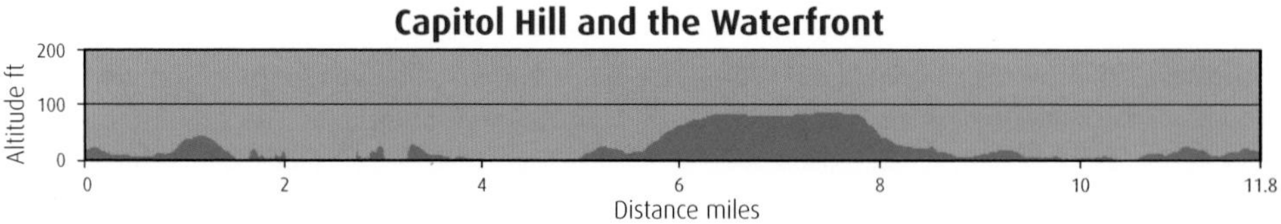

Capitol Hill and the Waterfront

Altitude ft: 0, 100, 200
Distance miles: 0, 2, 4, 6, 8, 10, 11.8

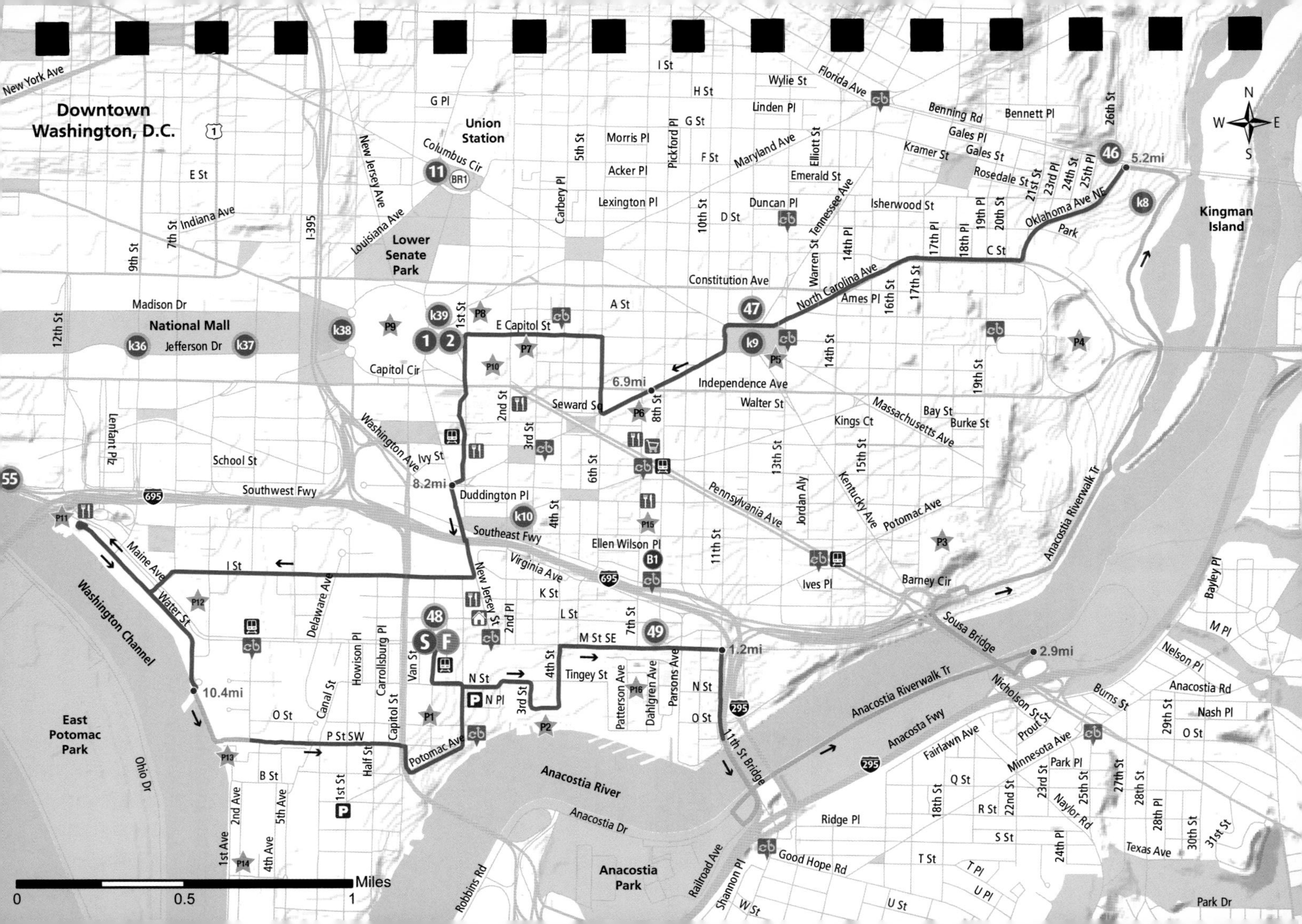
Downtown Washington, D.C.
Union Station
Columbus Cir
Lower Senate Park
National Mall
Jefferson Dr
Madison Dr
Capitol Cir
E Capitol St
Constitution Ave
Independence Ave
North Carolina Ave
Oklahoma Ave NE
Park
Kingman Island
Pennsylvania Ave
Massachusetts Ave
Kentucky Ave
Potomac Ave
Barney Cir
Sousa Bridge
11th St Bridge
Anacostia Riverwalk Tr
Anacostia Fwy
Anacostia River
Anacostia Dr
Anacostia Park
Southeast Fwy
Southwest Fwy
Virginia Ave
New Jersey Ave
Washington Ave
Maine Ave
Water St
Washington Channel
East Potomac Park
Ohio Dr
M St SE
Tingey St
Patterson Ave
Dahlgren Ave
Parsons Ave
Potomac Ave
P St SW
Good Hope Rd
Minnesota Ave
Nicholson St
Benning Rd
Florida Ave
New York Ave
Seward Sq
Duddington Pl
Ellen Wilson Pl
Ives Pl
Jordan Aly
Robbins Rd
Railroad Ave
Shannon Pl
Texas Ave
Naylor Rd
Fairlawn Ave
Anacostia Rd
Park Dr
1.2mi
2.9mi
5.2mi
6.9mi
8.2mi
10.4mi
Miles
0
0.5
1
N
E
S
W

Options include breaking for a cold one on 11th through Columbia Heights.

At a Glance

Distance 12.0 miles **Total Elevation** 370 feet

Terrain

A dozen on-road bicycle lanes linked by well-maintained city streets and sidewalks complement a wonderful stretch of Metro Branch Trail. One steep grade announces a steady uphill on 11th into Columbia Heights.

Traffic

This is an urban ride. Cars, trucks, buses and all their attendant danger and disruption will be present, especially around Chinatown, and on 14th. But the design, and its occasionally overwrought twists and turns, is made with that in mind. Take it slow when and if you have to, and my guess is you'll come away surprised by your skills.

How to Get There

Metro is exceptionally well-represented on this loop. If you choose not to begin at Union Station, or decide to finish elsewhere, you certainly won't be left out in the cold. If driving, access Massachusetts Avenue. If arriving by bus, check schedules and aim to connect to the D.C. Circulator.

Food and Drink

Heavily concentrated around Union Station, Chinatown, and 14th Street and never more than a few blocks away on the ride's first half. Much harder to come by the second six miles.

Side Trip

Visit Lincoln's Cottage three blocks uphill from Fifth and Upshur, or slip over the bridge on Monroe Street to explore Brookland at mile nine.

Links to 1 2 12 46 47 48 49 54

Where to Bike Rating

About...

It would take you days to thoroughly explore all the possible stops along this rich route, encompassing as it does so much of the fresh vitality and seasoned cultural attractions D.C. has on offer. Passing through at least six distinctive neighborhoods and by a bevy of monumental homes, churches, schools, buildings, and museums, it manages to take in the new, the old, the commercial, the residential, the industrial and the ultra-urban, all in about an hour-and-a-half.

A glimpse of D.C.'s eye-catching Bikestation.

This ride's first stretch brings you alongside the National Law Enforcement Memorial and Museum and its striking, symmetrical backdrop, the National Building Museum. Have a look around if you're at your leisure. The interior views from the upper floors of the NBM are stunning.

A brief peddle onward pushes you toward downtown. Here the Verizon Center rises above you, traffic picks up, and travelers, professionals, street folk and frisky teens all augment the bustle. Soon you're swinging by two Smithsonian Museums housed in the Reynolds Center for American Art and Portraiture. Make sure to glance right crossing H Street to eyeball Chinatown's impressive Friendship Gate.

Mount Vernon Square at K and Seventh is home to the Historical Society of Washington, D.C. Prepare here for the possibility of dense traffic as you make your way toward the relative tranquility of the bike lanes on Fifth, R and 11th streets, where you'll pass the 19th century Victorian row houses of Shaw, a neighborhood notable as an historic center of African-American intellectual and cultural life. The grand mansions of Logan Circle await.

Resurgent 14th Street tours you past the boutiques, nightclubs, and eateries of U Street, long the center of Washington's music scene. Busboys and Poet's one block south of the W Street turn toward 11th is a place to step out, see and be seen.

After a climb, expect hellos from the laid-back mix of porch-dwellers, bar-hoppers, and hipsters in Columbia Heights. Turns then take you through parts of Petworth to Sherman Circle, the ride's farthest northern reach. Once you hit the Fifth Street bike lane off Grant Circle, the pleasure of a near peddle-free mile past the grounds of the Armed Forces Retirement Home is often all yours.

Then it's out of neighborhoods, down safe sidewalks, and past a complex of National Medical Centers toward Brookland and the campus of The Catholic University of America. Beckoning will be the Basilica of the National Shrine, one of the 10 largest churches in the world.

Soon you'll join a wide stretch of the MBT, the long-awaited trail taking shape to Silver Spring, MD. Follow it home. But not before admiring Union Station, a masterpiece both inside and out.

Ride Log

0.0 Begin at the entrance of Union Station's Bikestation. Cross Massachusetts Ave to E St.

.15 Cross North Capitol St to continue on E St. Bike lane now available.

.85 Right onto Seventh St.

1.0 Left to G St bike lane then a quick right onto Eighth.

1.15 Go straight across H St.

1.2 Continue across I St through plaza to K St.

1.35 Left on Seventh followed by a quick right to continue on K. Use crosswalks if necessary.

1.55 Left on Fifth soon to cross New York Ave and begin bike lane.

2.25 Left onto R St bike lane.

2.35 Continue straight across Rhode Island Ave.

2.7 Left onto 11th St soon to re-cross R.I. Ave.

2.9 Right at P St to cut through Logan Circle. Use sidewalks and crosswalks to re-access R.I. Ave on other side.

3.15 Right onto 14th St bike lane.

3.7 Cross U St.

3.9 Right onto bike lane at W St.

4.15 A left onto L St initiates climb to Columbia Heights.

5.1 Right onto Monroe St before a quick left onto 10th.

5.5 Left when 10th ends at Randolph St then a quick right onto Kansas Ave.

5.75 Right on Taylor to cross Georgia Ave before a quick right onto Ninth.

5.95 Right onto Upshur St.

6.1 Left onto Seventh St bike lane.

6.4 Curl right at Sherman Circle to join Illinois Ave.

6.7 Cut across Grant Circle to join Fifth St bike lane.

7.1 Straight across Rock Creek Church Rd.

7.65 Left onto Irving St then cross it as it curves to continue left on far sidewalk.

8.2 Begin series of four road crossings. Be cautious!

8.6 Cross Michigan Ave to go left along far sidewalk.

8.9 Look to merge onto Monroe St bike lane.

9.05 Turn right onto Eighth St.

9.5 Dip left at overpass onto Metro Branch Trail.

10.9 Pass over Red Line New York Ave Metro Station.

11.2 Caution!! Steps. Dismount. Left on sidewalk at bottom then right to cross L St and continue on sidewalk/bikepath.

11.7 Turn right on F St toward Union Station. Bikes allowed.

11.8 A final right grants access to Union Station's grand archway. Dismount.

12.0 Return to Bikestation.

P
P1 Union Station
P2 National Law Enforcement Memorial and Museum/National Building Museum
P3 Verizon Center
P4 Reynolds Center for American Art and Portraiture
P5 Friendship Gate
P6 Historical Society of Washington, D.C.
P7 Watha T. Daniel-Shaw Library
P8 Logan Circle
P9 thebikehouse.org—a cooperative
P10 Lincoln's Cottage
P11 Basilica of the National Shrine

B
B1 BicycleSPACE, 459 I St, NW
B2 Rollin' Cycles, 1314-A, 14th St, NW
B3 The Bike Rack, 1412 Q St, NW
B4 City Bikes, 2501 Champlain St, NW

BR
BR1 Bike and Roll Union Station, 50 Massachusetts Ave, NE

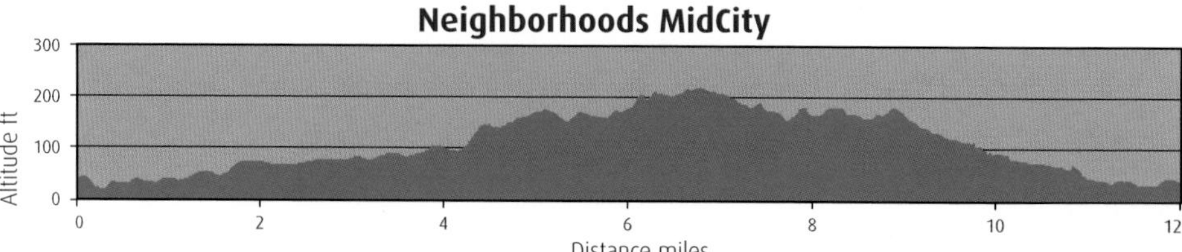

N
W
E
S
k2
Iowa Ave
Buchanan St
Arkansas Ave
US 29
7th St
Illinois Ave
Fort Totten Dr
Brookland Ave
Hawaii Ave
Fort Dr
Upshur St
Taylor St
P10
Rock Creek Church Rd
John Mccormack Rd
Piney Branch Pky
Kansas Ave
P9
Randolph St
Quincy St
Spring Rd
10th St
New Hampshire Ave
7.1mi
5th St
Armed Forces Retirement Home
The Catholic University of America
Harewood Rd
Perry St
Otis Pl
16th St
Georgia Ave
Pershing Dr
Monroe St
5.1mi
Park Rd
Warder St
Park Pl
Washington Hospital Center Dr
P11
46
Monroe St
Michigan Ave
Irving St
Mount Pleasant St
13th St
Kenyon St
Columbia Rd
Hobart Pl
4th St
8th St
10th St
14th St
McMillan Reservoir
Sherman Ave
Capitol St
Franklin St
9.5mi
Euclid St
Edgewood St
Lincoln Rd
Clifton St
11th St
k4
Howard University
Barry Pl
Bryant St
Adams St
To
B4
W St
V St
U St
Brentwood Rd
Metropolitan Branch Trail
Rhode Island Ave
T St
12
15th St
13th St
S St
Vermont Ave
R St
Corcoran St
14th St
P7
54
Florida Ave
R St
B3
Q St
New Jersey Ave
Eckington Pl
P St
2.9mi
P8
O St
Gallaudet University
B2
N St
1st St
M St
New York Ave
3rd St
Florida Ave
W Virginia Ave
Massachusetts Ave
9th St
5th St
50
11.2mi
Vermont Ave
395
L St
P6
K St
K St
6th St
7th St
8th St
New York Ave
B1
Massachusetts Ave
I St
2nd St
k32
H St
8th St
P5
New Jersey Ave
Capitol St
2
White House
15th St
G St
BR1
G St
1
P4
7th St
F St
F St
S
F
P1
P3
E St
P2
47
Columbus Cir
Maryland Ave
49
48
Delaware Ave
D St
k33
Pennsylvania Ave
C St
Miles
0
0.25
0.5
1

Sun-dappled houses in Georgetown.

At a Glance

Distance 9.4 miles **Total Elevation** 530 feet

Terrain

There are merely minor hills on this ride's first third to and through Georgetown, but the mid-section's climb to the National Cathedral will tax you a bit. It's worth it though. The way down is a coaster's dream.

Traffic

The number of turns in some parts of this jaunt shouldn't be a turn-off. They're there for a reason, as they take you down quieter streets with a higher density of sites. Georgetown's street plan dates to the second half of the 1700s so be prepared for some tight, occasionally bumpy riding there, without the help of bike lanes.

How to Get There

Metro's Red Line serves Dupont Circle. If busing, check current schedules. Drivers should aim for the confluence of Connecticut, Massachusetts, and New Hampshire avenues.

Food and Drink

Plan pit stops in and around Dupont Circle at ride's beginning and end, as well as the areas within this route's 7.5-8.5 mile mark extending from Connecticut Avenue in Woodley Park to Columbia Road in Adams Morgan.

Side Trip

Lock up and lose yourself inside the museum, research library, and gardens of Georgetown's Dumbarton Oaks.

Links to 3 6 11 28 47 48 51

Where to Bike Rating 

About...

Dupont carries itself like the cosmopolitan center of D.C., and indeed, this loop aims to take you through quite a few of the capital's richest historic and cultural treasures. From the diverse bustle in and around the Circle, to the polos and painted-brick facades of classy Georgetown, up to the manicured grandeur of the National Cathedral, and down past yet more million-dollar homes to Adams Morgan's youthful, ethnic-influenced entertainment corridor, this ride makes remembering to keep at least one eye on the road remarkably difficult.

The Croatian Embassy on Massachusetts Avenue.

Take it slow and stay alert as you trace this ride's first mile-and-a-half toward the Dumbarton Bridge. You'll want to see a lot and stay safe doing it. Houses are the key sites all along this loop and nowhere more than here, for even the embassies you'll be passing were once residences of D.C. high society.

Some former Gilded Age mansions are public treasures as well. Opened in 1921, The Phillips Collection is America's first museum of modern art. Drop in and experience its renowned intimacy.

The short climb into Sheridan-Kalorama takes you through arguably the most affluent neighborhood in Washington, studded as it is with chanceries and ambassadorial residences. Then drop down to the Islamic Center and its striking, white minaret.

After 'Buffalo Bridge', Georgetown begins to make itself known by its own inimitable houses bunched on narrow, shaded streets and fronted by buckling red-brick sidewalks. Some are huge affairs, some seemingly small as garages. Two along Q, Dumbarton House and Tudor Place, are justly celebrated for their elegant décor and gardens.

A few brief jogs enable you to absorb the neighborhood and avoid one-ways or trolley tracks long-unused. Soon Georgetown University's gothic gray Healy Hall rises before you.

Then, as you pass Visitation Preparatory School and The Duke Ellington School of the Arts, you'll begin climbing, gradually at first, before a steady half-mile or so brings you to a well-deserved break up on Calvert.

A turn onto Wisconsin Avenue, routed around until now, brings heavy traffic at high speeds. Do be careful. After a final uphill push, it's thankfully only a short sprint to the National Cathedral's commanding site on Mount Saint Albans, one of D.C.'s highest points.

Construction on this, the sixth largest cathedral in the world, began in 1907 and wasn't finished until the presidency of George H. W. Bush some 83 years later. Take a moment inside to appreciate its stunning size.

Now spin around the eclectic mix of homes in Cleveland Park before beginning a near peddle-free descent through Woodley Park to the Ellington Bridge. After the vibrant crossroads of Adams Morgan, another long downhill takes you to New Hampshire and a flat return to Dupont Circle.

Ride Log

0.0 Begin at the Dupont Circle Fountain. Take Massachusetts Ave heading past 20th St along Embassy Row. (Use caution and sidewalks if necessary.)

.3 Swing right part-way around Sheridan Circle to continue on Massachusetts Ave.

.6 Right on 24th. Continue straight.

.9 Left at Kalorama Rd.

1.0 Right onto Tracy Place then left toward Massachusetts Ave.

1.1 Left onto Massachusetts Ave to proceed along Embassy Row (Consider using sidewalk).

1.6 Swing right around Sheridan Circle to a right on 23rd and right again onto Q St over Dumbarton Bridge.

2.4 Left onto 32nd to right onto P to right onto Wisconsin to left on Volta Place.

2.7 Left onto 34th then right onto N.

3.2 Right onto 37th to right on O St to left on 35th.

4.0 Left onto Whitehaven to right on 37th to soft left onto Tunlaw Rd (steady climb).

4.6 Turn right onto Calvert St then left onto Wisconsin Ave.

5.1 Cross Massachusetts Ave looking to turn right into National Cathedral grounds on South Rd.

5.3 After passing directly in front of cathedral, continue right around sidewalk to exit on North Rd before heading straight across Woodley Rd onto 36th St.

5.8 Right onto Ordway St then right onto 34th Place.

6.0 Right onto Newark to a left onto 35th.

6.3 Left onto Woodley Rd.

6.8 Left onto Cathedral Ave to a right onto 29th/Woodley Rd.

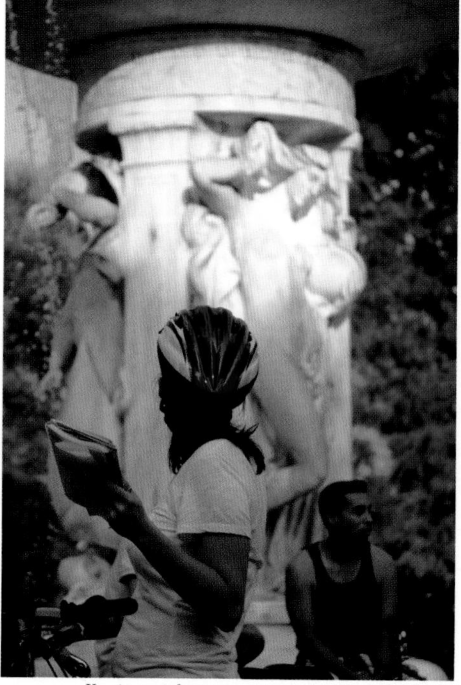

You just might meet your match at Dupont Circle.

7.5 Left on Cleveland/Calvert St toward Connecticut Ave crossing.

8.2 Prepare to briefly go left on Columbia Rd before quickly sliding right onto Euclid St to a sharp right onto Champlain (use caution).

8.6 Left onto Florida then right onto 17th.

9.0 Right onto New Hampshire bike lane.

9.4 Arrive back at Dupont Circle.

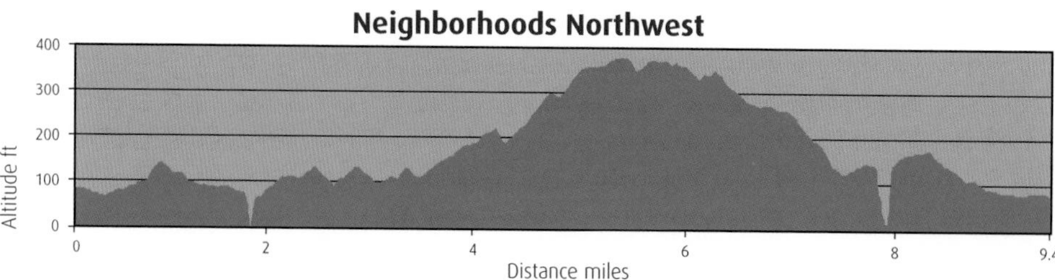

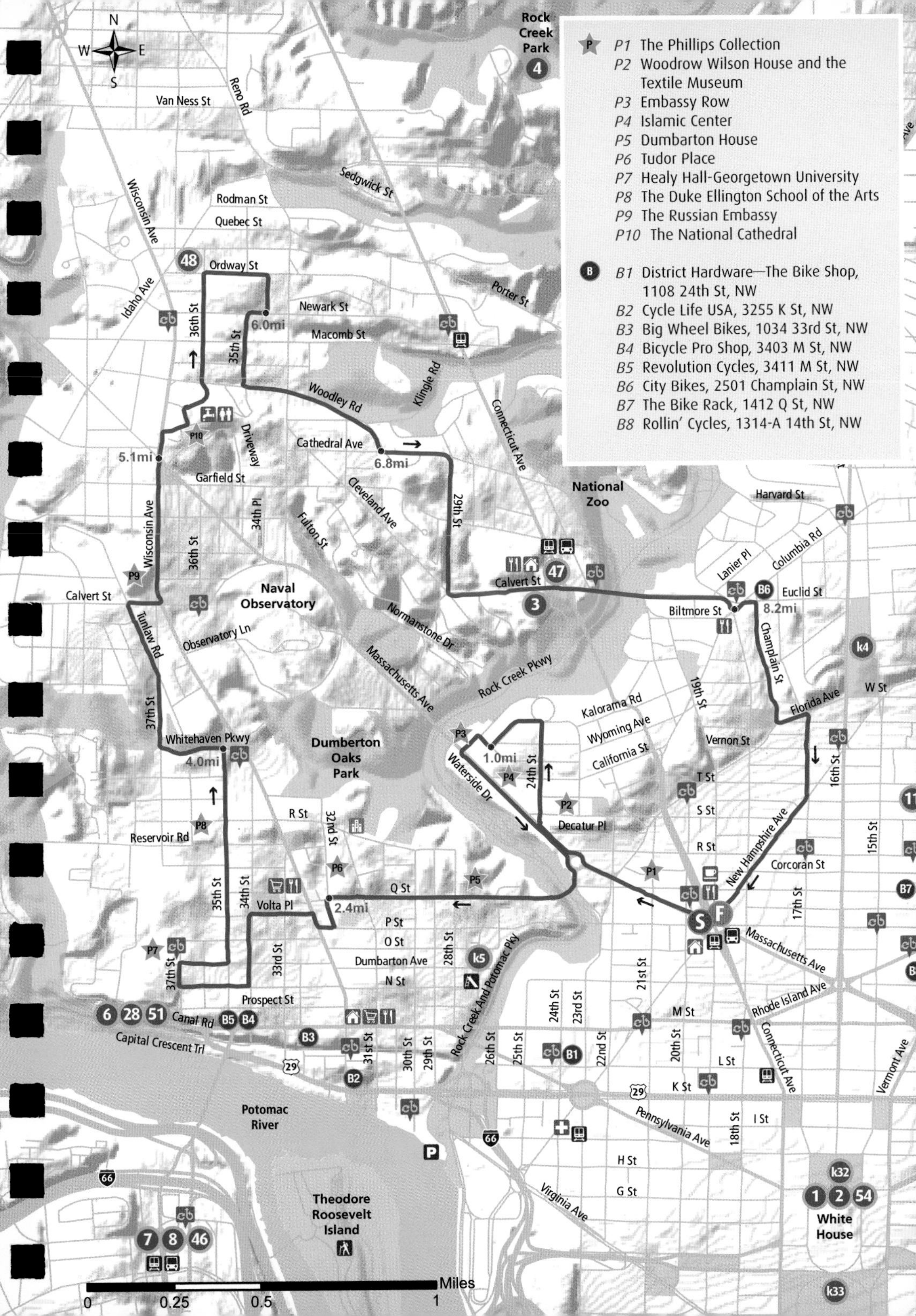
P1 The Phillips Collection
P2 Woodrow Wilson House and the Textile Museum
P3 Embassy Row
P4 Islamic Center
P5 Dumbarton House
P6 Tudor Place
P7 Healy Hall-Georgetown University
P8 The Duke Ellington School of the Arts
P9 The Russian Embassy
P10 The National Cathedral
B1 District Hardware—The Bike Shop, 1108 24th St, NW
B2 Cycle Life USA, 3255 K St, NW
B3 Big Wheel Bikes, 1034 33rd St, NW
B4 Bicycle Pro Shop, 3403 M St, NW
B5 Revolution Cycles, 3411 M St, NW
B6 City Bikes, 2501 Champlain St, NW
B7 The Bike Rack, 1412 Q St, NW
B8 Rollin' Cycles, 1314-A 14th St, NW
Rock Creek Park
National Zoo
Naval Observatory
Dumberton Oaks Park
Potomac River
Theodore Roosevelt Island
White House
Van Ness St
Reno Rd
Sedgwick St
Rodman St
Quebec St
Ordway St
Newark St
Macomb St
Porter St
Wisconsin Ave
Idaho Ave
36th St
35th St
Woodley Rd
Klingle Rd
Connecticut Ave
Driveway
Cathedral Ave
Garfield St
34th Pl
Cleveland Ave
Fulton St
29th St
Calvert St
Normanstone Dr
Observatory Ln
Tunlaw Rd
Massachusetts Ave
Rock Creek Pkwy
37th St
Whitehaven Pkwy
Waterside Dr
24th St
Kalorama Rd
Wyoming Ave
California St
19th St
Vernon St
Harvard St
Lanier Pl
Columbia Rd
Euclid St
Biltmore St
Champlain St
Florida Ave
W St
16th St
T St
S St
R St
New Hampshire Ave
Corcoran St
15th St
17th St
Decatur Pl
Reservoir Rd
32nd St
34th St
Volta Pl
Q St
P St
O St
Dumbarton Ave
N St
33rd St
28th St
Rock Creek And Potomac Pky
Prospect St
Canal Rd
Capital Crescent Trl
31st St
30th St
29th St
26th St
25th St
24th St
23rd St
22nd St
21st St
20th St
M St
Rhode Island Ave
L St
K St
Pennsylvania Ave
18th St
I St
H St
G St
Virginia Ave
Vermont Ave
1.0mi
2.4mi
4.0mi
5.1mi
6.0mi
6.8mi
8.2mi
Miles
0
0.25
0.5
1

Giro

Northern Virginia

Combining the historic heart of the Confederacy with the patriotic soul of the Founding Fathers, northern Virginia is a proud world unto itself where affluent suburbs share space with some of the region's most beautiful scenery. Here, wooded trails and winding roads, rolling hills and gorgeous green pastureland treat cyclists to routes ranging from easy cruises and classic riverside tours to intense hilltop adventures along the easternmost edge of the Blue Ridge. Accordingly, it's also here where this book makes its furthest forays into the countryside.

First, a note of clarification. This section details rides to the west and south of the District of Columbia's original boundaries. Tours specific to Arlington County and the City of Alexandria can be found in 'D.C., Inside the Diamond.'

The only comparable rival to this area's deep history and natural beauty is its astounding composite wealth and recent growth. Enriched by private sector government contracting, and buoyed by a rising tide of immigration, the population of Fairfax County now tops one million and pushes strongly west.

Progressive planners have done their best to keep pace and point contentedly to two grand trails, the expansive W&OD and the rugged CCT, which highlight a well-designed suburban system. But while commuting cyclists can now cling quite easily to extensive paths alongside the biggest highways in the suburbs, roadies increasingly look beyond the boundary-making ridges of the Catoctin and Bull Run mountains for northern Virginia's best recreational rides. There, in the hills of traditional Hunt Country, huge horse farms flank friendly byways connecting small towns intent on maintaining their links with the past.

Flatter terrain means speed rules the route south of Manassas, and shorter spins back east toward the suburbs attract families to famed Colonial plantations along the Potomac. The trail to Washington's Mount Vernon is simply a must, while lesser-known Mason Neck and Prince William Forest invite exploration within preserved natural settings.

Seen as one, these 11 rides incorporate five counties and 275 miles. And somehow, a section of superlatives gets better no matter where you begin.

A view across hills from Milltown Road.

At a Glance

Distance 31.3 miles **Total Elevation** 2095 feet

Terrain

This ride rolls over smooth, country two-lanes and hard surface trail. Expect some intense hills on Milltown Road (VA 681).

Traffic

Rush hours on VA 690 between Purcellville and Hillsboro can get busy, but things aren't bad at all out on the back roads.

How to Get There

Ride the Washington and Old Dominion Trail. There's no better way. Otherwise, exit 45 off the Beltway brings you to Dulles Toll Road (VA 267). Stay off its airport access section and continue on the Dulles Greenway to a left on the Leesburg Bypass (U.S. 15, VA 7). Now go west toward Purcellville, exit left onto the Berlin Pike (VA 287), and go right on East Main (VA 7) through town looking for another right onto North 21st or 23rd streets. Trail's End Cycling Company and the end of the W&OD are one block ahead.

Food and Drink

There are options in Purcellville, Lovettsville and Waterford.

Side Trip

If you'd like to lengthen this jaunt and take in some outstanding scenery (and climbing) in the process, take Lovettsville Road (VA 672) left at this ride's right turn onto Milltown Road (VA 673). A sharp right on Taylorstown Road (VA 668) and another onto Loyalty Road (VA 665) will bring you through Waterford.

Links to   14 19 52

Where to Bike Rating 

About...

Why not begin your Virginia experience with a nifty, country cruise taking the tip top of the state as its venue? This ride begins in Purcellville at the western terminus of the W&OD. Setting off speedily north alongside Appalachian hills and touching its halfway point two miles shy of the Potomac, it then turns back south climbing crumpled terrain through the historic milling village of Waterford before easing home on a recuperative stretch of trail.

A foldy and a ten-speed against a stone wall.

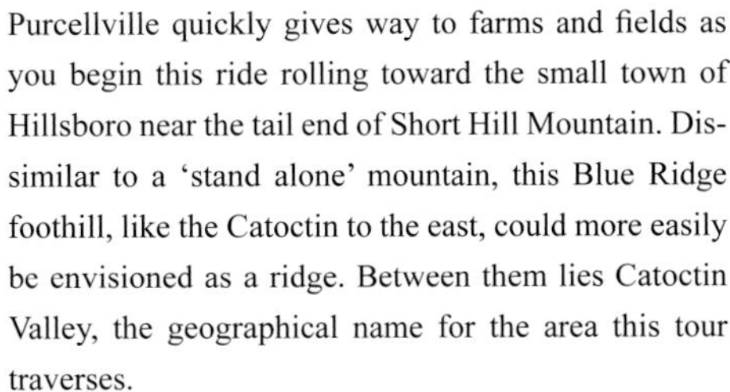

Purcellville quickly gives way to farms and fields as you begin this ride rolling toward the small town of Hillsboro near the tail end of Short Hill Mountain. Dissimilar to a 'stand alone' mountain, this Blue Ridge foothill, like the Catoctin to the east, could more easily be envisioned as a ridge. Between them lies Catoctin Valley, the geographical name for the area this tour traverses.

Soon, you've turned onto Mountain Road and though the name hints strongly at a major climb, the coming miles parallel rather than cross Short Hill as both make their way north.

Roll on now past Doukenie Winery and alternating woods and fields before a significant descent past mile 10 sets up a gradual climb into Lovettsville.

As opposed to the pro-Confederate southern and eastern sections of Loudoun County, this spin covers land settled primarily by German and Quaker immigrants strongly against the practice of slave-owning, plantation-style farming. Such belief in an area staunchly dissimilar made for fierce partisan fighting during the Civil War, namely an early skirmish seven miles down the road. Read up on the Loudoun Rangers, a unique bunch of Virginia Unionists, while you rest and recuperate in the town circle.

Let's hope you've saved some legs as this ride's second half begins with branches of Catoctin Creek forcing you steeply up and down. Before too long though, it's left you in Waterford, the site of said battle and one of only three towns in the United States whose entire area (and in this case surrounding farmland) has been designated a National Historic Landmark District. Take some time here as this small village looks and feels almost wholly true to its 19th century flour milling past. Founded way back in 1733, today it is best known for its annual homes and crafts fair early each October.

Now a nearly unbroken three-mile climb to Charlestown Pike and the W&OD, has you cresting at a historic sign for the village of Paeonian Springs and gliding another three miles down a wonderful tree-lined trail. Then, two more miles of gradual ascent and you're rolling level back into Purcellville, your destination.

Ride Log

P1 Doukenie Winery, 14727 Mountain Road
P2 Civil War history—Loudoun County Rangers
P3 Historic Waterford
P4 Paeonian Springs commemoration

B1 Trail's End Cycling Company, 201 N 23rd St

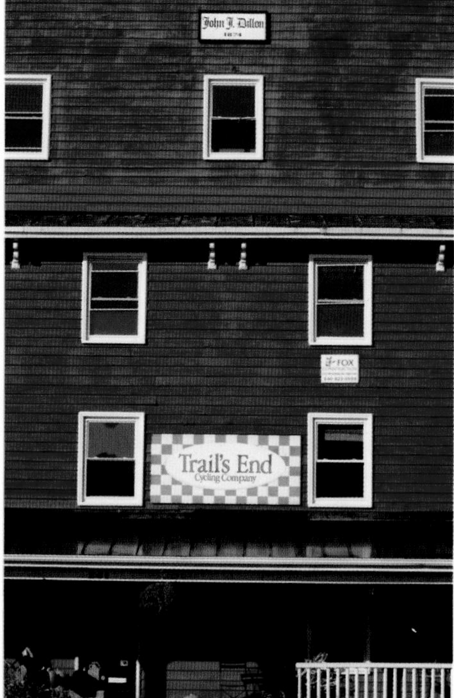

It's hard to miss Trail's End Cycling Company in Purcellville.

0.0 Begin by going right at extreme end of W&OD Trail in Purcellville. (Across from Trail's End Cycling Company.)

2.0 Go halfway around traffic circle to join Hillsboro Rd.

4.95 Right at Charlestown Pike to left on Mountain Rd. (Remain on VA 690.)

6.1 Pass Doukenie Winery.

8.35 Left to continue on Mountain Rd (VA 690).

12.2 Mountain Rd becomes Irish Corner Rd.

12.5 Bear right.

14.6 Go right at circle to another right on Lovettsville. (Or cut straight through circle on sidewalk.) Food and some history.

15.3 Bear right onto Milltown Rd (VA 673).

17.2 Stay straight. Milltown becomes VA 681.

21.5 Left on Old Wheatland Rd. (VA 698).

21.9 Bear right.

22.4 Take a right.

24.8 Left on Charlestown Pike.

25.2 Right on W&OD Trail.

25.9 Pass Paeonian Springs.

31.3 Finish.

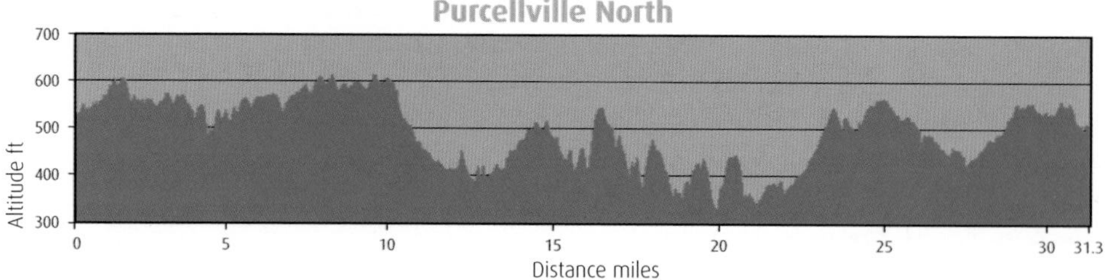

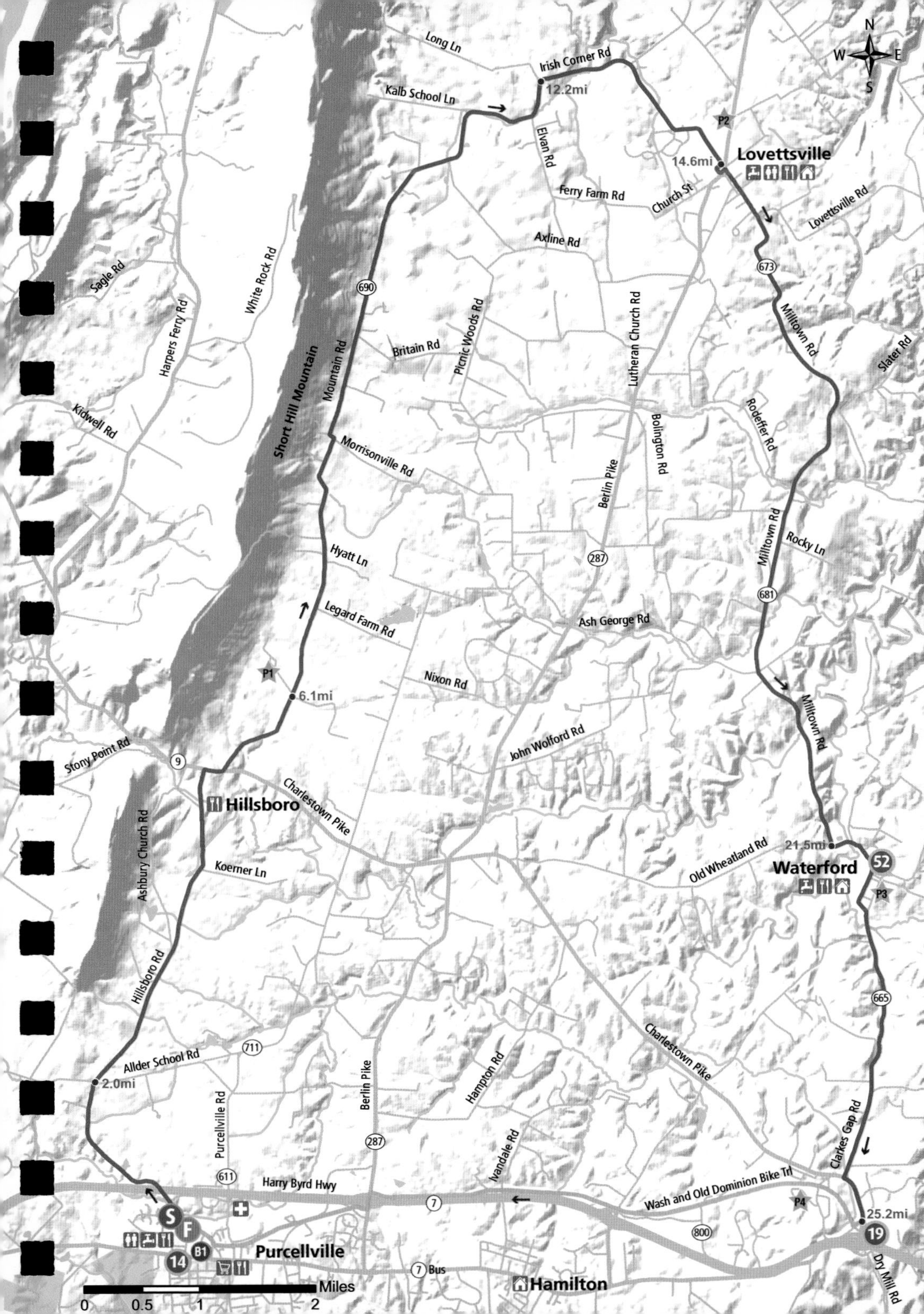

Long Ln
Irish Corner Rd
12.2mi
Kalb School Ln
Elvan Rd
P2
Lovettsville
14.6mi
Ferry Farm Rd
Church St
Lovettsville Rd
Axline Rd
673
Sagle Rd
White Rock Rd
690
Harpers Ferry Rd
Picnic Woods Rd
Lutheran Church Rd
Milltown Rd
Slater Rd
Britain Rd
Short Hill Mountain
Mountain Rd
Kidwell Rd
Rodeffer Rd
Bolington Rd
Morrisonville Rd
Berlin Pike
Milltown Rd
Rocky Ln
Hyatt Ln
287
681
Legard Farm Rd
Ash George Rd
P1
Nixon Rd
6.1mi
Milltown Rd
John Wolford Rd
Stony Point Rd
9
Hillsboro
Charlestown Pike
Ashbury Church Rd
21.5mi
Old Wheatland Rd
52
Waterford
Koerner Ln
P3
Hillsboro Rd
665
Allder School Rd
711
2.0mi
Charlestown Pike
Hampton Rd
Purcellville Rd
Berlin Pike
Clarkes Gap Rd
287
Ivandale Rd
611
Harry Byrd Hwy
Wash and Old Dominion Bike Trl
S
7
P4
F
800
25.2mi
B1
19
14
Purcellville
Dry Mill Rd
7 Bus
Miles
Hamilton
0
0.5
1
2
N
W
E
S

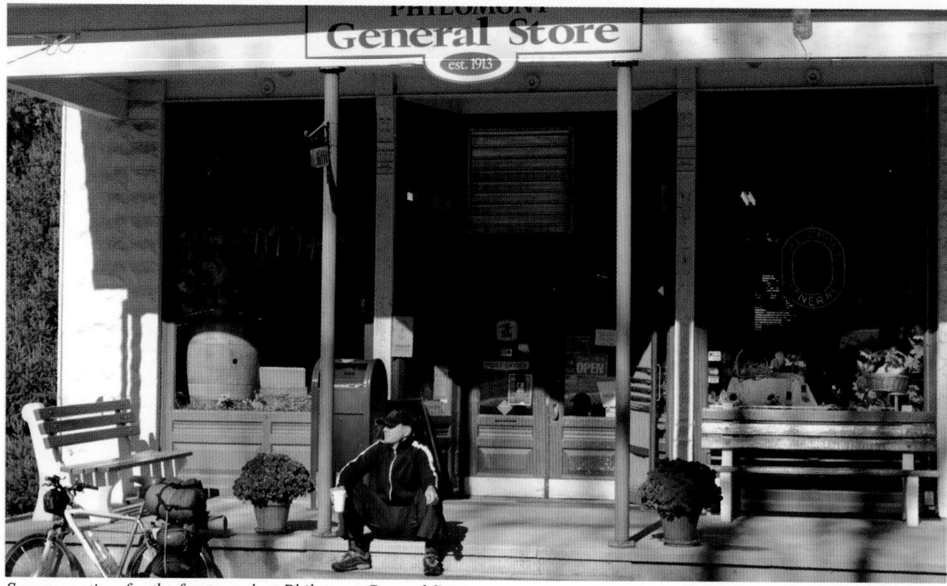

Save some time for the front porch at Philomont General Store.

At a Glance

Distance 35.2 miles **Total Elevation** 3085 feet

Terrain

One word, hilly. Roads are smooth, if narrow.

Traffic

Business Route 7 back into Purcellville will be the busiest road of the day. The others tend to bring brief waves of two and three vehicles followed by long periods of peace.

How to Get There

Ride the Washington and Old Dominion Trail. Otherwise, exit 45 off the Beltway brings you to Dulles Toll Road (VA 267). Stay off its airport access section and continue on the Dulles Greenway to a left on the Leesburg Bypass (U.S. 15, VA 7). Now go west toward Purcellville, exit left onto the Berlin Pike (VA 287), and go right on East Main (VA 7) through town looking for another right onto North 21st or 23rd streets. Trail's End Cycling Company and the end of the W&OD are one block ahead.

Food and Drink

Try Magnolias at the Mill in Purcellville, the Red Fox Inn and Restaurant in Middleburg, or sip on the porch at the Philomont and Airmont general stores.

Side Trip

Visit the National Sporting Library and Museum in Middleburg.

Links to   

Where to Bike Rating  

About...

When you finally make the time for that batch of weekend riding you've been wanting to do all year, you'd be mistaken leaving Virginia's Hunt Country off your list of possible destinations. Think rolling country roads and sweeping vistas by day and big meals, local wines, and intimate little inns by night. This particular spin alone passes five bed and breakfasts, a holiday's worth of good food, and enough wine to warrant another saddle bag. The area oozes history too, with more of everything in all directions.

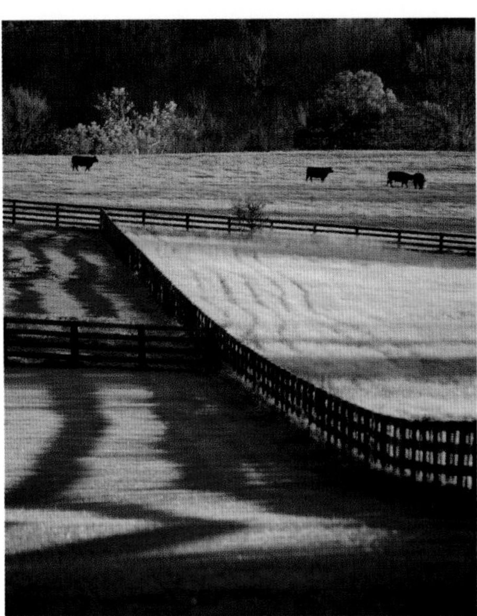

Fields and fence shadows near sundown.

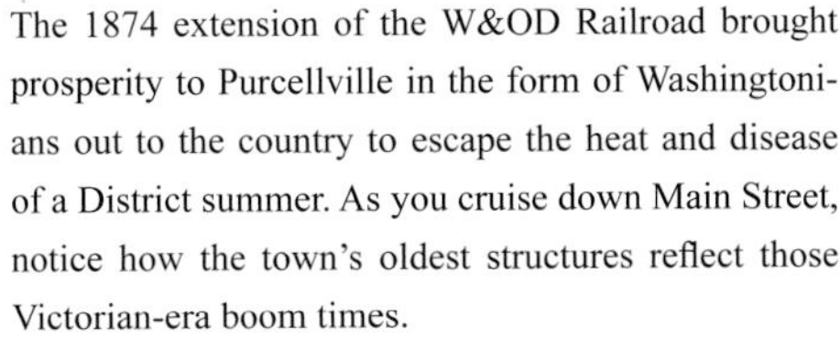

The 1874 extension of the W&OD Railroad brought prosperity to Purcellville in the form of Washingtonians out to the country to escape the heat and disease of a District summer. As you cruise down Main Street, notice how the town's oldest structures reflect those Victorian-era boom times.

South Maple brings you past newer developments before directing you downhill through Lincoln, a village at the center of a district celebrating Virginia's largest concentration of historic Quaker settlements.

Much of today's ride travels a rugged landscape criss-crossed by numerous creeks and streams, a fact which becomes readily apparent as you bounce your way to Crooked Run, then elevate before dropping again to the deep woods around 180-year-old Hibbs Bridge.

And just as soon as you fell, here's the Snickersville Turnpike to pick you up again. Expect lung-busting climbs and wind-whipped descents on this old road hemmed in by huge trees and fieldstone fences.

Sam Fred Road, then, seems comparatively relaxed, even as it begins to jump a bit nearing Middleburg. And while the route doesn't linger here long, you should feel free to. It's a place unique unto itself, the center of Hunt Country, where the wealthy and famous stable their thoroughbreds and each fall and spring bring steeplechase races and fox hunts.

Essentially a one road town, Foxcroft School angles you back north into the woods as the day's craggiest stretch sandwiches a second encounter with Goose Creek. Off Mountville, Snickersville again brings its deep grooves and high ridges to this ride's broken record before a potential rest stop in Philomont.

The turnpike runs from Aldie to Bluemont before crossing the mountains through Snickers' Gap. An Iroquois hunting path turned toll road, it's managed to remain rural to this day and can be imagined as the wavy spine of southwestern Loudoun County cycling.

The landscape opens up continuing northwestward, offering lovely views of the Blue Ridge. Airmont Road then beckons both ways, and while splendid to the south, home lies the opposite way today over rollers to Round Hill. It's preferable, then, to beat the traffic back into Purcellville, but if you don't, ride with the assurance that others have ridden this way before you.

Ride Log

0.0 Begin by going left onto N 23rd St from the extreme end of the W&OD Trail in Purcellville, VA.

0.15 Left onto E Main St.

0.75 Right onto S Maple Ave (VA 722). Becomes Lincoln Rd.

6.2 Right onto N Fork Rd (VA 728).

6.95 Left onto Watermill Rd (VA 731).

9.1 Left onto Snickersville Turnpike (VA 734).

10.8 Right to remain on Snickersville.

11.9 Right onto Sam Fred Rd (VA 748).

15.2 Right onto John S Mosby (U.S. Hwy 50).

15.8 Right onto Foxcroft Rd (VA 626).

19.7 Right onto Mountville Rd (VA 745/733).

22.7 Left onto Snickersville.

28.6 Right onto Airmont Rd (VA 719).

32.1 Right onto E Loudoun St (U.S. Business 7) to Purcellville.

35.2 Left onto N 21st St.

P1 Creek Crossing Farm Bed and Breakfast, 37768 Chappelle Hill Rd
P2 Montrose Bed and Breakfast, 19060 Lincoln Rd
P3 Hibbs Bridge
P4 Red Fox Inn and Restaurant
P5 National Sporting Library and Museum
P6 J. Patrick House Bed and Breakfast, 37110 Snickersville Turnpike
P7 Philomont General Store

B B1 Trail's End Cycling Company, 201 N 23rd St

A Japanese Maple roadside.

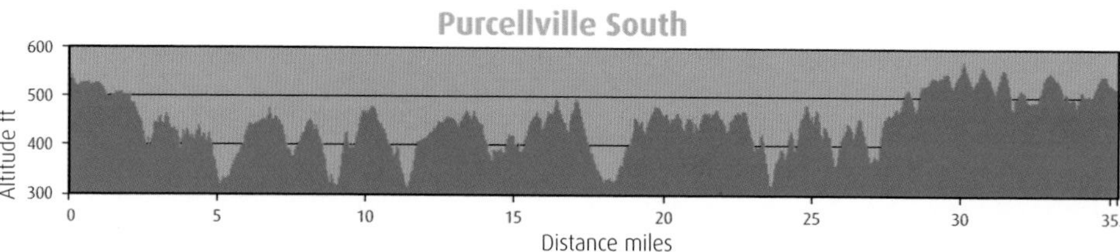

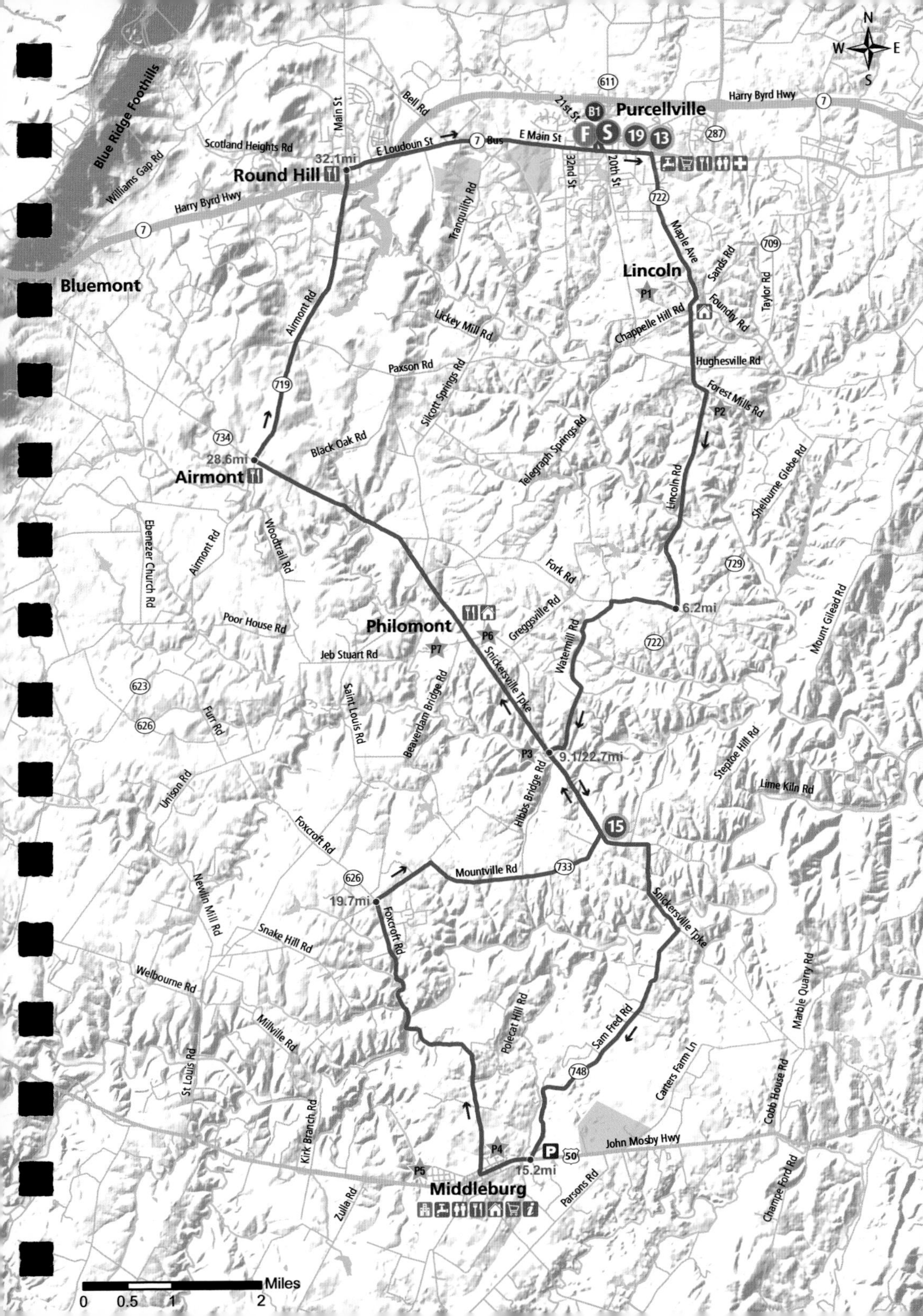

Purcellville
Round Hill
Lincoln
Bluemont
Airmont
Philomont
Middleburg
Blue Ridge Foothills
Harry Byrd Hwy
E Loudoun St
E Main St
Bus
Main St
Bell Rd
21st St
32nd St
20th St
Scotland Heights Rd
Williams Gap Rd
Tranquility Rd
Maple Ave
Sands Rd
Taylor Rd
Foundry Rd
Chappelle Hill Rd
Hughesville Rd
Forest Mills Rd
Lickey Mill Rd
Paxson Rd
Silcott Springs Rd
Airmont Rd
Black Oak Rd
Telegraph Springs Rd
Lincoln Rd
Shelburne Glebe Rd
Ebenezer Church Rd
Woodtrail Rd
Fork Rd
Greggsville Rd
Watermill Rd
Mount Gilead Rd
Poor House Rd
Jeb Stuart Rd
Snickersville Tpke
Saint Louis Rd
Beaverdam Bridge Rd
Furr Rd
Steptoe Hill Rd
Lime Kiln Rd
Unison Rd
Hibbs Bridge Rd
Foxcroft Rd
Mountville Rd
Newlin Mill Rd
Snake Hill Rd
Welbourne Rd
Millville Rd
Polecat Hill Rd
Sam Fred Rd
Marble Quarry Rd
Carters Farm Ln
St Louis Rd
Kirk Branch Rd
Cobb House Rd
John Mosby Hwy
Zulla Rd
Parsons Rd
Champe Ford Rd
32.1mi
28.6mi
6.2mi
9.1/22.7mi
19.7mi
15.2mi
P1
P2
P3
P4
P5
P6
P7
B1
F
S
19
13
15
611
7
287
722
709
719
734
729
623
626
733
748
50
N
E
S
W
Miles
0
0.5
1
2

This is horse country.

At a Glance

Distance 24.8 miles **Total Elevation** 1995 feet

Terrain

Rolling hills, some steep, over good country roads.

Traffic

While The Plains/Halfway Road (VA 626) carries the fastest moving vehicles, use caution and keep your ears open, as all these roads have blind curves.

How to Get There

Take Interstate 66 off the Beltway to U.S. Highway 50 west. Look to turn right onto Sam Fred Road down the hill before entering Middleburg proper. Park at St. Stephen's Catholic Church almost immediately to the left.

Food and Drink

Try the Red Fox or Hidden Horse Tavern on or near Madison Street or, for lighter fare, Dank's Deli at Liberty and Marshall, the Market Salamander along U.S. 50 near Pickering, or the sandwiches and baked goods of Upper Crust, across Pendleton from Safeway.

Side Trip

There are plenty of breathtaking scenic stretches throughout this rich cycling area, with prime miles along Atoka and Zulla roads chief among them. Go explore, perhaps during Memorial Day weekend's annual Hunt Country Stable Tour. Just be sure to consider safety first, as some roads are much more heavily trafficked and less amenable to cyclists than others.

Links to 

Where to Bike Rating 

About...

Though this may be the shortest ride in these parts, it's blessed with great roads, splendid scenery, and one heck of a winning personality. A trip to Middleburg is like that once-a-year visit to your charmingly eccentric aunt's. She never ceases to surprise, and introduces you to things you wouldn't have the chance to do anywhere else, like visit the exquisite horse stables of the super-wealthy, rub shoulders with the rich and famous, or take in Landmark School Road's spectacular views of the Bull Run Mountains.

An old barn backed by green fields.

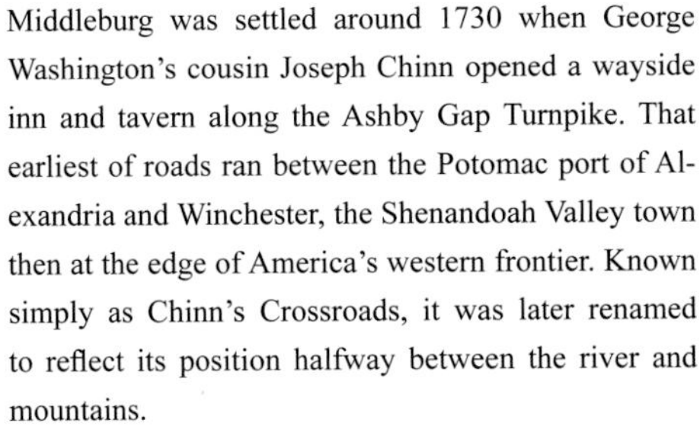

Middleburg was settled around 1730 when George Washington's cousin Joseph Chinn opened a wayside inn and tavern along the Ashby Gap Turnpike. That earliest of roads ran between the Potomac port of Alexandria and Winchester, the Shenandoah Valley town then at the edge of America's western frontier. Known simply as Chinn's Crossroads, it was later renamed to reflect its position halfway between the river and mountains.

The Civil War brought the lawyer John Singleton Mosby to town. Having made a name for himself as a scout under General J.E.B. Stuart, Mosby rose to Colonel in the Confederate States Army and recruited a small band of die-hard partisans whose lightning-quick raids wreaked havoc throughout the war on all things Union in the counties of northern Virginia. Known as the Gray Ghost for his seemingly supernatural ability to elude being captured, or even seen, his legend looms large in these parts and nowhere more than Middleburg.

After a period of post-war decline, the 20th century brought the fabulous wealth of the Gilded Age to Loudoun and Fauquier Counties. Enticed by the area's natural beauty and sporting potential, dynastic families including the Mellon's began buying property, raising thoroughbreds and reviving the Colonial tradition of the foxhunt. Later, Hollywood, Washington politicos, and the jet set became commonplace guests, and today, that Middleburg remains. Don't be surprised to see employees of old money or nouveau riche alike making quick runs to Safeway in jodhpurs and riding boots.

Riders of our stripe have frequented the region for years now as well, and you can expect to see a few of them out along this well-trod path. Though it traverses some ground covered in Ride 14, the truly splendid roads north of town deserve more than a backwards glance. Spin the other way, then, down pleasant Sam Fred and mild Mountville as they line you up for the rollercoaster ride that is Foxcroft School Road.

Landmark's southeastward gallop out of town toward the Bull Run Mountains is the day's most extraordinary stretch. There, a mile of climbing crests at 700 feet before rolling through lush green pastures to Halfway Road. Soon, you're passing Piedmont Vineyards and Winery, among the first of Virginia's modern, wine-making revival, located on the pre-Revolutionary estate of Waverly. And then, it's back to town for dinner.

Ride Log

0.0 Head left from the St Stephen's Catholic Church parking lot onto Sam Fred Rd (VA 748).
3.2 Left onto Snickersville Pike (VA 734).
4.3 Bear left.
4.8 Left onto Mountville Rd (VA 733).
6.95 Bear left (VA 745).
7.75 Left onto Foxcroft Rd (VA 626).
9.1 Stay left.
11.6 Left onto N Madison St to cross Hwy 50. Becomes Landmark School Rd (VA 776).
15.8 Bear right.
19.4 Right onto The Plains/Halfway Rd (VA 626).
23.8 Right onto John S Mosby Hwy (U.S. 50).
24.8 Left onto Sam Fred Rd (VA 748).

P1 Goodstone Inn and Estate 36205 Snake Hill Rd
P2 Glenwood Park—equine venue, 36787 Glenwood Park Ln
P3 Red Fox Inn and Restaurant, 2 E Washington St
P4 Piedmont Vineyards and Winery, 2546 Halfway Rd #D
P5 The Boxwood Winery, 2042 Burrland Rd
P6 The National Sporting Library and Museum, 102 The Plains Rd
P7 Swedenburg Estate Vineyard, 23595 Winery Ln

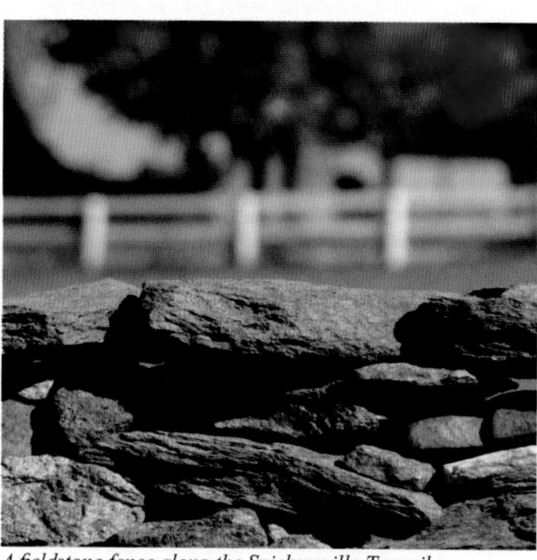

A fieldstone fence along the Snickersville Turnpike.

Outside the Red Fox Inn and Restaurant.

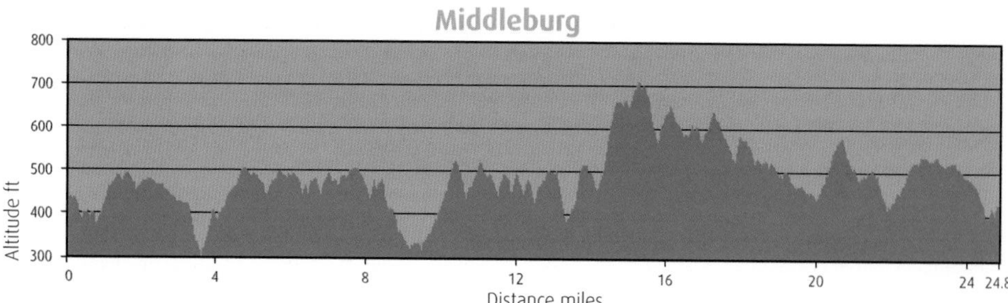

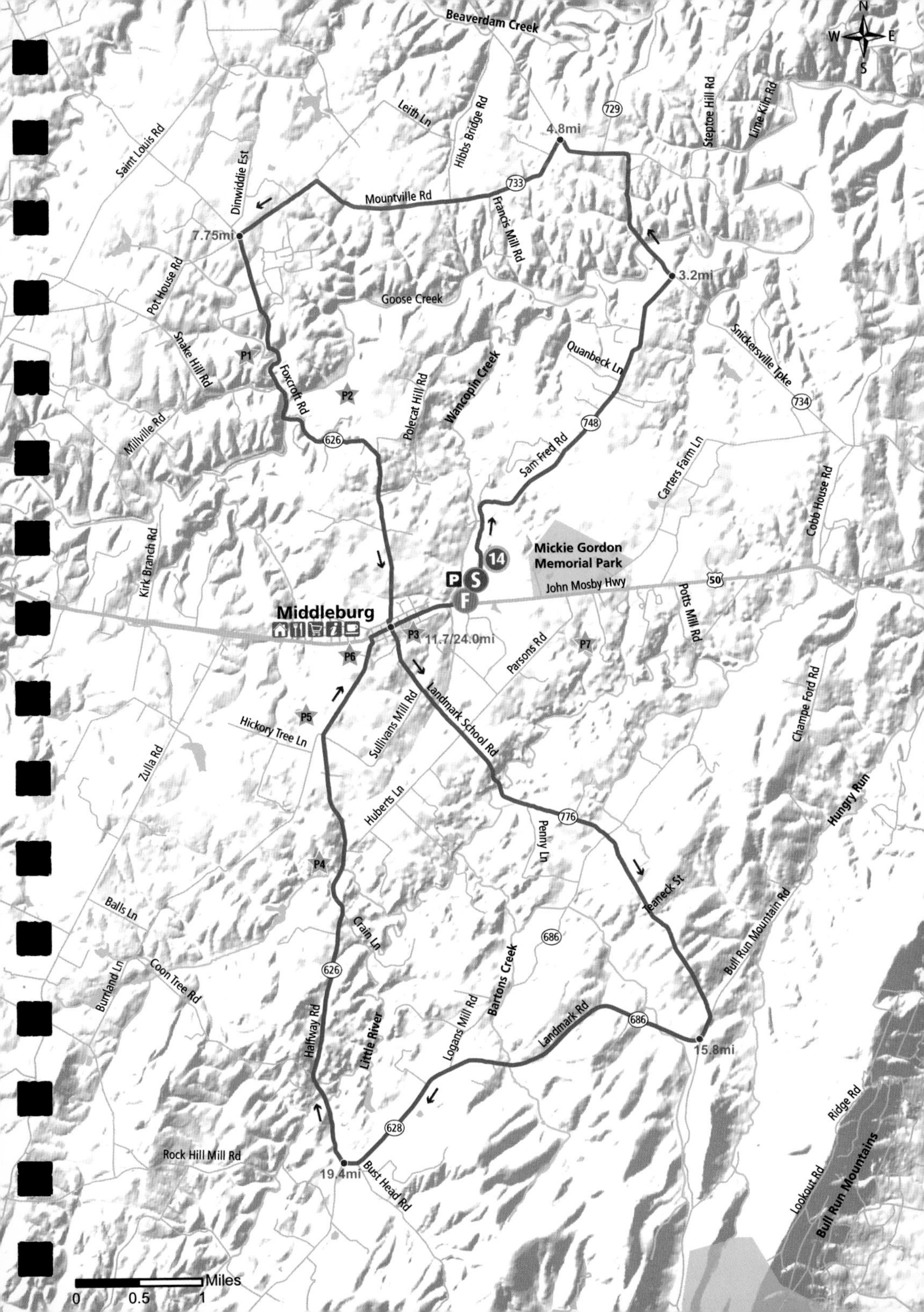

Beaverdam Creek
Leith Ln
Hibbs Bridge Rd
729
4.8mi
Steptoe Hill Rd
Line Kiln Rd
Saint Louis Rd
Dinwiddie Est
733
Mountville Rd
Francis Mill Rd
7.75mi
3.2mi
Pot House Rd
Goose Creek
Snickersville Tpke
Snake Hill Rd
P1
Foxcroft Rd
Quanbeck Ln
Wancopin Creek
P2
Polecat Hill Rd
734
Millville Rd
748
626
Sam Fred Rd
Carters Farm Ln
Cobb House Rd
Kirk Branch Rd
14
Mickie Gordon Memorial Park
P
S
F
50
John Mosby Hwy
Potts Mill Rd
Middleburg
P3
11.7/24.0mi
Parsons Rd
P7
P6
Champe Ford Rd
Landmark School Rd
Sullivans Mill Rd
P5
Hickory Tree Ln
Zulla Rd
Hungry Run
Huberts Ln
776
Penny Ln
P4
Teaneck St
Bull Run Mountain Rd
Balls Ln
Crain Ln
686
Bartons Creek
626
Burrland Ln
Coon Tree Rd
Little River
Halfway Rd
Logans Mill Rd
Landmark Rd
686
15.8mi
Ridge Rd
628
Rock Hill Mill Rd
19.4mi
Bust Head Rd
Lookout Rd
Bull Run Mountains
Miles
0
0.5
1

This ride brings miles of smiles.

At a Glance

Distance 34.6 miles **Total Elevation** 2640 feet

Terrain

Smooth country roads over rolling hills.

Traffic

U.S. Highway 50 is busy, as is the John Marshall Highway (VA 55).

How to Get There

Take Interstate 66 off the Beltway through Centreville and Haymarket to exit 31. Your destination is briefly right down Old Tavern/Fauquier Avenue (VA 245). Go right at Main Street then immediately left onto Loudoun Avenue (VA 626). Look to park left down Stuart Street just past Girasole Restaurant.

Food and Drink

Snack in Upperville, fuel up in Marshall, and feast in The Plains. Try the aforementioned Girasole or The Rail Stop on Main Street across from this ride's beginning.

Side Trip

Hopewell (VA 601) east into the Bull Run Mountains is a gorgeous stretch of road. Or visit Great Meadow Park south of town by going right just shy of mile 33 on Old Tavern instead of left. Catch a polo match or plan your ride around two of its fabled steeplechase races, the Virginia Gold Cup in May and the International Gold Cup in October.

Where to Bike Rating 

About...

As its name suggests, The Plains travels through more open country and entails less climbing (though still plenty) than its woodsier, hillier neighbors to the north. Beginning and ending in a town high on D.C. cycling's list of one-day getaways, visitors can expect nothing but the best food, amenities, and overall bikeability the region has to offer. Stretching northwestward from the Bull Run Mountains toward the foothills of the Blue Ridge, this elegantly-designed, double loop boasts continuous good views plus the necessary peace to enjoy them.

Washington, busted in Rectortown.

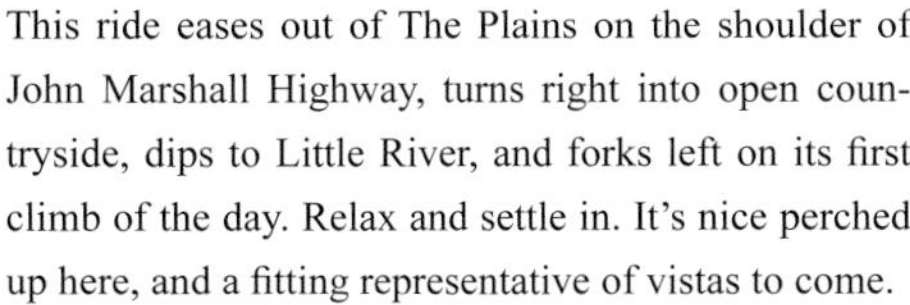

This ride eases out of The Plains on the shoulder of John Marshall Highway, turns right into open countryside, dips to Little River, and forks left on its first climb of the day. Relax and settle in. It's nice perched up here, and a fitting representative of vistas to come.

Soon you've dropped to a small stream, risen, and dropped again to Cromwell's Run, only to rise once more to the more heavily trafficked VA 710. Ride worry free though, enjoying a fast three miles down to tiny Rectortown sunken and shaded among surrounding hills. Climbing then once again, it's as if into the second act of a stunning natural play with wide open country extending westward to Lost Mountain and Sky Meadows State Park in the Blue Ridge beyond. Topping even that, the roll then turns north on a truly dreamy stretch of road past the impeccable grounds (and private airstrip) of the 4000-acre Mellon dynasty's Oak Spring Farms.

Paul Mellon was a philanthropist, a racehorse owner and breeder, and an heir to the Mellon banking fortune. His father Andrew was U.S. Secretary of the Treasury from 1921 to 1932 and founder of the National Gallery of Art.

Rokeby Road is perhaps too good to be true and all too soon gives way to the faster cars and bigger trucks of U.S. Highway 50. It's a two-mile ascending sprint, then, to another of this area's tony little towns. Notable as the site of the country's oldest colt and horse show, Upperville sits surrounded by the lands of heirs and heiresses. It is home, as well, to lovely Trinity Episcopal Church, built with Mellon money in an adaptation of the 12th century French provincial style. There are other pleasures here too, so have a look around before riding on.

The inspirational views return after a healthy half-mile climb on Delaplane Grade, and while you may pass a few rogue vehicles along this gorgeous stretch of road, it won't be enough to dampen the experience. Then, reversing your path on VA 710 brings you through busy Marshall and briefly back onto U.S. Highway 55 before unreining you south to enjoy Harrison Road, the day's final unmitigated gem.

Ride Log

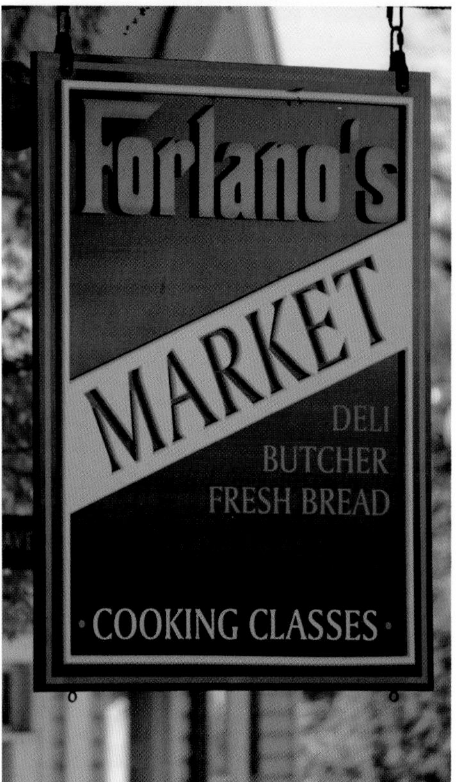

The Plains is the place for foodies.

0.0 Begin by going west on Main St/The John Marshall Hwy (VA 55) where it meets Old Tavern Rd/Fauquier Ave in The Plains. Food.

1.0 Right onto Whitewood Rd (704).

1.5 Bear left onto Lear/Milestone Rd (707).

2.8 Right onto Zulla Rd (709).

4.0 Left onto Rock Hill Mill Rd (702).

5.2 Stay left on RH Mill/Frogtown Rd (702).

7.5 Right onto Rectortown Rd (710).

11.2 Right onto Rokeby Rd (623).

14.9 Left onto John S Mosby Hwy (U.S. 50).

17.3 Left on Delaplane Grade Rd (712). Food.

18.8 Left onto Old Tavern Rd/Fauquier Ave (VA 245).

19.9 Left onto Rectortown Rd (710).

28.2 Left onto Hwy 55 East. Food.

30.3 Right onto Belvoir Rd (709).

31.3 Left onto Harrison Rd (750).

32.8 Left onto Old Tavern Rd.

34.6 End at the beginning.

P1 The Grey Horse Inn Bed and Breakfast, 4350 Fauquier Ave
P2 Mellon Estate—Oak Spring Farms
P3 Trinity Episcopal Church
P4 Great Meadows Park

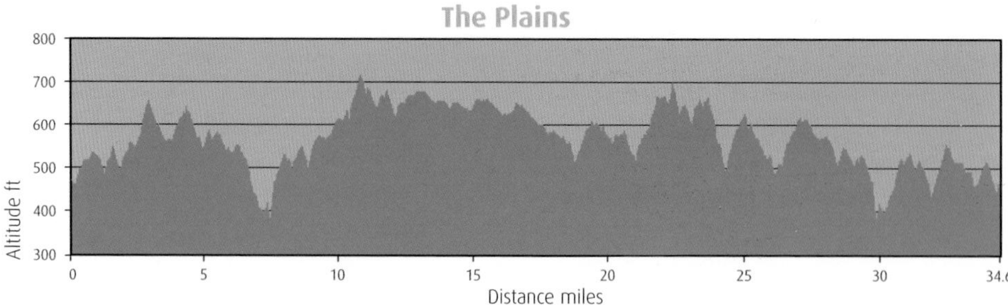

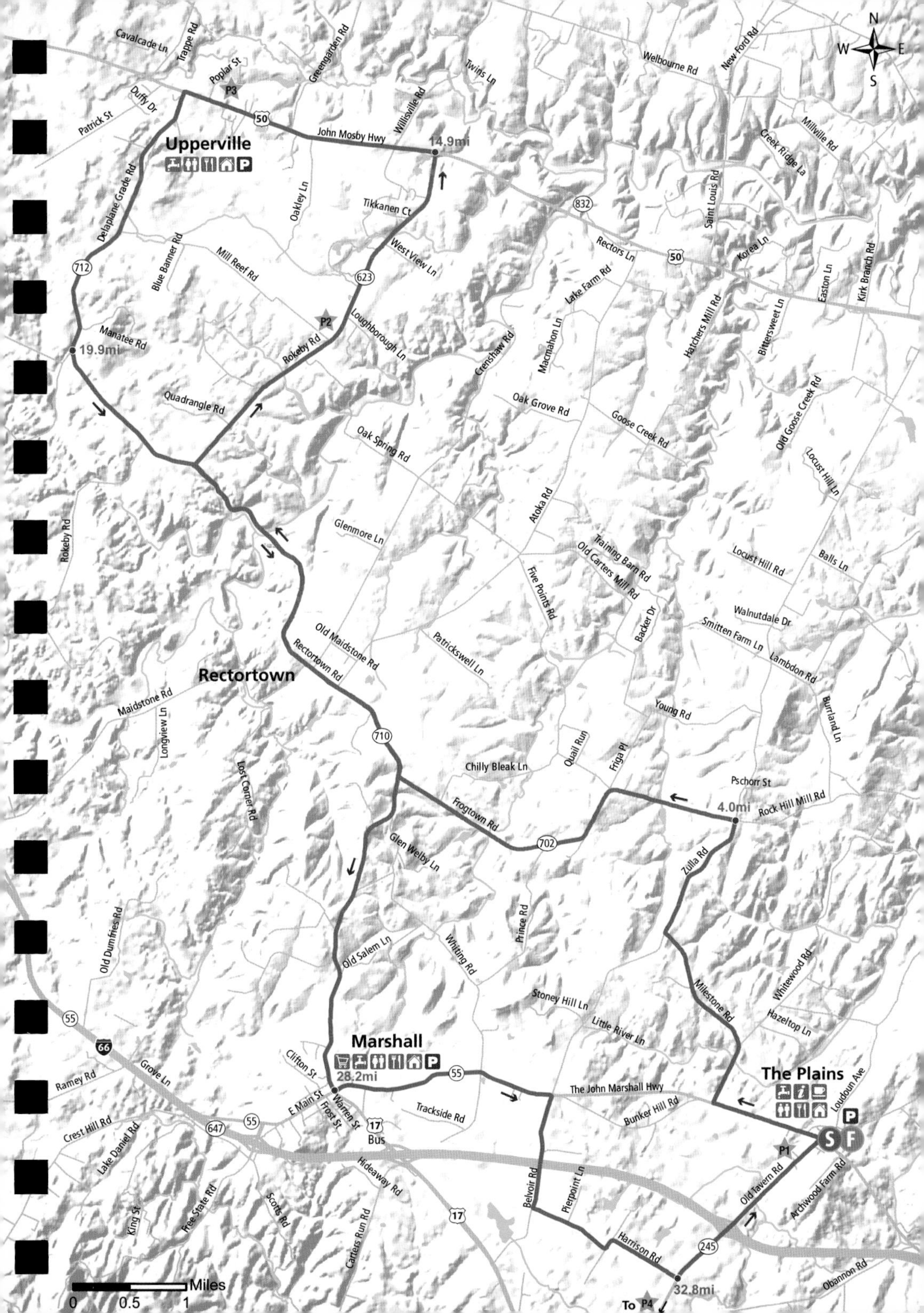

Upperville
Rectortown
Marshall
The Plains
14.9mi
19.9mi
4.0mi
28.2mi
32.8mi
P1
P2
P3
To P4
S
F
Miles
0
0.5
1
N
S
E
W

A museum's worth of yard ornaments outside Nokesville.

At a Glance

Distance 43.1 miles **Total Elevation** 1860 feet

Terrain

Moderate hills, substantial flat stretches, and smooth country roads.

Traffic

Trucks can sometimes crowd riders, and the way is narrow.

How to Get There

If you're up for the adventure, the Virginia Railway Express (VRE) allows bicycles at specific times daily. Jump on in Union Station or at multiple points west and take its Blue Manassas Line all the way to the terminal station at Broad Run, then ride here by way of Nokesville Road (VA 28).

If driving, use Interstate 66 west off the Beltway to exit 44 and the Prince William Parkway (VA 234). Take it about five miles to a right on Nokesville Road. Turn left onto Fitzwater Drive after about four-and-a-half miles, continue through town, and turn right onto Aden Road (VA 646). Park left at Brentsville District High School.

Food and Drink

Country stores are noted in the ride log or try the Chuckwagon Restaurant in Nokesville. Otherwise, retreat to nearby Bristow Center at Bristow and Nokesville roads, or deeper into Manassas.

Side Trip

Peddle with the locals along Linton Hall Road and Prince William Parkway side paths or visit Bristoe Station Battlefield Historic Park east off Nokesville Road and Bristow on Iron Brigade Unit Avenue. It preserves a few acres of cherished ground.

Where to Bike Rating

About...

Significantly flatter than many of its lengthy northern Virginia counterparts, this ride begins a few miles southwest of Manassas in the small town of Nokesville and races south on fast, lean country roads. And although Civil War history runs deep all around, the route here is notable for nothing so much as its speed and the sparsely populated region through which it passes. Less scenery than substance, come here for a rural experience and a tour designed to take your training to the next level.

Could be that old thing still rolls.

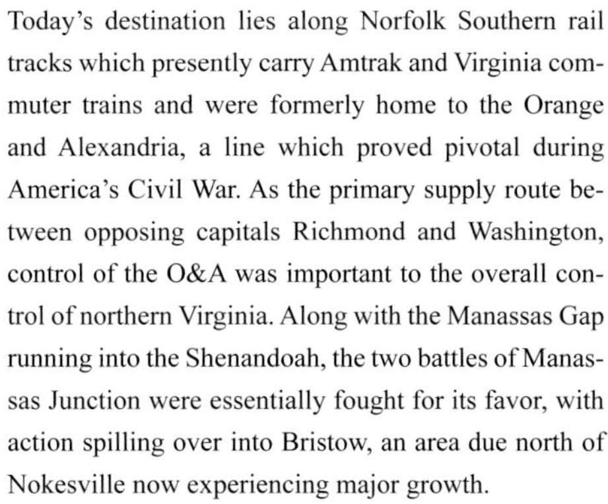

Today's destination lies along Norfolk Southern rail tracks which presently carry Amtrak and Virginia commuter trains and were formerly home to the Orange and Alexandria, a line which proved pivotal during America's Civil War. As the primary supply route between opposing capitals Richmond and Washington, control of the O&A was important to the overall control of northern Virginia. Along with the Manassas Gap running into the Shenandoah, the two battles of Manassas Junction were essentially fought for its favor, with action spilling over into Bristow, an area due north of Nokesville now experiencing major growth.

By contrast, the farming region stretching to its south resisted so much as a skirmish 150 years ago and is managing to escape significant sprawl so far this century. Still off the beaten track, it remains a great place to do some long-distance biking.

This tour begins easily past Nokesville Community Park, the Prince William County Criminal Justice Academy and scattered clusters of homes and family farms. Fleetwood Road then ushers in a faster pace, a brush with the forested, far western edge of Quantico Marine Corps Base, and several joint miles with southward-leading U.S. Bicycle Route 1.

Recognized by the American Association of State Highway and Transportation Officials way back in 1982, the number of (USBRS) routes has remained fixed at its initial two ever since. East-west (76), which originally followed Bikecentennial's TransAmerica Trail through Virginia, Kentucky and Illinois, and this one, which initially followed the Adventure Cycling Associaton's Atlantic Coast Route into North Carolina.

Thankfully, the system has recently been reinvigorated in large part due to the efforts of the (ACA), new designations are currently being made, and cyclists should be prepared for major national additions in the near future.

Past a market at mile 12.5, you'll come upon a cluster of buildings inside a copse of trees. Feel free to shorten this ride to an even 30 miles by continuing straight then right on VA 616 in less than half a mile. Both distances continue along rolling road past patches of forest, country homes, and open farmland through the crossroads at Calverton and beyond. And soon, a pleasant stretch on VA 603 prepares you for your return to Nokesville.

Ride Log

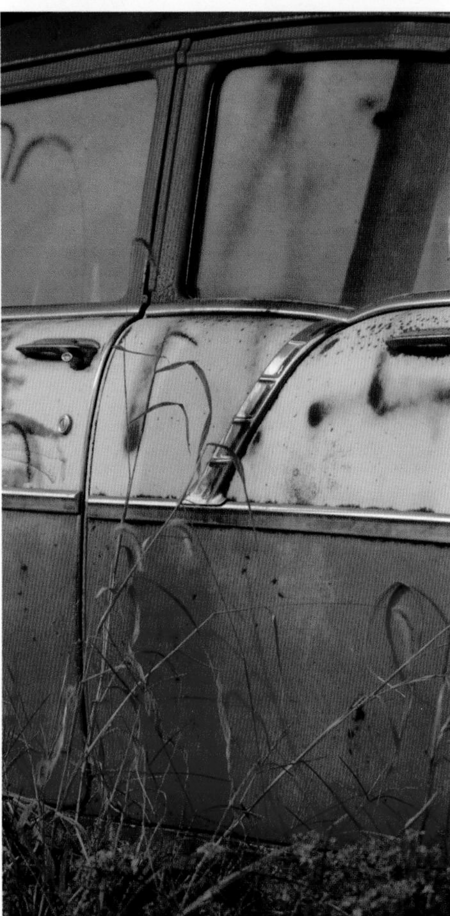

Gone the way of the dinosaur.

0.0 Begin at Brentsville District High School in Nokesville. Set your odometer and go left where the entrance to its main parking lot meets Aden Rd.

0.95 Right on Carriage Ford Rd.

3.4 Bear left onto Hazelwood.

5.6 Right on Fleetwood Dr.

7.45 Bear right to stay on Fleetwood Dr.

9.15 Right on Sowego.

10.8 Left on Elk Run.

12.3 Bear right. Handy Mart to left.

12.5 Left on VA 616. Or, to shorten ride to 30 miles, continue straight to go right on VA 616 within a half mile.

17.1 Right on Midland Rd. Grove's Store.

21.5 Right on VA 806. Elk Run Store.

25.5 Left on VA 616.

30.6 Straight onto VA 603. Market.

33.7 Right on VA 667.

33.9 Left on VA 603.

37.3 Right on VA 652.

38.8 Right on 604. Bear left to resume VA 652.

42.1 Cross VA 28. Food. ATM.

42.4 Chuck Wagon Restaurant.

43.0 Right on Aden.

43.1 Finish by turning left into Brentsville District High School.

P1 Bristoe Station Battlefield Historic Park

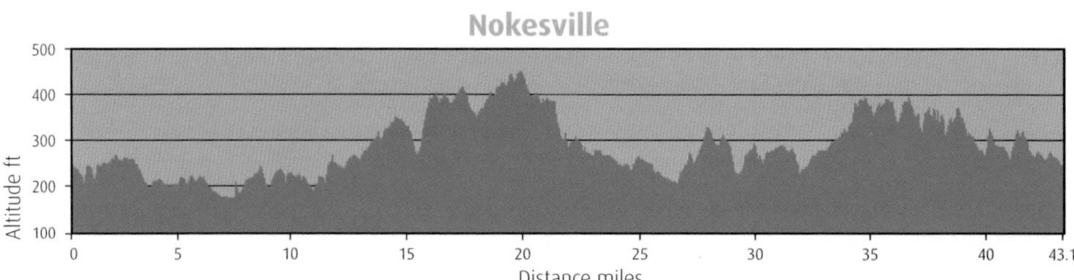

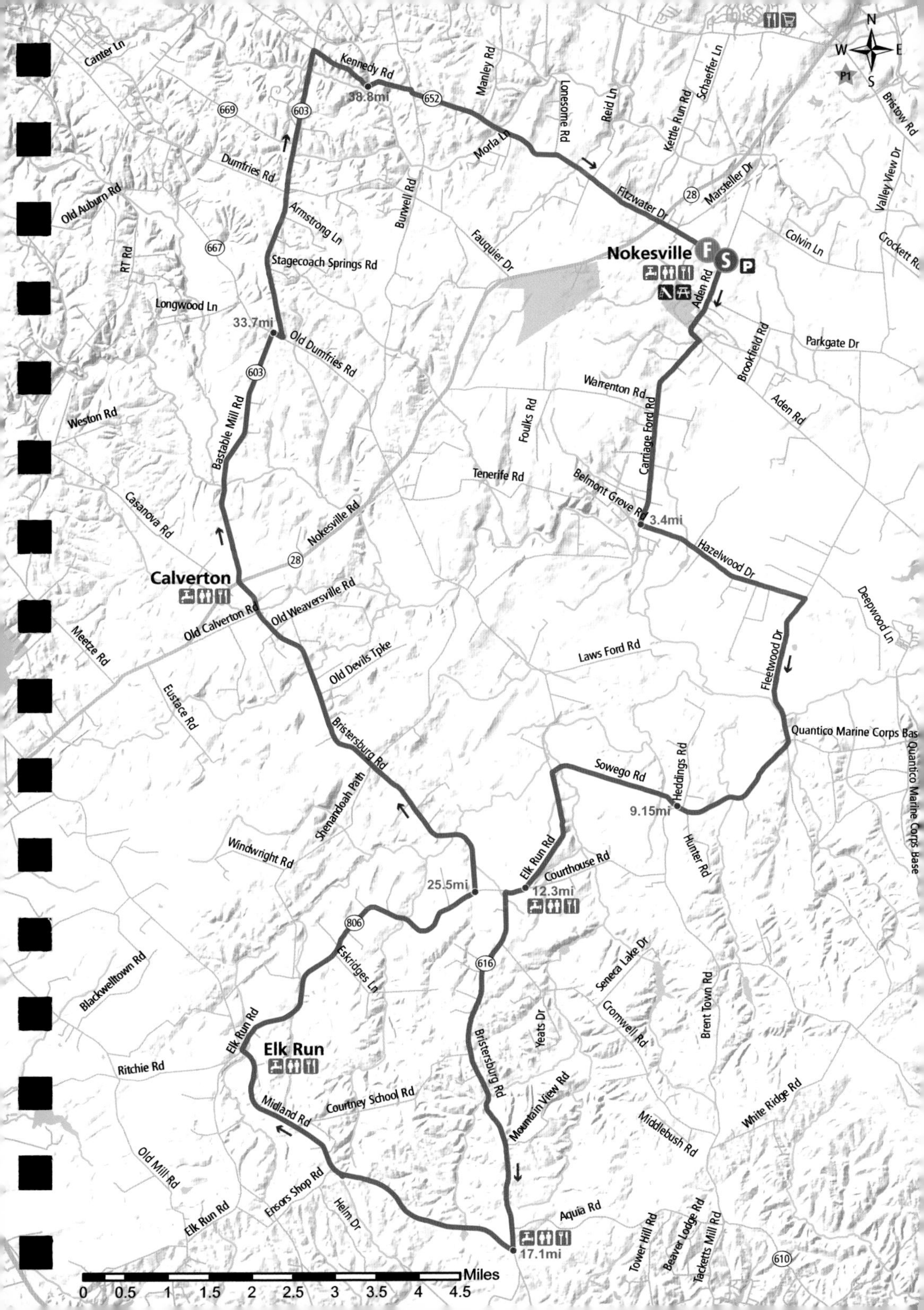

N
W
E
S
P1
Canter Ln
Kennedy Rd
38.8mi
652
Manley Rd
Lonesome Rd
Reid Ln
Kettle Run Rd
Schaeffer Ln
Bristow Rd
669
603
Dumfries Rd
Morla Ln
Fitzwater Dr
28
Marsteller Dr
Valley View Dr
Old Auburn Rd
Armstrong Ln
Burwell Rd
Fauquier Dr
Colvin Ln
Crockett Rd
RT Rd
667
Stagecoach Springs Rd
Nokesville
Aden Rd
Longwood Ln
33.7mi
Old Dumfries Rd
Brookfield Rd
Parkgate Dr
Warrenton Rd
Aden Rd
Weston Rd
Bastable Mill Rd
Foulks Rd
Carriage Ford Rd
Tenerife Rd
Belmont Grove Rd
3.4mi
Casanova Rd
Nokesville Rd
Hazelwood Dr
Calverton
Old Weaversville Rd
Old Calverton Rd
Deepwood Ln
Meetze Rd
Laws Ford Rd
Old Devils Tpke
Fleetwood Dr
Eustace Rd
Quantico Marine Corps Bas
Quantico Marine Corps Base
Bristersburg Rd
Sowego Rd
Heddings Rd
9.15mi
Shenandoah Path
Windwright Rd
Hunter Rd
Elk Run Rd
Courthouse Rd
25.5mi
12.3mi
806
Eskridges Ln
616
Seneca Lake Dr
Blackwelltown Rd
Brent Town Rd
Cromwell Rd
Elk Run Rd
Yeats Dr
Bristersburg Rd
Elk Run
Ritchie Rd
Mountain View Rd
White Ridge Rd
Midland Rd
Courtney School Rd
Middlebush Rd
Old Mill Rd
Ensors Shop Rd
Helm Dr
Aquia Rd
Elk Run Rd
17.1mi
Tower Hill Rd
Beaver Lodge Rd
Tacketts Mill Rd
610
Miles
0
0.5
1
1.5
2
2.5
3
3.5
4
4.5

A particularly beautiful section of the CCT near Lorton.

At a Glance

Distance 8.45 miles **Total Elevation** 150 feet

Terrain

A near-flat, paved trail through suburban woods with some sections of crushed stone.

Traffic

None, aside from a few road crossings.

How to Get There

Access this route from one of three directions. If biking, take Metro to the Orange Line terminus at Vienna, curl left out of its exit toward Vaden Drive, and cross Interstate 66 looking to link up to the CCT south to Arlington Boulevard (U.S. 50).

If driving, use exit 50 off the Beltway to go west onto Arlington Boulevard (U.S. 50). After two-and-a-half miles look to turn right onto Pickett Road then immediately left into Thaiss Park. To begin near Annandale (at the ride log's turnaround) use exit 52 off the Beltway to briefly go west on the Little River Turnpike (VA 236). Turn left the first chance you get onto Pineridge Drive and immediately left again onto Accotink Parkway. It will take you to another left and your start in Americana Park.

Food and Drink

Bring your own or choose among options near the corner of U.S. 50 and Pickett Road, and east of the Beltway along MD 236 in Annandale.

Side Trip

Explore the CCT in either direction.

Where to Bike Rating 

About...

The ambitious Cross County Trail is the primary north-south, multi-use path through Fairfax County, and it functions as a rustic counterpoint to the region's other signature, long-distance trail, the W&OD. The easy route detailed here, meanwhile, covers only a fraction of the CCT's entire 40 miles and is designed to serve as an accessible, road bike ready introduction to the trail as a whole. Having whetted your appetite, the hope is you'll be back to give some of its other sections a go sometime soon.

Bruce in Americana Park.

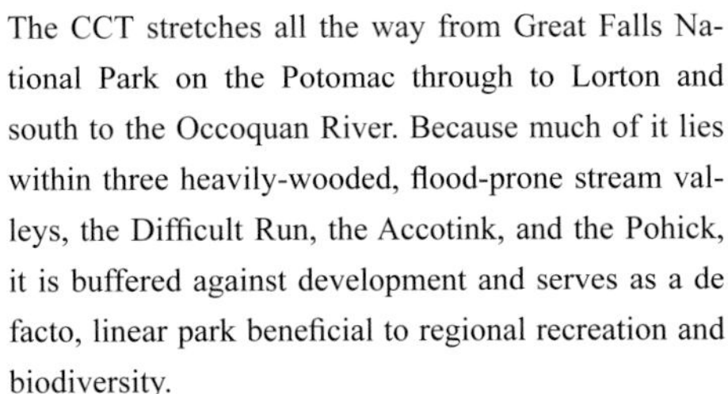

The CCT stretches all the way from Great Falls National Park on the Potomac through to Lorton and south to the Occoquan River. Because much of it lies within three heavily-wooded, flood-prone stream valleys, the Difficult Run, the Accotink, and the Pohick, it is buffered against development and serves as a de facto, linear park beneficial to regional recreation and biodiversity.

Though a large portion of the entire trail is essentially a moderate to extremely challenging mountain biking course, today's way is paved, near-flat, and easy, beginning outside the City of Fairfax, cutting southeast through the forested parks which run alongside Accotink Creek, and finishing at Americana Park after passing under the Little River Turnpike (MD 236) beside its junction with the Beltway.

Expect further exploration to be variable in all respects, and prepare for all types of terrain and conditions. There are a number of fair-weather stream crossings along the CCT, not all of which employ stepping stones, and during any given cycling session, a tree-lined, park-like spin might give way to a steeply-pitched mudfest and again to suburban sidewalk. Ultimately, a full, end-to-end ride across the trail is an amazing way to experience northern Virginia and will leave you surprised at the rugged landscape beyond your doorstep, insistent that such wilds remain untouched, and thankful for those who initially thought to preserve them.

It was outdoor enthusiast Bill Niedringhaus who first proposed the linkage of existing trails throughout Fairfax County. After obtaining an area map and highlighting all its public land, he noticed a near-continuous line snaking through the region and began the process of convincing authorities his visionary idea was justifiably feasible as a government-funded project. They reasoned it was, and volunteers, county agencies, and a few million dollars combined to bring it slowly to life.

Overall, the trail can be thought to include two major pieces, the northern Difficult Run section and the southern Accotink Creek portion, both of which descend from Interstate 66. And though durable, plastic and fiberglass trail signs do mark its way at pivotal locations, be sure to pick up or download a copy of the splendid Fairfax County Bicycle Map for greater access to the detailed information you'll need before setting out.

Ride Log

0.0 Begin at Thaiss Park where parking lot meets trail.
0.55 Turn right.
0.95 Cross Barkley Dr into Sally Ormsby Park.
1.55 Cross Prosperity Ave (699) into Eakin Comm Park. Parking. Playground.
2.35 Cross Woodburn Rd.
2.9 Access to King Arthur Rd.
4.23 Turnaround at Americana Park.
7.9 Turn left.
8.45 Finish.

See if you can count the stripes.

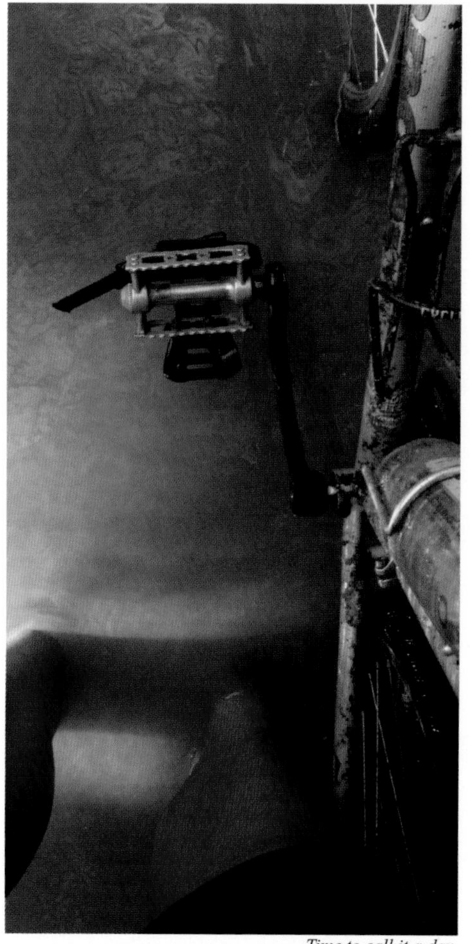

Time to call it a day.

B
B1 Performance Bicycles, 9504 Arlington Blvd
B2 Hudson Trail Outfitters, 9488 Arlington Blvd

The Cross County Trail

Altitude ft: 400, 300, 200
Distance miles: 0, 2, 4, 6, 8, 8.45

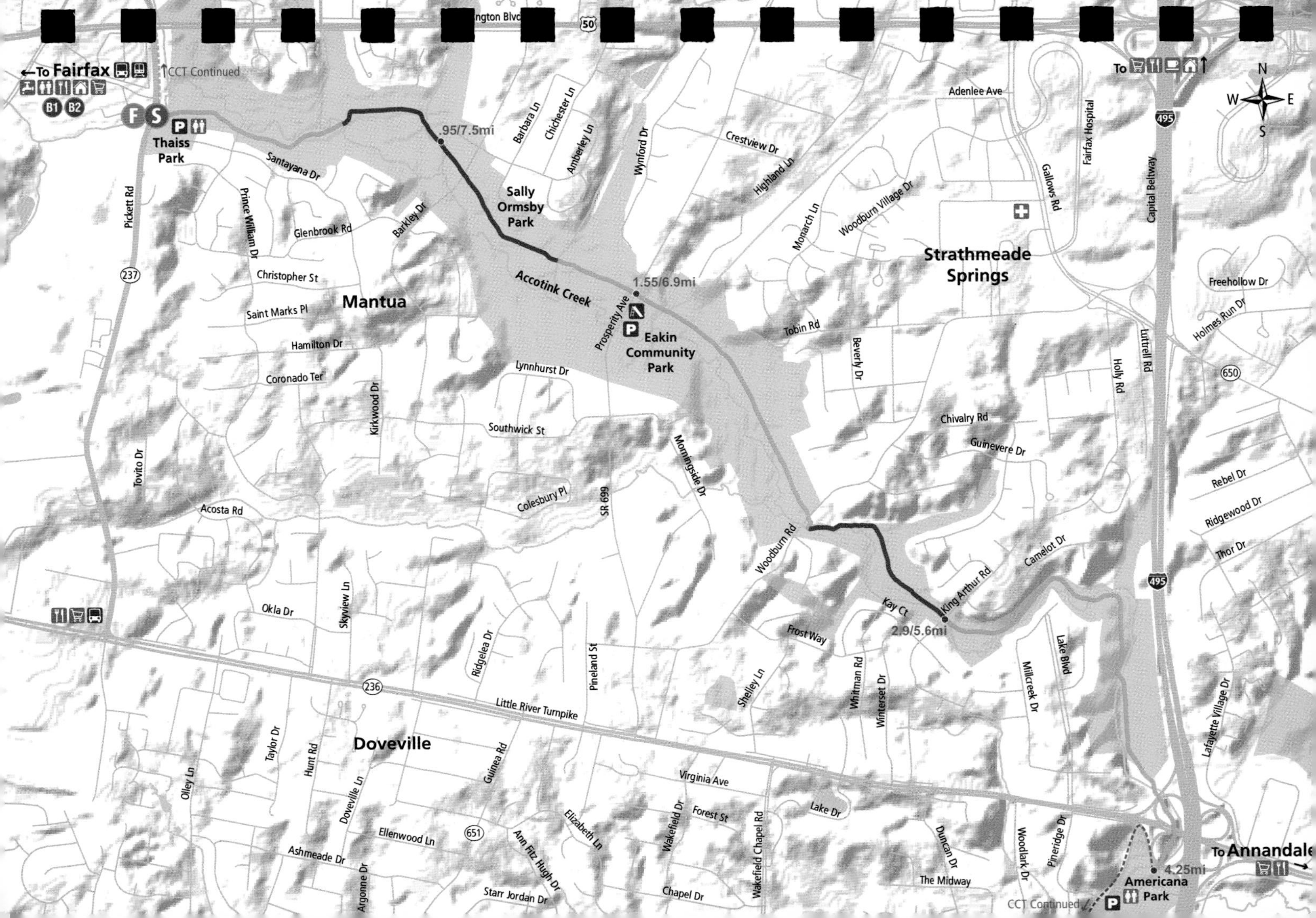

To Fairfax
CCT Continued
B1 B2
F S
Thaiss Park
Pickett Rd
237
Santayana Dr
Prince William Dr
Glenbrook Rd
Barkley Dr
Christopher St
Mantua
Saint Marks Pl
Hamilton Dr
Coronado Ter
Kirkwood Dr
Tovito Dr
Acosta Rd
Okla Dr
Skyview Ln
.95/7.5mi
Barbara Ln
Chichester Ln
Amberley Ln
Sally Ormsby Park
Wynford Dr
Accotink Creek
1.55/6.9mi
Prosperity Ave
Eakin Community Park
Lynnhurst Dr
Southwick St
Colesbury Pl
SR 699
Morningside Dr
Crestview Dr
Highland Ln
Monarch Ln
Woodburn Village Dr
Strathmeade Springs
Tobin Rd
Beverly Dr
Chivalry Rd
Guinevere Dr
Woodburn Rd
Camelot Dr
King Arthur Rd
Kay Ct
2.9/5.6mi
Frost Way
Shelley Ln
Whitman Rd
Winterset Dr
Millcreek Dr
Lake Blvd
Adenlee Ave
Fairfax Hospital
Gallows Rd
Capital Beltway
495
To
N
W
E
S
Freehollow Dr
Holmes Run Dr
650
Luttrell Rd
Holly Rd
Rebel Dr
Ridgewood Dr
Thor Dr
Lafayette Village Dr
50
Ridgelea Dr
Pineland St
236
Little River Turnpike
Doveville
Taylor Dr
Hunt Rd
Olley Ln
Doveville Ln
Guinea Rd
Virginia Ave
Wakefield Dr
Forest St
Lake Dr
Wakefield Chapel Rd
Elizabeth Ln
Ann Fitz Hugh Dr
651
Ellenwood Ln
Ashmeade Dr
Argonne Dr
Starr Jordan Dr
Chapel Dr
Duncan Dr
The Midway
Woodlark Dr
Pineridge Dr
CCT Continued
4.25mi
Americana Park
To Annandale

Riders emerge from the shadow of the stone arch at Clarke's Gap.

At a Glance

Distance 44.6 miles **Total Elevation** 2025 feet

Terrain

This route heads over nearly unblemished trail from coastal plains to piedmont plateau, through a gap in the Catoctin Mountain, and out into the Loudoun Valley. Expect several long, steady inclines broken by many lesser ups and downs.

Traffic

Your most significant negotiations will be done with walkers, runners, and fellow cyclists, but be cautious at road crossings as well. Some have poorer sight lines than others.

How to Get There

If you're beginning at the trail's eastern terminus, arrive by riding the Four Mile Run Trail. If driving, take Interstate 395 to Shirlington, bear right to head north, go to second stoplight and turn left on South Four Mile Run Drive, looking to park along the roadside. The trail parallels the road to the right. There are numerous other access points as well, including East Falls Church just past mile five by way of the Orange Line Metro. Check the friend's of the W&OD website for more detailed information.

Food and Drink

Water stops are frequent. Eat in Shirlington near the eastern trailhead, East and West Falls Church, the town of Vienna, or in each established community thereafter.

Side Trip

Enjoy a weekend of glorious riding in Loudoun County.

Links to 7 13 14 46

Where to Bike Rating

About...

If only they were all like this. The Washington & Old Dominion is just about the best trail you could hope to find rooted in an urban setting. Well-paved, well-designed, largely well-signed and well-maintained, with the ability to take you way out or just a few blocks to Safeway, it's our area's best example of a major cycling thoroughfare. Whatever you do, don't let its length mislead you. Get out and get moving. Going where you want to go, distance will take care of itself.

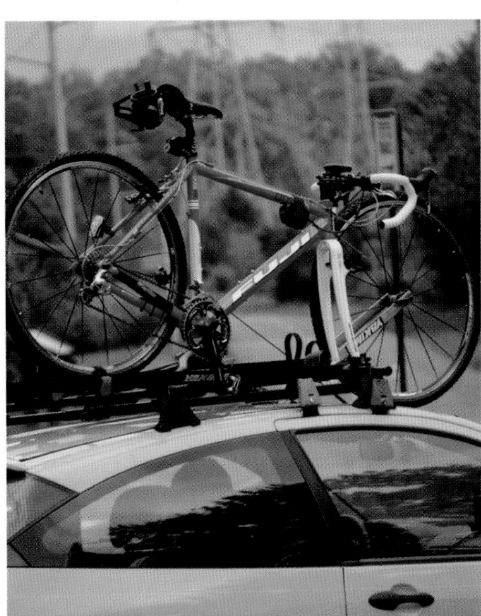

Park and ride at numerous spots along the trail.

The W&OD Trail takes its name from the railroad whose founders dreamed of linking Appalachian coal fields with the port of Alexandria. Though that idea never reached fruition and the Civil War nearly cost it its existence, the short-line was reenvisioned and found eventual success shuttling Washingtonians to resorts in the Blue Ridge foothills. At its peak early in the 20th century, service was provided from Potomac Yard out to Bluemont, with numerous stops in between. You'll become acquainted with some of these as you make your way west, and though many have been lost, several are preserved and function as historic sites and museums.

When the W&OD ceased operations in 1968, an electric company put power lines on the rail's right-of-way and local activists seized the opportunity to utilize the remaining space for a segment of test trail in Falls Church. Proving popular, the path was then incrementally expanded to its present length.

At 100 feet wide, this regional park could be one of the thinnest official playgrounds you've ever visited, and with a length of 45 miles, likely the longest. Regardless of its odd dimensions, however, it's a mainstream success and the region's shining example of the possibilities inherent in the partnership between trails and local business. A corridor of both recreation and transportation, offering equal opportunities to shoppers, sightseers, diners, and serious and not-so-serious cyclists alike, a ride here entails control and caution as lots of folks will be out to enjoy the day just as you wish to.

The tour's opening section paralells Four Mile Run and passes through a string of Arlington parks. A second stage then brings multiple road crossings as the busy life of the inner suburbs encroaches trailside. By this time, you've been steadily elevating and might consider a break in Vienna. The town has preserved the ambiance around its old depot, and amenities are thinner from here on as the trail becomes increasingly more countrified. Dropping through a pretty section past the Difficult Run, you'll climb to modern Reston, continue through Herndon's retro downtown, cross high above Goose Creek, and come to proud, old Leesburg. From there it's up to beautiful views through Clarke's Gap and onward to trail's end and the fresh air of Purcellville.

While Ride 19 has not been deemed kid-friendly in its entirety, it does include substantial sections which are entirely safe for family use.

Ride Log

0.0 The W&OD begins at the junction of S Shirlington Rd and Four Mile Run Dr.

2.2 Links to Four Mile Run Trail begin to appear here and ahead.

3.95 Intersect Custis Trail here and ahead.

4.9 Follow signs carefully through E Falls Church Park.

5.3 Pass E Falls Church Metro.

7.0 Falls Church.

11.5 Vienna. Bikeshop.

16.8 Reston. Food.

17.7 Performance Bike Center.

18.3 Bike Lane bike shop.

20.0 Herndon.

22.5 Sterling. The Bike Shop.

25.7 Ashburn.

34.3 Leesburg Historic District.

38.2 Clarke's Gap. Right to Waterford.

39.1 Sign for Paeonian Springs.

44.6 End in Purcellville at Trail's End Cycling Company.

B

- B1 Phoenix Bikes, 4200 S Four Mile Run Dr, Arlington
- B2 Spokes, Etc, 224 Maple Ave E, Vienna
- B3 bikes@vienna, 128 Church St NW, Vienna
- B4 Performance Bicycle Shop, 11634 Plaza America Dr, Reston
- B5 The Bike Lane, 11943 Democracy Dr, Reston
- B6 Eastern Mountain Sports, 22000 Dulles Retail Plaza Ste, Dulles
- B7 Bicycle Outfitters, 34-D, Catoctin Circle, Leesburg
- B8 Trail's End Cycling Company, 201 N 23rd St, Purcellville

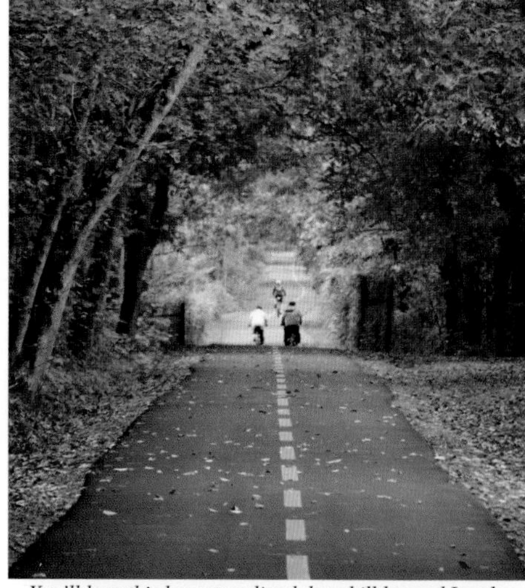

You'll love this long, tree-lined downhill beyond Leesburg.

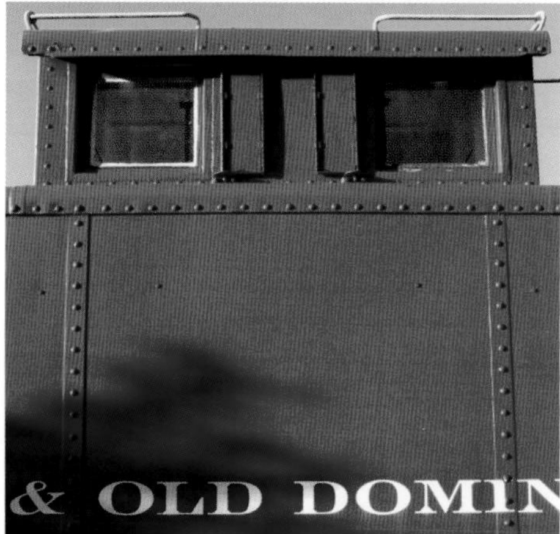

An antique caboose sits trailside.

The W&OD Rail Trail

Please note: the profile for Ride 19 is depicted in 200ft vertical increments due to unusually high elevation.

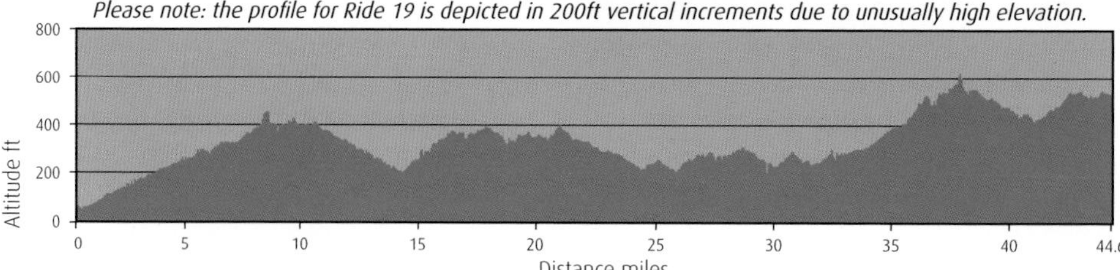

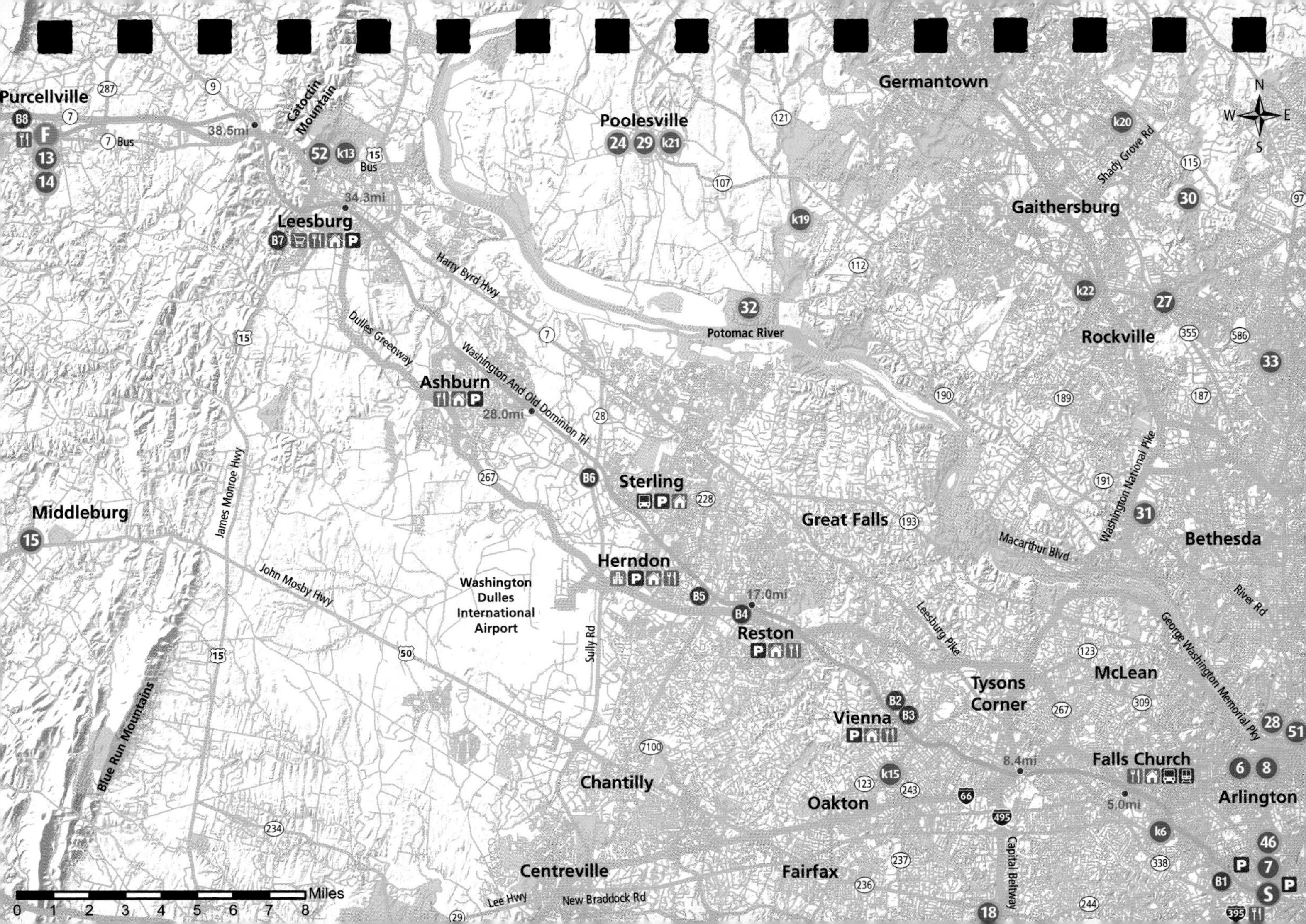

Purcellville
Catoctin Mountain
38.5mi
Poolesville
Germantown
Gaithersburg
Shady Grove Rd
34.3mi
Leesburg
Harry Byrd Hwy
Dulles Greenway
Potomac River
Rockville
Washington And Old Dominion Trl
Ashburn
28.0mi
Middleburg
James Monroe Hwy
Sterling
Great Falls
Washington National Pike
Macarthur Blvd
Bethesda
Herndon
John Mosby Hwy
Washington Dulles International Airport
Sully Rd
17.0mi
Reston
Leesburg Pike
River Rd
George Washington Memorial Pky
Tysons Corner
McLean
Vienna
Blue Run Mountains
Chantilly
8.4mi
Falls Church
Oakton
5.0mi
Arlington
Capital Beltway
Centreville
Fairfax
Lee Hwy
New Braddock Rd
Miles
0 1 2 3 4 5 6 7 8

The first First Family.

At a Glance

Distance 20.6 miles **Total Elevation** 935 feet

Terrain

This modestly hilly ride parallels the Potomac and passes through suburban woods, parks and wetlands. Its biggest climb brings you up to Mount Vernon Estate and Gardens.

Traffic

You'll have to share, but not to the extent you did on this trail's northern half. The short stretch on-road is mellow, as are all road crossings.

How to Get There

Cycle here by exiting the Yellow King Street Metro elevator to a soft right off King onto Daingerfield. After a left on Prince, take it all the way downtown to a left on South Lee. Go one block back to King and another block right to begin at Union. Drivers should use the Beltway to exit 176, Telegraph Road, turn right on Duke, follow it to South Lee, and look to park at metered street spaces or in designated garages and pay lots. King is two blocks north.

Food and Drink

There's a heap of options in Alexandria, and a food court inside Mount Vernon, but only water stops directly along the way.

Side Trip

Visit the American Horticultural Society at River Farm by continuing straight onto Southdown Lane at mile five and bearing right onto Kent. Or tour Collingwood Library and Museum by going left on Collingwood Road at mile six, then right on East Boulevard Drive.

Links to 8 9 36 46

Where to Bike Rating 

About...

Called 'the best horseman of his age' by Thomas Jefferson, George Washington's diaries show he sometimes spent up to 60 miles a day in the saddle. Riding this comparatively short route from Alexandria to Mount Vernon would have seemed relatively relaxed in comparison. And he would have made the commute an untold number of times throughout his storied career, as it linked both his business affairs and two of his homes. Estimates place his trotting pace at around eight minutes a mile. What's yours?

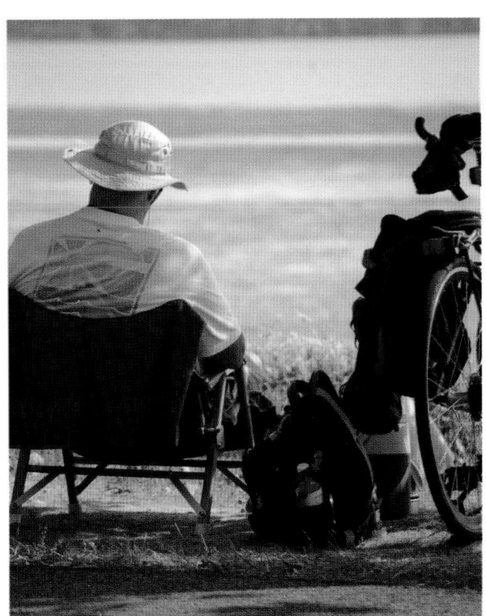

Nice idea.

This ride joins the Mount Vernon Trail at its epicenter along Union Street in Old Town Alexandria. Seven blocks south, the two become proper path, jog left to skirty Potomac shoreline, and travel under monumental Woodrow Wilson Bridge. After passing a path which offers introduction to D.C.'s southernmost boundary stone and Jones Point Lighthouse, it then ascends a ramp and cruises downhill past posh apartments and across Hunting Creek.

Belle Haven Park and Marina arrives with opportunities for sailing classes, boat rentals and a chance to hike 'Haul Road' into Dyke Marsh, one of the largest freshwater tidal wetlands in the metro area. The route itself edges the preserve and becomes elevated boardwalk. Stop and listen for the distinctive o-ka-leee of the red-winged blackbird as you look out over a sea of cattails toward Maryland. A birding hotspot, at least 300 species have been observed here within only 485 acres.

Continuing along your shaded way, you'll begin to encounter a few easy hills, jump briefly on-road, cross GW Parkway, and enter the northern reaches of River Farm, formerly one of George Washington's five linked properties. There, the trail fords a few neighborhood roads before star-shaped Fort Washington grandly positions itself into view across the Potomac.

After dipping under a handsome stone bridge, a chance then arrives to visit ruins along the Virginian riverside at old Fort Hunt. With a history stretching back to the Spanish-American War, it seems this military facility's greatest fame arrived only recently when it was revealed as the former headquarters of P.O. Box 1142, a secret American interrogation unit in operation during World War II.

Continuing onward, historic markers beside the path at sublimely positioned Riverside Park soon serve as appetizers for the feast to follow at this ride's namesake, only a hundred hard revolutions uphill beyond Little Hunting Creek.

Washington assumed possession of Mount Vernon late in 1754. An innovative agriculturalist throughout his more well-known military and political careers, he experimented over many years with crop rotation and soil conservation on holdings which eventually reached 8000 acres. And to the manner born, he enjoyed the aristocratic life of a plantation owner perched high above his beloved Potomac. Tour the impeccably-appointed estate and gardens before doubling back.

While Ride 20 has not been deemed kid-friendly in its entirety, it does include substantial sections which are entirely safe for family use.

Ride Log

0.0 Head south from the corner of King St and S Union in Alexandria.

0.55 A proper trail resumes, sliding left as S Union curves right.

1.0 Woodrow Wilson Bridge above. Jones Point Park and lighthouse at left.

1.3 Continue straight up ramp on bridge's south side.

1.5 At ramp's end, trail continues to left along sidewalk.

2.5 Pass through Belle Haven Park and Marina. Hike "Haul Road". Water. Bathrooms.

3.25 Begin boardwalk through Dyke Marsh Wildlife Preserve.

4.8 Continue straight on Northdown Ln. (Stay straight, right on Kent to visit American Horticultural Society.)

4.95 Right over GW Pkwy to immediate left as trail resumes on other side. Pass rest area with water, payphone, information.

7.3 Look right to enter Fort Hunt.

7.45 Water, rest area, info, before briefly joining road through tunnel and resuming trail to left.

9.05 Rest area. Bathrooms. Info.

10.3 Lock up at bicycle racks to left just before crossing parking lot entrance road. Take in Mt Vernon and begin here to retrace.

20.6 Finish at corner of King St and S Union.

Trailside bloom.

P1 Jones Point Lighthouse/ D.C.'s southernmost boundary stone
P2 Dyke Marsh Wildlife Preserve
P3 American Horticultural Society
P4 Collingwood Library and Museum
P5 Ft Hunt
P6 Ft Washington
P7 Mt Vernon Estate and Gardens

B1 Velocity Bicycle Cooperative, 204 S Union St
B2 Big Wheel Bikes, 2 Prince St
B3 Spokes, Etc, 1506 Belle View Blvd

BR1 Bike and Roll Alexandria, One Wales Alley

The Mount Vernon Trail South

Altitude ft: 0, 100, 200
Distance miles: 0, 4, 8, 12, 16, 20.6

Alexandria
Cameron St
Queen St
Prince St
King St
Eisenhower Bike Path
Eisenhower Ave
Elmwood Dr
Mill Rd
Wilkes St
Wolfe St
Gibbon St
Franklin St
Saint Asaph St
Pitt St
Royal St
S Union St
Payne St
Alfred St
Jefferson St
Green St
Burgundy Rd
Capital Beltway
Huntington Ave
Norton Rd
Ridge View Dr
Clermont Dr
Franconia Rd
Wilton Rd
Javins Dr
Fort Hill Dr
Huntington
1.5/
19.1mi
P1
Belle
Haven
Country
Club
Potomac
River
Old Telegraph Rd
Telegraph Rd
Florence Ln
Gentle Ln
Hillview Ave
The Pky
Windsor Rd
Belle Haven Rd
Olde Towne Rd
2.5/18.1mi
H St
Belle View Blvd
Potomac Ave
10th St
Rosier Rd
Dorset Dr
Kings Hwy
Groveton
Beacon Hill Rd
Quander Rd
Groveton St
P2
Stoneybrooke Ln
Harrison Ln
Vantage Dr
Bedrock Rd
Popkins Ln
Rollins Dr
Shiver Dr
Paul Spring Rd
Fort
Foote
Bluffwood Ln
Fort Foote Rd
Lounghran Rd
Richmond Hwy
Huntley
Meadows
Park
Range Rd
Mason Hill Dr
Whiteoaks Dr
Park Terrace Dr
George Washington Memorial Pky
Ridgecrest Dr
Elba Rd
Courtland Rd
Hybla
Valley
Paul Spring Pky
Alexandria Ave
5.0/15.6mi
Audubon Ave
Fordson Rd
Sherwood Hall Ln
Midday Ln
Lee Ave
Fielding St
Martha Washington St
Janna Lee Ave
Ashton St
Russell Rd
Little Hunting Creek Dr
Holland Rd
Candlewood Dr
Bainbridge Rd
Shenandoah Rd
Wellington Rd
Boulevard Dr
P3
Little Hunting Creek
Collingwood Rd
Fort Hunt Rd
Cool Spring Dr
Rampart Dr
P4
Buckman Rd
Washington Ave
Old Mount Vernon Rd
Wagon Wheel Rd
Bound Brook Ln
Stirrup Ln
Riverside Rd
Old Stage Rd
Neal Dr
Croton Dr
Riverview Rd
Amer Dr
Sero Estates Dr
Othman Dr
Londonderry Rd
Fort
Hunt
Waynewood Blvd
Mount Vernon View Hwy
Swan Creek Rd
Laurel Rd
Woodley Dr
Batter Sea Ln
Wessynton Way
Potomac Ln
Dalebrook Dr
Stockton Pky
Wittington Blvd
Adrienne Dr
Camden St
Linton Ln
Priscilla Ln
Cunningham Dr
Old Mill Rd
Mount
Vernon
Fort
Hunt
Park
P5
7.3/13.3mi
P6
Fort
Washington
National
Park
Fort Washington Rd
Warburton Dr
10.3mi
P7
Miles
0
0.5
1
1.5
2
2.5
3

Gunston Hall, George Mason's Georgian-style home.

At a Glance

Distance 9.0 miles **Total Elevation** 285 feet

Terrain

This route incorporates smooth, hard surface trail, some boardwalk, and a portion of roadway. The way is flat but for one moderate climb.

Traffic

Minimal to none.

How to Get There

Exit 163 off Interstate 95 brings you to Lorton Road. Briefly take it east beneath the rail tracks to Lorton Market Street. Go right. Follow it as it curves uphill, crosses Jefferson Davis Highway (U.S. 1), and becomes Gunston Road (VA 242). Turn left onto the Gunston Hall Plantation access drive after about three-and-a-half miles. Or continue downhill and turn right to visit Mason Neck State Park.

Food and Drink

There are restaurants and a supermarket around I-95 in Lorton.

Side Trip

For stretches of unbroken pedaling, take Gunston Road in either direction. Visit Pirate's Cove Waterpark. Hike Meadowood Special Recreation Area.

Where to Bike Rating

About...

Think of this place as a package deal for the family that plays together. History? Got that covered. Nature? In abundance. A safe, scenic place to cycle? Yup. Throw in the amenities of next door Pohick Bay Regional Park, and you've all got yourself a weekend to remember. Off the bike highlights include a tour of Gunston Hall, a glimpse of nature by the bay, or a paddle in search of an elusive bald eagle.

Big ideas call for bigger helmets.

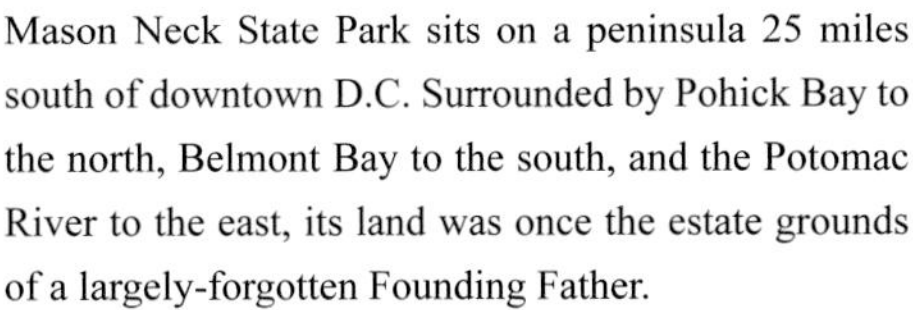

Mason Neck State Park sits on a peninsula 25 miles south of downtown D.C. Surrounded by Pohick Bay to the north, Belmont Bay to the south, and the Potomac River to the east, its land was once the estate grounds of a largely-forgotten Founding Father.

George Mason was hugely influential. An American patriot and statesman, it was he who authored the Virginia Declaration of Rights in 1776, a document crucial to the ensuing U.S. Bill of Rights and France's Declaration of the Rights of Man.

You've probably driven over the bridge named in his honor (14th Street), and you're likely familiar with the university which bears his name. You may have even visited his memorial near Jefferson's along the Tidal Basin. But for all practical purposes, he's been lost to history. Find him here.

Outdoors, expect a birder's paradise. The neck supports an active heron rookery along with 200 other species. What's more, it is known for the frequency of its bald eagle sightings, perhaps the nearest natural space to the capital with that distinction. Its beginnings can, in fact, be traced back to 1965 when the spotting of two bald eagles became the groundswell which eventually led to the park's opening 20 years later.

This ride is fun, leisurely, and easily navigated. Start at the Gunston Hall visitor's center and exit the grounds by way of a tree-lined, plantation drive. A bike path presents itself just past the estate's gates. Take it left as it crosses the road and drops downhill. Continue right through dense forest, ending in open parkland near Belmont Bay.

Some cyclists use High Point Road as a training route. Recreational riders should consider it too, as it's smooth as silk, lightly-trafficked, and straighter than the mapped trail. Above all, enjoy yourselves, and don't forget the three or so bikes for rent at the Elizabeth S. Hartwell Environmental Center for $5/hour.

Ride Log

0.0 Begin at the entrance to the Gunston Hall Plantation visitor's center.

0.5 Turn left onto the path between entry gates and Gunston Rd.

0.7 Follow path as it crosses Gunston Rd.

1.35 Cross High Point Rd to continue on trail.

2.1 Cross entrance to Woodmarsh Trail. Bathrooms. Info.

2.5 One of two successive road crossings.

3.9 Road crossing.

4.1 Wilson Spring Trail crossing.

4.25 Trail ends. Right to Elizabeth S. Hartwell Environmental Center.

4.5 Stop at park office entranceway. Retrace when ready.

9.0 Finish at Gunston Hall Plantation visitor's center.

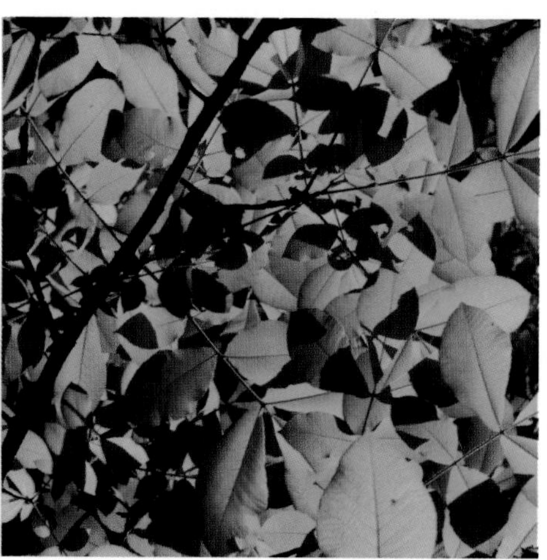

Looking up through spring's first green.

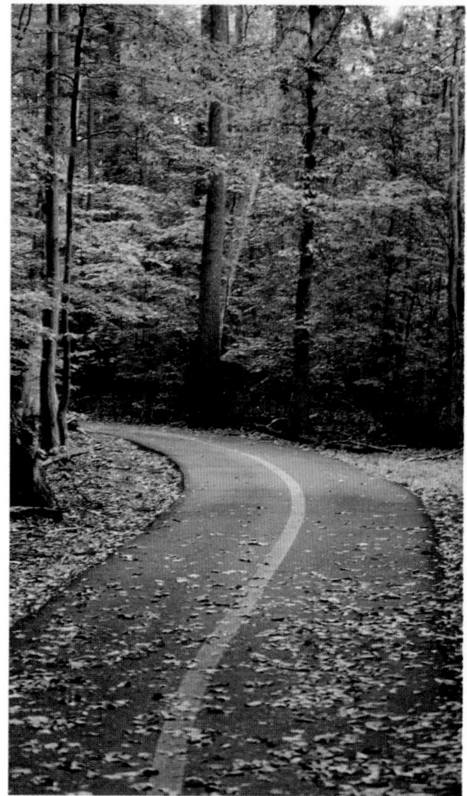

High Point Trail through Mason Neck State Park.

P1 Gunston Hall Plantation
P2 Elizabeth S. Hartwell Environmental Center
P3 Pirate's Cove Water Park

BR1 Inside visitor's center

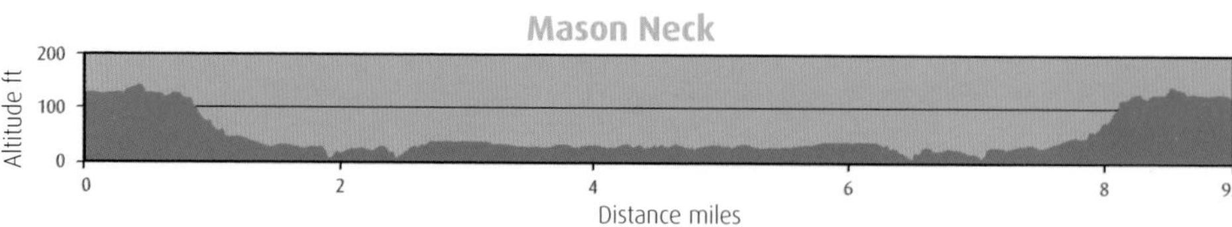

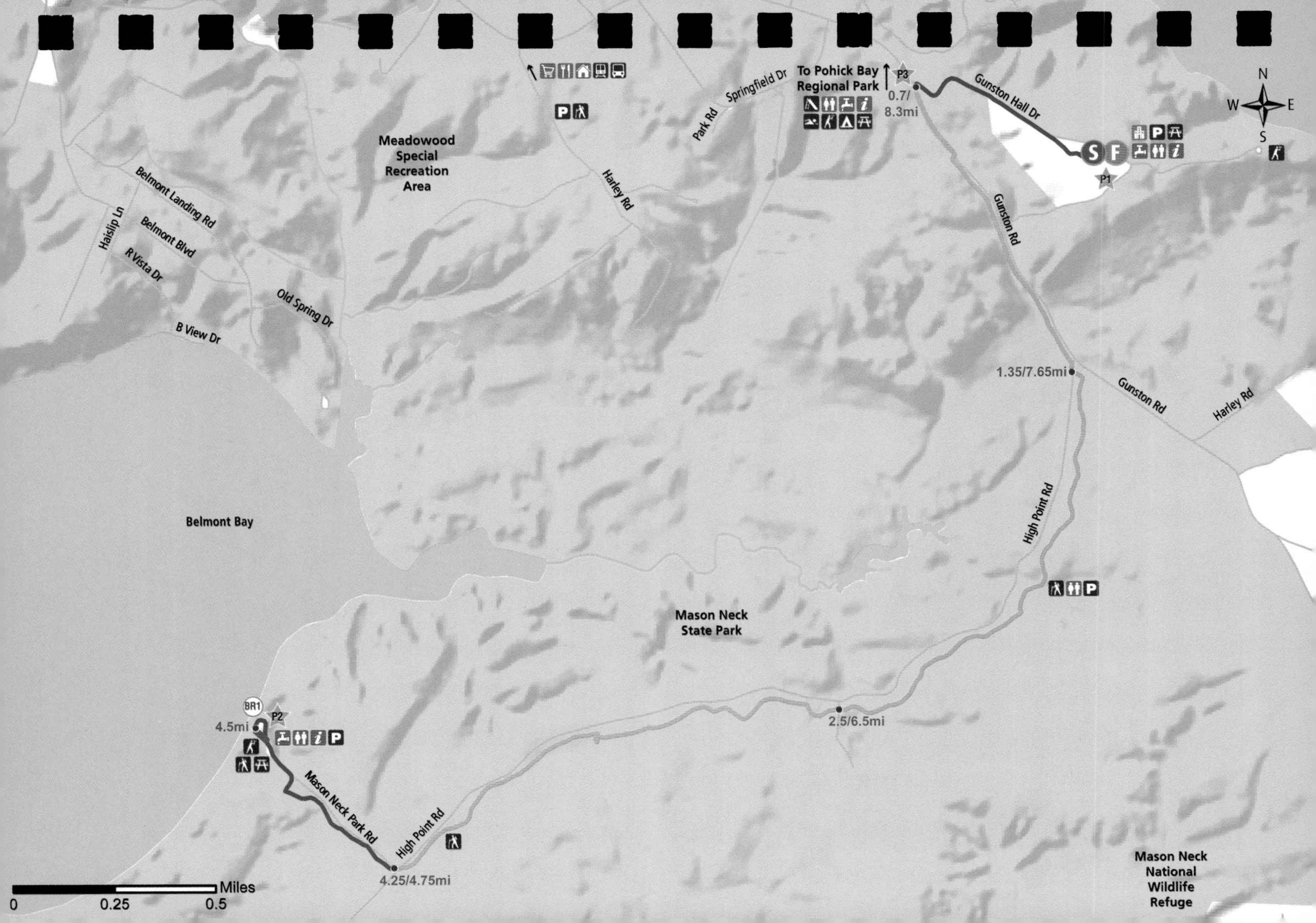
Meadowood
Special
Recreation
Area
To Pohick Bay
Regional Park
Springfield Dr
Park Rd
Harley Rd
Gunston Hall Dr
S
F
P1
P3
0.7/
8.3mi
N
W
E
S
Belmont Landing Rd
Haislip Ln
Belmont Blvd
R Vista Dr
Old Spring Dr
B View Dr
Gunston Rd
1.35/7.65mi
Gunston Rd
Harley Rd
Belmont Bay
High Point Rd
Mason Neck
State Park
2.5/6.5mi
BR1
P2
4.5mi
Mason Neck Park Rd
High Point Rd
4.25/4.75mi
Miles
0
0.25
0.5
Mason Neck
National
Wildlife
Refuge

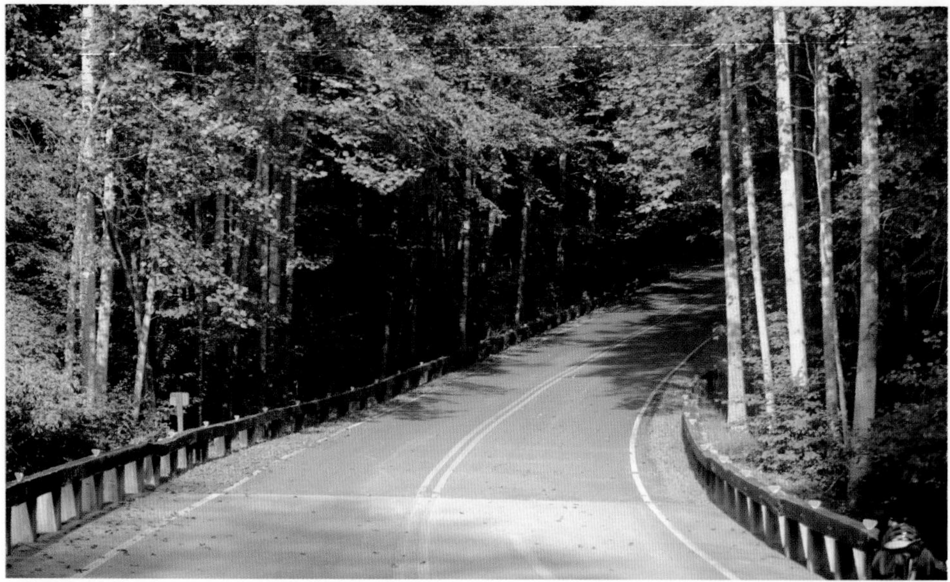

Yellow Poplar line the road down along South Quantico Creek.

At a Glance

Distance 11.6 miles **Total Elevation** 890 feet

Terrain

The identical first and last two miles of this loop are quite hilly, with the remainder of the course much less so. Its surface throughout is excellent.

Traffic

Very light.

How to Get There

Take exit 150 off Interstate 95 onto Joplin Road going west briefly to a right on Park Entrance Road. Follow it to a left toward Pine Grove picnic area just past Park Scenic Drive. Parking is then available immediately to the right. Prepare for a $5 drive-in/ $3 bike-in fee.

Food and Drink

Stock up before you get here, as the visitor center offers scant selection. Try the convenience stores just past Joplin/Fuller Road (VA 619) at its junction with Jefferson Davis Highway (U.S. 1).

Side Trip

Bring your mountain bike to explore the park's miles of crushed stone fire roads. Also worth mentioning, but certainly not for the faint-hearted, is a short, pulse-quickening ride to arrive at the National Museum of the Marine Corps. Go east on VA 619 to a right (south) on U.S. 1. Its entrance drive is one quarter-mile ahead on your right. Alternatively, Quantico National Cemetery is a half-mile west on VA 619 from this park's entrance, though you'll have to lock your bike and pay your respects on foot.

Where to Bike Rating 

Optional MTB side-trips

About...

This peaceful ride offers the chance to cycle through a section of the capital region as it once appeared centuries ago. Come and be transported into the largest remaining tract of Eastern Piedmont forest ecosystem in America's national parks. Whether you prefer road or mountain, easy or challenging, any of Prince William's family pedaling options is bound to be fun and memorable, and more than likely result in an encounter with one of its thousands of wild inhabitants.

A rider turns onto the park's bike lane.

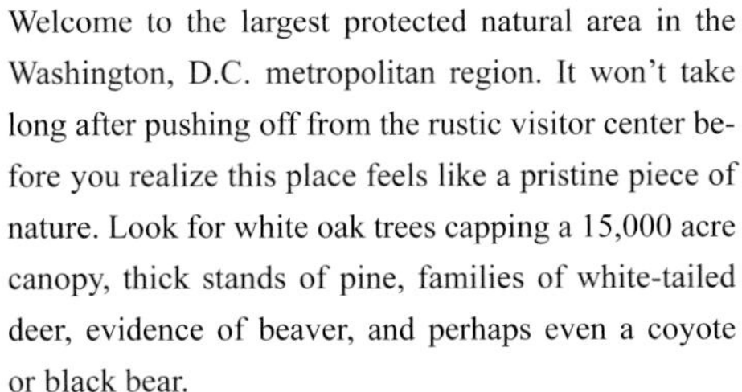

Welcome to the largest protected natural area in the Washington, D.C. metropolitan region. It won't take long after pushing off from the rustic visitor center before you realize this place feels like a pristine piece of nature. Look for white oak trees capping a 15,000 acre canopy, thick stands of pine, families of white-tailed deer, evidence of beaver, and perhaps even a coyote or black bear.

The map details a route with steep hills in its first and last two identical miles. It's nothing a moderately experienced rider can't handle, but if you'd like to keep things a bit more mellow, drive that initial section, park at any one of many lettered lots, and stick to the ride's inner, 7.2-mile scenic loop. A third even more relaxed option has you parking at lot D and limiting yourself to the beginner-level three mile bike lane running to Oak Ridge Campground Road. Whatever your choice, view any distance here as a chance to ride uninterrupted with minimal traffic. The scenic loop winds and undulates between a wall of trees, occasionally passing fire roads and hiking trails. Then, within its last quarter, prepare for two more miles of hills around lovely South Quantico Creek.

Post-ride leaves you plenty of options. Perhaps hiking through the forest's 37 miles of trail is the order of the afternoon. Otherwise fish, orienteer, bird watch or tap into one of the park's intriguing layers of history. Visit the Civil War-era pyrite mine or look for evidence of the land's heyday, when it was known as the Chopawamsic Recreational Demonstration Area.

In the 1930s, FDR's Civilian Conservation Corps put men to work here planting trees, blazing trails, and building shelters. The resulting cabin camps were first used 'to bring the character-building benefits of camping to under-privileged urban children'. Later, they were used by the pre-CIA, Office of Strategic Services as a training ground for spies. And now, if you decide to stay, they're yours. Other camping choices run from pack-it-in-pack-it-out primitive to an RV park with pool and laundry. So be on the lookout for events such as the Chopawamsic Cycling Challenge and get yourself down here.

While Ride 22 has not been deemed kid-friendly in its entirety, it does include substantial sections which are entirely safe for family use.

Ride Log

Cruising along...

0.0 Start in the visitor center circle loop. Bathrooms, snacks, water, maps, and other information are available.

0.15 Go right at Park Scenic Dr.

1.35 Stay right.

1.75 Pass parking for Scott Valley Trail.

2.2 Continue right.

2.55 Orenda fire road to right.

2.6 A separated bicycle lane begins to left.

4.0 Cross Taylor Farm Rd.

5.75 Bicycle lane ends at Oak Ridge Rd. Straight to continue loop. Right to campsites.

6.55 Mawavi Rd to right. Cabin camping available.

7.6 High Meadows Trail.

8.75 Cross S Fork Quantico Creek.

9.05 Continue straight. A left leads to Turkey Run Education Center.

9.4 Right.

11.4 Left.

11.6 Finish.

P1 Weems-Botts Museum, 3944 Cameron St
P2 National Museum of the Marine Corps
P3 Quantico National Cemetery
P4 Turkey Run Education Center
P5 Cabin Branch Pyrite Mine

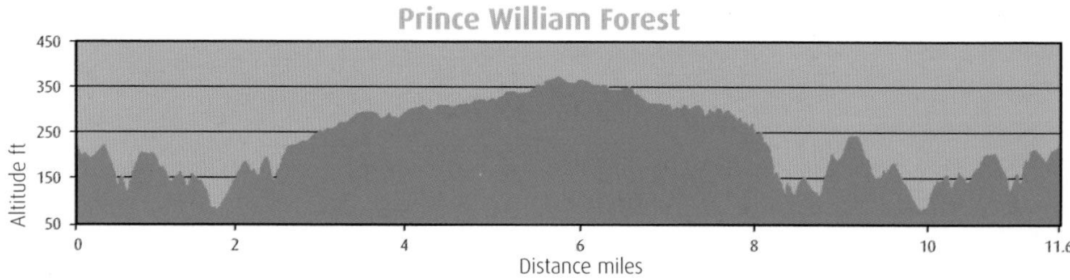

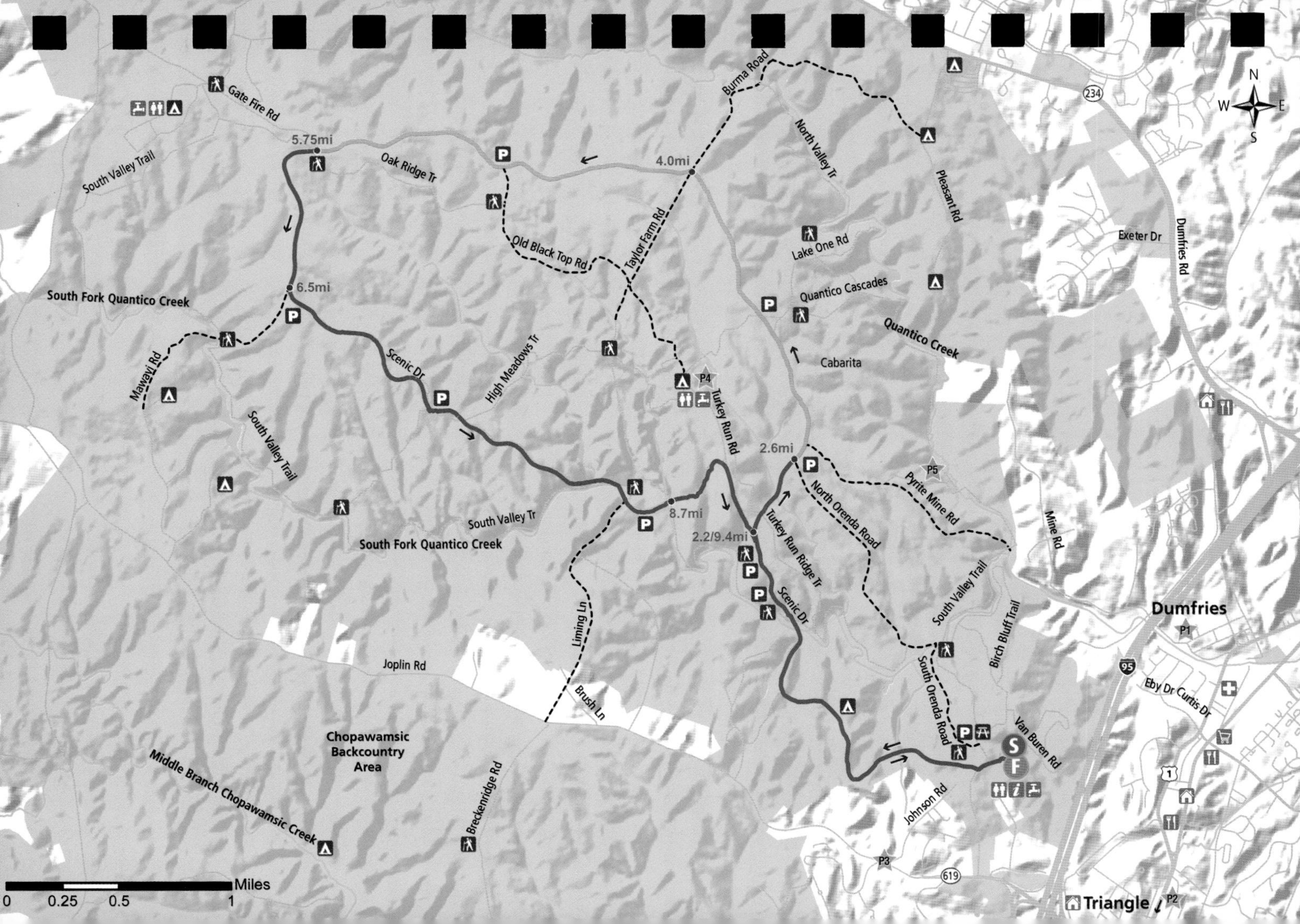
Gate Fire Rd
5.75mi
South Valley Trail
Oak Ridge Tr
4.0mi
Burma Road
North Valley Tr
Pleasant Rd
Taylor Farm Rd
Old Black Top Rd
Lake One Rd
Exeter Dr
Dumfries Rd
234
6.5mi
South Fork Quantico Creek
Quantico Cascades
Quantico Creek
Scenic Dr
High Meadows Tr
P4
Turkey Run Rd
Cabarita
Mawavi Rd
South Valley Trail
2.6mi
P5
Pyrite Mine Rd
North Orenda Road
Mine Rd
8.7mi
2.2/9.4mi
South Valley Tr
South Fork Quantico Creek
Turkey Run Ridge Tr
Scenic Dr
South Valley Trail
Birch Bluff Trail
Dumfries
P1
Liming Ln
Joplin Rd
Brush Ln
95
Eby Dr Curtis Dr
South Orenda Road
Van Buren Rd
S
F
Chopawamsic Backcountry Area
Middle Branch Chopawamsic Creek
Breckenridge Rd
Johnson Rd
1
P3
619
Miles
0 0.25 0.5 1
Triangle
P2
N
W
E
S

'Melancholy is incompatible with biking.' James E. Starrs

At a Glance

Distance 11.5 miles **Total Elevation** 575 feet

Terrain

Expect some hills around Lake Mercer, and the South Run Trail is bumpy. The crushed stone path around Burke Lake is flat.

Traffic

No cars, but the lakes attract a large amount of runners, riders, and walkers.

How to Get There

Using a combination of the Beltway, Interstate 95, and the Franconia Springfield/Fairfax County Parkway, take a left onto Hooes Road. Look to park as you go downhill past Newington Forest Avenue. If you come to Triple Ridge Road, you've gone too far.

Food and Drink

There's an ice cream parlor with snacks and drinks at Burke Lake as well as a campground store and a clubhouse at its 18-hole, par-3 golf course.

Side Trip

Subdued lake loops not quite enough for you? Did you know there was a trail running alongside the Fairfax County Parkway? Did you realize that trail runs from the Blue Line Springfield-Franconia Metro station all the way out to Hooes Road (and beyond)? Well... there's your side trip if you choose to accept it. (Check out a Fairfax County Bicycle Map for more adventures).

Where to Bike Rating

About...

This satisfying spin linking Lake Mercer to Lake Burke in central southern Fairfax County is a great destination ride for the family. There's a lot to do once you get here, and whether you prefer the water and wonderful views of the lakes or easing through the shade of the South Run stream valley, consider this yet another pleasant, bucolic getaway within the confines of the greater metropolitan region.

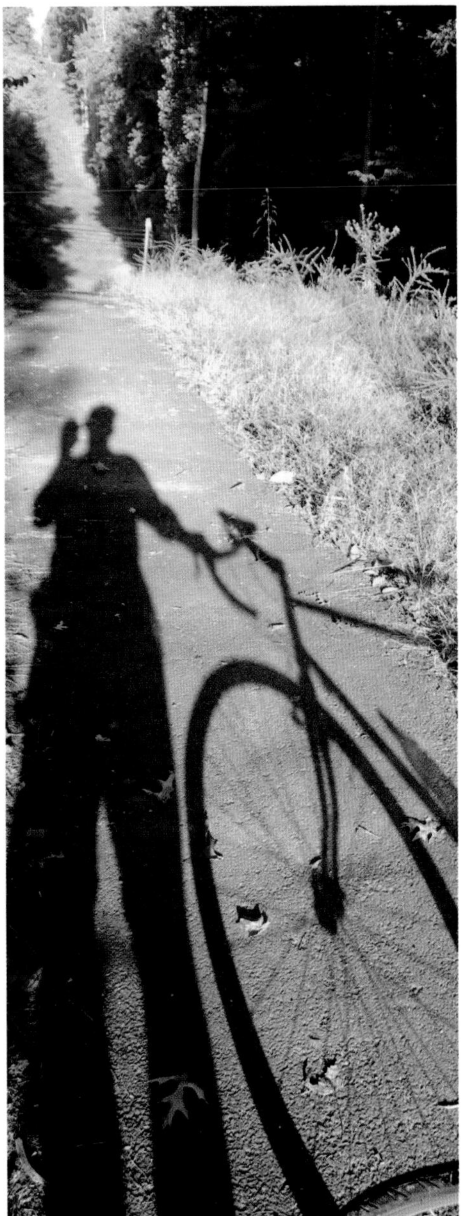

Self-portrait with shadow.

Begin with a climb to 43-acre Lake Mercer. After enjoying the dam's treetop view, attack the brief, steeply-pitched hills around the lake's south side, turning right as the path levels into a stream valley and crosses a footbridge. South Run District Park is sign-posted to the right down a spur at mile two. Continue left. The trail grades gradually uphill as you make your way upstream through patches of suburban forest. Ignore the paths leading left or right into neighborhoods, and keep moving forward.

Soon, you've arrived at 888-acre Burke Lake Park. After curving right and climbing to water's edge, stay right to begin circling the four-and-a-half mile crushed stone trail around the lake. You'll be tracing the shoreline's jagged contours as the water ducks in and out of view. Benches and vista points abound. Rest as required and relax into the scene.

Taking up nearly a quarter of the park, lovely, tree-lined Burke Lake is the most heavily fished reservoir in Virginia. It's also home to Vesper Island, a refuge for waterfowl. Visitors can camp, picnic, boat, hike, ride the miniature train and carousel, use the 18-hole, par-3 golf course and driving range, play miniature golf and disk golf, pitch horseshoes, or pass the time at one of the park's three playgrounds.

As you finish your loop, you may wish to make another. Many people do. Retrace your path back to Lake Mercer at your leisure.

Ride Log

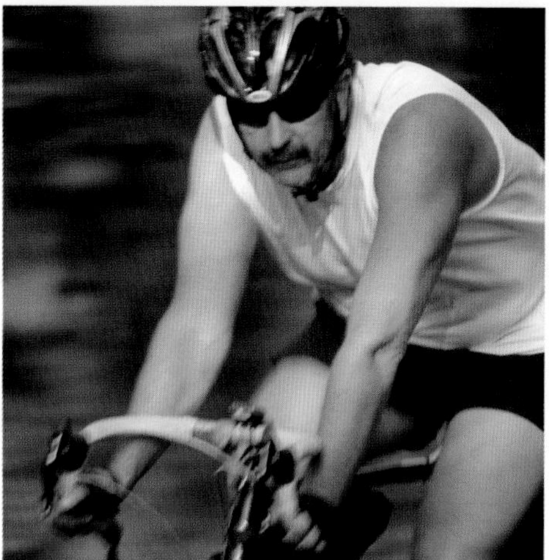

Out for an afternoon spin.

Somebody loves this trail.

0.0 Start even with the Mercer Lake regulation sign before bearing right to access dam.

0.2 Left onto path above lake.

0.7 Continue straight.

2.0 Right to go over bridge then bear left. Pass sign for South Run Recreation Center.

2.25 Left to Burke Lake.

2.45 Continue straight.

2.8 Continue straight.

3.5 Go right to begin circling lake.

6.15 Continue along lake perimeter.

7.1 As trail forks, turn right away from lake to cross parking lot. Food, snacks, drinks, bathrooms, boat rental to left.

7.25 Playground and more bathrooms to right.

8.05 Lake loop ends.

9.25 Right to return to Lake Mercer.

9.5 Right then quick left after bridge.

10.8 Stay left.

11.3 Right to return to parking along Hooes Rd.

11.5 End.

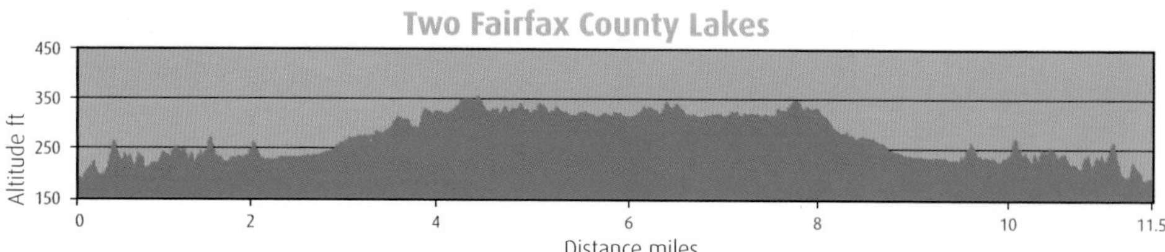

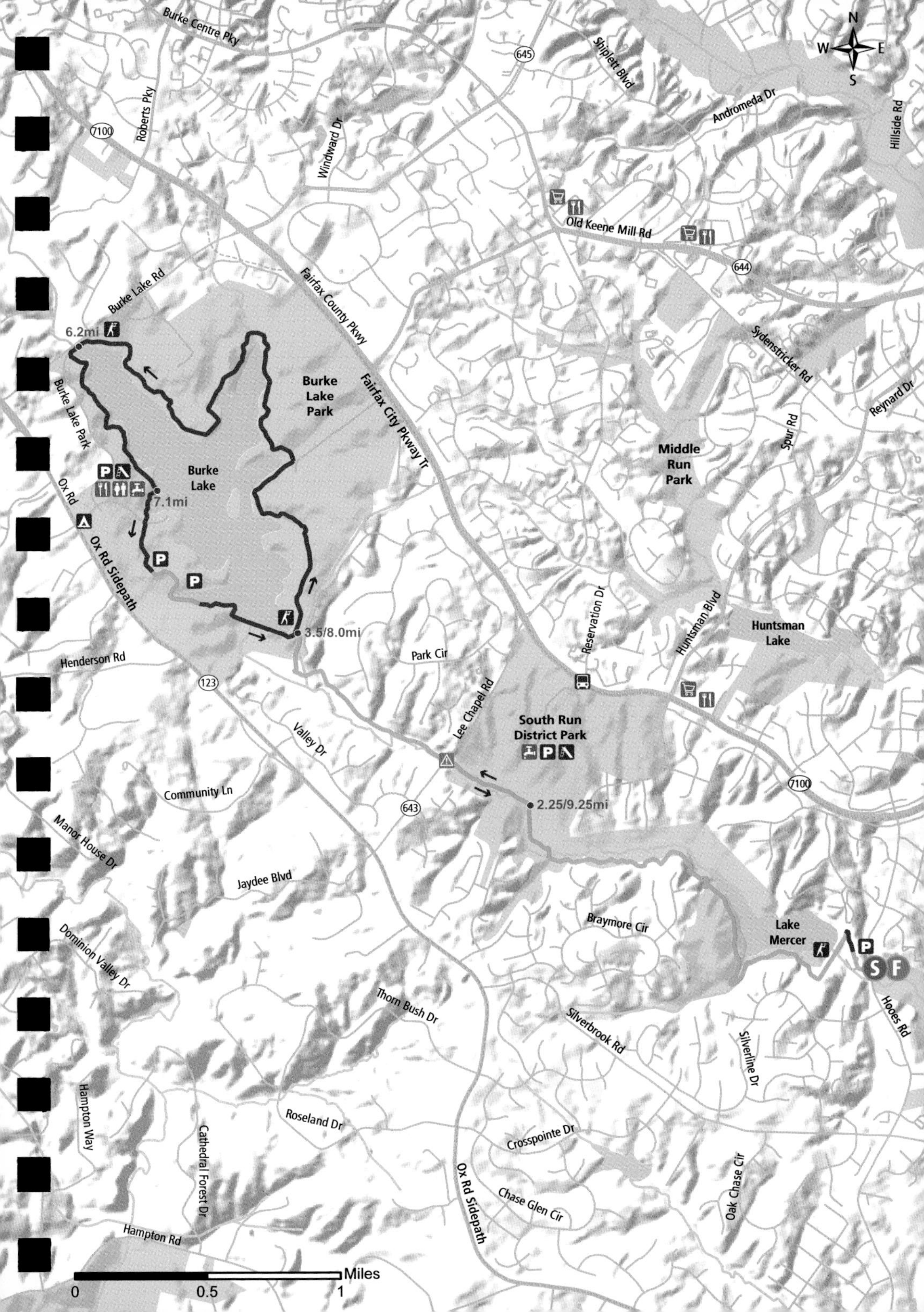

Burke Centre Pky
645
Shiplett Blvd
N
W
E
S
Andromeda Dr
Hillside Rd
7100
Roberts Pky
Windward Dr
Old Keene Mill Rd
644
Fairfax County Pkwy
Burke Lake Rd
Sydenstricker Rd
6.2mi
Burke Lake Park
Fairfax City Pkway Tr
Reynard Dr
Burke Lake Park
Spur Rd
Middle Run Park
Burke Lake
Ox Rd
7.1mi
Ox Rd Sidepath
Reservation Dr
Huntsman Blvd
Huntsman Lake
3.5/8.0mi
Henderson Rd
Park Cir
123
Lee Chapel Rd
South Run District Park
Valley Dr
7100
Community Ln
643
2.25/9.25mi
Manor House Dr
Jaydee Blvd
Braymore Cir
Lake Mercer
Dominion Valley Dr
Thorn Bush Dr
Silverbrook Rd
Silverline Dr
Hooes Rd
Hampton Way
Roseland Dr
Cathedral Forest Dr
Crosspointe Dr
Oak Chase Cir
Ox Rd Sidepath
Chase Glen Cir
Hampton Rd
Miles
0
0.5
1

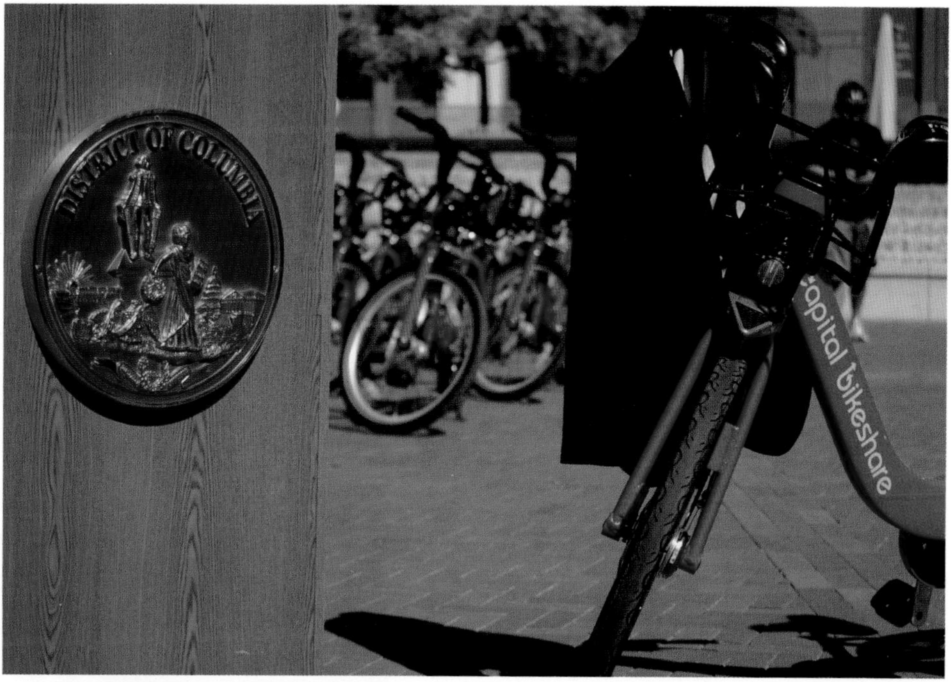
DISTRICT OF COLUMBIA
capital bikeshare

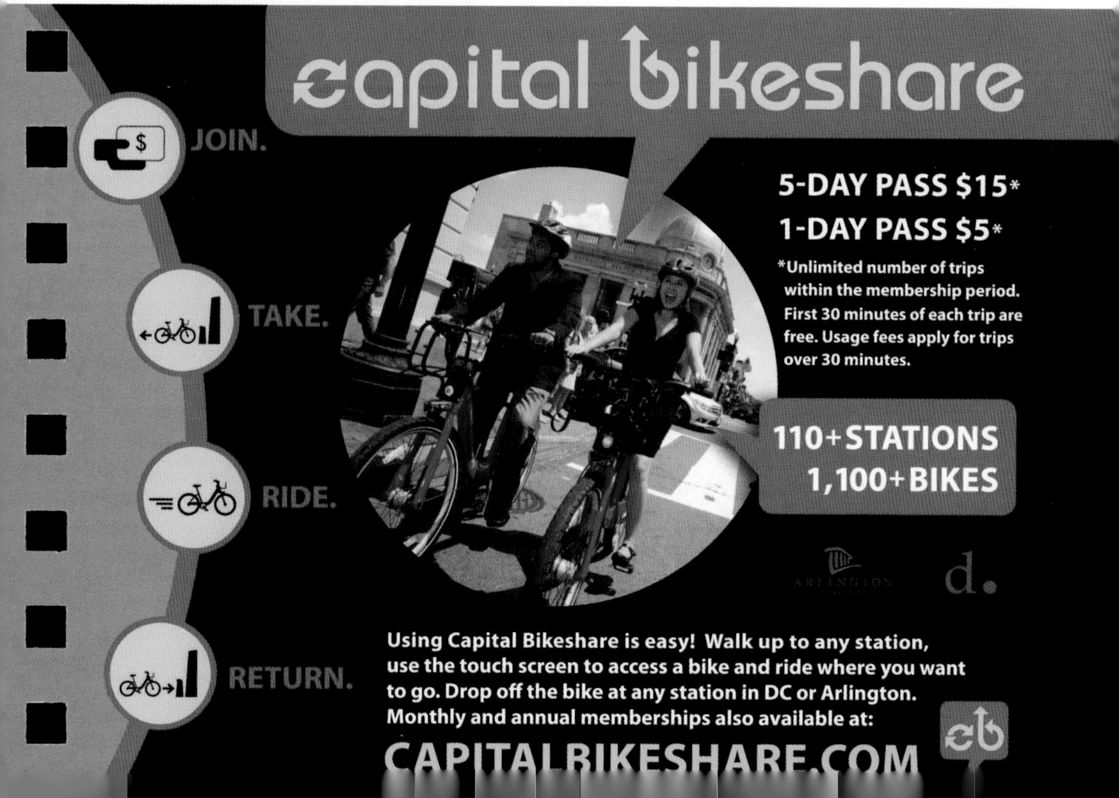
capital bikeshare
JOIN.
TAKE.
RIDE.
RETURN.
5-DAY PASS $15*
1-DAY PASS $5*
*Unlimited number of trips within the membership period. First 30 minutes of each trip are free. Usage fees apply for trips over 30 minutes.
110+STATIONS
1,100+BIKES
Using Capital Bikeshare is easy! Walk up to any station, use the touch screen to access a bike and ride where you want to go. Drop off the bike at any station in DC or Arlington. Monthly and annual memberships also available at:
CAPITALBIKESHARE.COM

Maryland: North by Northwest

This section's 11 offerings lie to the north and northwest of the District of Columbia and can be found throughout Montgomery County, Maryland. Once home to prosperous mills and dairy farms, the region still harbors an agrarian past along its periphery while its inner suburbs thrive off wealth created at the leading edge of medical and biotechnological research. Here, numerous creeks cut their way to the Potomac and Patuxent rivers and rolling roads invite cyclists on simple spins to unique destinations, restorative, natural rides nestled inside forested parks, and major rural tours.

Take a look at a satellite image of the entire D.C. metro area. Pretty much green, wouldn't you say? Not too bad for a multi-tentacled mega-city of six million people. Montgomery County, for one, seems to have bought into the idea that happy citizens need ample play space, and you'll find four ribbons of trail running through its preserves in the following pages. Flat, relatively short, and accessible to all, families return time and again to these specific stream valley selections, and a glance at the county's comprehensive parks and trails website proves it hasn't forgotten about riders looking to get a little dirt under their wheels either.

Rolling onward, distinct routes detailing the work hard/play hard Capital Crescent Trail and the practical Rockville Millennium Trail highlight the area's ever-growing infrastructure of business and pleasure paths, a fun jaunt takes in 100-year old Glen Echo Park, and the book's longest Metro-accessible ride loops due north over 50 challenging miles around Triadelphia Reservoir.

Eventually, riders new to the region reach its outskirts and realize why the pleasant, scenic two-lanes tucked away in the high land between Germantown and the Potomac have sustained cyclists for so long. The area centers itself around Poolesville and holds the highest concentration of countryside routes in WTB D.C. One of the book's loveliest rides rounds the nearest mountain to Washington, while other beauties reach down to the riverside by way of a splendid series of low-traffic roads.

VOLPE
Bianchi

Breathe it in.

At a Glance

Distance 34.3 miles **Total Elevation** 2635 feet

Terrain

This ride goes around the mountain, not over it. There are numerous hills however, and many roads that lack a proper shoulder. Thurston is especially twisty.

Traffic

Mostly light. Heavier and faster on Dickerson (MD 28), though you are afforded more space.

How to Get There

Using exit 39 north off the Beltway, take River Road (MD 190) around nine miles beyond the town of Potomac to its intersection with Seneca Road (MD 112). Head left looking for a right onto Partnership Road. A left at Fisher Road (MD 107) brings you into Poolesville. Continue past Elgin Road (MD 109) to a left on West Willard Road. Parking should be available in the high school's back lot near the football field.

Food and Drink

Refresh in Poolesville along Fisher Avenue/White's Ferry Road (MD 107) or at Dickerson Market as you turn onto Big Woods Road about twenty-seven-and-a-half miles into the ride.

Side Trip

Ready for an extra challenge? Bear left just past mile 21 off Park Mills Road to climb up Sugarloaf on Mount Ephraim Road. Want something more relaxing? Turn right a mile further down Park Mills onto Lilypons Road and visit the water gardens of the same name.

Links to 29 32 52

Where to Bike Rating 

About...

If nothing else, this excursion will teach you the meaning of the geologic term 'monadnock' and give you the chance to circle one. The hoped-for result, however, is a memorable trip through beautiful country. And perhaps more than any other offering in the region, this tour around the D.C.-area's only mountain tops the scenic scale. Heading north from its basecamp at Poolesville, prepare to experience the smooth cruising and sweeping views that make this one of the best rides around for years running.

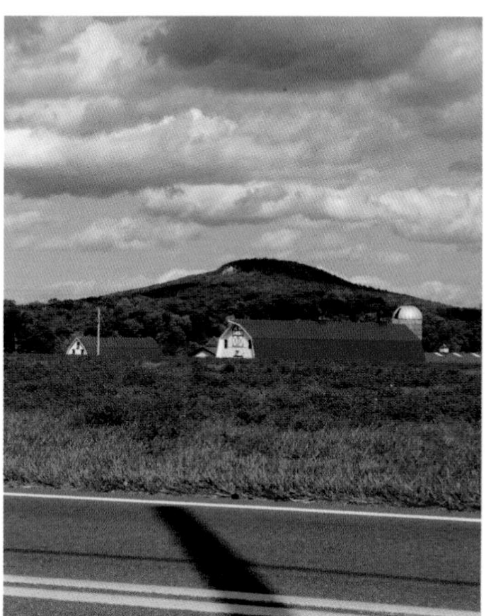

Sugarloaf from MD 28.

Whereas Ride 29 stays straight past Lewis Orchards after three miles north out of Poolesville, this tour heads right down Peach Tree Road for its next six miles. You'll begin catching glimpses of Sugarloaf as your elevation gradually increases to Comus Road. Here, then, is your first full view of the ride's namesake before you descend rapidly and climb sharply to the corner of Old Hundred Road, where there's often seasonal produce for sale. The fetching, red-roofed Comus Inn, though worth a picture, and perhaps a weekend, is most likely a touch posh for today's proceedings, so ride on.

Now peak before plunging, climbing sharply, and plunging again, an exhilarating beginning to what could well be the best five miles of the day. Thurston Road dips and dives its way into Frederick County and around Sugarloaf's northern side then leaves you to trace the remaining distance to Park Mills Road and its relatively straight, yet decisively rolling, shot down to the Monocacy River.

That river, and said mountain by which it flows, both played geographic roles in the Civil War. While the Battle of Monocacy Junction was fought up near Frederick, Sugarloaf was used as an observation point and signal station due to its status as a monadnock, that is, an isolated hill or small mountain rising abruptly from generally level surrounding land. Acting as such, it served as the spot from which Union troops observed Confederate General Robert E. Lee's Army of Northern Virginia crossing the Potomac on its way to what would become the Battle of Antietam.

Presently, Sugarloaf Mountain exists as a free, privately-owned, scenic park, though the FDR administration did consider it as a potential presidential retreat, a designation it lost in favor of a site then named Shangri-la (and now Camp David) farther north in the Catoctin Mountain.

Traffic will pick up on Dickerson Road (MD 28) as you get your last, leftward looks of Sugarloaf and climb from the Monocacy Valley. Stay focused. It's only a short distance to a possible pit stop in Dickerson and the ride's final, long climb towards Beallsville on narrow Big Woods Road. Once that's behind you, it's nearly all downhill from there.

Ride Log

0.0 Begin by going right where Poolesville High School back parking lot meets W Willard.
0.3 Right on Fisher Ave.
0.8 Left on Cattail Rd one block then right at next stop sign to continue on Cattail.
2.9 Left on Darnestown Rd (MD 28).
3.15 Right on Peach Tree.
7.3 Cross Barnesville Rd to continue straight on Peach Tree.
8.75 Bucklodge Forest Conservation Park to right.
9.8 Left on Comus Rd.
11.1 Right on Old Hundred Rd.
12.4 Left on Thurston Rd.
17.4 Stay straight to join Fingerboard Rd (80 West).
18.8 Left on Park Mills Rd.
25.4 Left on Dickerson Rd.
25.8 Monocacy Natural Resource Area to left.
27.6 Left on Big Woods Rd just past railroad overpass. Dickerson Market.
30.2 Right on Beallsville Rd.
33.9 Right on Fisher to quick left on W Willard.
34.3 Left to finish in back parking lot of Poolesville High School.

P *P1* John Poole House
P2 Lewis Orchards
P3 Comus Inn
P4 Sugarloaf Mountain Vineyard
P5 Mt Ephraim Rd up Sugarloaf Mt
P6 Lilypons Water Garden
P7 Monocacy Cemetery

B *B1* Bob's Bikes, 19961 Fisher Ave

The Monocacy River.

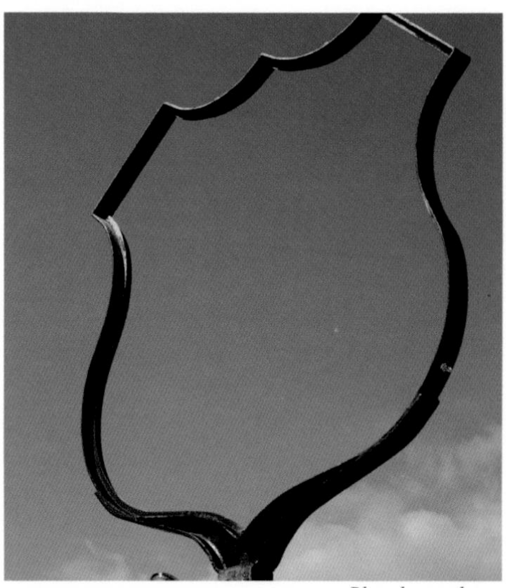

Blue sky up above.

Sugarloaf Mountain

Altitude ft: 200, 300, 400, 500, 600, 700
Distance miles: 0, 5, 10, 15, 20, 25, 30, 34.3

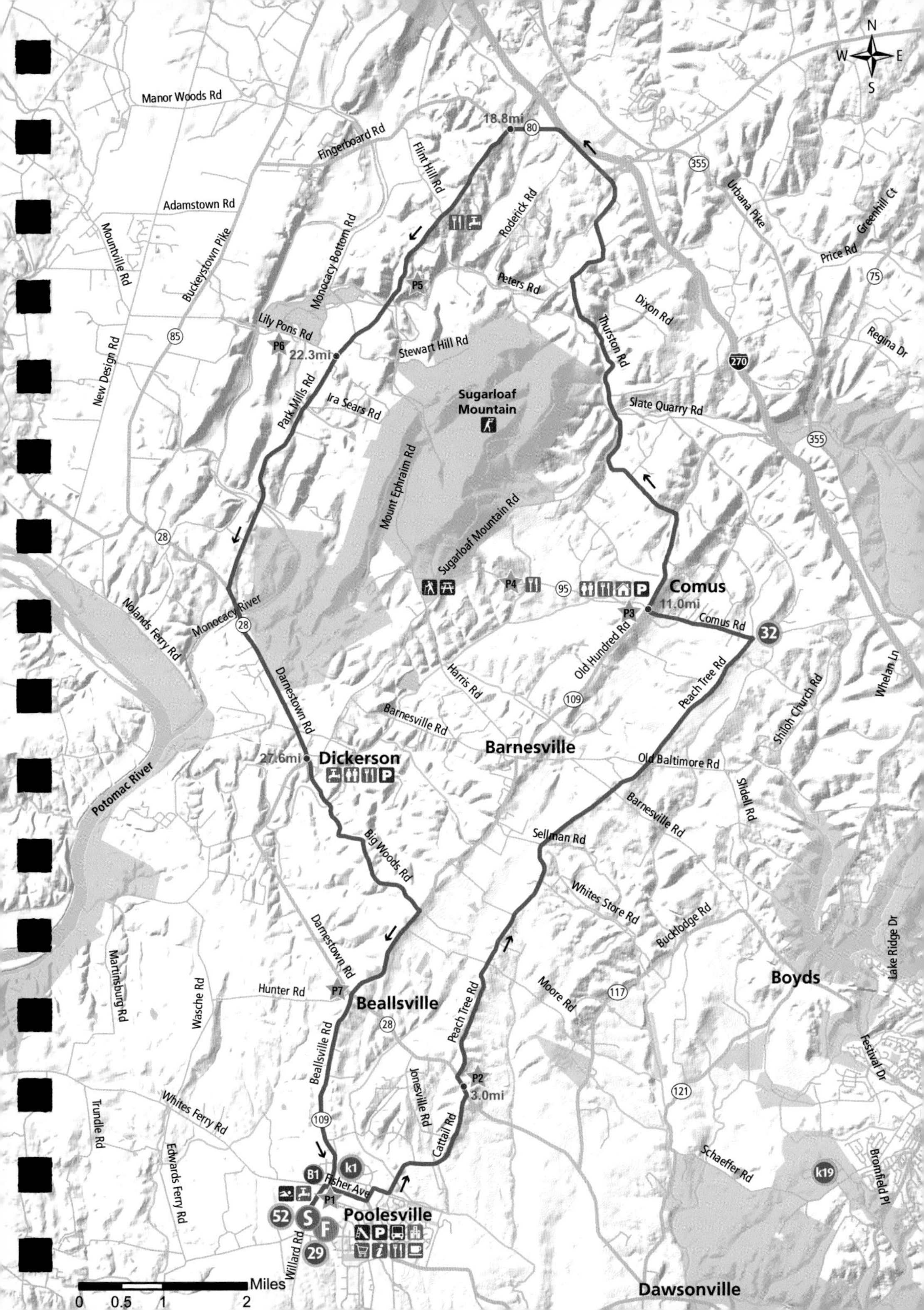

N
W
E
S
Manor Woods Rd
Fingerboard Rd
18.8mi
80
355
Flint Hill Rd
Adamstown Rd
Roderick Rd
Urbana Pike
Greenhill Ct
Mountville Rd
Buckeystown Pike
Monocacy Bottom Rd
Price Rd
75
P5
Peters Rd
Dixon Rd
Lily Pons Rd
85
P6
22.3mi
Stewart Hill Rd
Thurston Rd
Regina Dr
New Design Rd
270
Park Mills Rd
Ira Sears Rd
Sugarloaf Mountain
Slate Quarry Rd
355
Mount Ephraim Rd
Sugarloaf Mountain Rd
28
P4
95
Comus
11.0mi
P3
Nolands Ferry Rd
Monocacy River
28
Comus Rd
32
Old Hundred Rd
Peach Tree Rd
Harris Rd
109
Darnestown Rd
Shiloh Church Rd
Whelan Ln
Barnesville Rd
Barnesville
27.6mi
Dickerson
Old Baltimore Rd
Potomac River
Shidell Rd
Barnesville Rd
Sellman Rd
Big Woods Rd
Whites Store Rd
Bucklodge Rd
Darnestown Rd
Martinsburg Rd
Lake Ridge Dr
Boyds
Hunter Rd
P7
Beallsville
Moore Rd
117
Wasche Rd
28
Peach Tree Rd
Beallsville Rd
Jonesville Rd
Festival Dr
P2
3.0mi
Trundle Rd
Whites Ferry Rd
Cattail Rd
109
121
Edwards Ferry Rd
Schaeffer Rd
k1
B1
Fisher Ave
P1
k19
Bromfield Pl
52
S
F
Poolesville
29
Willard Rd
Miles
0
0.5
1
2
Dawsonville

Blissed out along Brooke Road.

At a Glance

Distance 53.0 miles **Total Elevation** 4165 feet

Terrain

Lots of hills interspersed with many nice, rolling stretches.

Traffic

Given the rapid pace of recent area development, this ride's overall vehicle count is surprisingly low. Though most roads have minimal to zero shoulder, the route has been designed to avoid as many major throughways as possible.

How to Get There

Take the Red Line Metro to its terminus at Glenmont. Drivers should center upon Georgia Avenue (MD 97) and Randolph Road, looking to park in a Metro lot or, after asking kindly, perhaps next door at Georgia Avenue Baptist Church. An alternate start has you shaving 14 miles off the route by driving to Sandy Spring and parking at Urban Bar-B-Que. Use a combination of MD 28, 108, 182, and 650 to get there, depending on direction of travel.

Food and Drink

Stop within the ride's first three miles at the corner of Layhill and Bel Pre/Bonifont roads or at the Crossroads Pub at mile 17. And if that BBQ in Sandy Spring's not your thing, try the French Confection across the street.

Side Trip

Stop by the Sandy Spring Museum on Bentley Road off MD 108 or visit the National Capital Trolley Museum off Layhill about three-quarters-of-a-mile down Bonifont Road. Be sure to check hours, but the latter is normally open weekend afternoons.

Links to 33

Where to Bike Rating 

About...

One of the longest and hilliest offerings in the book, this tour through the diminishing countryside due north of the District is certain to challenge even highly experienced enthusiasts. Combining a Metro beginning with a handful of possible recreational and historical stops, and lengthy, quiet stretches long-populated by area joy-riders with steep ascents perfect for serious road warriors, this route around the reservoir promises just about all you could hope to handle on a single given day. Come prepared for a serious session of cycling.

You gotta' love these two!

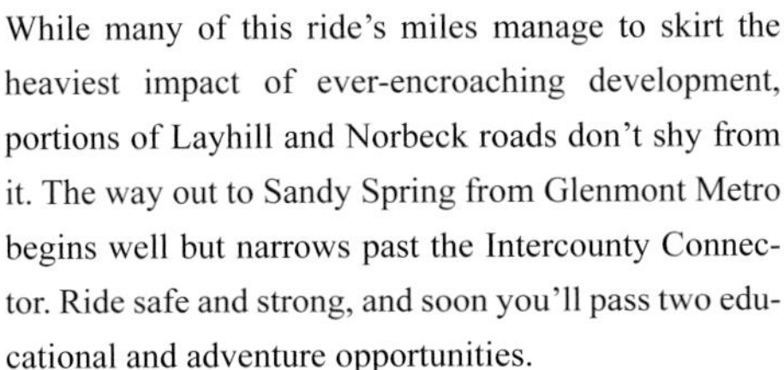

While many of this ride's miles manage to skirt the heaviest impact of ever-encroaching development, portions of Layhill and Norbeck roads don't shy from it. The way out to Sandy Spring from Glenmont Metro begins well but narrows past the Intercounty Connector. Ride safe and strong, and soon you'll pass two educational and adventure opportunities.

Woodlawn Manor, thought to be a stop along the Underground Railroad, is an 18th century brick house and farm complete with tours and trails. Neighboring Sandy Spring Adventure Park boasts five acres of hanging cables, zip lines and bridges, with courses designed to challenge all levels of participants.

The route heads toward rurality along Brooke and Haviland Mill roads, and its occasionally steep way is marked by alternating forests, fields, and country homes. You've now begun your broad loop of the Triadelphia Reservoir, and though within reach, it never makes an explicit appearance. Burntwoods Road bounces you easily toward a brief segment of MD 197 and inaugurates an overall 200 foot drop to lovely Union Chapel Road and Cattail Creek. The ensuing miles then offer some of the day's best riding as you make your way beyond two successive ups and downs through densely-wooded Patuxent River State Park.

Damascus Road, in turn, glides you past beautiful, open countryside toward Sundown Road and within reach of a web of nature trails inside the 650 undeveloped acres of Rachel Carson Conservation Park. Honoring the former Montgomery County resident, marine biologist and nature writer credited with greatly advancing the global environmental movement, it is one of three exploration points along this ride's homeward stretch.

The others are Oakley Cabin, a 19th century African-American historic site, and the community of Brookeville, the place where fourth President James Madison fled as the British burned the White House in 1814. Both the home where he stayed and the stone-walled Brookeville Academy are worth a look, but do remember to honor any pleas to privacy.

After dipping out of town and down to James Creek, a nice climb completes your loop back to Brooke Road and Sandy Spring. Eat, hydrate, and be merry, but be sure to save some daylight if making your way back to Metro.

Ride Log

0.0 Exit the east Glenmont Metro elevator to left, passing bike racks to join Georgia Ave Baptist Church driveway, then go right onto Glenallan Ave.
0.3 Left onto Layhill Rd.
1.65 Cross Matthew Henson Trail.
5.05 Left on Norwood Rd (MD 182).
6.0 Right to continue on Norwood Rd.
6.8 Right on Olney-Sandy Spring Rd (MD 108).
6.95 Left on Brooke Rd.
9.05 Left on New Hampshire Ave.
9.2 Right on Haviland Mill Rd.
12.2 Right on Brighton Dam Rd.
12.7 Left on Highland Rd.
13.8 Use traffic circle to left on Triadelphia Mill Rd.
15.6 Straight on Greenbridge Rd.
17.0 Left on Linthicum Rd soon to bear right to remain on it. Crossroads Pub.
18.8 Right on Triadelphia Mill Rd.
19.1 Left on Ivory Rd.
19.7 Left on Ten Oaks then use traffic circle to go left on Burntwoods Rd.
20.7 Continue straight on Burntwoods at traffic circle.
21.7 Bear left to stay on Burntwoods.
22.5 Right on Roxbury Mills Rd.
23.5 Left on Union Chapel Rd.
26.2 Jog left on Daisy to immediate right onto Ed Warfield Rd. Ben's Performance Bicycles.
26.8 Stay left on Ed Warfield.
27.7 Left onto Jennings Chapel.

P1 National Capital Trolley Museum
P2 Woodlawn Manor
P3 Sandy Spring Adventure Park
P4 Oakley Cabin
P5 The Madison House

B1 Ben's Performance Bicycles, 2878 Daisy Rd
B2 Just Riding Along Bicycle Shop, 6860-4 Olney-Laytonsville Rd

27.9 Right onto Hipsley Mill Rd. Pass Patuxent River State Park.
31.6 Left onto Damascus Rd (MD 650).
35.6 Right onto Howard Chapel Rd.
35.8 Right onto Sundown Rd.
36.3 Left onto Zion Rd. Rachel Carson Conservation Park soon to left.
39.1 Left onto Brookeville Rd.
41.3 Right onto Georgia Ave (MD 97).
41.5 Right to stay on Georgia through Brookeville.
42.1 Left onto Gold Mine Rd.
43.7 Right at Chandlee Mill Rd.
44.9 Right at Brooke Rd.
46.0 Right onto Olney-Sandy Spring Rd to begin retracing to Glenmont Metro.
46.2 Left onto Norwood Rd.
47.0 Left to stay on Norwood Rd (MD 182).
48.0 Right to return to Layhill Rd.
52.6 Right at Glenallan Ave.
52.9 Left toward Glenmont Metro east elevator.
53.0 Finish and descend.

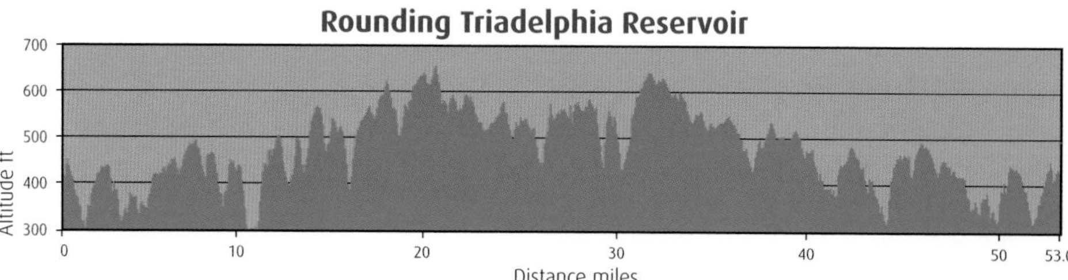

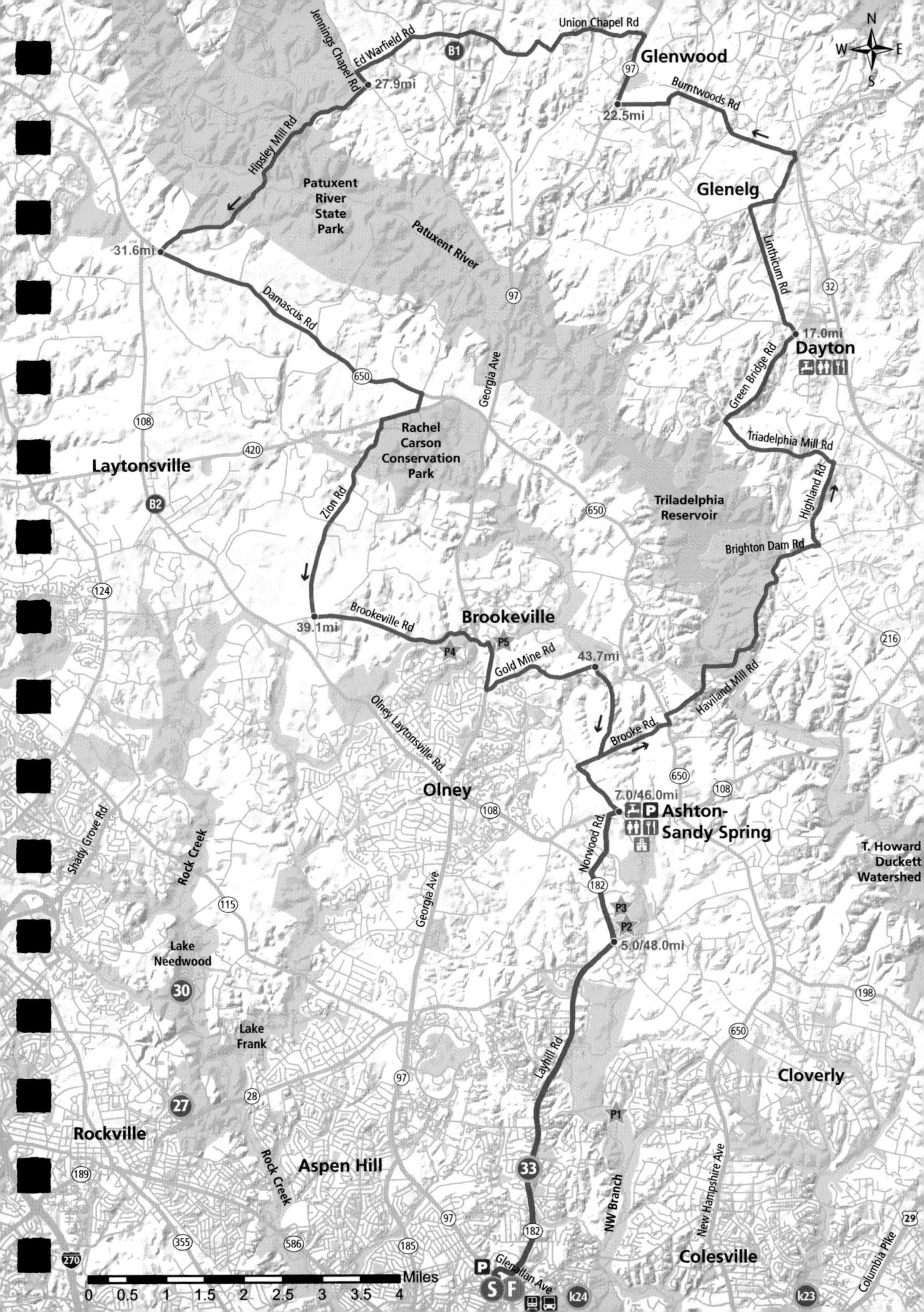

Union Chapel Rd
Jennings Chapel Rd
Ed Warfield Rd
B1
Glenwood
97
27.9mi
Burntwoods Rd
22.5mi
Hipsley Mill Rd
Patuxent River State Park
Glenelg
Patuxent River
31.6mi
Linthicum Rd
Damascus Rd
97
32
17.0mi
Dayton
Green Bridge Rd
650
Georgia Ave
108
Rachel Carson Conservation Park
Triadelphia Mill Rd
420
Laytonsville
Highland Rd
Zion Rd
B2
650
Triladelphia Reservoir
Brighton Dam Rd
124
39.1mi
Brookeville Rd
Brookeville
216
P5
P4
Gold Mine Rd
43.7mi
Haviland Mill Rd
Olney Laytonsville Rd.
Brooke Rd.
Shady Grove Rd
650
Olney
108
7.0/46.0mi
Ashton-Sandy Spring
108
Rock Creek
Norwood Rd.
T. Howard Duckett Watershed
182
115
P3
P2
5.0/48.0mi
Lake Needwood
Georgia Ave
30
198
Lake Frank
Layhill Rd
650
97
Cloverly
28
27
P1
Rockville
Aspen Hill
33
189
Rock Creek
NW Branch
New Hampshire Ave
97
29
182
355
586
185
270
Colesville
Columbia Pike
Glenallan Ave
Miles
0 0.5 1 1.5 2 2.5 3 3.5 4
k24
k23

A golden fall day around Damascus.

At a Glance

Distance 6.4 miles **Total Elevation** 350 feet

Terrain

Expect climbs on both ends and a mellow gradient down along the river. The hard surface trail is almost entirely smooth and interspersed with sections of wooden boardwalk.

Traffic

Zero, but do take caution crossing Sweepstakes Road as fast-moving vehicles sometimes plunge into the valley with little warning.

How to Get There

Use Interstate 270 off the Beltway to exit 16, Ridge Road (MD 27). After about four miles, look to turn right onto Kings Valley Road. The trail begins a half mile beyond, to the left off the second entrance to Damascus Recreational Park. Its opposite end is a few miles north along Ridge Road, to the right down Valley Drive.

Food and Drink

Get it on your way through Montgomery Village or continue the short way into Damascus.

Side Trip

Spin north and explore the town of Damascus or bring your wide wheels to experience the natural surface of the Lower Magruder all the way through its connection to the rugged Seneca Creek Greenway Trail.

Where to Bike Rating 

About...

As the population north of the District continues to surge upward and some areas once friendly to cyclists inevitably become less so, it's nice to know stream valley paths like the Magruder Branch will remain preserved for public use. This family-friendly selection exists for those times when the desire arrives to explore new ground. Pack some lunch, break the city's boundaries, and come experience the fresh air, cool forest, and safe, accessible riding here in far northern Montgomery County.

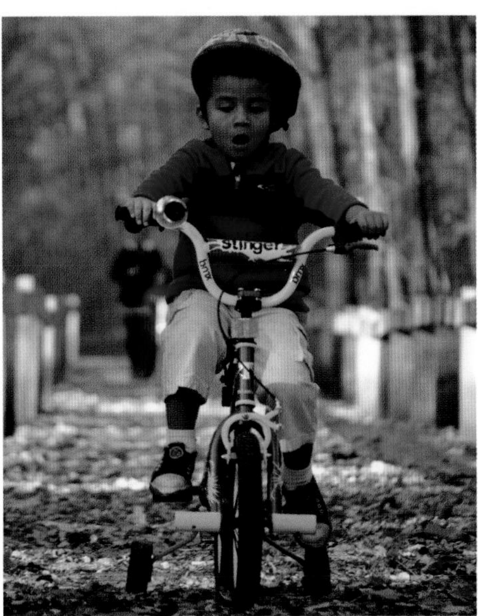

It's such a yawn being so far out in front of the pack.

This easy spin begins by rolling through Damascus Regional Park alongside tennis courts and ballfields, and past pavilions and picnic opportunities. Use water fountains and restrooms here as there are no chances along the route.

After winding, climbing, and reaching a ridge under open sky, the trail enters woodland and drops precipitously into a narrow, shaded valley. Turning sharply left it begins making its way upstream either beside the meandering Magruder Branch or periodically crossing it and adjacent wetlands on raised boardwalk.

Though the elevation you quickly lost is regained within the next two miles, it occurs gradually enough as to be nearly undetected. The forest here is lush with subtle life, and occasional benches offer the perfect opportunity for observing, snacking, or sitting in solitude. The trail naturally carries more traffic on weekends, but there are moments each and every day when it should belong only to you.

Turn around after a steep switchback brings you to your highest point of the day, above 750 feet along Valley Park Drive. If you'd like to make your way the short distance into central Damascus, the path does continue across the road. Otherwise, retrace back to your starting point.

Like its southern companion, the approximately 231 acres of Upper Magruder Branch Park remain undeveloped upland forest. Both provide singular birding opportunities and frequent deer sightings along with the myriad pleasures of the great outdoors.

If this ride's not quite enough in the way of adventure, however, bring your mountain bike and look to take the natural surface path shooting southeast off this trail down along the stream. It begins to the right after you've descended to the Magruder Branch from Damascus Recreational Park and just before you reach the water.

Crossing open fields, lush wetlands, and dense woodland, expect a challenging ride over variable terrain with moderate steepness. After 3.3 miles, the Lower Magruder meets the Seneca Creek Greenway where it inherits eight more miles of demanding, highly scenic trail. This path is in turn part of a larger planned connection between the Potomac and Patuxent rivers. Check the outstanding Montgomery Parks website for detailed updates and information.

Ride Log

0.0 Begin at trailhead off parking lot at Damascus Recreational Park.
1.75 Cross Sweepstakes Rd.
3.2 Turnaround at Valley Dr.
6.4 Finish.

An apple (and a trail) a day.

Interpretations welcome.

B *B1* All-American Bicycle Center
26039 Ridge Road

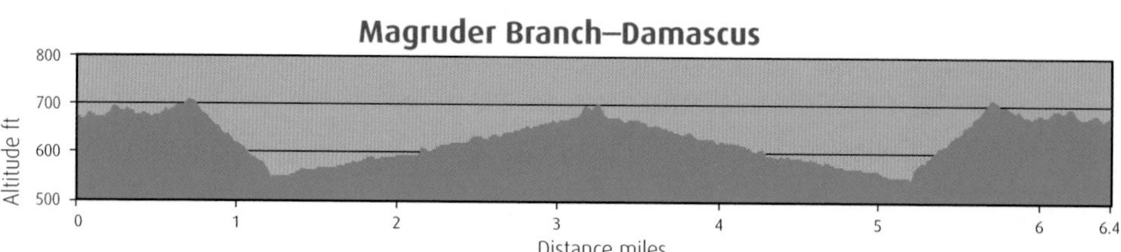

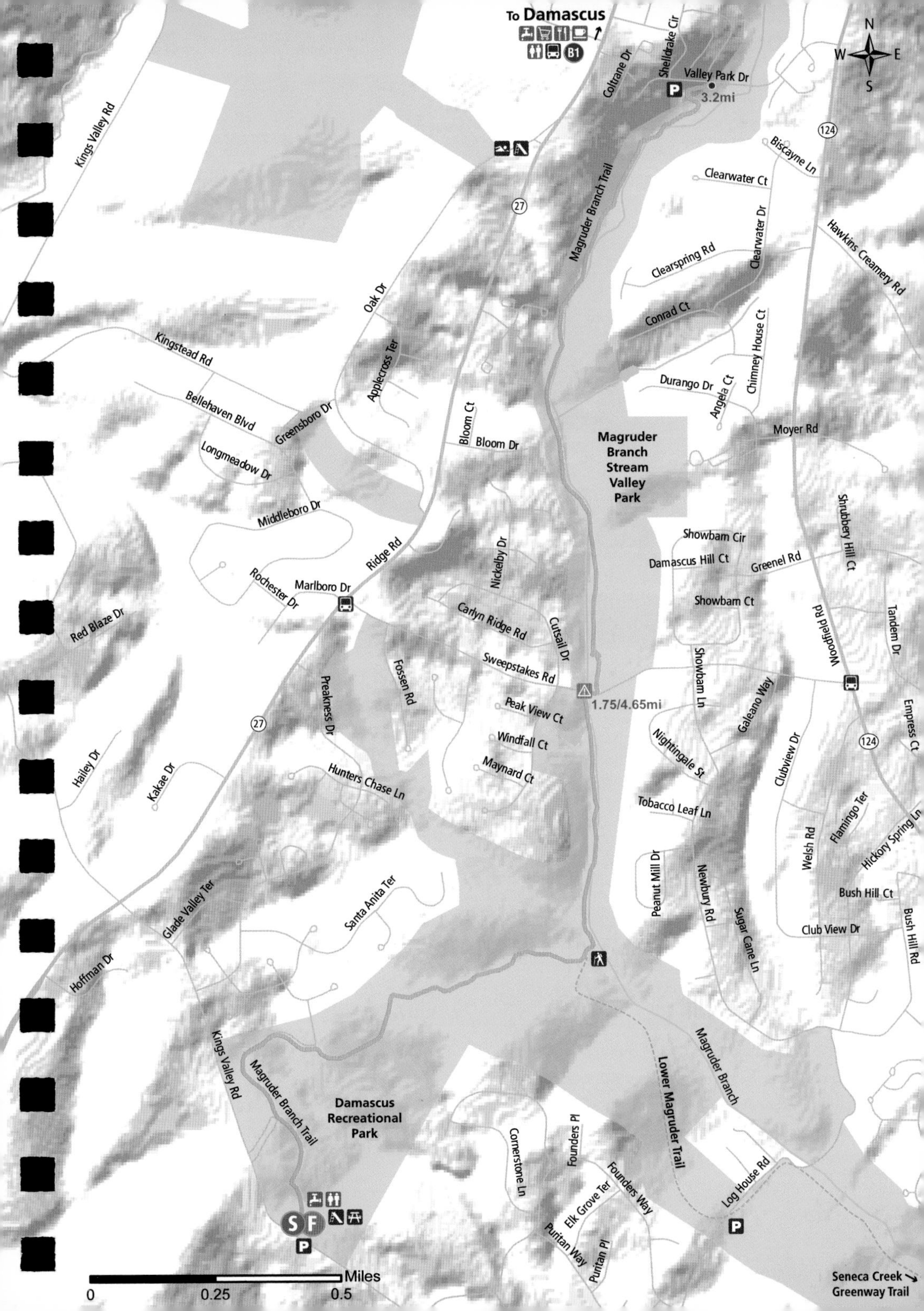

To Damascus
B1
N
W
E
S
Kings Valley Rd
Coltrane Dr
Shelldrake Cir
Valley Park Dr
3.2mi
124
Biscayne Ln
Clearwater Ct
27
Magruder Branch Trail
Hawkins Creamery Rd
Clearwater Dr
Clearspring Rd
Oak Dr
Conrad Ct
Chimney House Ct
Kingstead Rd
Applecross Ter
Durango Dr
Angela Ct
Bellehaven Blvd
Greensboro Dr
Bloom Ct
Bloom Dr
Moyer Rd
Longmeadow Dr
Magruder Branch Stream Valley Park
Middleboro Dr
Ridge Rd
Nickelby Dr
Showbarn Cir
Damascus Hill Ct
Greenel Rd
Shrubbery Hill Ct
Rochester Dr
Marlboro Dr
Showbarn Ct
Red Blaze Dr
Carlyn Ridge Rd
Cutsail Dr
Woodfield Rd
Tandem Dr
Fossen Rd
Sweepstakes Rd
Showbarn Ln
Preakness Dr
1.75/4.65mi
Peak View Ct
Galeano Way
Empress Ct
27
Windfall Ct
Nightingale St
Clubview Dr
124
Hailey Dr
Kakae Dr
Hunters Chase Ln
Maynard Ct
Tobacco Leaf Ln
Flamingo Ter
Hickory Spring Ln
Welsh Rd
Peanut Mill Dr
Newbury Rd
Bush Hill Ct
Santa Anita Ter
Sugar Cane Ln
Bush Hill Rd
Club View Dr
Glade Valley Ter
Hoffman Dr
Magruder Branch
Kings Valley Rd
Lower Magruder Trail
Magruder Branch Trail
Damascus Recreational Park
Founders Pl
Cornerstone Ln
Founders Way
Log House Rd
Elk Grove Ter
S
F
Puritan Way
Puritan Pl
0
0.25
0.5
Miles
Seneca Creek Greenway Trail

Jue ma on his way to Florida.

At a Glance

Distance 13.35 miles **Total Elevation** 670 feet

Terrain

This route rolls pleasantly over trail, sidewalk, and well-maintained city streets.

Traffic

Though you'll share two-and-a-half miles with cars getting to and from Metro, the bulk of the ride is set away on sidepath. Road crossings are signaled and well-marked.

How to Get There

Take the Red Line Metro to Rockville. Or, if driving, use the Rockville Pike (MD 355) north off the Beltway to access Park Road in downtown Rockville. Go right and begin looking for parking. Veirs Mill Road, Norbeck Road, and Interstate 270 to West Montgomery Avenue will also get you in the vicinity.

Food and Drink

Many options are available in downtown Rockville, with others along East Gude Drive, or at miles 2.75, 6.3, or 7.25 in the ride log.

Side Trip

Visit F. Scott Fitzgerald's grave down Church Street from Metro or hang your hat in Rockville's retro downtown district.

Where to Bike Rating 

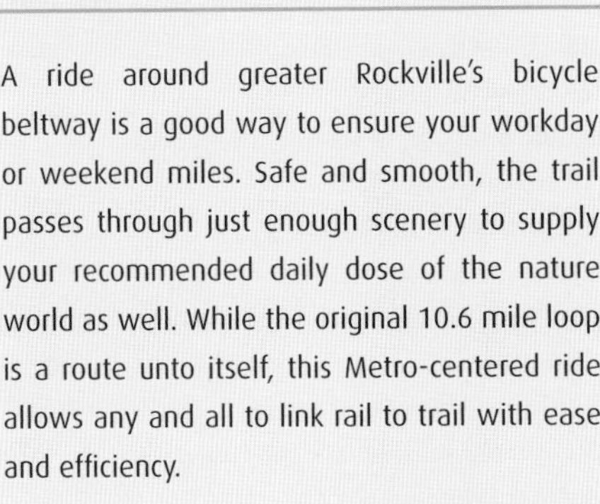

About...

A ride around greater Rockville's bicycle beltway is a good way to ensure your workday or weekend miles. Safe and smooth, the trail passes through just enough scenery to supply your recommended daily dose of the nature world as well. While the original 10.6 mile loop is a route unto itself, this Metro-centered ride allows any and all to link rail to trail with ease and efficiency.

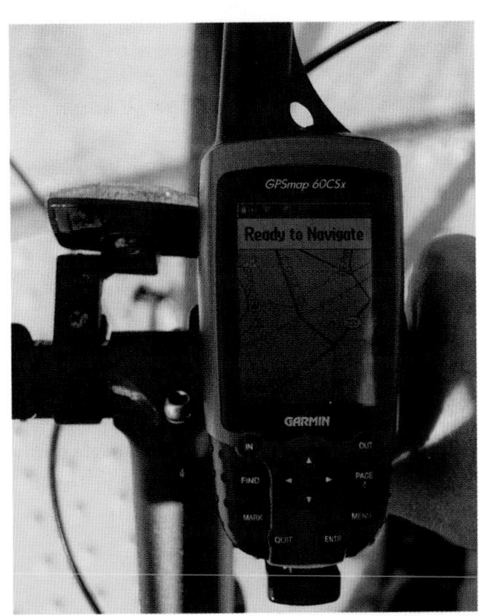

An important tool of the trade.

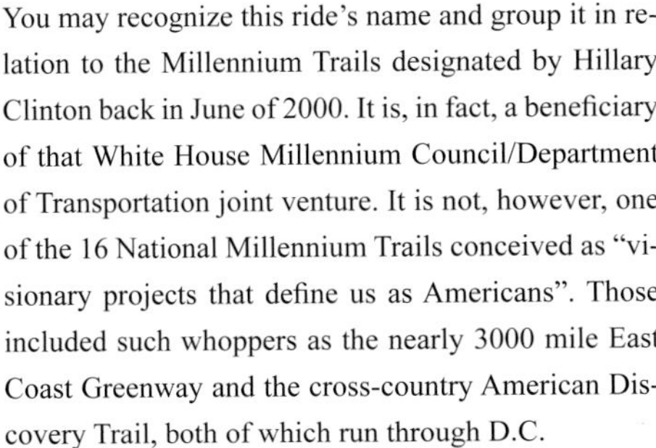

You may recognize this ride's name and group it in relation to the Millennium Trails designated by Hillary Clinton back in June of 2000. It is, in fact, a beneficiary of that White House Millennium Council/Department of Transportation joint venture. It is not, however, one of the 16 National Millennium Trails conceived as "visionary projects that define us as Americans". Those included such whoppers as the nearly 3000 mile East Coast Greenway and the cross-country American Discovery Trail, both of which run through D.C.

While those signature selections gobbled attention, the initiative's focus on sparking the creation and enhancement of trails nationwide was best realized at the local level, and even then not all that successfully. Ask Rockville. It's quite a process bringing a trail off paper and into reality. Conceived all the way back in 1998, it was eight years before this path unique to the region opened and was named in honor of the first grant it received in 2000.

Begin your experience at the Rockville Metro, working your way north and east. After North Horner's Lane the surface streets widen into those of a suburban industrial park, and before too long you'll have joined the trail, flowing right.

Traffic is heavy along East Gude Drive, and the path may not impress you all that much here. Don't fret. It improves. Just have faith and roll. And while this trail is contiguous and clearly marked, (and has, in fact, been renamed the Carl Henn Millennium Trail after the man who most made it so) keep a good eye on that ride log so as not to miss any sneaky turns, one of which comes within a mile as First Street banks right and splits. Follow it left.

After a few major road crossings, you should be moving swimmingly along Wootton Parkway, one of this route's particularly pleasant stretches. Not until a right after crossing Darnestown Road is that forward motion broken. Then, after a few turns and a dip through a preserved woodland, arrive to rest and refresh as needed at Fallsgrove Park and the adjacent Thomas Farm Community Center. Once back beside Gude, it's a straight, undulating shot to close this millennium's loop and return to Metro.

While Ride 27 has not been deemed kid-friendly in its entirety, it does include substantial sections which are entirely safe for family use.

Ride Log

P1 thebiketex.com—pick-up, repair, and delivery
P2 Beall-Dawson Historical Park
P3 F. Scott Fitzgerald's grave

B1 Revolution Cycles, 1066 Rockville Pike
B2 Performance Bicycles, Congressional Plaza Sunoco, 1667 Rockville Pike
B3 REI, 1701 Rockville Pike
B4 Fitness Resource, 12232 Rockville Pike

0.0 Exit turnstiles to right and set odometer at Rockville Metro sign near bicycle racks. Go straight briefly before following sidewalk as it curves left to Park Rd.

.10 Bear left to stay on Park (becomes N Horner's Ln) at light.

.65 Right onto Southlawn Ln.

.80 Right onto Lofstrand Ln.

1.0 Right onto Taft St.

1.3 Begin Millennium Trail loop by going right along E Gude Dr sidepath.

1.45 Continue straight.

1.6 Curve left to follow trail along Norbeck Rd.

2.0 Right on First St then immediate left at forked intersection to remain on First (now unmarked).

2.2 Cross Baltimore Rd. Continue straight.

2.55 Cross Maryland Rt 28 (MD 28).

2.75 Cross Rockville Pike. Now moving along Wootton Pkwy.

2.85 Cross Fleet to continue.

3.25 Cross Edmonston.

3.8 Side trail to right leads to town center.

4.1 Cross Tower Oaks Blvd.

4.5 Cross Seven Locks Rd.

4.7 Cross Henstowe Rd.

5.05 Cross Falls Rd to continue. (No sign, not completely obvious.)

5.85 Cross Greenplace Terrace.

6.3 Giant supermarket at right.

7.4 Cross Darnestown Rd.

7.6 Fork left to follow trail.

8.15 Again left at fork in trail.

8.45 Fallsgrove Park at left.

8.6 Fork left then cross W Montgomery Ave to right to continue straight along trail. Thomas Farm Community Center at left.

10.25 Cross Frederick Rd.

11.55 Dover Rd (optional way back to Metro).

12.05 End Millennium Trail loop at Taft St.

12.35 Left onto Lofstrand Ln.

12.55 Left onto Southlawn Ln.

12.7 Left onto N Horner's Ln (becomes Park).

13.25 Straight through light before a left onto Metro sidewalk.

13.35 Finish at Rockville Metro sign.

The Rockville Millennium Trail

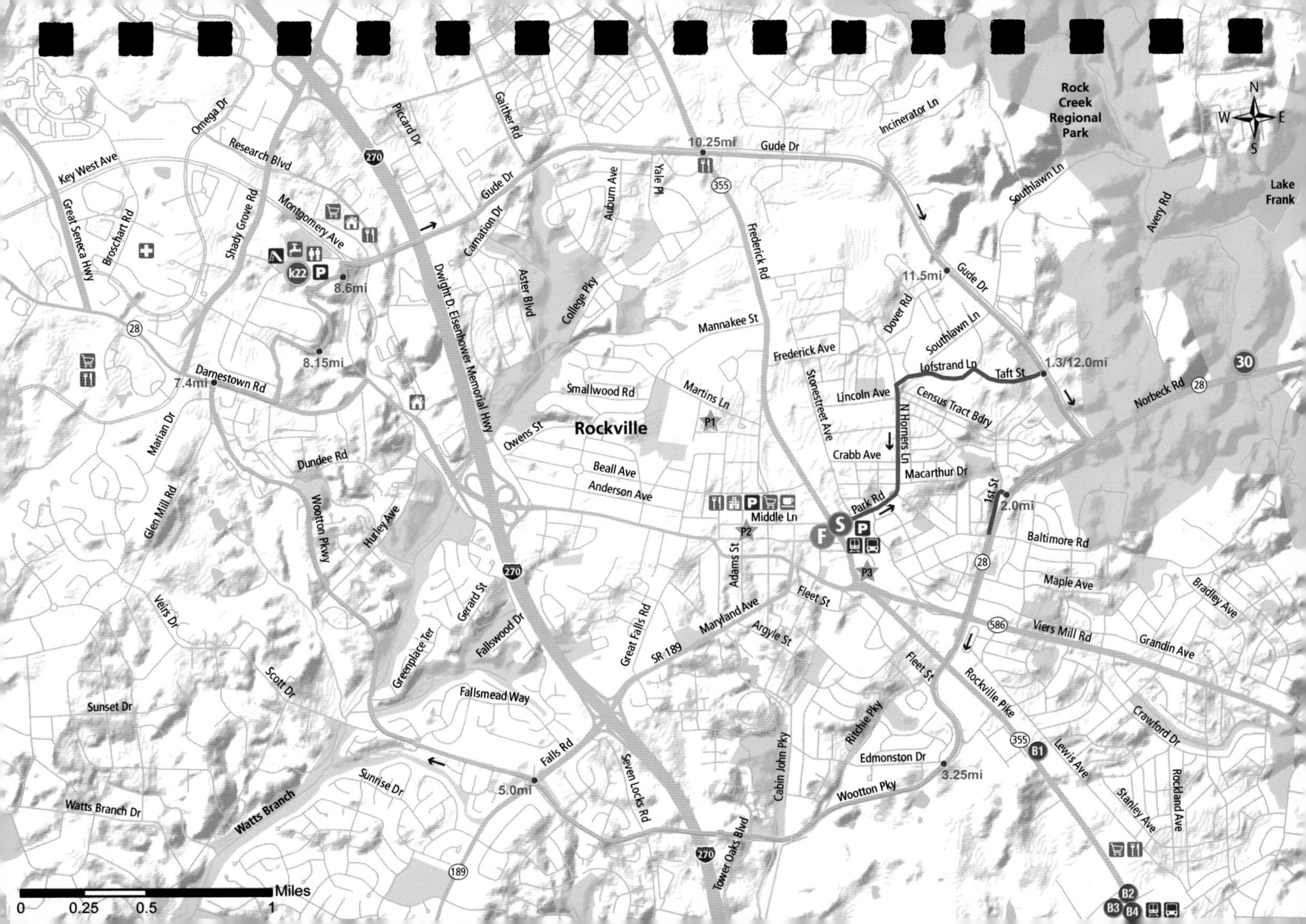

Rock Creek Regional Park
Lake Frank
Avery Rd
Southlawn Ln
Incinerator Ln
Gaither Rd
Piccard Dr
Omega Dr
Research Blvd
Key West Ave
Great Seneca Hwy
Broschart Rd
Shady Grove Rd
Montgomery Ave
K22
8.6mi
270
Gude Dr
10.25mi
355
Yale Pl
Auburn Ave
Carnation Dr
Aster Blvd
College Pky
Frederick Rd
11.5mi
Dover Rd
Southlawn Ln
Lofstrand Ln
Taft St
1.3/12.0mi
30
Norbeck Rd
28
Mannakee St
Frederick Ave
8.15mi
Darnestown Rd
7.4mi
Smallwood Rd
Martins Ln
P1
Lincoln Ave
Census Tract Bdry
Stonestreet Ave
N Horners Ln
Rockville
Owens St
Dwight D. Eisenhower Memorial Hwy
Marian Dr
Crabb Ave
Macarthur Dr
1st St
2.0mi
Dundee Rd
Beall Ave
Anderson Ave
Park Rd
Middle Ln
P2
F
S
P
P3
Baltimore Rd
Glen Mill Rd
Wootton Pkwy
Hurley Ave
Adams St
Maple Ave
Bradley Ave
Veirs Dr
Gerard St
Fleet St
Maryland Ave
586
Viers Mill Rd
Grandin Ave
Greenplace Ter
Fallswood Dr
Great Falls Rd
SR 189
Argyle St
Scott Dr
Fleet St
Rockville Pike
Crawford Dr
Sunset Dr
Fallsmead Way
Ritchie Pky
Cabin John Pky
Edmonston Dr
B1
Lewis Ave
Rockland Ave
Falls Rd
5.0mi
3.25mi
Wootton Pky
Sunrise Dr
Stanley Ave
Watts Branch Dr
Watts Branch
Seven Locks Rd
Tower Oaks Blvd
189
B2
B3
B4
Miles
0
0.25
0.5
1

Blur the line between your workout and your commute.

At a Glance

Distance 23.5 miles **Total Elevation** 520 feet

Terrain

Fourteen miles are asphalt, six are crushed stone, and three traverse city streets. Though the trail rises over 300 feet to Bethesda from the banks of the Potomac, the grade is gradual enough in most areas as to be largely indiscernible. The remainder is flat or slightly downhill.

Traffic

Statistically one of the most heavily used rail-trails in the entire country, the Crescent is proof that car-free doesn't mean traffic-free. Take special care at intersections, during rush hours (yes, these do exist), and on weekends.

How to Get There

If coming by Metro, exit at the Orange/Blue Rosslyn stop and cross the Key Bridge before descending. Drivers use Interstate 66 to the Lee Highway if arriving from Virginia, Wisconsin Avenue if coming from Maryland, and the Rock Creek Parkway if approaching from within the District. Take Water/K Street (below Whitehurst Freeway/U.S.29) to its end and look to park.

Food and Drink

The most convenient options are along Water/K Street near ride's beginning, in Bethesda at mile seven, or near ride's turnaround at the Silver Spring Metro. There are some water fountains along the course as well.

Side Trip

Check out Bethesda and Silver Spring, and chill out post-ride at Georgetown Waterfront Park.

Links to 

Where to Bike Rating 

About...

Befitting its status as one of the premier, urban, rail-to-trail projects in the nation, the Capital Crescent is a hugely popular and heavily utilized recreational thoroughfare connecting affluent Maryland suburbs nearly the entire distance to downtown. Built within the forested corridor of the old Georgetown Branch railroad, it functions as a highly effective balance between business and pleasure. Enjoying its four historic bridges, two cool tunnels and handsome vistas of the Potomac goes hand-in-hand with the satisfaction of joining D.C.'s people of purpose moving dynamically about.

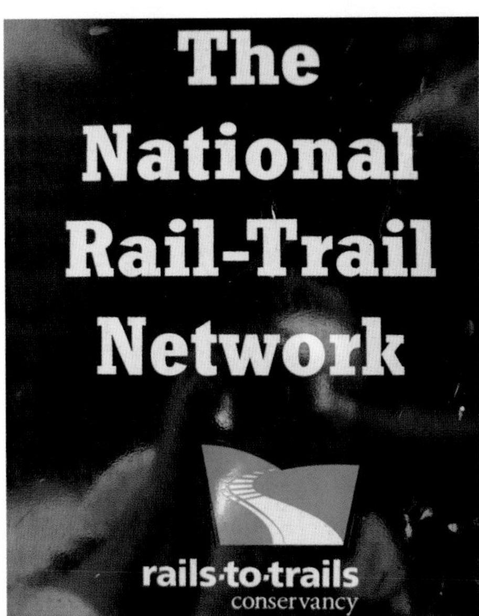

Advocating mobile lifestyles since 1986.

The old Georgetown Branch was a line of the Baltimore and Ohio Railroad which carried coal and building supplies from 1910 to 1985. Its subsequent transformation from disused single-track to first-class rail-trail was a feather in the cooperative cap of local civic groups and government.

Despite that and other successes, the trail remains a work in progress, having existed in three distinct sections throughout its history. And it seems only through the ultimate realization of a proposed, Maryland-owned, Metro-linking Purple Line can it hope to reach its final form. One thing is certain though. The first seven miles of the current Capital Crescent are undoubtedly its signature, as well as a hopeful blueprint for its future.

Beginning at the Georgetown boat houses, you'll parallel the Potomac and the historic C&O Canal (passing possible bike and boat rental at Fletcher's Cove) before crossing the Arizona Avenue Railway Bridge and motoring toward the Dalecarlia Tunnel. There's water straight from the Washington Aqueduct around here as well as benches and a historical panel.

The route soon crosses paths with the Little Falls Hiker-Biker Trail and the site of old Loughborough Mill, all the while elevating its way ever so slightly through residential woods. Take advantage of more water and local history, before spilling into the welcome busyness of Bethesda.

By now you will have noticed signs indicating the Georgetown Branch Trail. After a spot of people-watching, it's on to this, the second section, beginning just beyond the Wisconsin Avenue tunnel. Though not quite the silly-smooth ride you once enjoyed, continue your buzz among the wooded backyards of ritzy Chevy Chase and on through its country club.

Suddenly then, trail abruptly gives way to industry, and it's a series of surface streets from here on out. Welcome to the Crescent's third section, the one most easily labeled interim. It's far from unpleasant however, as designers have done well to maintain safety. That means lots of turns though. Keep your eye out for directional signs. Silver Spring and the chance to shop, eat, or jump on Metro's Red Line, come soon. If not, retrace your tracks to take it all in again.

While Ride 28 has not been deemed kid-friendly in its entirety, it does include substantial sections which are entirely safe for family use.

Ride Log

0.0 Begin at extreme northern end of Water/K St at Capital Crescent Trail map beyond Aqueduct Arch and Potomac Boat Club.

2.0 Fletcher's Cove.

4.0 Pass through Dalecarlia Tunnel.

6.95 Paved section of trail ends. Use Georgetown Branch Trail signs to cross Bethesda and Woodmont avenues and continue toward Wisconsin Ave tunnel.

8.45 Jog right to cross Connecticut Ave then left to reaccess trail.

10.1 Crushed stone trail ends. Right onto Stewart Ave. Follow signs.

10.2 Left on Kansas to right on Pennsylvania to left on Michigan to right on Talbot (over rail trestle) to right onto Grace Church Rd. Way is well-marked.

10.8 Right onto Second Ave to cross 16th Ave.

P *P1* Abner Cloud House—circa 1802
P2 Arizona Avenue trestle
P3 Former location of Loughborough Mill
P4 Rock Creek trestle

B *B1* Revolution Cycles, 3411 M St, NW
B2 Bicycle Pro Shop, 3403 M St, NW
B3 Big Wheel Bikes, 1034 33rd St, NW
B4 Cycle Life USA, 3255 K St, NW
B5 District Hardware—The Bike Shop, 1108 24th St, NW
B6 Big Wheel Bikes, 6917 Arlington Rd #B
B7 Griffin Cycle Inc, 4949 Bethesda Avenue
B8 Conte's, 7626 Old Georgetown Road
B9 City Bikes, 8401 Connecticut Avenue #111
B10 The Bicycle Place, 8313 Grubb Rd
B11 Silver Cycles, 9332 Georgia Ave

BR *BR1* Fletcher's Boathouse

11.35 Cross Spring St.

11.7 End at Silver Spring Metro sign at junction of Second Ave and Colesville Rd. Turn around to retrace route.

23.5 End at Capital Crescent Trail map.

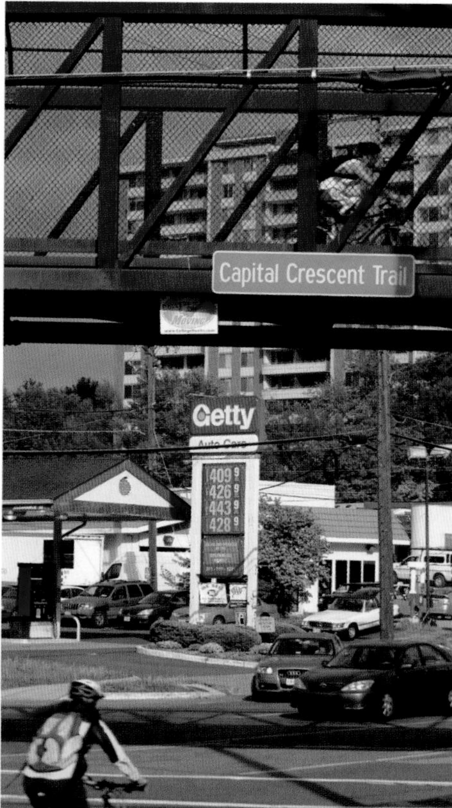

Take the high road.

The Capital Crescent

Altitude ft: 0, 100, 200, 300, 400
Distance miles: 0, 4, 8, 12, 16, 20, 23.5

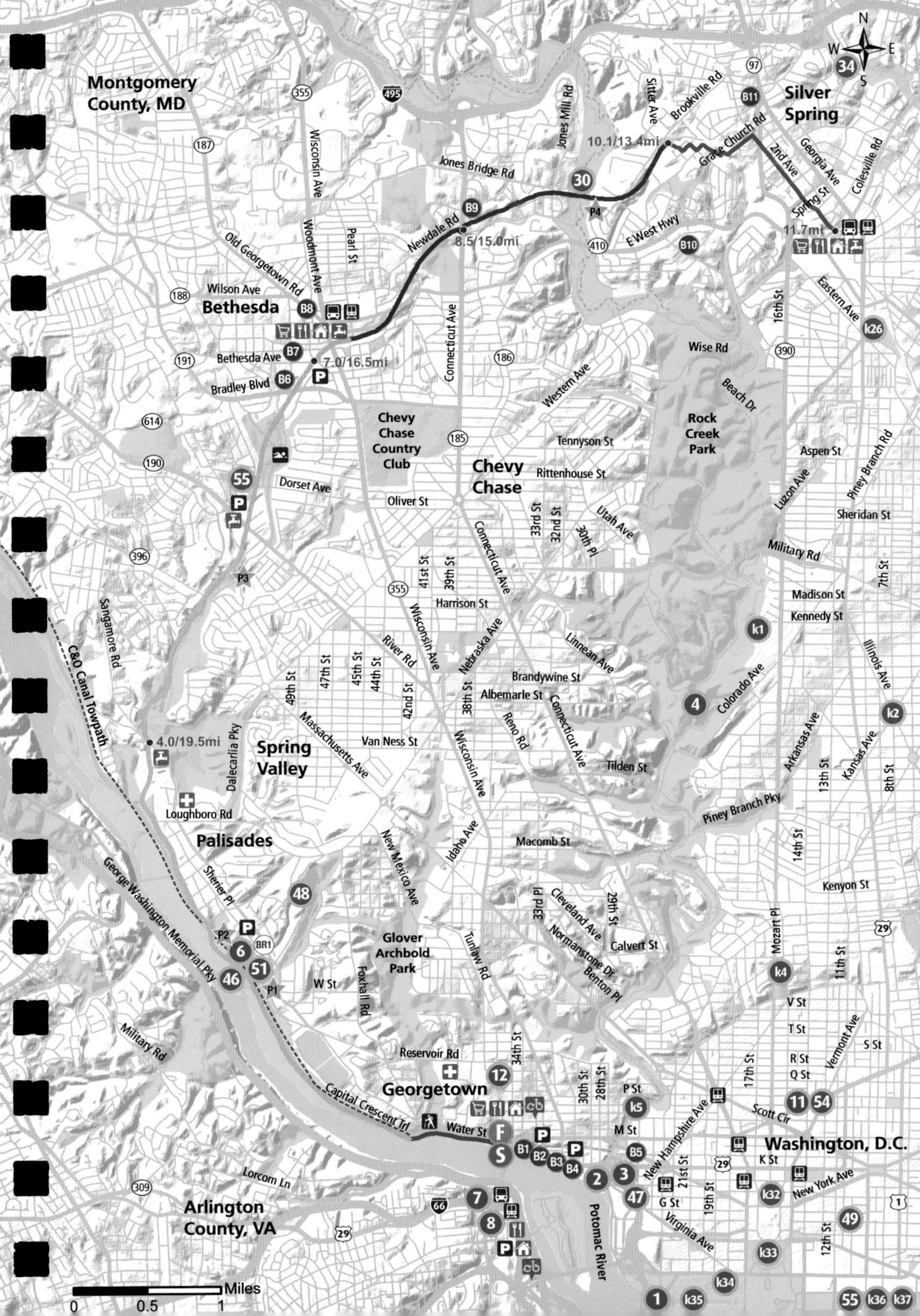

Montgomery County, MD
Bethesda
Silver Spring
Chevy Chase
Chevy Chase Country Club
Rock Creek Park
Spring Valley
Palisades
Glover Archbold Park
Georgetown
Washington, D.C.
Arlington County, VA
Potomac River
C&O Canal Towpath
Capital Crescent Trl
George Washington Memorial Pky
10.1/13.4mi
8.5/15.0mi
7.0/16.5mi
4.0/19.5mi
11.7mi
Jones Bridge Rd
Newdale Rd
Old Georgetown Rd
Wilson Ave
Bethesda Ave
Bradley Blvd
Wisconsin Ave
Woodmont Ave
Pearl St
Connecticut Ave
Jones Mill Rd
Sitter Ave
Brookville Rd
Grace Church Rd
2nd Ave
Georgia Ave
Colesville Rd
Spring St
E West Hwy
Eastern Ave
16th St
Wise Rd
Beach Dr
Western Ave
Tennyson St
Rittenhouse St
Dorset Ave
Oliver St
Utah Ave
33rd St
32nd St
30th Pl
Military Rd
Aspen St
Luzon Ave
Piney Branch Rd
Sheridan St
7th St
Madison St
Kennedy St
Harrison St
41st St
39th St
River Rd
Nebraska Ave
Linnean Ave
Brandywine St
Albemarle St
Reno Rd
Colorado Ave
Illinois Ave
Arkansas Ave
Kansas Ave
13th St
8th St
Tilden St
Piney Branch Pky
49th St
47th St
45th St
44th St
42nd St
38th St
Massachusetts Ave
Van Ness St
Sangamore Rd
Dalecarlia Pky
Loughboro Rd
Macomb St
14th St
Idaho Ave
New Mexico Ave
Sherier Pl
Kenyon St
33rd Pl
Cleveland Ave
29th St
Normanstone Dr
Calvert St
Benton Pl
Mozart Pl
11th St
Tunlaw Rd
Foxhall Rd
W St
V St
T St
Vermont Ave
S St
R St
Q St
Military Rd
Reservoir Rd
34th St
30th St
28th St
P St
17th St
New Hampshire Ave
Scott Cir
Water St
M St
K St
21st St
19th St
G St
New York Ave
Virginia Ave
12th St
Lorcom Ln
Miles
0
0.5
1

Snack break at Lewis Orchards.

At a Glance

Distance 26.1 miles **Total Elevation** 1410 feet

Terrain

Rolling hills over smooth, country roads.

Traffic

Mostly light, increasing along Darnestown (MD 28) and River roads.

How to Get There

Take River Road (MD 190) north off the Beltway using exit 39. Go around nine miles beyond the town of Potomac before coming to a T-intersection with Seneca Road (MD 112). Go left past Poole's Store in Seneca looking for Partnership Road to the right. A left at Fisher Road (MD 107) brings you into Poolesville. Continue past the town square (Whalen Commons) and through Elgin Road (MD 109) to a left on West Willard Road. Parking should be available in the high school's back lot near the football field.

Food and Drink

In Poolesville along Fisher Avenue/White's Ferry Road (MD 107).

Side Trip

Visit John Poole's house, the town's original structure off Fisher near Elgin, and go next door to the Poolesville Museum.

Links to

Where to Bike Rating

About...

This accessible jaunt explores some of the best country roads in the region. With a modest amount of low-traffic climbing, it rolls among the fields, horse farms, and homes just beyond the exurb's ever-encroaching grasp. And once you've cycled this area stretching primarily south of Poolesville to the Potomac, you may find your new favorite destination outside the city. All told, here's a fantastic way to get a taste of this place minus the rigor of other rides.

Riding with purpose.

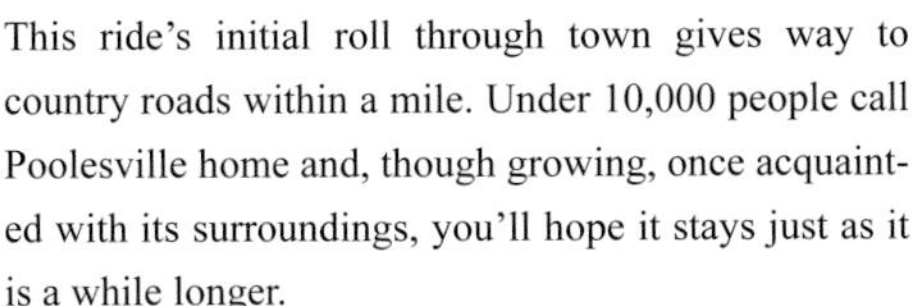

This ride's initial roll through town gives way to country roads within a mile. Under 10,000 people call Poolesville home and, though growing, once acquainted with its surroundings, you'll hope it stays just as it is a while longer.

The way out Cattail Road drops a bit initially before climbing toward Darnestown Road. Expect traffic here, and some big trucks, but enough shoulder to operate with peace of mind. You've gained ground now and, immediately right, there's a nice view over Lewis Orchards, as well as a chance to stop and sample its harvest. After dropping to the Dry Seneca creek bed, you'll rise to reach the ride's highest destination at Beallsville. Monocacy Cemetery offers peace, shade, and history before a beckoning stretch of downhill brings you through to beautiful, wooded Wasche Road and its nearly consistent, three-mile descent.

Then, after regaining much of the ground you just flew down, exit Poolesville stage south this time as you take in a second appealing vista. Sugarloaf Mountain is that distant, green bump due north over your shoulder while the Potomac, though obscured, sits straight ahead. The next four miles angle downhill among broad, tree-lined fields and are only broken briefly by a moderate climb midway.

The following three-and-a-half miles, however, have the potential to be the most harrying of the day. Traffic moves fast on River Road, and space is at a premium. Experienced cyclists do frequent this road though, and while not very busy to begin with, the route calms significantly during the workday. So, ride assured. You're still in the country, and by avoiding rush hours you've gone a long way toward ensuring your safety. The terrain itself undulates lightly as it leads you beyond River and down Partnership Road.

Consider the significant climb to reach Sugarland Road a toll well-spent as you're basically home-free now on lovely, quiet roads. Past St. Paul Community Church and its signs commemorating a settlement founded by freed slaves in the late 1800s, a hump hill to Hughes Road grants a western-facing view of Virginia's Catoctin Mountain. It's an ideal spot to enjoy the sunset before the ride's relaxed four-mile finish.

Ride Log

0.0 Begin by going right out of Poolesville High School's back parking lot onto W Willard Rd.
0.3 Go right onto Fisher Ave.
0.8 Left onto Cattail (across from CVS) then right at 1.0 to remain on it.
2.9 Left onto Darnestown Rd. Pass Lewis Orchards.
4.8 Go through Beallsville Rd sliding immediately left onto W Hunter.
6.5 Left onto Wasche Rd.
7.9 Cross White's Ferry Rd. (Wasche becomes Edward's Ferry Rd).
9.8 Left onto Westerly Rd. (Had enough? Left to return to PHS).
11.2 Right onto W Willard Rd.
15.1 Left onto River Rd.
18.7 Left onto Partnership Rd.
20.5 Left onto Sugarland Rd.
21.2 Right to stay on Sugarland Rd.
22.4 Right at Hughes Rd.
25.0 Left onto Westerly.
25.7 Right onto W Willard Rd.
26.1 Right to finish at Poolesville High School.

P1 John Poole House
P2 Lewis Orchards
P3 Monocacy Cemetery
P4 Seneca Creek Schoolhouse Museum
P5 St. Paul Community Church

B1 Bob's Bikes, 19961 Fisher Ave

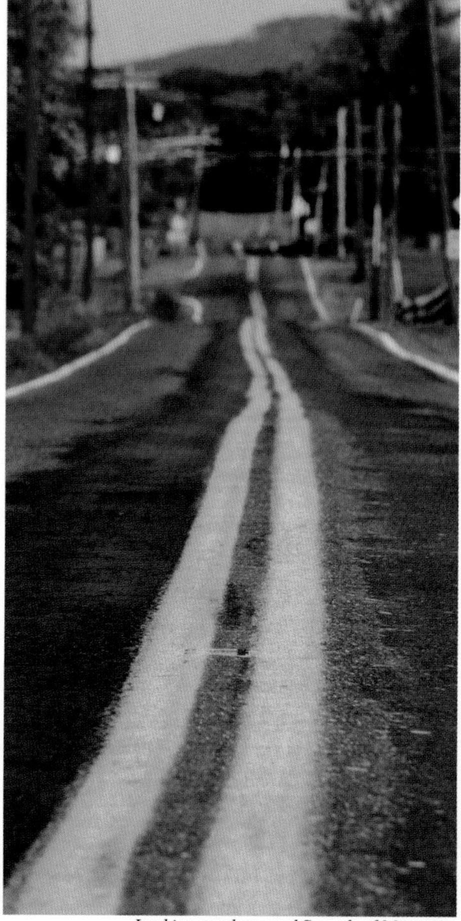

Looking north toward Sugarloaf Mountain.

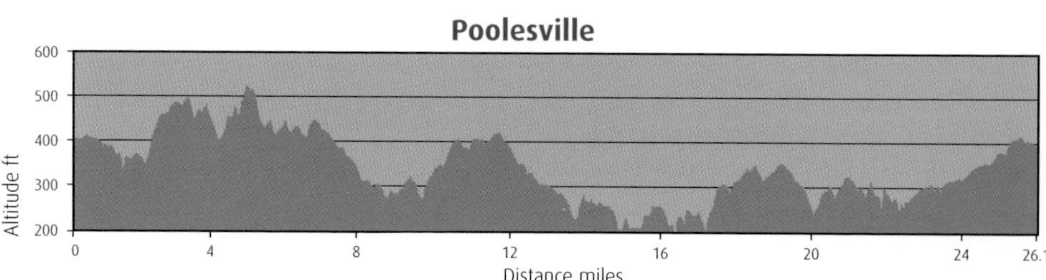

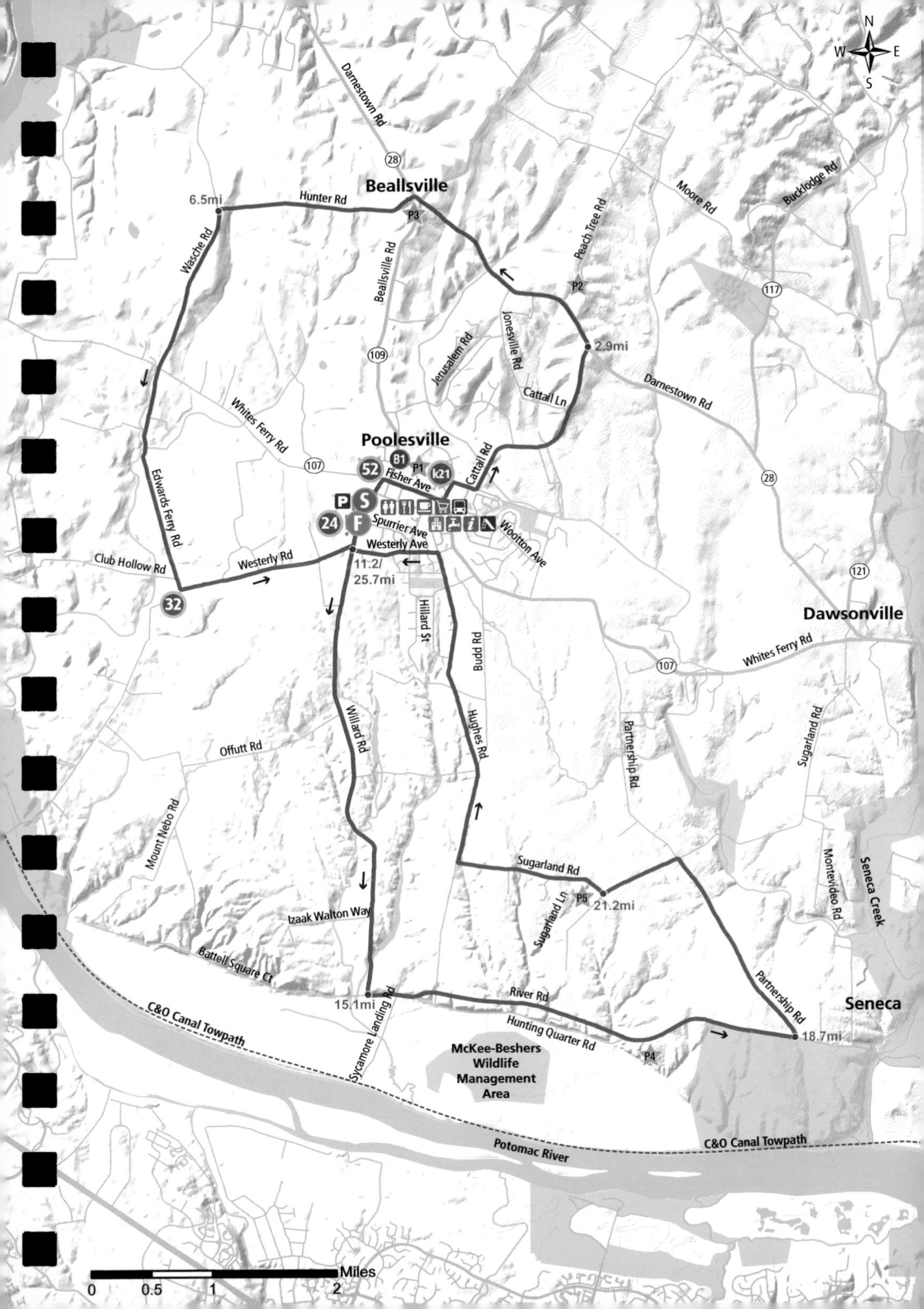
N
W
E
S
Darnestown Rd
28
Beallsville
Hunter Rd
6.5mi
P3
Moore Rd
Bucklodge Rd
Peach Tree Rd
Wasche Rd
Beallsville Rd
P2
117
Jonesville Rd
Jerusalem Rd
109
2.9mi
Cattail Ln
Darnestown Rd
Whites Ferry Rd
Poolesville
107
B1
P1
52
k21
Cattail Rd
Fisher Ave
28
P
S
24
F
Spurrier Ave
Wootton Ave
Westerly Ave
Edwards Ferry Rd
Club Hollow Rd
Westerly Rd
11.2/
25.7mi
121
32
Hillard St
Budd Rd
Dawsonville
Whites Ferry Rd
107
Hughes Rd
Willard Rd
Sugarland Rd
Partnership Rd
Offutt Rd
Mount Nebo Rd
Montevideo Rd
Sugarland Rd
Seneca Creek
P5
21.2mi
Sugarland Ln
Izaak Walton Way
Battell Square Ct
Partnership Rd
15.1mi
Sycamore Landing Rd
River Rd
Seneca
C&O Canal Towpath
Hunting Quarter Rd
18.7mi
McKee-Beshers
Wildlife
Management
Area
P4
Potomac River
C&O Canal Towpath
Miles
0
0.5
1
2

Sunshine and solitude at Lake Needwood.

At a Glance

Distance 28.6 miles **Total Elevation** 1380 feet

Terrain

Mostly flat trail with modest ups and downs and only a handful of longer inclines.

Traffic

None, aside from numerous road crossings.

How to Get There

This ride begins in Maryland at the northwest D.C. line. Arrive by taking Beach Drive off Military Road through Rock Creek Park a bit beyond the Wise Road intersection, or use Western Avenue or Oregon on Rock Creek Park's western side to a right on Beach. The trail begins off a small parking lot on the northern side of the road.

Food and Drink

There's a summer snack bar at Needwood and water fountains at intervals along the way. Otherwise, plan ahead.

Side Trip

Stop by the Washington, D.C. LDS Temple visitor's center up Stoneybrook Drive beside the Beltway; take the fork in the trail to Needwood's companion, Lake Frank; or visit the 40 acres of Woodend Nature Sanctuary, the headquarters of the regional Audubon Naturalist Society. It's off Jones Mill Road about a half-mile north of this ride's intersection with the Capital Crescent Trail.

Links to   4 28 33

Where to Bike Rating  

About...

The establishment of a park system to protect this portion of Rock Creek long-ago led to the creation of the Maryland-National Capital Park and Planning Commission. Today the mostly wooded trail running through that preserved slice of land extends northward from the Washington, D.C. line to Lake Needwood and is one of only a few area routes designated a National Recreation Trail. Offering refuge to road-weary commuters and recreational riders alike, it also exists to provide a surprisingly deep natural experience near and dear to many.

A detail of the bike/ped bridge over Veirs Mill Road.

This relaxed ride serves as an extension of the book's two other Rock Creek Park offerings, yet maintains a flavor all its own. Begin by weaving through slices of suburban woods beyond ball fields and tennis courts. You'll pass Meadowbrook Stables in these initial miles and travel under the impressive wooden trestle which carries the Capital Crescent Trail high above. A third sight follows not far along as the Washington, D.C. Mormon Temple shoots its spires skyward just past the Beltway.

At this point you'll likely see cyclists seeking a bit more speed beside you out on Beach Drive. Feel free to join them if you think you'd be comfortable. The road here isn't too heavily trafficked, and its way has been blazed by two-wheelers for years. The trail itself becomes increasingly winding in this section and trades freer rolling for security and contention with walkers and joggers.

Settle in wherever you choose as the day's make-up has now been established. Expect periods of easy pedaling broken by road crossings, recreation areas, and neighborhood spurs. Though narrow, the coming sections of thick woods are transportive, and you'll likely lose track of the fact you're no more than hundreds of feet beyond backyards at any given moment.

Certain sections of the path have suffered a bit in the past from a lack of directional signs. And while the ride log obviously aims to eliminate those pains, if you do find yourself errant, fear not. You're never far from correcting the situation. Bearing left, then right uphill out of Winding Creek Park brings you past Park Lawn Cemetery, over the Veirs Mill bike/ped bridge, and into the wilder forest nearer Lake Needwood.

Part of Rock Creek Regional Park, the reservoir is located just east of Rockville in Dermont. Visitors can fish, picnic, rent boats and canoes, or take a ride on the Needwood Queen, a flat-bottomed, passenger pontoon. The park also features a visitor's center, hiking and natural surface biking trails, playgrounds, an archery range, and a nearby golf course. Facilities are seasonal. Bidding farewell to Rock Creek as it climbs on upstream to its source spring near Laytonsville, your journey, only half-complete, now retraces southward back to D.C.

While Ride 30 has not been deemed kid-friendly in its entirety, it does include substantial sections which are entirely safe for family use.

Ride Log

0.0 Begin at Rock Creek—Lake Needwood trailhead off Beach Dr parking lot.

1.8 Possible connection to Capital Crescent Trail.

3.8 Trail forks (left goes under Connecticut, right crosses it) but unifies ahead.

5.15 Stay straight.

5.5 Cross Beach Dr then follow trail to right away from parking spaces.

6.0 Bear left.

6.3 Bear left.

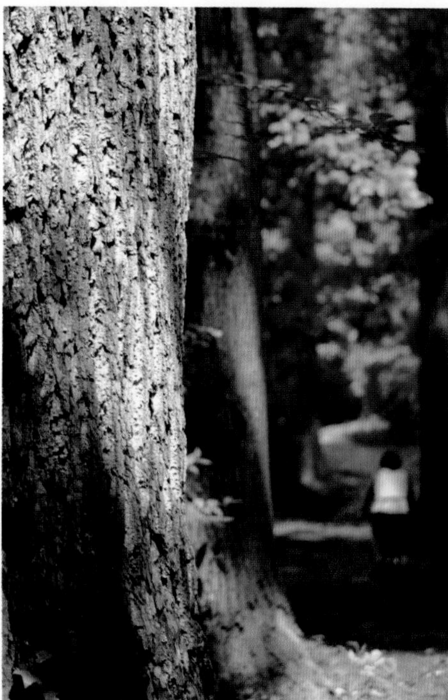

Into the woods.

8.3 Bear right twice in succession.

8.6 Bear right to cross Randolph.

9.0 Bear left to continue over bridge away from Winding Creek Park, then right to go uphill. A right before bridge accesses Matthew Henson Trail.

12.5 Bear left.

14.2 Bicycle rack and maps near Lake Needwood parking lot. Recreational opportunities and amenities. Retrace when ready.

16.9 Stay left.

19.4 Left over footbridge, then right.

19.8 Cross Randolph then go right along sidewalk to re-engage trail.

20.2 Stay left through Dewey Park.

22.2 Bear right.

28.0 Bear left over bridge.

28.6 Finish.

P

P1 Audubon Naturalist Society—Woodend Nature Sanctuary
P2 LDS Temple
P3 Lake Frank
P4 Lake Needwood

B

B1 The Bicycle Place, 8313 Grubb Rd
B2 City Bikes, 8401 Connecticut Avenue #111
B3 Silver Cycles, 9332 Georgia Ave
B4 Bike Express, 3731 University Blvd W, Ste B
B5 Sports Authority, 12055 Rockville Pike
B6 Hudson Trail Outfitters Ltd, 12085 Rockville Pike
B7 REI, 1701 Rockville Pike
B8 Performance Bicycle, 1667 Rockville Pike
B9 Revolution Cycles, 1066 Rockville Pike
B10 Conte's, 7626 Old Georgetown Road
B11 Griffin Cycle Inc, 4949 Bethesda Avenue
B12 Big Wheel Bikes, 6917 Arlington Rd #B

Rock Creek–Lake Needwood

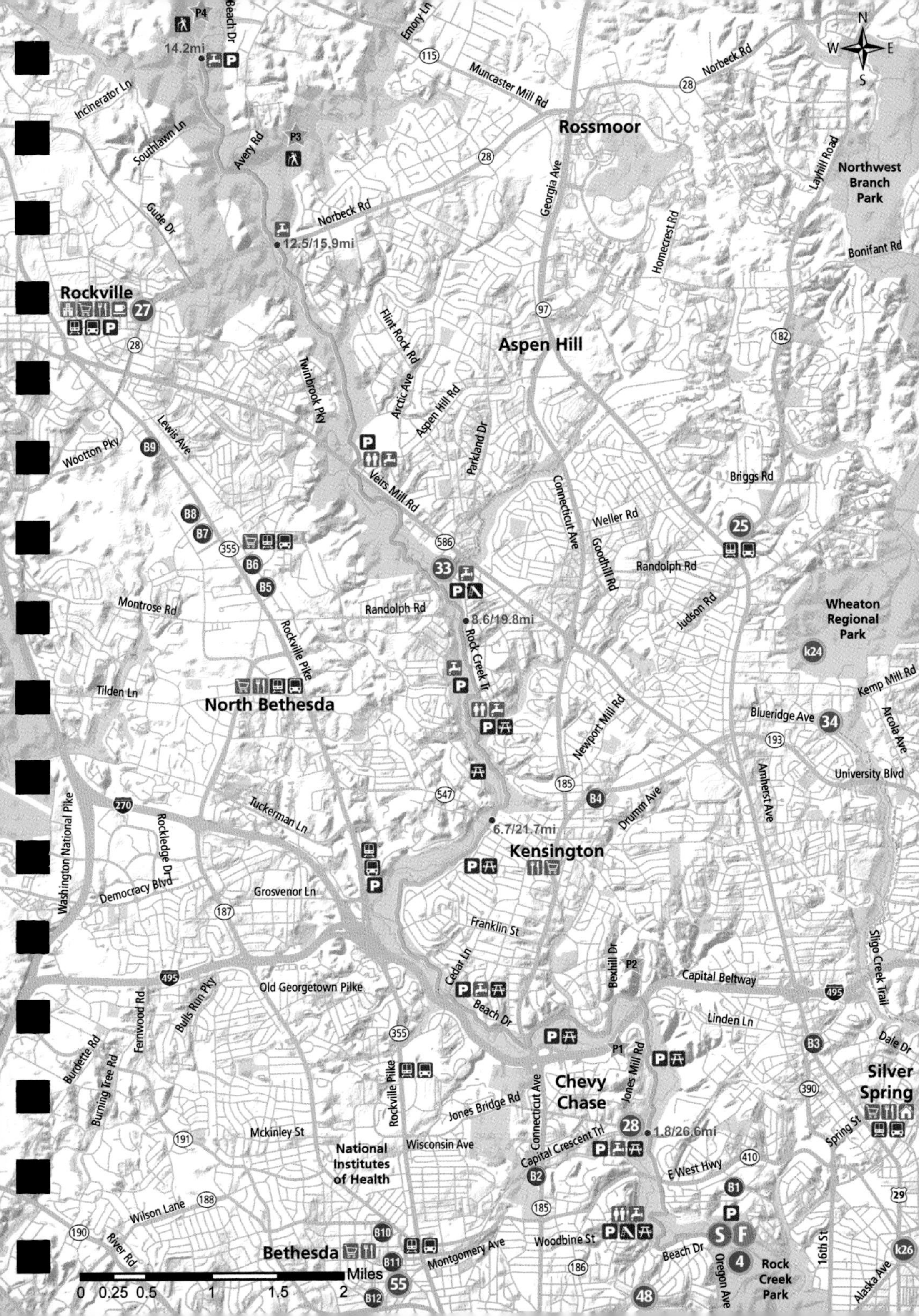

P4
Beach Dr
Emory Ln
14.2mi
115
Norbeck Rd
Muncaster Mill Rd
28
Incinerator Ln
Rossmoor
P3
Southlawn Ln
Avery Rd
28
Layhill Road
Northwest Branch Park
Georgia Ave
Gude Dr
Norbeck Rd
Homecrest Rd
12.5/15.9mi
Bonifant Rd
Rockville
27
97
28
Flint Rock Rd
182
Aspen Hill
Twinbrook Pky
Arctic Ave
Aspen Hill Rd
Lewis Ave
B9
Wootton Pky
Parkland Dr
Veirs Mill Rd
Connecticut Ave
Briggs Rd
B8
B7
Weller Rd
25
355
586
Goodhill Rd
B6
33
Randolph Rd
B5
Montrose Rd
Randolph Rd
Judson Rd
8.6/19.8mi
Wheaton Regional Park
Rock Creek Tr
Rockville Pike
k24
Tilden Ln
Kemp Mill Rd
North Bethesda
Newport Mill Rd
Blueridge Ave
34
Arcola Ave
193
University Blvd
185
B4
Drumm Ave
547
Amherst Ave
270
Rockledge Dr
Tuckerman Ln
6.7/21.7mi
Washington National Pike
Kensington
Democracy Blvd
Grosvenor Ln
187
Franklin St
Sligo Creek Trail
Bexhill Dr
P2
Cedar Ln
Capital Beltway
495
Old Georgetown Pilke
495
Bulls Run Pky
Fernwood Rd
Beach Dr
Linden Ln
355
Burdette Rd
Burning Tree Rd
P1
B3
Dale Dr
Jones Mill Rd
Silver Spring
Chevy Chase
390
Rockville Pike
Jones Bridge Rd
Connecticut Ave
28
1.8/26.6mi
191
Mckinley St
Spring St
National Institutes of Health
Wisconsin Ave
Capital Crescent Trl
E West Hwy
410
B2
B1
29
Wilson Lane
188
185
190
River Rd
B10
Woodbine St
S
F
Beach Dr
Bethesda
Montgomery Ave
186
4
Rock Creek Park
16th St
k26
Alaska Ave
Oregon Ave
B11
Miles
55
0 0.25 0.5 1 1.5 2
B12
48
N
W
E
S

Glen Echo and Art Deco go together like bikes and MacArthur Boulevard.

At a Glance

Distance 13.55 miles **Total Elevation** 595 feet

Terrain

Flat to rolling sidepath aside from a hefty, narrow-shouldered ascent up MacArthur.

Traffic

You'll be safely segregated on cycling lanes aside from the hectic eight mile mark through busy Potomac and short, on-roads stretches along MacArthur and Persimmon Tree. Use sidewalks and crosswalks through that busy junction of Falls and River roads or, better yet, sneak across Safeway's parking lot to Counselman Road to continue.

How to Get There

MacArthur Boulevard's your aim here. Use the Clara Barton Parkway off the Beltway to reach it from the north or Canal Road NW off K Street out of Georgetown to get to it from D.C.

Food and Drink

There's a three-season café at Glen Echo Park itself, the Irish Inn and a convenience store or two near ride's start, and a supermarket, restaurants, and cafés in Potomac.

Side Trip

Visit Great Falls and the Chesapeake and Ohio Canal National Historical Park by staying on MacArthur Boulevard at mile six instead of joining the Falls Road sidepath.

Links to 51

Where to Bike Rating 

About...

Here's a ramble that could hardly be more made to order. Beginning and ending at a place of recreation cherished by generations of area residents and moving safely through a section of the region developed by folks with bicycles in mind, this easy-to-follow loop practically rides itself. Starting flat, it rises past country homes with big lawns to the classy town of Potomac before finishing with a sprint through the rolling terrain of old horse country cum multi-million dollar development.

Taking a break in Potomac.

Glen Echo Park got its start thanks to a better egg beater. It was 1889 when the Baltzley brothers invested proceeds from their new invention in a development along the Potomac. The site was quickly chosen to host the first-ever, D.C.-area Chautauqua, a summer camp movement in bloom at the time which aimed to bring education, culture, and personal enrichment to the masses. Though foul weather and economic issues doomed those proceedings after only two years, the life of the park itself was just beginning. Soon, a wide variety of entertainments began to be offered, rides were built, and a trolley line was established to transport urbanites out to the burgeoning suburbs for a day of amusement.

Rising to peak popularity during WWII, and surviving many leaner intervening years, Glen Echo Park thrives again today as a place of arts, culture, and play. Its historic carousel and exquisite Spanish Ballroom are must sees, while the adjacent Clara Barton National Historic Site honors the founder of the American Red Cross.

Your initial miles here will take you along MacArthur Boulevard (and over the one-lane Cabin John Bridge). Expect company as its flat, segregated bikeway is an area training favorite. After an on-road intermission, the Falls Road sidepath presents itself and ushers you lightly over hill and dale into Potomac, one of the most affluent towns in America and a good place to stop, sit, sip, and people watch.

River Road then links with Persimmon Tree Road, and quickly, you're racing downhill past parcels of old farms and horse pastures given over to gates, fences and manicured greenery. The community has taken good care of cyclists here too though, as yet another multiuse path presents itself and offers to bring you pleasantly onward through the grounds of Congressional Country Club. Then it's a bridge over the Beltway, another streaking downhill stretch to MacArthur, and a return on its bikeway back to Glen Echo.

If you'd like a modified, even ritzier, experience, turn right past mile seven off Falls onto Oaklyn Drive. It will wind you through the luxury residential community of Avenel before linking you back to the mapped route along Persimmon Tree.

While Ride 31 has not been deemed kid-friendly in its entirety, it does include substantial sections which are entirely safe for family use.

Ride Log

P1 Glen Echo Park
P2 Clara Barton National Historic Site
P3 Cabin John Bridge
P4 Old Angler's Inn
P5 Great Falls

B *B1* Big Wheel Bikes, 9931 Falls Rd

A couple rides the MacArthur bikeway.

0.0 Begin where Oxford Ln (the entrance road to Glen Echo Park and the Clara Barton Historic Site) meets MacArthur Ave. Go left on the sidepath adjacent to MacArthur.

0.55 Cross Cabin John Bridge.

0.75 Be cautious crossing Ericsson Rd.

1.75 Follow bike signs to cross then re-cross MacArthur Ave.

2.5 Continue straight along path at Eggert Dr intersection.

4.9 MacArthur sidepath ends. Cross MacArthur to begin riding with traffic uphill.

6.0 Slide onto Falls Rd sidepath to right.

7.0 Possible left onto Oaklyn Dr.

7.3 Follow bike path to cross Falls Rd.

8.0 Use light at River Rd to cross Falls Rd to the right. Alternatively, cut across Safeway parking lot to use Counselman Rd exit to cross River Rd. A sidepath is available on its far side.

8.4 Cross River Rd to join Persimmon Tree Rd.

9.95 Cross Oaklyn Dr. (Sidepath again available.)

11.35 Cross Eggert and soon, the Beltway.

11.9 A long downhill brings you back to MacArthur. Go left.

13.55 End where you started.

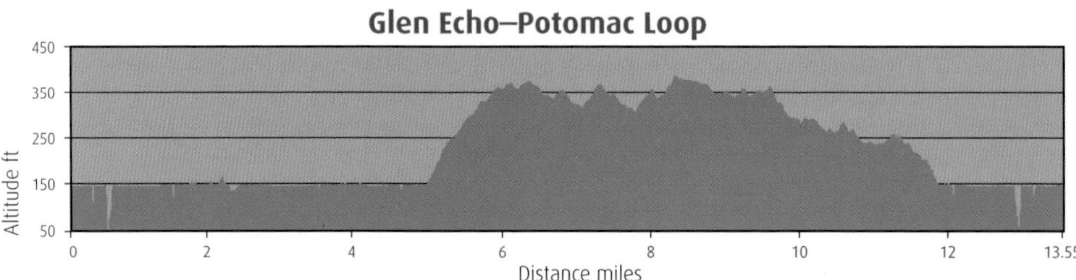

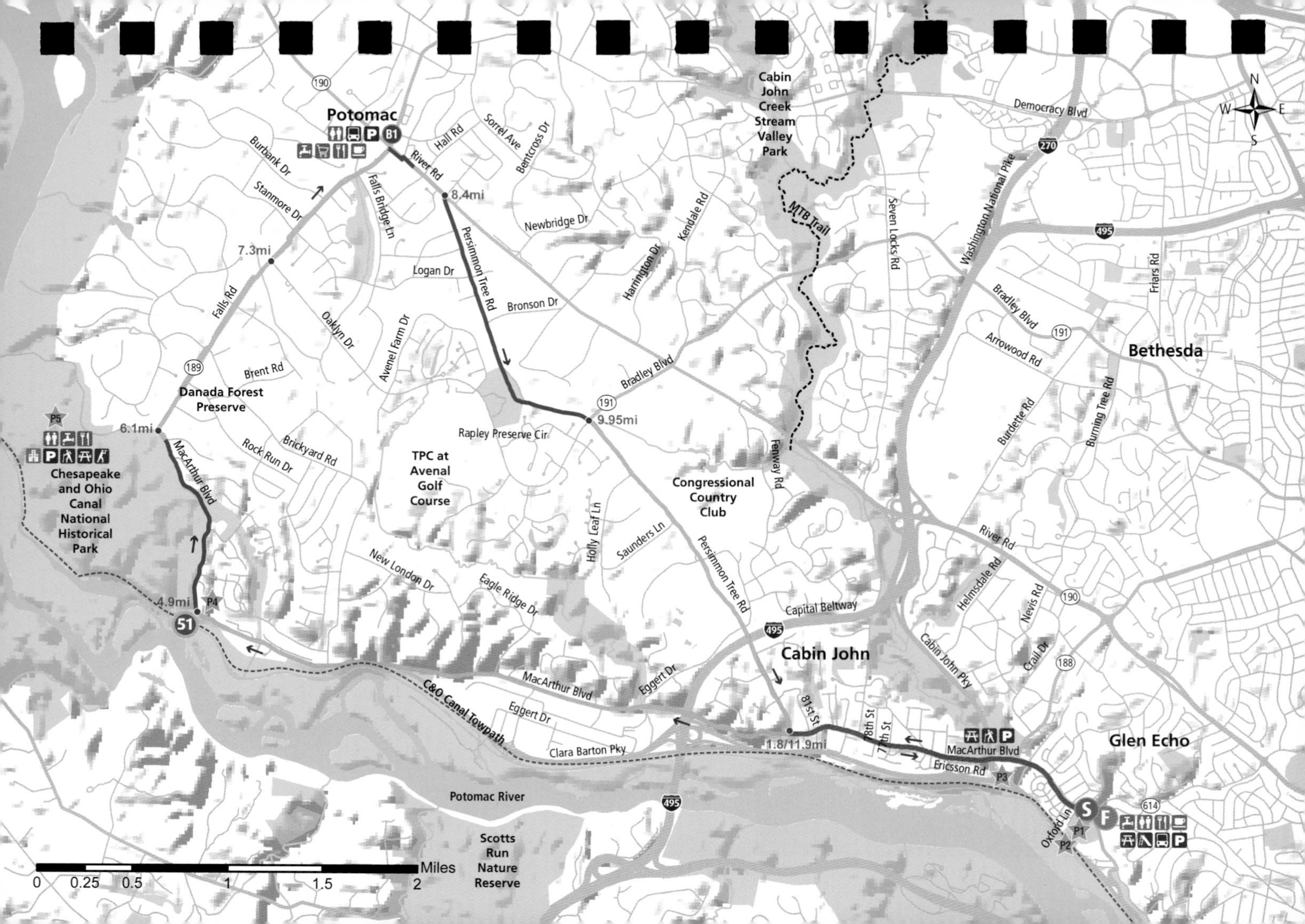

Potomac
Cabin John Creek Stream Valley Park
Democracy Blvd
Bethesda
Glen Echo
Cabin John
Congressional Country Club
TPC at Avenal Golf Course
Danada Forest Preserve
Chesapeake and Ohio Canal National Historical Park
Scotts Run Nature Reserve
Potomac River
C&O Canal Towpath
MTB Trail
Burbank Dr
Stanmore Dr
Hall Rd
Sorrel Ave
Bentcross Dr
River Rd
Falls Bridge Ln
Newbridge Dr
Kendale Rd
Harrington Dr
Logan Dr
Persimmon Tree Rd
Bronson Dr
Falls Rd
Oaklyn Dr
Avenel Farm Dr
Brent Rd
Bradley Blvd
Rapley Preserve Cir
Brickyard Rd
Rock Run Dr
MacArthur Blvd
New London Dr
Eagle Ridge Dr
Holly Leaf Ln
Saunders Ln
Fenway Rd
Seven Locks Rd
Washington National Pike
Friars Rd
Arrowood Rd
Burdette Rd
Burning Tree Rd
River Rd
Helmsdale Rd
Nevis Rd
Crail Dr
Cabin John Pky
Capital Beltway
Eggert Dr
Clara Barton Pky
81st St
78th St
77th St
Ericsson Rd
Oxford Ln
8.4mi
7.3mi
9.95mi
6.1mi
4.9mi
1.8/11.9mi
B1
51
S
F
P1
P2
P3
P4
P5
190
189
191
188
614
270
495
N
E
S
W
0
0.25
0.5
1
1.5
2
Miles

Worth a second look.

At a Glance

Distance 41.5 miles **Total Elevation** 3150 feet

Terrain

The first two-thirds of this ride traverses rolling hills and demands a lot of climbing. Its roads are good throughout.

Traffic

There is no shoulder on River Road, and while vehicles do move quickly, their frequency drops considerably outside rush hours. Dickerson Road (MD 28) carries big trucks but provides more space. All else should be much calmer.

How to Get There

Using exit 39 north off the Beltway, take River Road (MD 190) around nine miles beyond the town of Potomac to a T-intersection with Seneca Road (MD 112). Go left looking to go left again within a mile onto Riley's Lock Road. Take it a short way to its end and park near the lockhouse.

Food and Drink

Stop by historic Poole's Store in Seneca at ride's beginning and end and Dickerson Market halfway through.

Side Trip

Consider cruising past Ride 51's turnaround at Great Falls to camp at the Horsepen Branch Hiker-Biker Campsite at mile 26 of the C&O Towpath. Build a fire, get some zzzz's and retrace to this ride's beginning the next morning just past mile 23.

Links to 24  29  52

Where to Bike Rating  

About...

Named after the landmark at which it begins and ends, this third and most challenging far western Montgomery County ride attempts to survey the best remaining roads in the region while linking the lowland along the Potomac River with the higher elevations sitting in sight of Sugarloaf Mountain. Mostly rolling throughout, but punctuated with occasionally intense climbs and thrilling downhills, this route doubly rewards the experienced rider with consistently low-traffic roads through gorgeous countryside.

Think about saving this ride for fall.

Beginning here where Seneca Creek meets the Potomac is not only a convenient place to launch a grand tour of the area, it also provides a chance for post-ride exploration. The C&O Canal once fortified a local economy famous for its production of the red sandstone used to construct the Smithsonian Castle on the National Mall. Seneca's was one of 11 aqueducts needed to bring the canal across Potomac tributaries along its journey from Georgetown to Cumberland, and, Riley's Lock, the 24th upstream along the canal, is named after the last lockkeeper to live and work here.

Flat ever-so-briefly, this tour soon rises sharply from Seneca Creek before settling onto an undulating portion of River Road past McKee-Besher's Wildlife Area. Narrowing over a single-lane bridge at mile five, the road ducks deeper into woods, and soon brings another bruising hill before leveling out to a descent. Consider yourself properly introduced to today's offering, then, as you drop, rise and roll along Club Hollow Road.

Continue by ascending gradually to meet White's Ferry Road, then turning twice and spilling three, twisting miles down a lovely stretch of shaded country lane capped off by a mile-long climb to an historic fieldstone fence. Take care at the initial downhill onto heavily trafficked Dickerson Road (MD 28) and stop at the ride's exact halfway point for a much-deserved bit of rest and refreshment.

Mount Ephraim Road grants a wide, open survey of surrounding farms and fields as it calmly elevates toward a peaceful crossroads at the base of Sugarloaf Mountain. Trail maps are available, but the road beckons, taking you past a lovely vineyard and mounting upward through a series of rolling inclines. It's work, but the tree-lined way is pleasant and, soon, you've passed the Comus Inn and reached the day's highest elevation just before your turn onto Slidell Road. And though it's not quite all downhill from here, calm back roads now drop you consistently over eight miles to thick woods beside Little Seneca Creek. Then, only an occasional climb breaks long stretches of level ground and descent before you're back down to Riley's Lock Road and your starting point.

Ride Log

0.0 Begin at the Seneca Creek Aqueduct sign where Riley's Lock Rd meets the parking lot nearest the lock-house. Bathrooms are available.

0.65 Left on River Rd.

5.1 Continue past W Willard. River Rd becomes Mt Nebo Rd.

9.0 Right on Edward's Ferry.

10.5 Left on Club Hollow.

12.5 Right on Elmer School.

14.6 Right at White's Ferry to a left at Martinsburg.

17.1 Pass Dickerson Conservation Park.

18.2 Bear left to stay on Martinsburg.

19.5 Left on MD 28.

20.7 Right after train overpass on Mt Ephraim.

23.5 Right on Comus Rd.

26.0 Straight across Old Hundred Rd.

27.6 Right on Slidell.

29.5 Cross W Old Baltimore.

31.2 Right on MD 117.

34.0 Right on White Ground Rd.

34.9 Bear right to stay on White Ground.

36.6 Left on MD 28 to quick right onto Sugarland Rd.

38.3 Right on Montevideo Rd.

40.5 Left on River Rd.

40.8 Right on Riley's Lock Rd.

41.5 End at Seneca Creek Aqueduct.

P1 Seneca Creek Aqueduct
P2 Poole's Store
P3 Seneca Creek Schoolhouse Museum
P4 Sugarloaf Mountain Vineyard

B *B1* Bob's Bikes, 19961 Fisher Ave

Rising to the challenge.

The Seneca Aqueduct Loop

Please note: the profile for Ride 32 is depicted in 200ft vertical increments due to unusually high elevation.

Altitude ft: 750, 550, 350, 150

Distance miles: 0, 4, 8, 12, 16, 20, 24, 28, 32, 36, 40, 41.5

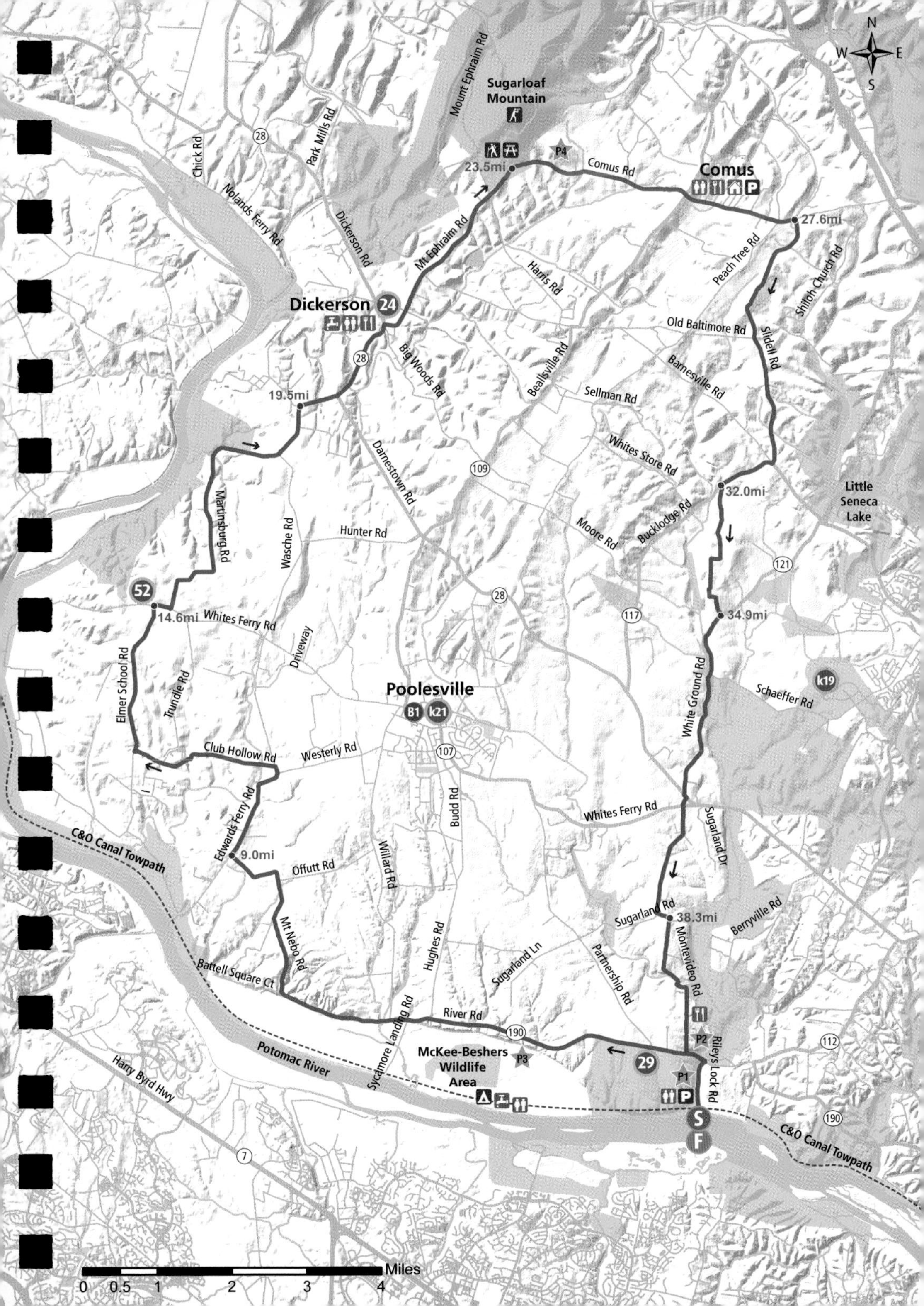

N
W
E
S
Sugarloaf Mountain
Mount Ephraim Rd
Park Mills Rd
Chick Rd
28
Nolands Ferry Rd
Dickerson Rd
Mt Ephraim Rd
23.5mi
P4
Comus Rd
Comus
27.6mi
Peach Tree Rd
Shiloh Church Rd
Harris Rd
Dickerson
24
Big Woods Rd
Old Baltimore Rd
Bealsville Rd
Barnesville Rd
Slidell Rd
19.5mi
Sellman Rd
Darnestown Rd
109
Whites Store Rd
32.0mi
Little Seneca Lake
Martinsburg Rd
Wasche Rd
Hunter Rd
Moore Rd
Bucklodge Rd
121
52
14.6mi
Whites Ferry Rd
28
117
34.9mi
Elmer School Rd
Trundle Rd
Driveway
White Ground Rd
Poolesville
B1
k21
k19
Schaeffer Rd
Club Hollow Rd
Westerly Rd
107
Edwards Ferry Rd
Budd Rd
Whites Ferry Rd
Sugarland Dr
C&O Canal Towpath
9.0mi
Offutt Rd
Willard Rd
Berryville Rd
Sugarland Rd
38.3mi
Mt Nebo Rd
Hughes Rd
Sugarland Ln
Partnership Rd
Monteviideo Rd
Battell Square Ct
Sycamore Landing Rd
River Rd
190
P2
Rileys Lock Rd
112
McKee-Beshers Wildlife Area
P3
29
P1
Potomac River
Harry Byrd Hwy
S
F
C&O Canal Towpath
190
7
Miles
0 0.5 1 2 3 4

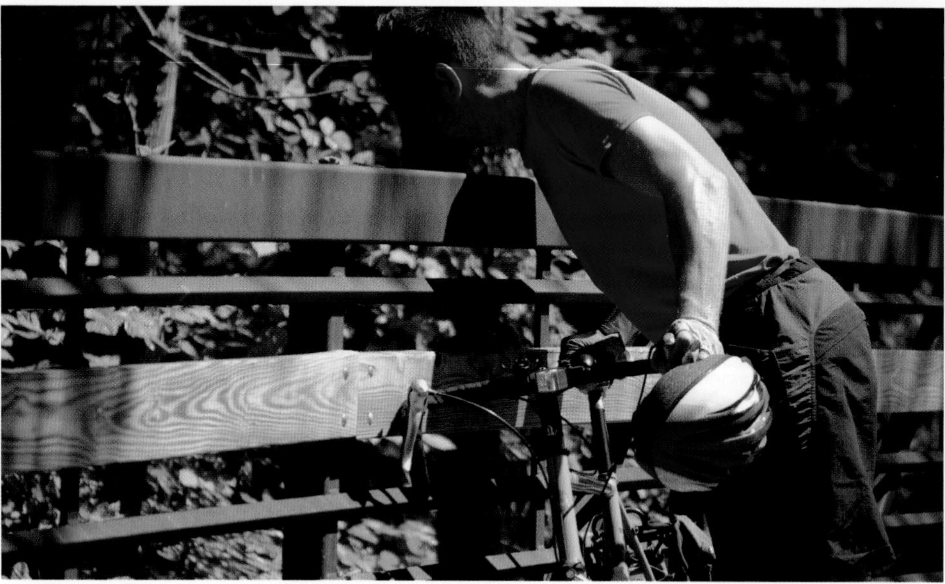

Cycling is exploring.

At a Glance

Distance 8.95 miles **Total Elevation** 405 feet

Terrain

This smooth asphalt trail includes .6 miles of elevated boardwalk and has one nice-size hill halfway.

Traffic

None, aside from a few road crossings.

How to Get There

Cycle here by way of Ride 30 or drive and use exit 33 to access Connecticut Avenue (MD 185) off the Beltway. Take it north to a left onto Veirs Mill Road (MD 586). Another left onto Edgebrook Road brings you three blocks to Winding Creek Park.

Food and Drink

At the corner of Veirs Mill Road and Randolph Road, not far from the Edgebrook turnoff.

Links to  

Where to Bike Rating

About...

This short spin on one of the newest of D.C.'s ever-growing family of stream valley trails begins at an intersection with Maryland's Rock Creek Trail to Lake Needwood. Its course follows the Turkey Branch safely east, crosses several major arterial roads, and moves through a wooded suburban corridor. And while you won't finish with fame identical to that of its namesake, at least you'll enjoy the satisfaction of having found another fresh slice of preserved peace right near your own backyard.

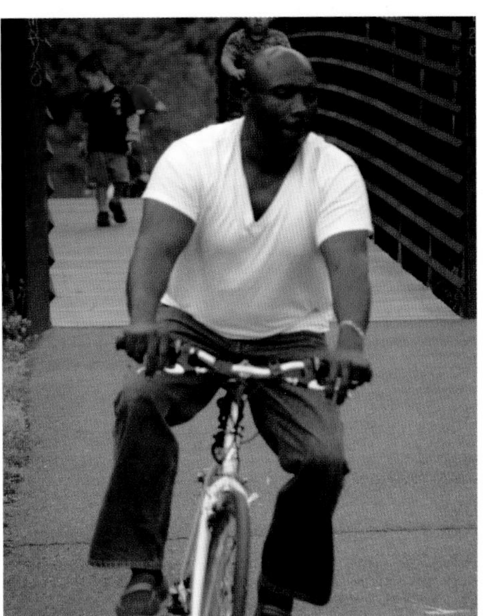

Beginning the trail in Winding Creek Park.

It's true this linear green space bears absolutely no relation to the fabled white north which earned Matthew Henson his fame. His Maryland birth, in fact, is just about the only thing connecting the explorer to the state park and trail which bear his name. The story of the first African-American believed to have reached the Geographic North Pole is one of great accomplishment however, and perhaps bears repeating if only for encouragement along your way.

Already a veteran seaman by his late teens, Henson met Naval Commander Robert E. Peary in the late 1880s and went on to accompany him on many adventures. In 1909, after multiple attempts, the two finally reached the North Pole. And though their claim was widely contested, Peary went on to lasting fame. Henson, instead, faded into the obscurity of a clerk's position and not until he reached his seventies did he begin to get the recognition he deserved. As fate would have it, it took yet another 30 years after his death before his body was exhumed and placed in a position of honor near Peary's in Arlington National Cemetery.

While it's no Arctic expedition to be sure, the Matthew Henson is certainly a pleasant enough way to get some quality outdoor time with the family. After beginning in Winding Creek Park and crossing Veirs Mill Road, continue through one of the trail's prettiest sections as it skirts alongside the Turkey Branch before crossing Connecticut Avenue. At Georgia, be prepared to climb for a third-of-a-mile before a fun descent zips you across two long stretches of elevated boardwalk. Not long after Layhill Road, the trail ends abruptly at Alderton Road. It's quite possible there's connection in its future, but for now, turn around and retrace your path back to Winding Creek Park.

Ride Log

Keep connecting the dots.

0.0 Begin at trailhead near parking lot of Winding Creek Park.

0.25 Jog left then right while crossing Veirs Mill Rd.

1.5 Cross Connecticut Ave.

2.65 Cross Georgia Ave then proceed right along sidewalk to re-engage trail.

3.55 Cross Layhill Rd at Middlevale Ln.

4.45 Trail ends at Alderton Rd. Turnaround to retrace.

5.3 Layhill Rd at Middlevale Ln.

6.7 Big downhill. Begin slowing to prepare for Georgia Ave crossing.

8.7 Veirs Mill Rd.

8.95 End.

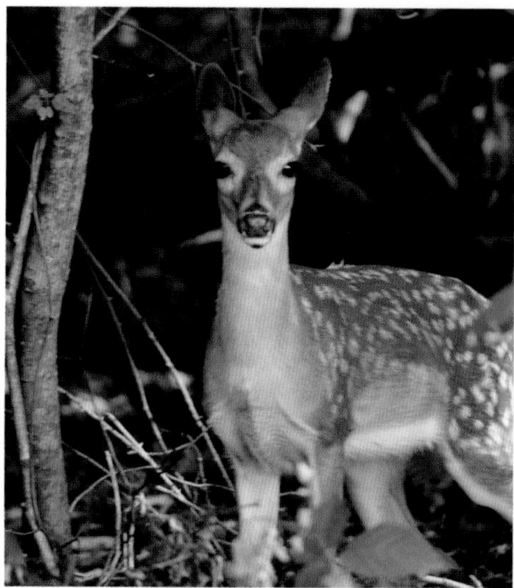
A white-tailed fawn looks on.

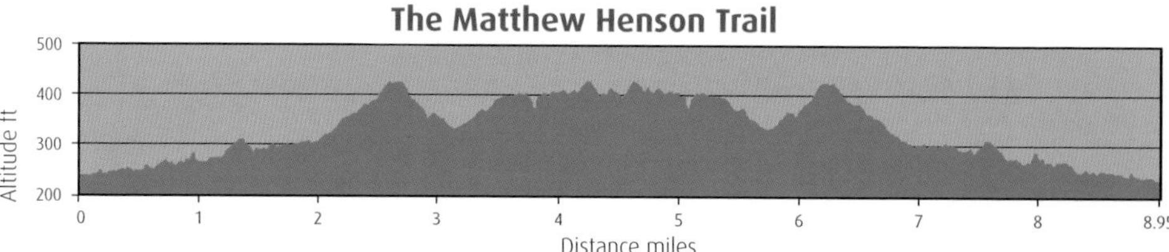

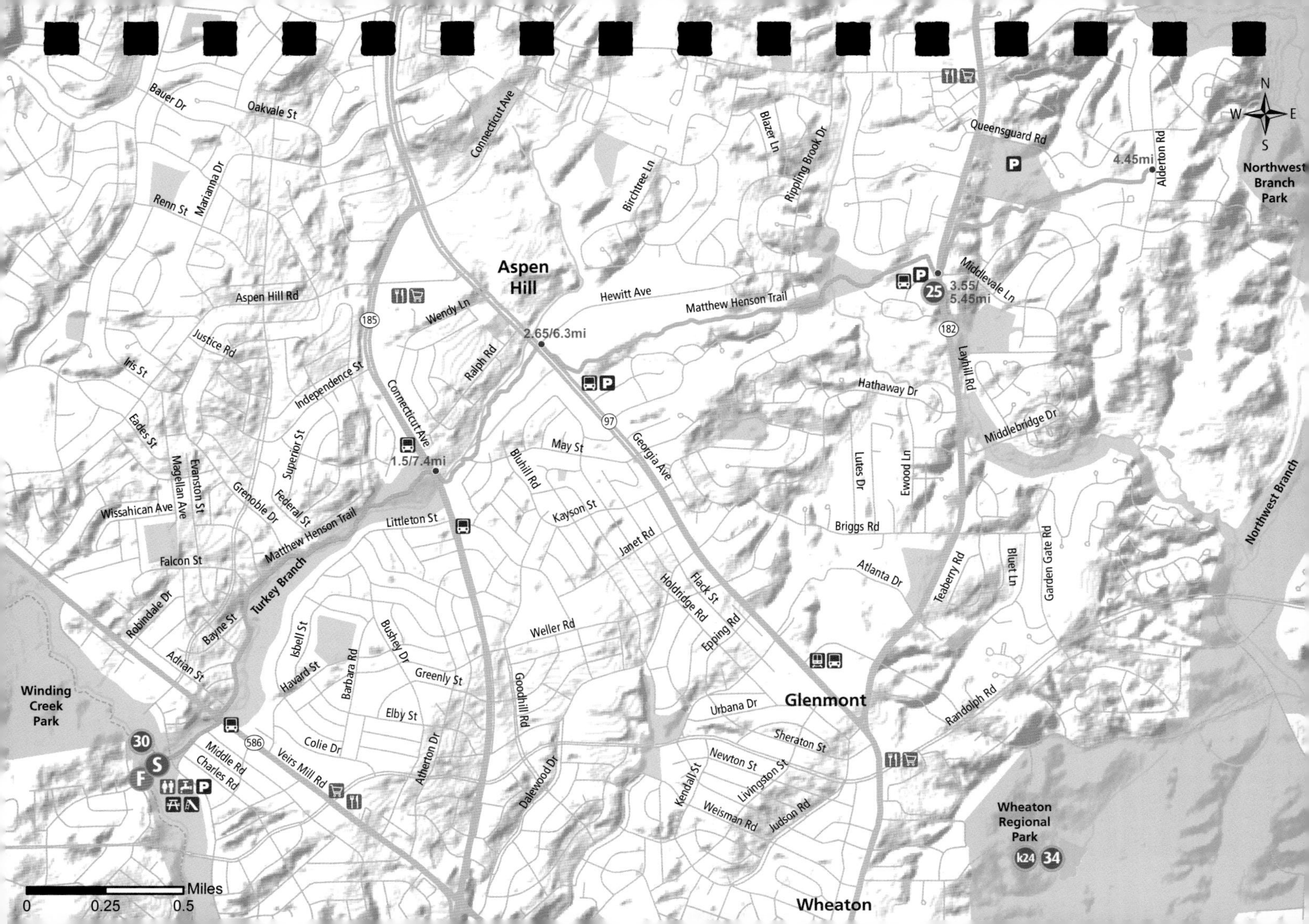

Northwest Branch Park
Aspen Hill
Glenmont
Wheaton
Wheaton Regional Park
Winding Creek Park
Northwest Branch
Turkey Branch
Matthew Henson Trail
Alderton Rd
4.45mi
Queensguard Rd
Middlevale Ln
3.55/ 5.45mi
25
182
Layhill Rd
Middlebridge Dr
Hathaway Dr
Lutes Dr
Ewood Ln
Briggs Rd
Garden Gate Rd
Bluet Ln
Teaberry Rd
Atlanta Dr
Randolph Rd
Blazer Ln
Rippling Brook Dr
Birchtree Ln
Hewitt Ave
2.65/6.3mi
97
Georgia Ave
Connecticut Ave
185
Aspen Hill Rd
Wendy Ln
Ralph Rd
May St
Bluhill Rd
Kayson St
Janet Rd
Flack St
Holdridge Rd
Epping Rd
Urbana Dr
Sheraton St
Newton St
Livingston St
Kendall St
Weisman Rd
Judson Rd
1.5/7.4mi
Littleton St
Weller Rd
Goodhill Rd
Dalewood Dr
Atherton Dr
Bushey Dr
Greenly St
Elby St
Barbara Rd
Isbell St
Havard St
Colie Dr
586
Veirs Mill Rd
Middle Rd
Charles Rd
30
S
F
Bauer Dr
Oakvale St
Marianna Dr
Renn St
Justice Rd
Iris St
Independence St
Eades St
Superior St
Federal St
Grenoble Dr
Magellan Ave
Evanston St
Wissahican Ave
Falcon St
Robindale Dr
Bayne St
Adrian St
k24
34
N
E
S
W
Miles
0
0.25
0.5

Sunlight, Camera, Action!

At a Glance

Distance 18.3 miles **Total Elevation** 815 feet

Terrain

The Sligo Creek Trail is smooth and rises gradually as it proceeds north. The loops in Takoma Park and Wheaton take in mostly modest hills with the largest coming early on Elm Street within the ride's second mile and again in the last mile on Cedar Avenue.

Traffic

Your progress will only be impeded by some major street crossings. Do expect a few cars at the outset on Carroll before dipping into quiet Takoma Park, as well as a few on Argosy on the northern loop back to the trailhead in Wheaton.

How to Get There

Take Metro's Red Line to Takoma, which is also served by multiple bus routes. Drivers, set your compasses to Eastern Avenue's crossing with Carroll Avenue and head west a block or so. Piney Branch Road also gets you in the vicinity.

Food and Drink

Get your grub at the outset and the end on Carroll and around said Metro in Takoma Park. The trail is isolated and free of convenience, providing refreshment of another kind.

Side Trip

Do some more cruising among the fanciful homes of Takoma Park's historic district or head south toward Hyattsville and the Sligo Trail's linkage with another Anacostia Tributary Trail, the Northwestern Branch, by turning right after mile 1.75 instead of left.

Where to Bike Rating 

About...

Here's a first-class out-and-back in among the tall trees on one of the area's most cherished stream valley trails. Throw in a dash of sightseeing in Takoma Park and a pinch of exploration at the turnaround in Wheaton, and you've found yourself a quality way to get some sylvan exposure smack dab in the suburbs.

Pausing to reflect.

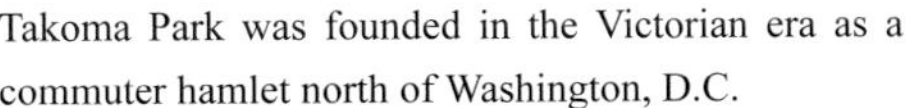

Takoma Park was founded in the Victorian era as a commuter hamlet north of Washington, D.C.

You'll be starting your ride, in fact, at the Metro station on the site of the former B&O Railroad stop around which the community was built. The Seventh-day Adventist Church spurred a fair amount of the area's early growth after moving its world headquarters here for a time, and establishing churches, schools, and a small college. And one can only imagine its long-lived, vegetarian health food co-op had a hand in Takoma Park's reincarnation as a hippy enclave in the 1960s.

You may get a pang of nostalgia yourself as you breeze through downtown. Notice the town clock, the hardware store, and the absence of anything but small, local business, and you're a long way toward understanding what makes this place tick. A dip into the historic district, here and at ride's end, provides another clue to the town's prevailing spirit. Now colorful homes, some turreted and multi-gabled, sit deep on tree-filled lots.

The area is very hilly, and though this ride skirts the biggest of them, there is one strenuous climb on Elm before a short, steep descent engages the Sligo Creek Hiker-Biker Trail. Once there, a sensation of being pleasantly hemmed in takes hold, as you've entered a deep, forested valley.

This won't always be the case. The Sligo Creek Parkway does at times creep alongside the trail and road crossings will pull you back to reality, but overall the greenspace remains unbroken to Wheaton and back. With the creek chattering beside you, and sunny spots to relax and play along the way, you could potentially be here a while without realizing the time.

The trail ends a few quiet residential blocks shy of Wheaton Regional Park, and the mini-loop here is designed to give you a chance to get a taste of one of the best recreational spaces in the entire region. Have fun, and a safe spin back to Takoma Metro.

While Ride 34 has not been deemed kid-friendly in its entirety, it does include substantial sections which are entirely safe for family use.

Ride Log

0.0 Begin at Takoma Metro Station's main gate. Take Carroll Ave up a slight hill toward 7-11 and continue straight through two traffic lights to downtown.

0.25 Left to continue on Carroll.

0.45 Right onto Columbia Ave just after Tulip St traffic light.

0.65 Right onto Poplar Ave.

0.85 Left onto Elm Ave.

1.2 Continue straight on Elm through Prince George's Ave and up a big hill.

1.35 Go straight across Ethan Allen Ave veering right at traffic circle to stay on Elm.

1.65 Right onto Heather Ave.

1.75 Take last available left on unmarked lane before cul-de-sac. Go down steep hill, crossing road at bottom and turning left onto Sligo Creek Hiker-Biker Trail. Expect road crossings and bridge and sidewalk connections. Keep an eye out for signage.

8.15 Stay straight to exit trail proper and enter upcoming street.

8.3 Go straight through both upcoming stop signs before crossing Argosy Ave. Sign for Wheaton Regional Park at right.

8.5 Continue as road proceeds deeper into park toward ice rink, turns right, then jogs left, and straightens past ball fields.

8.8 At stop sign, dip onto unnamed trail at left.

9.6 Prepare to bear left over bridge to enter open parkland. Carousel is straight ahead.

9.7 Turn left to climb gradual hill out of park and enter neighborhood on Henderson Ave.

10.15 Take a left onto Georgia Ave sidewalk proceeding past Wheaton Library.

10.4 Turn left onto Argosy Ave.

10.9 Take a right onto Nairn Rd.

11.2 Turn left onto Blue Ridge Ave, and left again as it ends, looking to access trail to right behind schoolyard.

11.7 Go right to re-engage Sligo Creek Trail proper and retrace route.

15.7 Go left along sidewalk then quick right to cross road.

16.25 Cross Piney Branch to go right. Quick left back onto trail.

16.8 Jog left, followed by quick right to continue.

17.1 Take a right onto Maple Ave toward Takoma Community Center (Washington Adventist Hospital across road).

17.65 Take a right onto Philadelphia followed by a left onto Cedar Ave.

18.15 Merge right toward Metro to go left into parking lot.

18.3 Arrive back at Takoma Metro.

P1 Takoma Park Historic District
P2 Brookside Gardens and Nature Center

B1 Takoma Bicycle, 7030 Carroll Ave
B2 Silver Cycles, 9332 Georgia
B3 Bicycle Place, 8813 Grubb

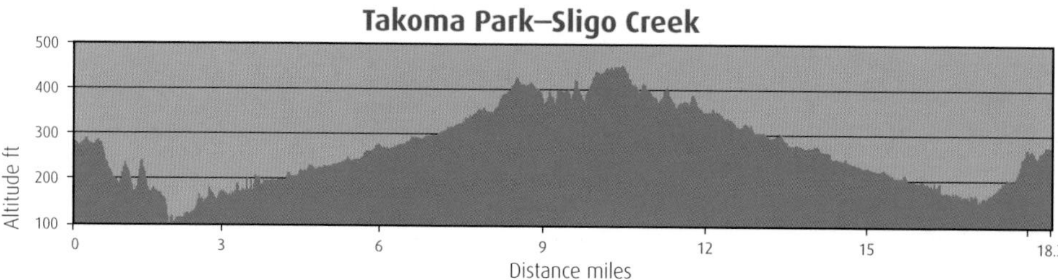

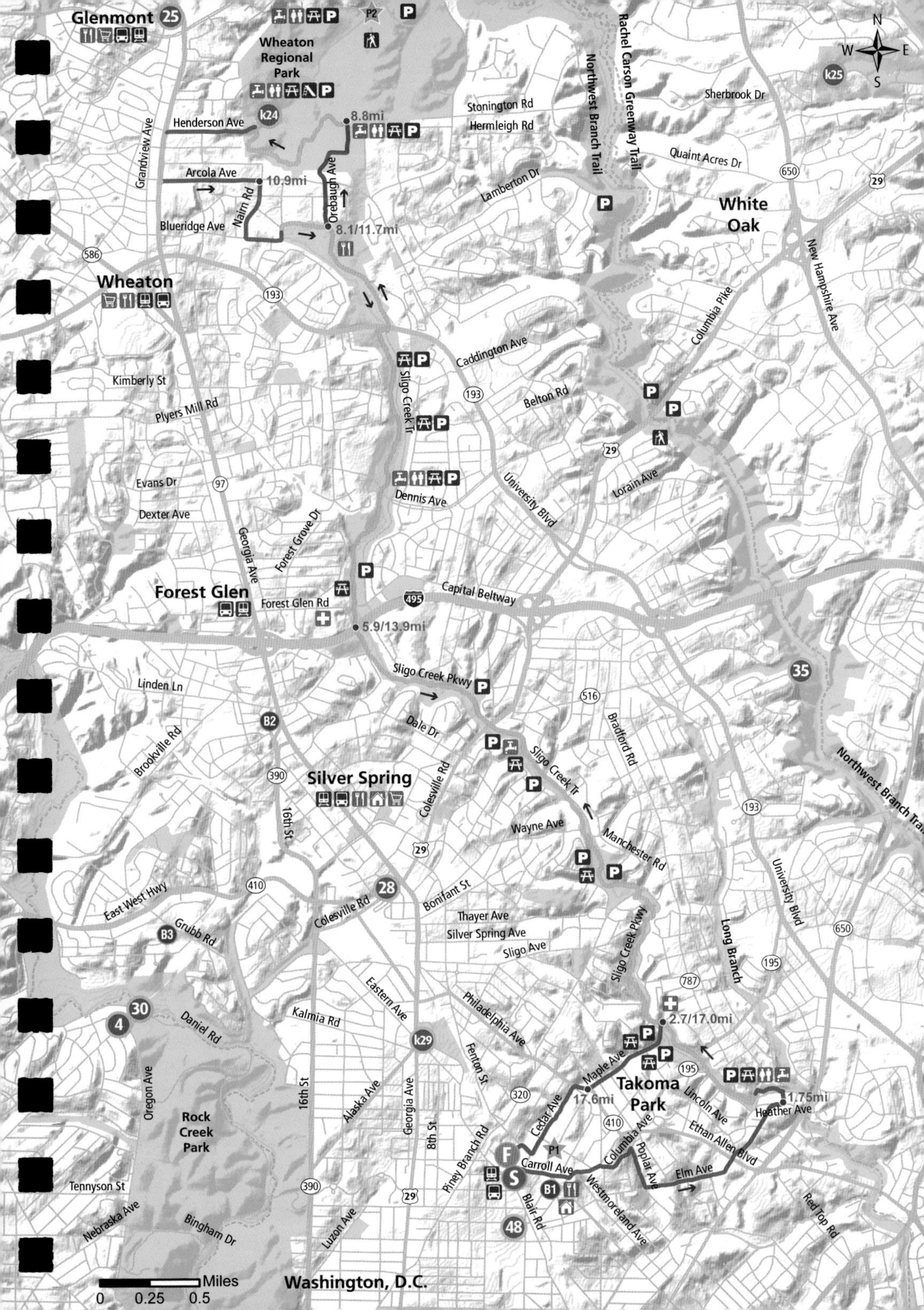

Glenmont
Wheaton Regional Park
Henderson Ave
Arcola Ave
10.9mi
8.8mi
Orebaugh Ave
Nairn Rd
Blueridge Ave
8.1/11.7mi
Grandview Ave
Stonington Rd
Hermleigh Rd
Northwest Branch Trail
Rachel Carson Greenway Trail
Sherbrook Dr
Quaint Acres Dr
Lamberton Dr
White Oak
Wheaton
New Hampshire Ave
Columbia Pike
Caddington Ave
Sligo Creek Tr
Kimberly St
Plyers Mill Rd
Belton Rd
Lorain Ave
University Blvd
Dennis Ave
Evans Dr
Dexter Ave
Forest Grove Dr
Georgia Ave
Forest Glen
Forest Glen Rd
Capital Beltway
5.9/13.9mi
Sligo Creek Pkwy
Linden Ln
Dale Dr
Bradford Rd
Brookville Rd
Silver Spring
Colesville Rd
16th St
Wayne Ave
Manchester Rd
Northwest Branch Trail
East West Hwy
Bonifant St
Thayer Ave
Silver Spring Ave
Sligo Ave
Grubb Rd
Long Branch
University Blvd
Daniel Rd
Kalmia Rd
Eastern Ave
Philadelphia Ave
2.7/17.0mi
Fenton St
Maple Ave
Takoma Park
Lincoln Ave
1.75mi
Heather Ave
17.6mi
Cedar Ave
Columbia Ave
Ethan Allen Blvd
Oregon Ave
Rock Creek Park
Alaska Ave
Georgia Ave
8th St
Piney Branch Rd
Carroll Ave
Poplar Ave
Elm Ave
Westmoreland Ave
Blair Rd
Red Top Rd
Tennyson St
Nebraska Ave
Bingham Dr
Luzon Ave
Miles
0
0.25
0.5
Washington, D.C.

Maryland: East and South

This region lies beyond the District of Columbia and extends northeasterly to the outskirts of Baltimore, easterly to Chesapeake Bay, and southerly into rural Maryland. Flatter overall than its respective counterparts in northern Virginia and northern Maryland, its selections can be grouped into two main categories: those traversing obsolete rail lines and those exploring landscapes defined by their relationship to surrounding waters. Read ahead, then roll on, to rides that run the gamut from couple's cruises to sunset loops to challenging half-day tours.

For a section covering such a broad area, the following 11 offerings are readily accessible. Three begin at Metro stops, two more can easily be reached by biking a short distance from terminal Metro stations, and the remaining six are either a mere half hour from downtown D.C. or located at a distance likely comparable to your workday commute.

The four counties here encompassed, Anne Arundel, Calvert, Charles, and Prince George's, trace their legacy to the arrival of British colonists in 1634, and are home to some of the oldest post-Native settlement in the United States. And while all of these routes encourage engagement with some layer of the area's rich past, it matters little whether each detailed historical opportunity strikes your fancy. The real beauty of these selections rests in the simple pleasure of the pedaling itself. If you like to bike, you'll savor this region as you have all the rest.

The suburban corridor between Washington, D.C. and Baltimore is densely populated, making good cycling difficult to find. As a result, courses there are specifically chosen to maximize safety without sacrificing enjoyment. Chances are you'll be surprised by what you find. Further to the southeast, the metropolis gives way to countryside and the landscape begins to resemble its younger self, before bicycles were born. Here, weathered tobacco barns populate rolling fields and farms, low-traffic roads link one tree-lined way to another, and speed suddenly makes no difference at all. Simply enjoy, and return with a friend.

Maryland: East and South

One of several fair-weather stream crossings along the NW Branch.

At a Glance

Distance 16.6 miles **Total Elevation** 625 feet

Terrain

Expect flat, primarily smooth rolling along the trails versus a few hills and a touch rougher riding on the roads. The gravel path leading down from Oakview's end (mile 11) to the NW Branch Trail is particularly steep. Don't hesitate to walk it.

Traffic

Take special care at mile 7.75, the Metzerott Road/University Avenue junction, and extra special care from miles nine to 10, along Adelphi Road.

How to Get There

Use the Green Line Metro to the West Hyattsville Station. If driving, aim for Ager Road off Queens Chapel Road (MD 500) not far beyond the eastern edge of the District.

Food and Drink

At ride's beginning and end near the Metro, and along Queen's Chapel, Hamilton Street, and Chillum Road.

Side Trip

Learn about the British (Naval) Invasion, or paddle along the Bladensburg Waterfront. Stop at the historic College Park Airport and Aviation Museum. Visit National Archives II. Picnic at Adelphi Mill.

Where to Bike Rating 

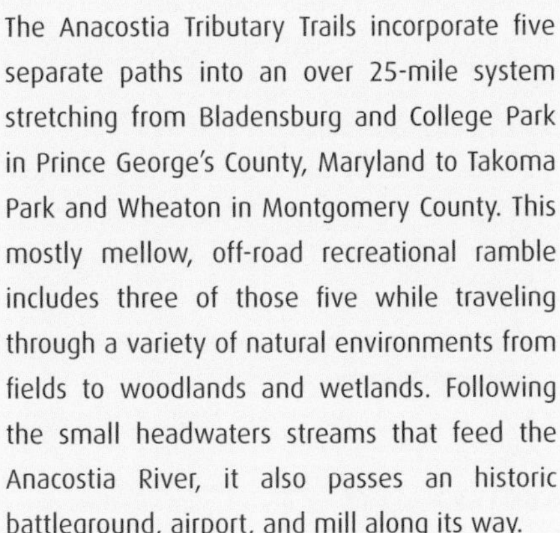

About...

The Anacostia Tributary Trails incorporate five separate paths into an over 25-mile system stretching from Bladensburg and College Park in Prince George's County, Maryland to Takoma Park and Wheaton in Montgomery County. This mostly mellow, off-road recreational ramble includes three of those five while traveling through a variety of natural environments from fields to woodlands and wetlands. Following the small headwaters streams that feed the Anacostia River, it also passes an historic battleground, airport, and mill along its way.

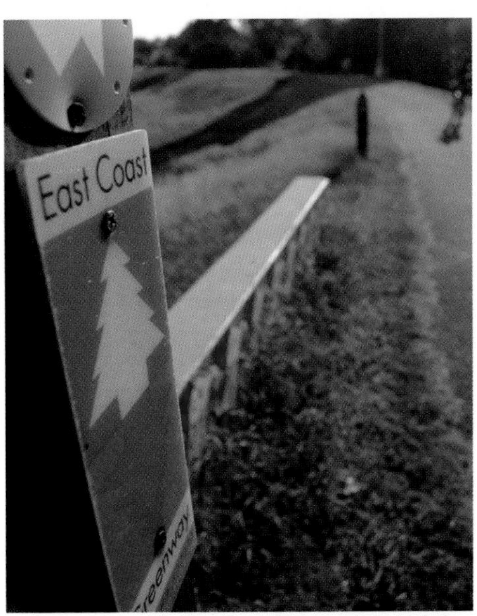

The East Coast Greenway links trails from Maine to Florida.

It's literally a minute off Metro and this ride has you cruising the Northwest Branch through flat greenspace toward Bladensburg. It was here, to your right, in 1814, where the British traded boats for boots and mounted their fiery march on Washington.

After another stretch of level, open pedaling beside the Northeast Branch, the trail ducks to shade before passing the perimeter of College Park Airport. Don't miss your unmarked turn to the Paint Branch. It brings you around the southern edge of Lake Artemesia toward the state's flagship university. Metzerott soon provides a quiet transition to this route's on-road portion, and after a busy crossing at University Boulevard, continue up a modest ascent on its bike lane past National Archives II, a second storehouse of important national documents. Then (see right) expect a mile of hilly, more hectic riding following your turn onto Adelphi. But, just as fast as it started, the traffic quiets and neighborhood streets poise you toward reengagement with the NW Branch. Here it flows through a deep ravine, and you'll begin to feel transported as you drop into its steeply wooded valley.

Continue onward now to Adelphi Mill on perhaps the day's loveliest section of trail and, all too soon, two fast, flat miles through parkland have brought you home.

An east-west tributary stream, and accompanying trail, would turn this ride into an easy, near traffic-free loop. Without the benefit of that pipe dream, however, the route is forced on-road. And while this way has been established for quite some time now, the roads on which it travels have only gotten busier. Much of its less than four miles is worry-free to be sure, but, as previously detailed, two rough sections do exist. The mile-long stretch along Adelphi tends to be heavily trafficked, and the steep gravel downhill connecting Oakview to the NW Branch is a doozy.

If you'd like to keep things more relaxed, continue straight on Metzerott just past mile nine instead of taking that right onto Adelphi. At New Hampshire, make your way carefully downhill by sidewalk if necessary, curving right as it connects with Piney Branch. Then use a sneaky little access ramp to join the NW Branch three-quarters of a mile above Adelphi Mill.

While Ride 35 has not been deemed kid-friendly in its entirety, it does include substantial sections which are entirely safe for family use.

Ride Log

0.0 Exit W Hyattsville Metro turnstiles to right. Access NW Branch Trail at far edge of right-hand parking lot. Set odometer and go left to begin.

1.9 Left onto NE Branch Trail.

2.4 Cross Decatur St to continue.

3.55 Stay right to continue around park's perimeter.

4.5 Stay right to continue on NE Branch Trail. Rest stop.

5.25 Left onto Paint Branch Trail.

5.35 Left to begin partial swing around Lake Artemesia.

5.6 Left to continue along Paint Branch Trail.

5.75 Another left to continue along PB Trail.

6.0 Bear right to continue.

A portion of Paint Branch near the University of Maryland.

6.45 Stay left on sidewalk over bridge to curl under and continue as trail makes its way on other side of creek.

7.25 Left on Metzerott.

7.75 Left onto University to continue right on Metzerott at light.

9.1 Right on Adelphi.

9.35 Cross Riggs.

10.1 Straight across New Hampshire Ave to immediate right onto Avenal.

10.4 As Avenal dead-ends use left-hand sidewalk to join Oakview.

11.05 Oakview ends at gravel path leading steeply downhill through woods.

11.3 Left onto NW Branch Trail.

13.3 Pass Adelphi Mill.

14.05 Cross University Blvd. Park. Bathrooms.

15.55 Left to Heurich Park.

16.15 Sligo Creek Trail junction.

16.3 Chillum Community Park.

16.6 Return to W Hyattsville Metro.

P1 British Invasion of 1814
P2 College Park Airport and Aviation Museum
P3 National Archives II
P4 Feeling like a shortcut?
P5 Adelphi Mill

B1 Arrow Bicycle, 5108 Baltimore Ave
B2 College Park Bicycle, 4360 Knox Rd
B3 Proteus Bicycles, 9217 Baltimore Ave
B4 REI, 9801 Rhode Island Ave
B5 Mt Rainier Bike Co-op, 3601 Bunker Hill Rd

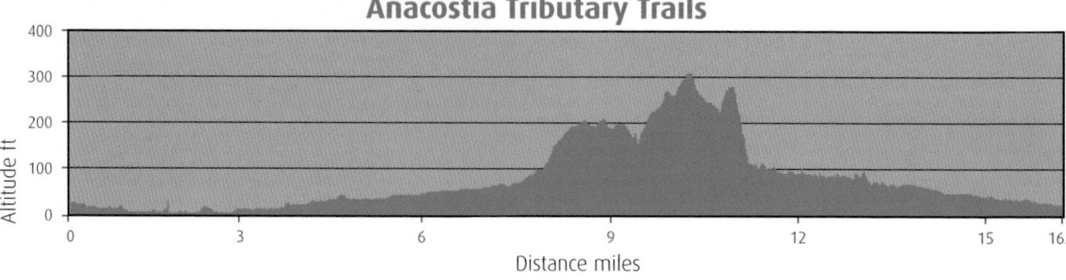

N
W
E
S
Northwest Branch
Royal Rd
Green Forest Dr
95
495
Cherry Hill Rd
Oakview Dr
11.3mi
10.4mi
Avenel Rd
516
Paint Branch
Baltimore Ave
Lackawanna St
B4
Adelphi Rd
New Hampshire Ave
Paint Branch Trail
B3
Rhode Island Ave
51st Ave
193
Riggs Rd
Metzerott Rd
7.75mi
P4
P3
320
650
Northwest Branch Tr
Quebec St
P5
Merrimac Dr
University Blvd
University of Maryland
Paint Branch Dr
58th Ave
55th Ave
Berwyn Rd
Cool Spring Rd
195
212
Union Dr
Paint Branch Tr
k30
Indian Creek Trail
14.0mi
Park Dr
Campus Dr
Hannon St
24th Ave
25th Ave
34
Erskine St
Knox Rd
B2
College Ave
Wells Pky
College Park
P2
Paint Branch Pky
5.35mi
Banning Pl
Adelphi Rd
College Heights Dr
410
Amherst Rd
Red Top Rd
Toledo Rd
River Rd
8th Ave
Riggs Rd
East-West Hwy
Sheridan St
Somerset Rd
Chillum
20th Ave
500
Ravenswood Rd
Riverdale Rd
Sargent Rd
Queens Chapel Rd
42nd Ave
Oglethorpe St
Ager Rd
54th Ave
16.15mi
41st Ave
Baltimore Ave
Taylor Rd
Northwest Branch Tr
Tanglewood Dr
501
Lafayette Pl
Jefferson St
208
Galloway St
F
S
P
Carters Ln
B1
Gallatin St
Arundel Rd
Rhode Island Ave
Burlington Rd
Decatur St
Sargent Rd
Emerson St
29th St
31st St
34th St
37th St
1.9mi
Alt
Kenilworth Ave
48
12th St
13th Pl
18th St
Eastern Ave
Mt Rainier
P1
54th St
56th Ave
57th Ave
295
B5
450
Northeast Washington, D.C.
S Dakota Ave
26th St
28th St
Bladensburg Waterfront Park
201
202
Miles
0
0.25
0.5
0.75
1
1.25
1.5
1.75
2

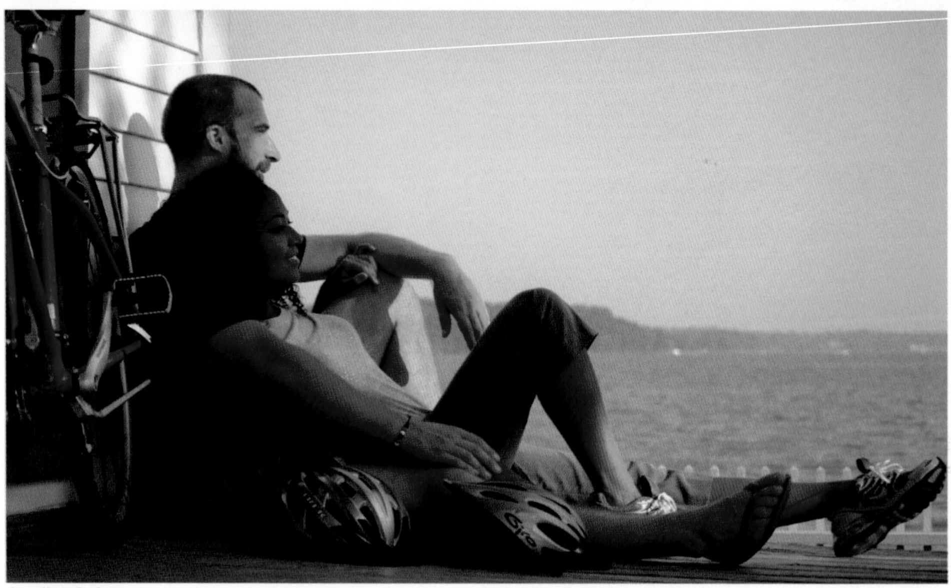

Don't rush this one.

At a Glance

Distance 6.5 miles **Total Elevation** 300 feet

Terrain

This ride begins on a stretch of crushed shells, and there's a short gravel and grass path to access the old lighthouse on the Potomac's Virginia side, but in between is smooth, wide multi-use path. Expect healthy climbs both ways to get up on the bridge's main expanse.

Traffic

Will be whooshing by up on the bridge. No worries, though, you'll be safely sequestered on your own mini-Beltway. Do expect other bicyclists, runners, and walkers.

How to Get There

Metro's a long shot this time, but if you insist, take its Green Line to Congress Heights, link up to nearby Ride 46 and follow it directly here. Want to play it cool? Drive the Beltway to Woodrow Wilson Bridge and let all those National Harbor signs guide you in, or jump on a bus destined specifically for the harbor at the Green Line's Branch Avenue station.

Food and Drink

There's an abundance of options all over National Harbor.

Side Trip

Take the path leading through the viaduct all the way uphill away from National Harbor on this ride's Maryland side (just beyond the crushed shell trail), go left briefly on Oxon Hill Road and left again to enjoy the goings-on at Oxon Hill Farm and its super-secret (and sadly, too short) bike trail.

Links to   

Where to Bike Rating 

About...

This short out-and-back begins and ends in fresh-faced National Harbor and takes in easily-forgotten Jones Point, twice traversing a truly awesome expanse of bridge. Along the way, you'll have the benefit of unimpeded views up and down the Potomac and the privilege of visiting the District's southernmost boundary stone at its 220-year old seat beside the purportedly oldest surviving inland lighthouse in the United States.

The Awakening at National Harbor.

Your very own bike highway.

This ride's first stretch curves around National Harbor's North Cove over a bed of crushed shells. Nearing a half-mile you meet the trail proper. It's an impressive sight, 12-feet wide, extending unbroken along Smoot's Cove before winding up and onto the Woodrow Wilson Bridge's bicycle/pedestrian deck positioned over the beltway on Rosalie Island.

There you'll enter a landscaped environment which acts as a sort of gateway to Maryland's Prince George's County. Read the well-presented natural and historical signs as cars stream below.

Then, continue down a switchback ramp to a seamless flow along the entire north side of the bridge. You'll climb, then descend, with the opportunity to rest, appreciate the panorama and read up a little more on pertinent D.C. and Virginia history.

Follow the ramp down the bridge's south side straight to your turnoff at picnic-worthy Jones Point Park. Here are yet more views, and, before retracing, don't forget to have a peek at the historical markers and boundary stone beside the old disused lighthouse at water's edge.

Ride Log

A sailboat fronts the WW Bridge and the Masonic National Memorial.

0.0 Start along National Harbor's northernmost waterfront where crushed shell trail begins near bicycle racks outside Pier House Restaurant.

.45 Bear left as trail widens and becomes asphalt.

1.3 Woodrow Wilson tribute.

1.9 District of Columbia informational sign.

2.1 Virginia informational sign.

2.65 First of two successive lefts takes you down ramp on bridge's other side. Engage Mt Vernon Trail.

2.85 Continue straight to Jones Point Park rather than turning under bridge.

3.1 Right to lighthouse on short stretch of gravel/grass.

3.3 Arrive at lighthouse with view of National Harbor. Begin retracing path.

6.1 Bear right to National Harbor. Prepare for shell trail.

6.5 Dismount, grab a bite, and have a look around.

Expect great views above the Potomac.

P *P1* The Awakening
P2 Jones Point Lighthouse
P3 D.C.'s southernmost boundary stone

B *B1* Big Wheel Bikes, 2 Prince St
B2 Velocity Bike Cooperative, 204 S Union St
BR *BR1* Bike and Roll Alexandria, One Wales Alley

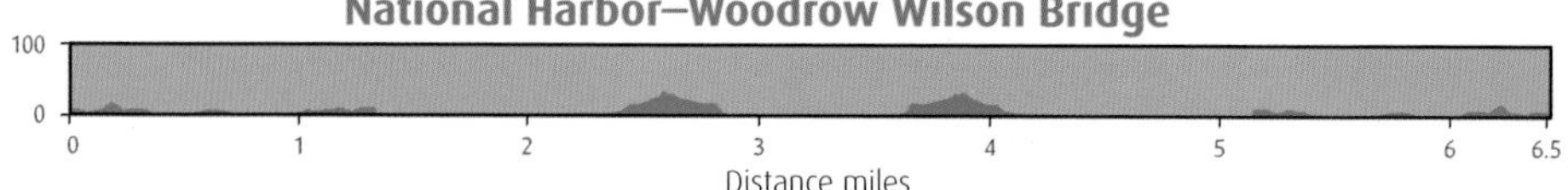

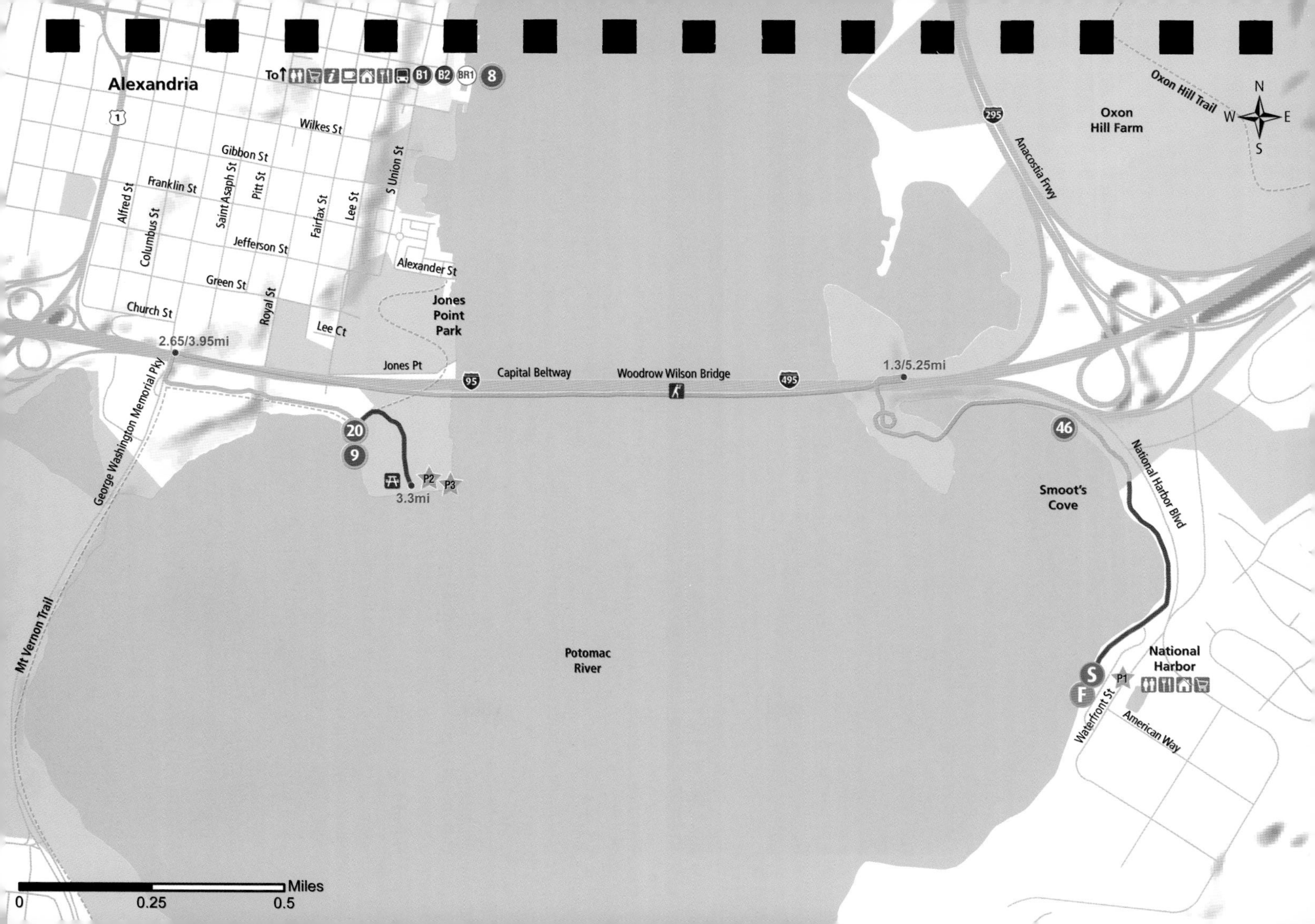

Alexandria
To
B1
B2
BR1
8
Wilkes St
Gibbon St
Franklin St
Saint Asaph St
Pitt St
Alfred St
Columbus St
Fairfax St
Lee St
S Union St
Jefferson St
Alexander St
Green St
Royal St
Church St
Lee Ct
Jones Point Park
2.65/3.95mi
Jones Pt
95
Capital Beltway
Woodrow Wilson Bridge
495
1.3/5.25mi
20
9
P2
P3
3.3mi
George Washington Memorial Pky
46
Smoot's Cove
National Harbor Blvd
Oxon Hill Trail
Oxon Hill Farm
295
Anacostia Frwy
N
W
E
S
Potomac River
Mt Vernon Trail
National Harbor
P1
S
F
Waterfront St
American Way
Miles
0
0.25
0.5

One last check of the map before lift-off.

At a Glance

Distance 23.0 miles **Total Elevation** 1460 feet

Terrain

Narrow country roads traverse moderately rolling hills.

Traffic

Minimal on most roads, with the propensity for a bit more along Duley Station and North Keys.

How to Get There

Use exit 11A off the Beltway heading south and east onto Pennsylvania Avenue (MD 4). Go right on Woodward Avenue (MD 223) continuing straight as it becomes Rosaryville Road. Cross MD 301 onto Old Indian Head Road and immediately bear right onto Duley Station Road. Look to park at Mattaponi Elementary School or Holy Rosary Church across the road.

Food and Drink

Stop at the country store in Croom just before St. Thomas Church.

Side Trip

Take the short, self-guided Chesapeake Bay Critical Area Tour connecting Merkle Wildlife Sanctuary with the Jug Bay Natural Area at Patuxent River Park. Be sure to check open and closing hours.

Where to Bike Rating 

About...

It's nice to know this variation of a classic, easy-going ramble through the gently undulating fields, farms, and preserves of Prince George's County manages to remain relatively unchanged decades past its creation. Getting here is still easy, the miles you travel aren't indicative of how far you've gone, and once you've arrived, the ride offers a chance to bone up on Chesapeake Bay area history, gear down from the pace of the city, and cruise the back roads to your heart's content.

Children, dogs, CYCLISTS and me.

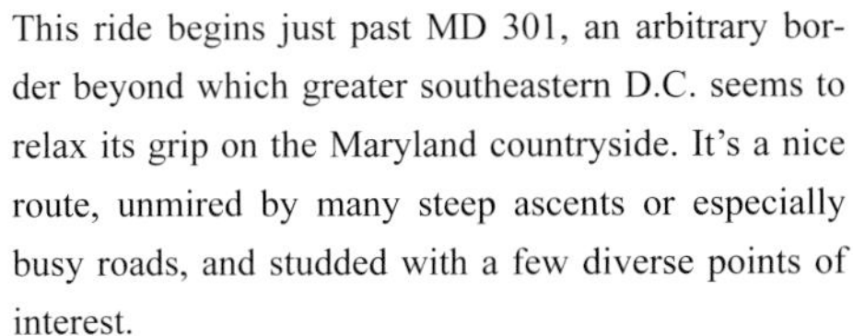

This ride begins just past MD 301, an arbitrary border beyond which greater southeastern D.C. seems to relax its grip on the Maryland countryside. It's a nice route, unmired by many steep ascents or especially busy roads, and studded with a few diverse points of interest.

St. Thomas Church arrives in a flash after a fast first three miles. It has survived since 1745 and features a memorial to former rector Thomas John Claggett, the first bishop of the United States Episcopal Church to have been consecrated on American soil. A few members of Maryland's founding families, Bowies and Calverts among them, are buried in the adjoining graveyard.

A gliding descent then brings you to seemingly forgotten Fenno Road and briefly back up to this ride's namesake, the largest wintering ground for Canada geese on the western shore of Chesapeake Bay. Named after Edgar Merkle, a successful D.C. publisher and conservationist, it was he who introduced a handful of breeding pairs here along the Patuxent River in the early 1930s. Both the flock and the farm grew and in 1970 Merkle sold his land to the state. The sanctuary now totals 1,670 acres and includes an observation tower, an education program, and hiking trails.

It sits directly south of the Jug Bay Natural Area and both properties are linked by a bikeable four-mile route featuring informational displays, scenic overlooks, and a 1000-foot bridge crossing Mattaponi Creek. You may encounter as many as 5000 geese here in December and January, and though they're gone by early March, you still stand a good chance of seeing groundhogs, red fox, white-tailed deer, osprey, hummingbirds, songbirds, and a select few wading birds inside the park's extensive network of woods, fields, and wetlands.

The route's next stop at old Nottingham could easily pass undetected were it not for a couple of roadside historical panels. Formerly a thriving port, the site was one of several places the British occupied as they prepared for their assault on Washington in August of 1814. Engage your imagination before pedaling on. Plenty of riding remains, along with the space and peace to sit back and enjoy it. Expect some hills, but nothing near enough to break your rolling reverie.

Ride Log

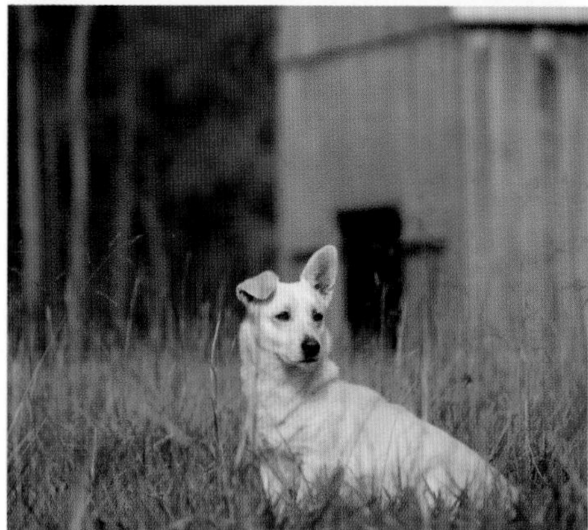

Cocking an ear to the wind outside Nottingham.

A relief of Bishop Thomas J. Claggett at St Thomas Church.

0.0 Begin by going right out of Mattaponi Elementary School parking lot and taking an immediate left onto Duley Station Rd.

0.35 Stay right to remain on Duley Station.

2.65 Right onto Croom Rd (MD 382). Food.

3.0 Left onto St Thomas Church Rd (becomes Fenno Rd).

5.9 Left onto Merkle Rd.

6.2 Bear right toward Merkle Wildlife Sanctuary visitor center.

7.25 Bear right to exit.

7.7 Left onto Fenno Rd.

8.6 Left onto Nottingham Rd.

9.75 Bear right onto Tanyard Rd.

11.6 Go straight across Croom Rd onto Brooks Chapel Rd.

12.1 Bear left onto Baden Naylor Rd.

12.9 Right onto Molly Berry Rd.

14.3 Left onto Martin Rd.

16.5 Right onto N Key Rd.

18.4 Left onto Molly Berry Rd.

19.5 Left on Van Brady Rd.

22.2 Bear right at Van Brady and Van Brady (no joke).

22.4 Right onto Old Indian Head Rd.

22.6 Right onto Cheltenham Rd.

23.0 Left onto Duley Station Rd to finish at Mattaponi Elementary.

P1 St Thomas Episcopal Church
P2 Chesapeake Bay Critical Area Tour
P3 Former location of Nottingham, MD

Merkle Wildlife Sanctuary

Altitude ft: 0, 100, 200, 300

Distance miles: 0, 2, 4, 6, 8, 10, 12, 14, 16, 18, 20, 22, 23.0

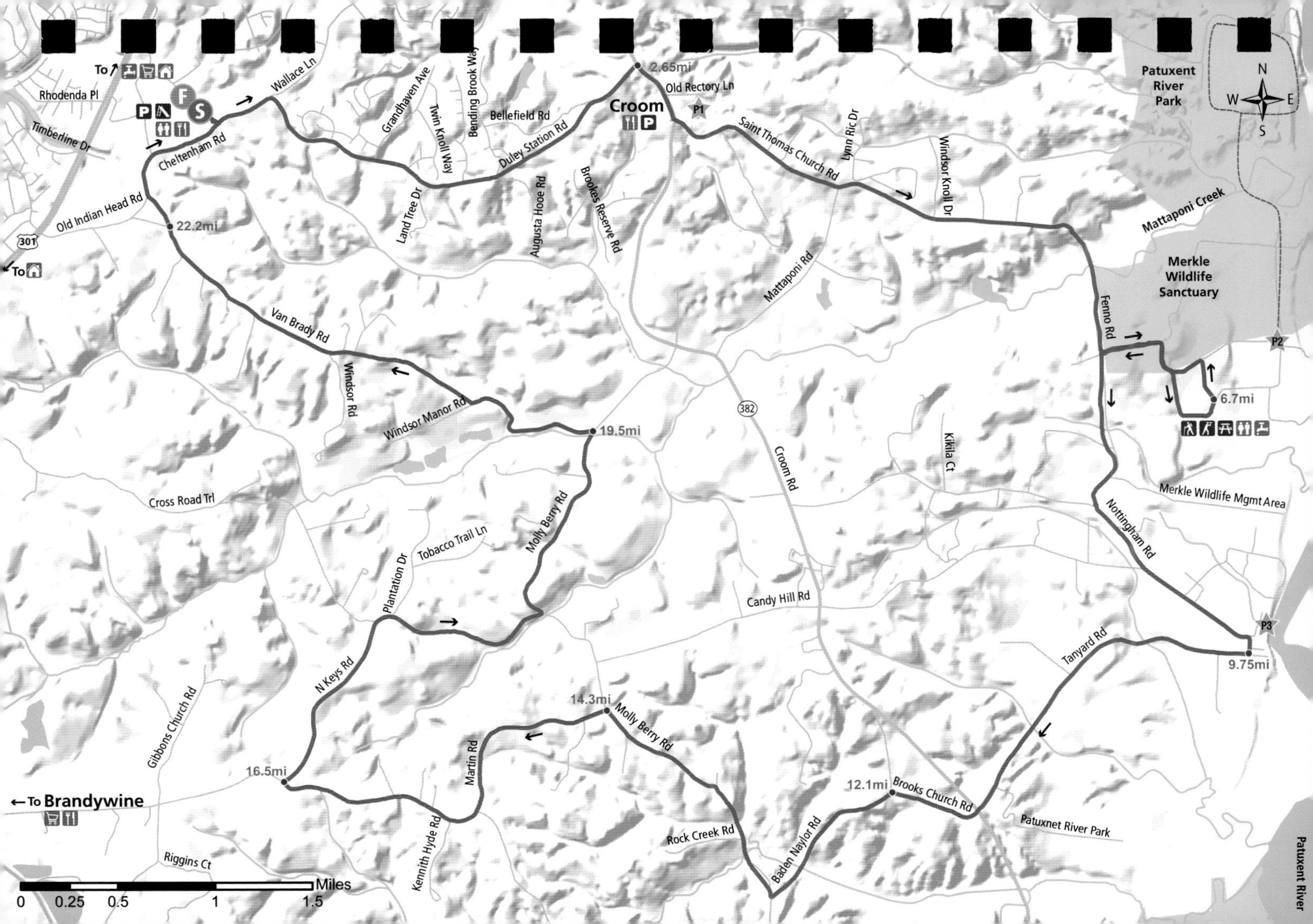

Patuxent River Park
N
E
S
W
Mattaponi Creek
Merkle Wildlife Sanctuary
P2
6.7mi
Fenno Rd
Merkle Wildlife Mgmt Area
Nottingham Rd
P3
9.75mi
Patuxent River
Tanyard Rd
Patuxnet River Park
Brooks Church Rd
12.1mi
Baden Naylor Rd
Rock Creek Rd
Molly Berry Rd
14.3mi
Martin Rd
Kennith Hyde Rd
16.5mi
N Keys Rd
Plantation Dr
Tobacco Trail Ln
Molly Berry Rd
19.5mi
Windsor Manor Rd
Windsor Rd
Van Brady Rd
22.2mi
Old Indian Head Rd
Cheltenham Rd
Wallace Ln
Grandhaven Ave
Twin Knoll Way
Bending Brook Way
Bellefield Rd
Land Tree Dr
Augusta Hooe Rd
Duley Station Rd
Brookes Reserve Rd
Croom
2.65mi
Old Rectory Ln
P1
Saint Thomas Church Rd
Lynn Ric Dr
Windsor Knoll Dr
Mattaponi Rd
Kikila Ct
Croom Rd
382
Candy Hill Rd
Cross Road Trl
Gibbons Church Rd
Riggins Ct
To Brandywine
Rhodenda Pl
Timberline Dr
301
To
To
F
S
Miles
0
0.25
0.5
1
1.5

Don't be surprised if you see these guys on the trail someday.

At a Glance

Distance 11.4 miles **Total Elevation** 400 feet

Terrain

Paved and flat aside from a few brief inclines.

Traffic

Though brief parts of this trail are shared with motorized vehicles, the possibility is rare, cautionary signs are prevalent, and car and truck speeds are extremely slow.

How to Get There

Use exits 19 or 20 off the Beltway to access the John Hanson Highway (U.S. 50) and Annapolis Road (MD 450), respectively. If using U.S. 50, exit at MLK, Jr. Highway (MD 704) and connect to Annapolis Road. The ride begins just north at Seltzer Street. Park there, or better yet, take Annapolis Road to a left on Glenn Dale Road. Another left at its junction with Electric Avenue brings you to a lot near mile one of the trail.

Food and Drink

Options run the gamut at the junction of Annapolis Road and MLK, Jr. Highway.

Side Trip

Turn right on Bell Station Road near mile one-and-a-half. Marietta Mansion sits to your right just over a half-mile distant. A second option offers signposted direction to Old Bowie around mile five.

Links to 53

Where to Bike Rating

About...

Despite its cumbersome official name, the Washington, Baltimore, & Annapolis Trail is actually a modest affair, albeit one with a colorful history and a potentially lengthened future. Once, state-of-the-art electric trains ran everybody (and everything) from commuters to bootlegged whiskey along this route at up to 70 mph. Today, in lieu of a bridge over the Patuxent River which will eventually provide connection to a sister section in Anne Arundel County, it still manages to offer pleasant, easy-going spinning from end to end.

Side trips are available.

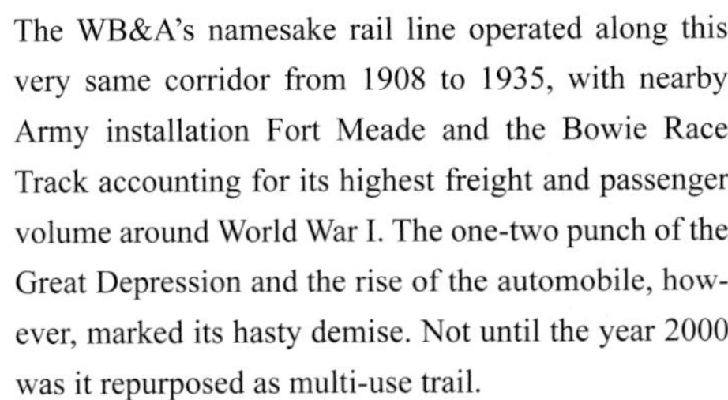

The WB&A's namesake rail line operated along this very same corridor from 1908 to 1935, with nearby Army installation Fort Meade and the Bowie Race Track accounting for its highest freight and passenger volume around World War I. The one-two punch of the Great Depression and the rise of the automobile, however, marked its hasty demise. Not until the year 2000 was it repurposed as multi-use trail.

Feel free, of course, to begin your ride wherever you like. Some will choose the trail's eastern end off Race Track Road, others the aforementioned parking area just shy of mile one.

The ride log's first mile crosses Folly Branch before running alongside Electric Avenue, soon arriving at a small pond and surrounding marsh. Continue onward after strolling the wooden boardwalk and perusing the informational kiosk. Then cross Glenn Dale Boulevard, jogging left immediately thereafter.

First, though, (if you've arrived prior to its planned demolition) pause to glimpse the cluster of abandoned buildings, pointed water tower, and tall red-brick incinerator to your right. These are the rather eerie ruins of Glenn Dale Hospital, a former tuberculosis sanitarium.

Now continue straight as a rail line past another marshy area, beyond Glenn Dale Splash Park (family fun during those hot, summer rides) and through the first of the route's two corrugated metal tunnels. Without much discernible change aside from a brief bit of shared road and some familiar backyard views, the trail then begins a quiet cut through suburbs for its next three miles.

After passing Temptation Horse Farm and bridging Laurel Bowie Road, a final section runs through dense woods. Don't let the popping noises (or the warning sign) make you flinch. That's just the members of the Berwyn Rod & Gun Club having fun behind the wall to your left.

End a short way ahead. And if you wish, before heading back, check out the Patuxent River further down the trail a few tenths.

Ride Log

0.0 Start at milepost zero just off Rt 450 (MD 450) near its junction with MLK Jr Hwy (MD 704).

0.9 Historical information. Bathrooms.

1.0 Left after crossing Glen Dale Rd.

A mailbox cocks its rusty head along the route.

P1 Glenn Dale Hospital ruins
P2 Marietta Manor
P3 Side trip to Old Bowie
P4 Patuxent River

B1 A & M Cycle, 13002 9th St

1.6 Cross Bell Station Rd.

1.75 Pass Glen Dale Splash Park.

3.25 Hit blacktop. Stay left in painted lane.

3.4 Jog left briefly uphill. Well-signposted.

5.0 Look for sign indicating 1.1 mile side-trip to Old Bowie.

5.65 Turnaround to retrace. Bathrooms and parking available

11.4 Return.

Close-up of mile-marker 0.0.

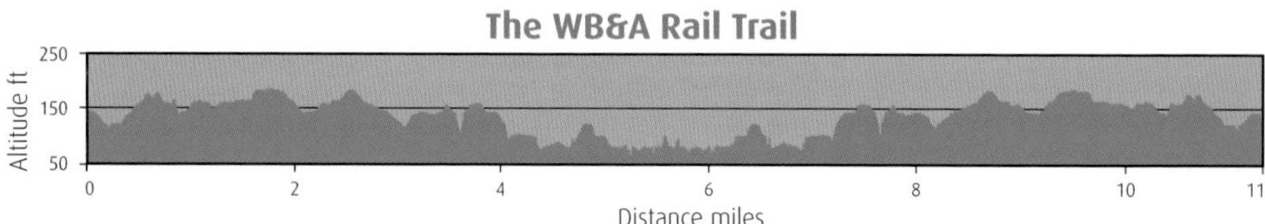

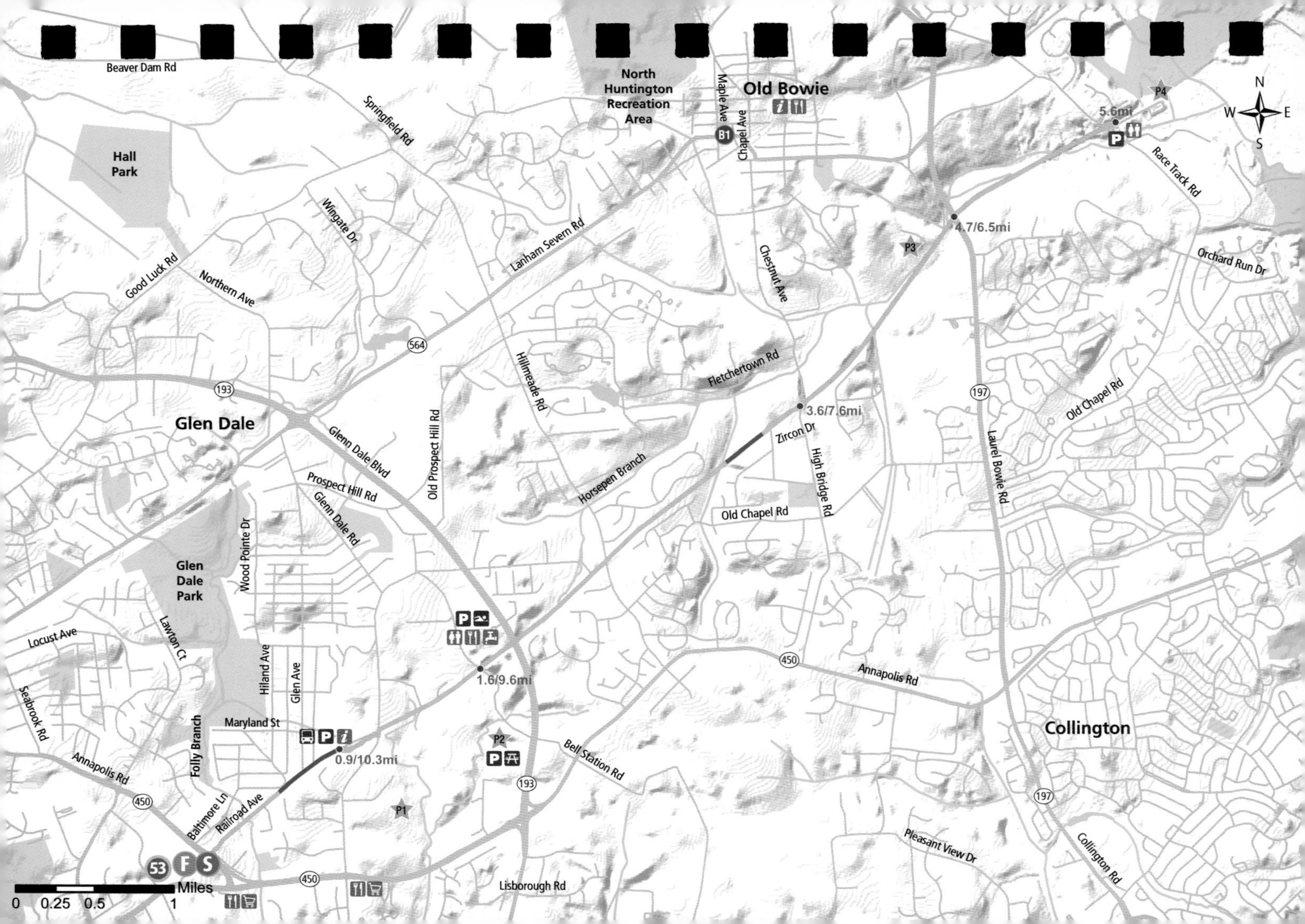

Old Bowie
North Huntington Recreation Area
Hall Park
Glen Dale
Glen Dale Park
Collington
Beaver Dam Rd
Springfield Rd
Maple Ave
Chapel Ave
Chestnut Ave
Wingate Dr
Lanham Severn Rd
Good Luck Rd
Northern Ave
564
193
197
450
Hillmeade Rd
Fletchertown Rd
Old Prospect Hill Rd
Glenn Dale Blvd
Prospect Hill Rd
Glenn Dale Rd
Horsepen Branch
Zircon Dr
High Bridge Rd
Old Chapel Rd
Laurel Bowie Rd
Orchard Run Dr
Race Track Rd
Wood Pointe Dr
Locust Ave
Lawton Ct
Hiland Ave
Glen Ave
Seabrook Rd
Maryland St
Folly Branch
Annapolis Rd
Baltimore Ln
Railroad Ave
Bell Station Rd
Pleasant View Dr
Lisborough Rd
Collington Rd
B1
P1
P2
P3
P4
5.6mi
4.7/6.5mi
3.6/7.6mi
1.6/9.6mi
0.9/10.3mi
53
F
S
N
E
S
W
0
0.25
0.5
1
Miles

The wheels and underbelly of a 25-ton Rodman Gun still located at Fort Foote.

At a Glance

Distance 35.0 miles **Total Elevation** 1425 feet

Terrain

Smooth, flat roads much of the way, though Temple Hill and Oxon Hill demand some climbing (go figure), as does Fort Washington Road before entering and upon leaving the park.

Traffic

Heavy along Allentown Road (MD 337), especially at its intersection with Branch Avenue (MD 5). Livingston Road is narrow and can also be busy.

How to Get There

Take the Green Line Metro to its southernmost stop at Branch Avenue. If driving, use the Beltway to exit 7 and Branch Avenue (MD 5), then take an immediate right onto Auth Road. A left at the traffic circle and you're ready to park. An alternate start has you eliminating this ride's busier first and last 4.3 miles, parking off Temple Hill Road, and beginning at the Henson Creek Trail's eastern end.

Food and Drink

Along Allentown Road and at the corner of Oxon Hill and Livingston roads.

Side Trip

Check out the 18th century buildings that make up the Broad Creek Historic District off Livingston Road. And bring lunch, lounge, and take some time to wander Fort Washington.

Links to 49

Where to Bike Rating

About...

Within 20 minutes of the District, this winning ride takes advantage of the best tools the area has to offer its cyclists. Beginning with a boost from Metro and utilizing six miles of sequestered stream valley trail, it manages to link two unique-to-D.C. destinations using portions of the Potomac Heritage Trail On-Road Bicycle Route. Bikes on trains, safe paths, and a scenic byway connecting 19th century fortifications? This pleasant peddle through Prince George's County flat-out gets you there.

Seven cannon carriages positioned over the Potomac.

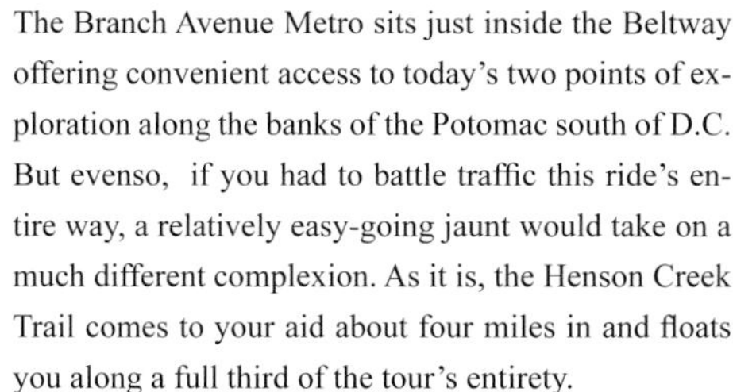

The Branch Avenue Metro sits just inside the Beltway offering convenient access to today's two points of exploration along the banks of the Potomac south of D.C. But evenso, if you had to battle traffic this ride's entire way, a relatively easy-going jaunt would take on a much different complexion. As it is, the Henson Creek Trail comes to your aid about four miles in and floats you along a full third of the tour's entirety.

Your most hectic miles here will occur on the stretches along Allentown Road (MD 337), a busy four-lane not exactly built for biking. Use the sidewalk if you need to, but it's best to put your brights on (clothes and lights) and command the given space. Take special care at the Branch Avenue (MD 5) underpass and in just a few minutes you're moving through residential neighborhoods on the way into a stream valley. A steady drop continues as you engage the trail and follow its gentle grade downstream through suburban woods and alongside lively, little Henson Creek.

The ride's first ascent in some time takes you to Oxon Hill Road where a steep, second uphill awaits, and just that fast, another residential stretch has you poised to enter Fort Foote. It's off the road and through the woods a short way, but worth a look. Constructed during the Civil War, its purpose was to close the ring of defenses then encircling Washington and defend the city from naval attack. As no such assault occurred, it was retired without ever having fired a shot. Two 25-ton Rodman Guns remain here though. It took hundreds of soldiers to get them up the bluff, and one supposes a little too much effort to move them along once the Confederacy disbanded.

The majority of the way onward toward Fort Washington is flat and fast, and it's always a bit of a shock encountering this large, imposing ruin in such lovely surroundings. The impressive structure has commanded its inspiring view since 1809 and remains the only permanent fortification built to defend a water approach to the nation's capital. Lock your bike up and have a look around, retracing your way back to Metro as your whims would have you.

Ride Log

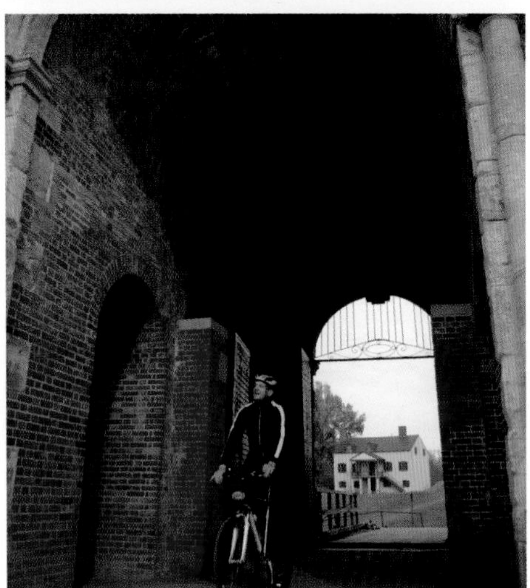

Riding through the entrance to Fort Washington.

0.0 Exit left from turnstiles, set odometer at gates, and head straight using crosswalk to access Metro car entrance road swinging left then right to exit the parking area.
0.15 Turn left using upcoming roundabout to continue straight on Auth Rd.
1.5 Right onto Allentown Rd (MD 337).
2.65 Right onto Brinkley Rd.
3.7 Right onto Temple Hill Rd.
4.3 Left to access trail at Henson Creek Neighborhood Park.
6.75 Cross Bock jogging left then right to continue.
7.0 Continue straight on maintenance road and through parking lot of Tucker Park to a left on Tucker Rd.
7.55 Right on Ferguson Ln to a left past community center. Re-engage trail at edge of parking lot.
10.2 Right on Oxon Hill Rd to an immediate left on Ft Foote Rd.
11.8 Ft Foote to left briefly through woods.
12.5 Right on Loughran Rd.
13.6 Left on Ft Foote Rd.
14.4 Right on Oxon Hill Rd.
14.9 Right onto Livingston Rd.
16.0 Right onto Ft Washington Rd.
17.2 Use roundabout to continue straight.
19.0 Enter Ft Washington curving way right then left toward fort and visitor's center.
19.7 Entrance walkway.
20.3 Exit Ft Washington. Retracing way to Metro minus Ft Foote departure.
23.3 Left onto Livingston.
24.4 Left on Oxon Hill Rd.
24.9 Right to return to Henson Creek Trail.
30.6 End Henson Trail. Right onto Temple Hill Rd.
31.3 Left onto Brinkley Rd.
32.4 Left onto Allentown Rd (MD 337).
33.5 Left onto Auth Rd.
35.0 Finish at Metro gates.

P1 Rosecroft Raceway
P2 Ft Foote
P3 Broad Creek Historic District
P4 Ft Washington

B1 Revolution Cycles City Hub, 220 20th Street South, Arlington
B2 Sports Authority, 3701 Jefferson Davis Hwy, Unit 3, Alexandria
B3 Wheel Nuts, 302 Montgomery St, Alexandria
B4 Big Wheel Bikes, 2 Prince St, Alexandria
B5 Velocity Bicycle Cooperative, 204 S Union St, Alexandria
BR1 Bike and Roll Alexandria, One Wales Alley

Henson Creek–Fort Washington

Altitude ft: 0, 100, 200, 300
Distance miles: 0, 5, 10, 15, 20, 25, 30, 35.0

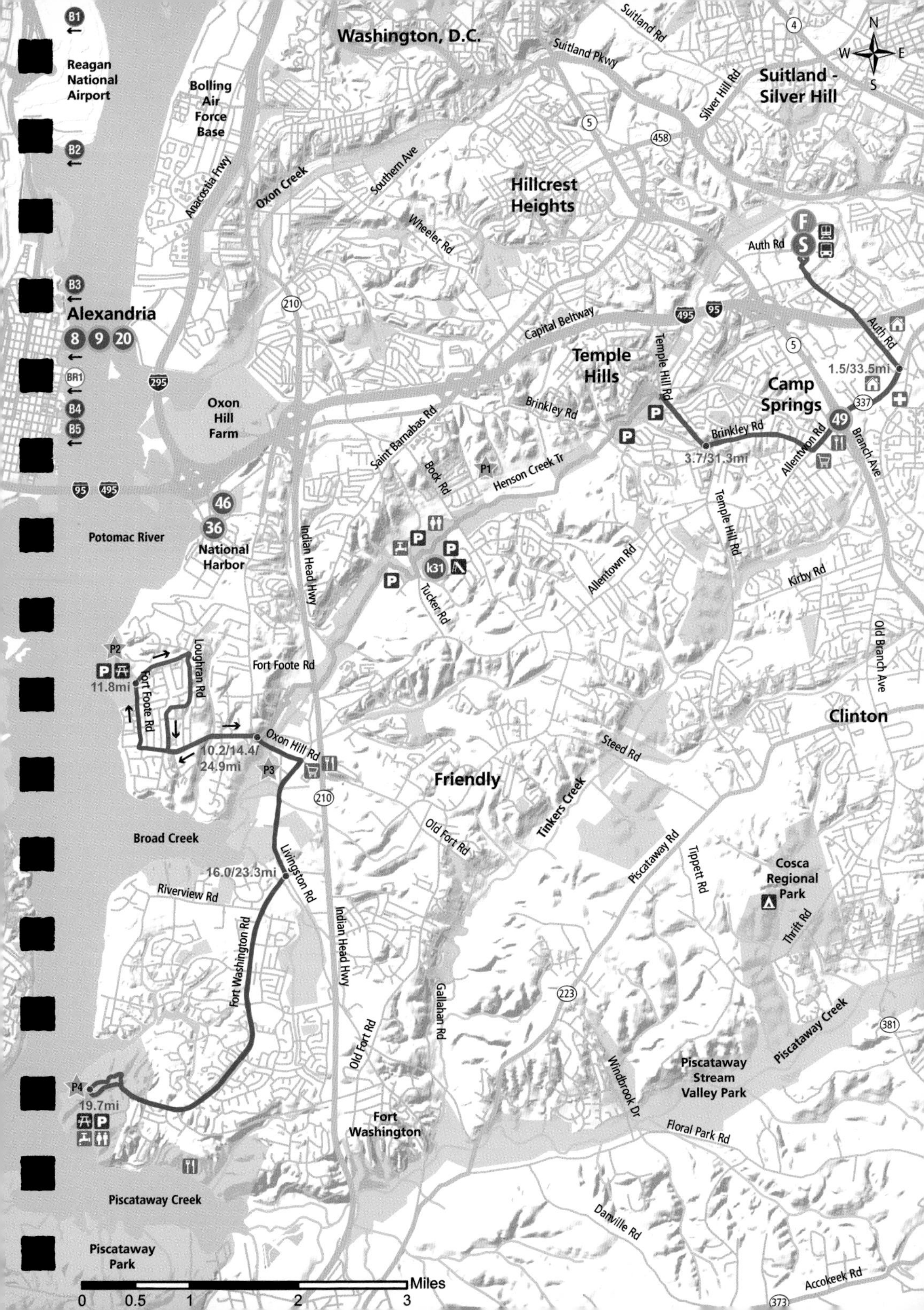

Washington, D.C.
Reagan National Airport
Bolling Air Force Base
Suitland - Silver Hill
Hillcrest Heights
Temple Hills
Camp Springs
Alexandria
Oxon Hill Farm
National Harbor
Potomac River
Friendly
Clinton
Broad Creek
Cosca Regional Park
Piscataway Stream Valley Park
Fort Washington
Piscataway Creek
Piscataway Park
Suitland Rd
Suitland Pkwy
Silver Hill Rd
Southern Ave
Oxon Creek
Anacostia Frwy
Wheeler Rd
Auth Rd
Capital Beltway
Temple Hill Rd
Brinkley Rd
Saint Barnabas Rd
Bock Rd
Henson Creek Tr
Allentown Rd
Branch Ave
Indian Head Hwy
Tucker Rd
Kirby Rd
Old Branch Ave
Fort Foote Rd
Loughran Rd
Oxon Hill Rd
Steed Rd
Tinkers Creek
Old Fort Rd
Piscataway Rd
Tippett Rd
Thrift Rd
Livingston Rd
Riverview Rd
Fort Washington Rd
Gallahan Rd
Windbrook Dr
Floral Park Rd
Danville Rd
Accokeek Rd
1.5/33.5mi
3.7/31.3mi
11.8mi
10.2/14.4/24.9mi
16.0/23.3mi
19.7mi
P1
P2
P3
P4
Miles
0 0.5 1 2 3

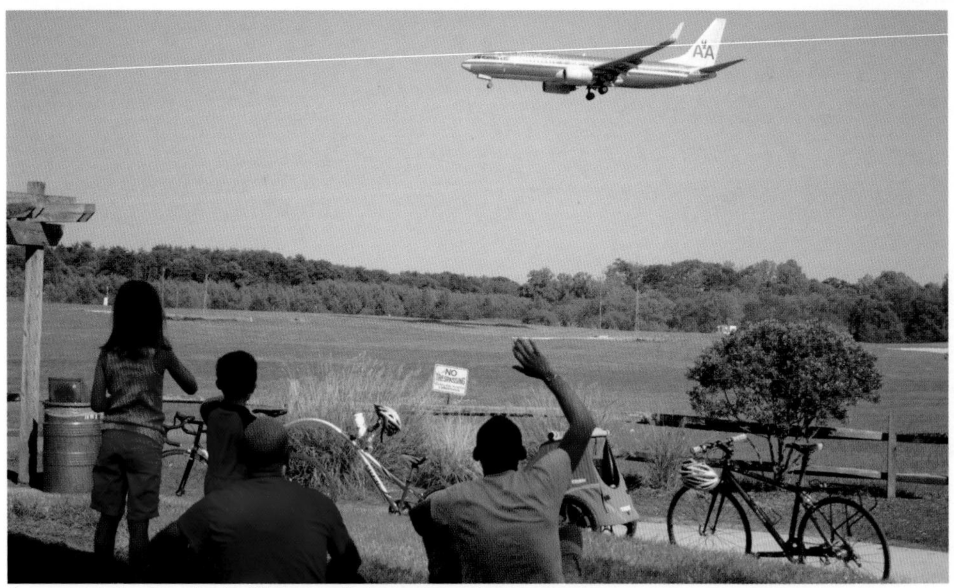

Stay to watch the planes land at BWI's aircraft observation park.

At a Glance

Distance 40.2 miles **Total Elevation** 1140 feet

Terrain

Both trails are well-maintained, traversing mostly flat ground with gradual ascents. The B&A is as straight as the tracks it replaced, while the BWI loops dips and dives and has a few more hills.

Traffic

No on-road sections here. Just watch yourself at intersections.

How to Get There

Take the Washington-Baltimore Parkway north off the Beltway to the Paul Pitcher Memorial Highway (MD 100). Follow it to Interstate 97 North, and soon, use exit 15 to go left (west) on Dorsey Road. The Thomas A. Dixon Aircraft Observation Park is not far ahead on your left. Park and ride.

Food and Drink

Possible stops along the B&A Trail are concentrated at numerous points adjacent to its passage through Glen Bernie, and at mile 11 (or 21) in Severna Park, or mile 15 (or 17) in Arnold. The BWI has options across Aviation Boulevard around mile 32 and later across Dorsey Road just past mile 39.

Side Trip

Span the short gap to Annapolis at the southern end of the B&A by swinging left on Boulter's Way, joining Ritchie Highway/Baltimore Boulevard (MD 450) right toward Jonas Point State Park, and following it over the U.S. Naval Academy Bridge. A left on King George Street brings you within sight of the Maryland State House.

Links to 50

Where to Bike Rating 

About...

The Baltimore-Washington International Airport loop and the Baltimore and Annapolis Trail are the long, clunky, linked title for this nice, smooth route over easy terrain. And though this may at first glance appear to be a ride within another guide's jurisdiction, don't make the mistake of judging it solely by its name or seemingly distant location. It's not that far away and has the benefit of being the lengthiest offering of the book that is also 100% off-road, as in pure, car-free bike path.

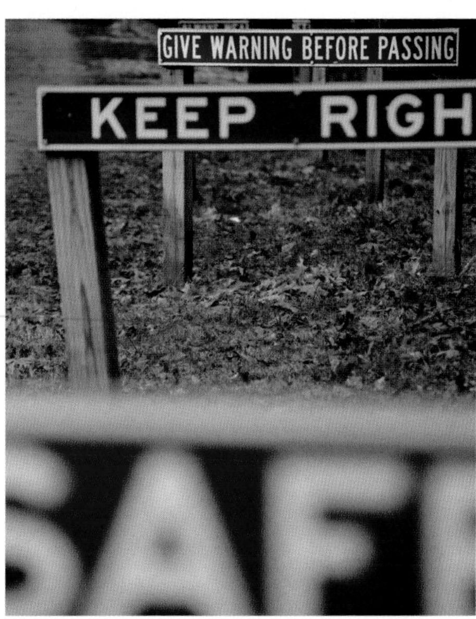

The rules, rules, rules of the road along the B&A Trail.

This route begins by moving through a refreshing slice of pine forest before heading briefly east on the well-signed John Overstreet Connector. The B&A Trail replaces a rail line which ran from the 1880s to the early 1950s, when competition from burgeoning highways forced its closure. After a period of decline, public interest in the deteriorated property increased until Anne Arundel County purchased the 66-foot wide corridor near the end of the 1970s and began implementing what you see today. The result includes some unique features.

Historical markers located at points along the path celebrate area history and extraordinary individual achievement. You can pick up a guide detailing each A to Z listing at the Earleigh Heights Ranger Station. It's also a good place to rest, picnic and play around, but you shouldn't limit yourself to just this single spot of relaxation. Numerous others exist too, with a short middle passage through Severna Park chief among them. As a means of comparison, the trail tends to shed any grit it initially rolls through in Glen Burnie as it makes its way south into the greener suburbs around Arnold.

Be sure to keep your eyes peeled for several antique railroad switch boxes, dozens of volunteer-tended flower planters, informational kiosks, and the 4.6 mile, high-concept Planet Walk, a linear museum and condensed solar system laid out precisely to scale and featuring sculptures and/or educational displays for each planet and the sun.

Blessed with the ability to take you places, the B&A was designated a Millennium Legacy Trail at the turn of the 21st century, and it also forms links in both the Maine to Florida East Coast Greenway, and the Delaware to California American Discovery Trail. Today though, restrict yourself to reconnecting to the BWI loop.

Though it's easy to be fooled by this trail's prosaic name, its 11 miles stand a good chance of surprising you. Less informational than its sister stretch, it benefits from moving over more varied terrain, including one especially beautiful crest when the airport spreads before you like a giant model on the floor of a basement rec room. Break here if you wish, then continue rolling past terminal and light rail access to your destination.

While Ride 40 has not been deemed kid-friendly in its entirety, it does include substantial sections which are entirely safe for family use.

Ride Log

0.0 Begin at BWI's Thomas A. Dixon, Jr. Observation Area where the path from the parking lot meets the BWI Trail. Go straight. Not right.
1.3 Turn right to use overpass toward B&A Trail.
1.5 Cross Stewart Rd to continue left toward B&A.
2.5 Cross Central Ave before turning right onto B&A.
3.15 Cross right then left to continue.
6.85 Cross Jumpers Hole Rd.
9.0 B&A Trail Park ranger station. Parking. Restrooms.
11.1 Severna Park. Food. Pedal Pushers Bike Shop.
16.1 Turnaround at Boulters Way.
29.5 Leave B&A left to return to BWI loop.
30.6 Cross Stewart Rd to connect to BWI.
30.8 Go straight to loop airport.
32.9 Cross Aviation Blvd. Benson-Hammond House.
33.8 Stay straight.
35.2 Bear Right. Left turn leads to terminal.
36.2 Bear right.
36.9 Turn left.
39.9 Cross Airport Loop then WB&A Rd.
40.2 Finish.

P
P1 Thomas A. Dixon Jr. Aircraft Observation Area
P2 Beginning of Planet Walk
P3 Earleigh Heights Ranger Station
P4 Benson-Hammond House
P5 Bike-friendly light rail to Baltimore

B
B1 Pedal Pusher Bike Shop, 546 Baltimore Annapolis Blvd
B2 Arnold Bike Doctor, 953 Ritchie Hwy
B3 Bike Doctor of Linthicum, 507 Camp Meade Rd
B4 Hudson Trail Outfitters, 1079 Annapolis Mall
B5 Bike Doctor Annapolis - 160-C, Jennifer Rd
B6 Eastern Mountain Sports, 200 Harker Place, Suite 105
B7 Capital Bicycle Inc, 436 Chinquapin Round Road

Crossing the light rail tracks around BWI.

The BWI to the B&A and Back

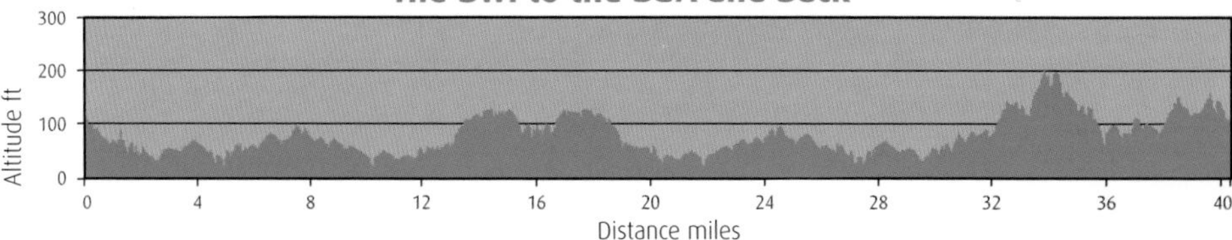

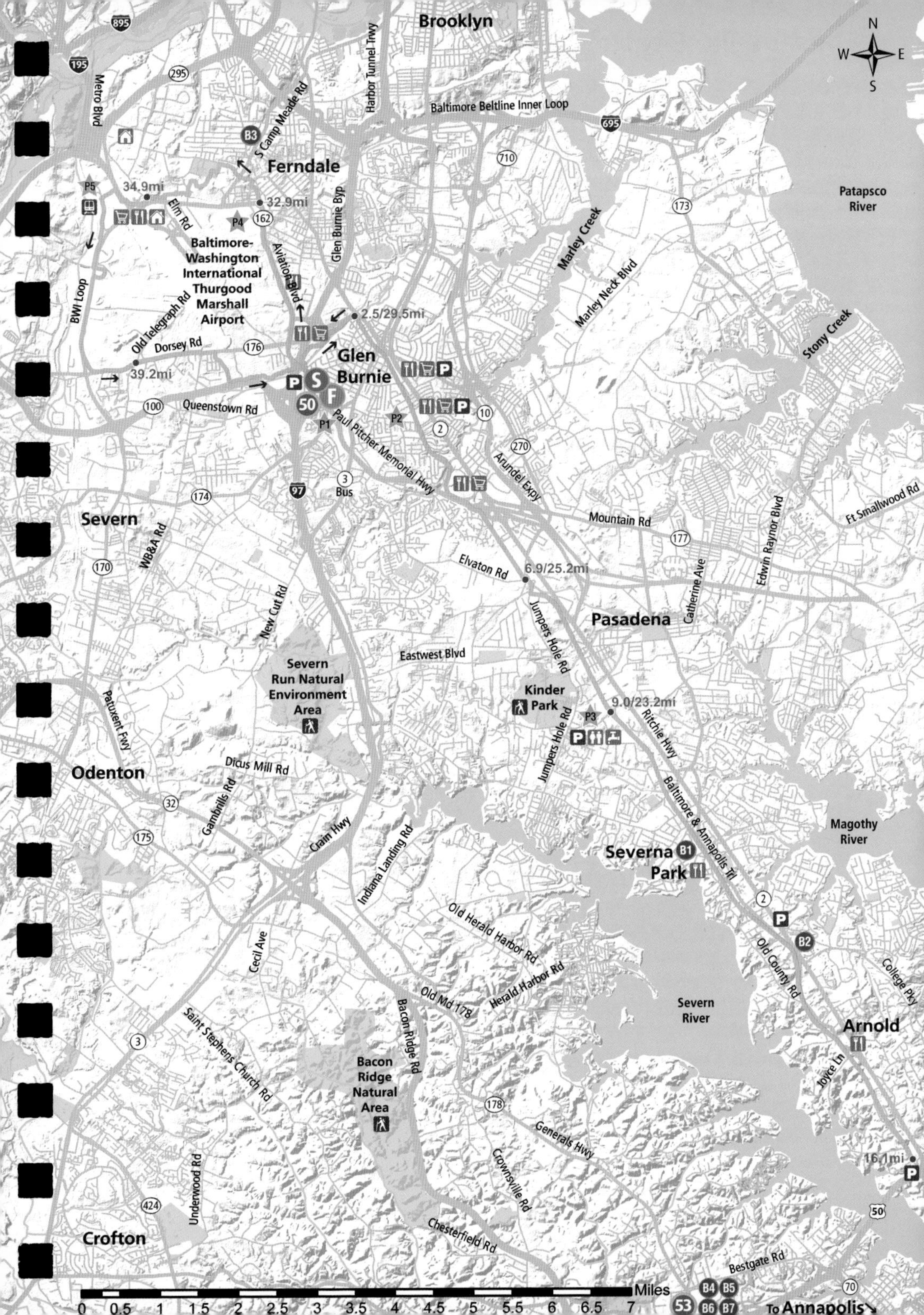

Brooklyn
Ferndale
Glen Burnie
Baltimore-Washington International Thurgood Marshall Airport
Severn
Odenton
Crofton
Pasadena
Severna Park
Arnold
Patapsco River
Magothy River
Severn River
Marley Creek
Stony Creek
Severn Run Natural Environment Area
Bacon Ridge Natural Area
Kinder Park
Metro Blvd
BWI Loop
S Camp Meade Rd
Harbor Tunnel Trwy
Baltimore Beltline Inner Loop
Glen Burnie Byp
Aviation Blvd
Elm Rd
Old Telegraph Rd
Dorsey Rd
Queenstown Rd
Paul Pitcher Memorial Hwy
Arundel Expy
Marley Neck Blvd
Mountain Rd
Ft Smallwood Rd
Edwin Raynor Blvd
Catherine Ave
Elvaton Rd
Jumpers Hole Rd
Ritchie Hwy
Baltimore & Annapolis Trl
Eastwest Blvd
New Cut Rd
WB&A Rd
Patuxent Fwy
Dicus Mill Rd
Gambrills Rd
Crain Hwy
Indiana Landing Rd
Old Herald Harbor Rd
Herald Harbor Rd
Old Md 178
Bacon Ridge Rd
Cecil Ave
Saint Stephens Church Rd
Generals Hwy
Crownsville Rd
Chesterfield Rd
Underwood Rd
Old County Rd
College Pky
Joyce Ln
Bestgate Rd
To Annapolis
34.9mi
32.9mi
2.5/29.5mi
39.2mi
6.9/25.2mi
9.0/23.2mi
16.1mi
P1
P2
P3
P4
P5
B1
B2
B3
B4
B5
B6
B7
53
50
895
195
295
695
710
173
162
176
100
10
2
270
3
Bus
97
174
177
170
32
175
178
424
70
Miles
0 0.5 1 1.5 2 2.5 3 3.5 4 4.5 5 5.5 6 6.5 7
N
W
E
S

Chesapeake Beach is well-positioned for post-ride relaxation. *Photo by Elena Wigelsworth.*

At a Glance

Rural Ride

Distance 36.4 miles **Total Elevation** 2050 feet

Terrain

A manageable amount of hills over winding country byways.

Traffic

Not too bad as the route sticks as much as possible to roads less traveled. The short stints on Bayside and Plum Point are a bit busier, as is winding MD 261. It tends to draw folks motoring to and from Rose Haven and North Beach on nice weekends.

How to Get There

Take Pennsylvania Avenue (MD 4) southeast off the Beltway through Upper Marlboro and MD 301 exiting onto Chesapeake Beach Road. It will take you all the way to the water and a right turn onto Bayside Road (MD 261). Now look to turn right past Trader's Seafood Steak and Ale onto Gordon Stinnett Avenue and left to park at the NE Community Center.

Food and Drink

Multiple options exist at the beginning and end of this ride in the twin towns of North Beach and Chesapeake Beach. Look for snack stops along the route around mile 14 in Huntington or at the mile 28 (MD 260) crossing.

Side Trip

Splash away at the Chesapeake Beach Water Park, tour the town's railway museum, or charter a fishing boat and hit the bay for a rod n' reel adventure.

Where to Bike Rating

About...

This route roams the northern part of a peninsula separated from Washington by the Patuxent River and bound by Chesapeake Bay. With the opportunity for fun, food, relaxation and a fresh-aired tour through the region's tobacco-centered past, it's a sweet ride which promises pleasure from beginning to end. Whether you make it a day trip or plan to stay the night, bring the family or arrive solo, the destination provides everything you'd want while the spin itself satisfies an appetite intent on some serious miles.

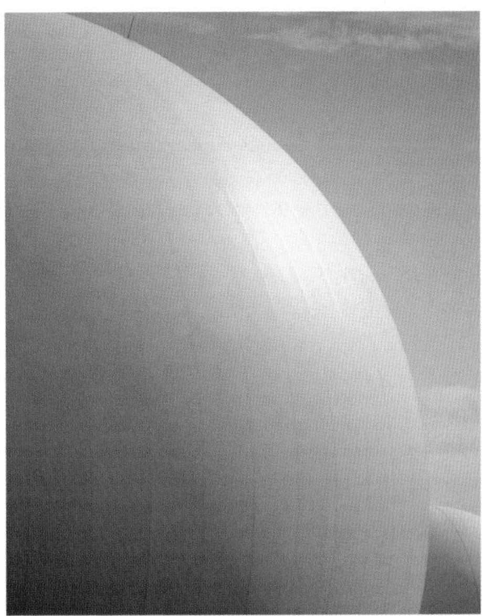

The white domes of the Chesapeake Bay Detachment.

Near the end of the 20th century, railroad baron Otto Mears took control of a planned short-line stretching from D.C. to an isolated spot in southern Maryland. He envisioned a resort at the end of that span, and Chesapeake Beach soon materialized from virgin bay front property into an entertainment center with casinos, an amusement park, a luxurious hotel, and a boardwalk extending out into the bay.

Vacationers arrived from the capital, steamships brought merrymakers from Baltimore, North Beach grew as a neighboring cottage community, and by the 1920s, the area's summer population often reached the 10,000s. The depression years hit hard however, the railroad went bust, and the party ended 35 years after it began. Today the tidy little town has a railway museum honoring its heritage and fresh new amenities to replace the old. Be sure to check it all out sometime before or after your spin.

Speaking of which, quite quickly here you've bobbed along beyond the striking white domes of a naval research facility, and into some nice, long sections of rolling hills past sporadic tree-lined residential streets and single homes nestled in fields or wooded lots set back off the road. Expect long relaxed spells of riding today, broken by shorter stretches along somewhat busier state roads.

Lower Marlboro may not be much more than a pretty memory, a pier, and a cluster of houses now, but a port of entry as early as the late 1600s, it grew to become an important tobacco shipping center during the 19th century. Though burned by the British during the War of 1812, you may still spot a surviving structure.

The way back to the bay from the Patuxent follows the ride's quasi-country trend, and after a satisfying series of wooded turns and buckled straightaways you've tripped through Friendship's one corner, dipped past classy Herrington Harbour, and slipped south from Holland Point to the happening little downtown of North Beach. Stop here and grab a treat at Sweet Sue's, shake your legs out on the boardwalk, or plant your feet in the sand and sit a while. Ostensibly home, it's only a matter of picking your lunch or dinner locale at this point, and wherever you choose, seafood comes highly recommended.

Ride Log

0.0 Exit the NE Community Center parking lot by going right on Gordon Stinnett Ave. Then go right immediately on Bayside Rd (MD 261). Food. Bathrooms.

0.7 Right onto Old Bayside Rd.

4.05 Left onto Christiana Parran Rd.

5.95 Right onto Bayside Rd.

7.4 Left onto Stinnett Rd.

9.45 Continue straight as Stinnett becomes Emmanuel Church Rd.

11.3 Left onto Plum Point Rd (MD 263).

A wooden clock reads quarter to five in Friendship.

11.8 Right onto Cox Rd.

14.1 Go straight across Hwy 2 then slide left onto Thanksgiving Ln. Food.

14.4 Left onto MD 521 S.

14.8 Stay straight as MD 521 S becomes Huntingtown Rd.

15.6 Go right to continue on Huntingtown Rd.

17.1 Left onto Mill Branch Rd.

18.3 Right onto Lower Marlboro Rd (MD 263).

20.5 Right onto Lower Marlboro Ln. Becomes Flint Hill Rd.

21.6 Follow road left. Becomes Chaneyville Rd.

24.9 Go straight across Hwy 2 then left on Jennifer Ln.

25.1 Right onto Fowler Rd.

26.4 Go straight across Mount Harmony Rd. Fowler becomes Grover's Turn Rd.

27.3 Go straight across Solomon's Island Rd to continue on Old Solomon's Island Rd (MD 778).

27.9 Go straight across MD 260 to continue on MD 778. Food.

29.4 Right onto Friendship Rd. Continue straight as it becomes Lake Shore and Walnut.

35.2 Right on Ninth St (MD 261) in North Beach then first left to stay on it. Food.

36.4 Right on Gordon Stinnett to return to NECC parking lot. Food. Bathrooms.

P1 Water park
P2 Railroad museum
P3 Historic Lower Marlboro
P4 Herrington Harbor

BR1 Paddle or Pedal, 4055 Gordon Stinnett Ave, behind the waterpark

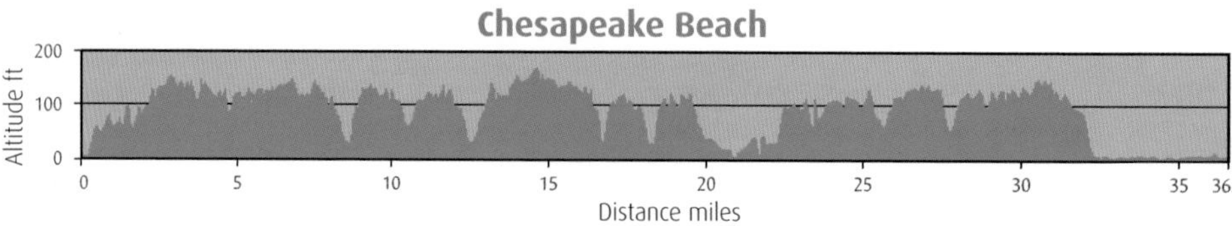

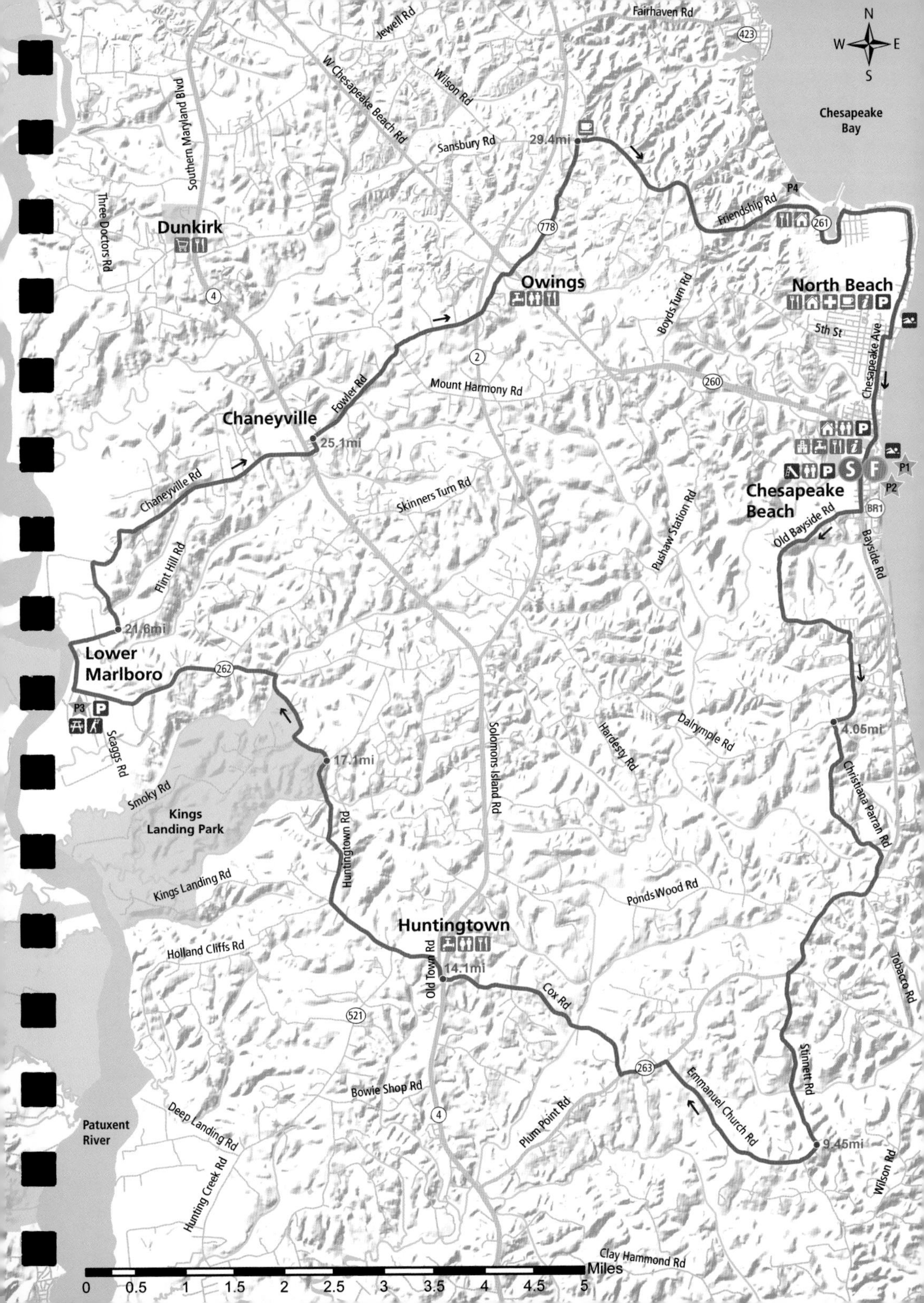

Fairhaven Rd
Jewell Rd
423
N
W
E
S
Chesapeake Bay
Wilson Rd
W Chesapeake Beach Rd
Southern Maryland Blvd
Sansbury Rd
29.4mi
Friendship Rd
P4
261
Three Doctors Rd
778
Dunkirk
Owings
Boyds Turn Rd
North Beach
4
5th St
Chesapeake Ave
2
260
Mount Harmony Rd
Fowler Rd
Chaneyville
25.1mi
Chesapeake Beach
P1
P2
BR1
Chaneyville Rd
Skinners Turn Rd
Pushaw Station Rd
Old Bayside Rd
Bayside Rd
Flint Hill Rd
21.6mi
Lower Marlboro
262
P3
Scaggs Rd
17.1mi
Hardesty Rd
Dalrymple Rd
4.05mi
Smoky Rd
Kings Landing Park
Huntingtown Rd
Solomons Island Rd
Christiana Parran Rd
Kings Landing Rd
Ponds Wood Rd
Huntingtown
Holland Cliffs Rd
Old Town Rd
14.1mi
Cox Rd
Tobacco Rd
521
263
Emmanuel Church Rd
Stinnett Rd
Bowie Shop Rd
Plum Point Rd
Deep Landing Rd
Patuxent River
9.45mi
Hunting Creek Rd
Clay Hammond Rd
Miles
0 0.5 1 1.5 2 2.5 3 3.5 4 4.5 5

Fourteen geese in flight.

At a Glance

Distance 17.7 miles **Total Elevation** 645 feet

Terrain

Pleasantly rolling hills and smooth riding aside from bumpy Beaver Dam Road.

Traffic

More than you'd wish for along Edmonston and Powder Mill roads. Diminishes significantly elsewhere.

How to Get There

Take the Green Line Metro to its last stop at Greenbelt Metro Station. Use the Beltway if arriving by car. Travelling clockwise? Use exit 24. It will bring you directly into Metro's parking lot. Counter-clockwise? Use exit 23 to MD 201, followed by lefts onto Ivy and Cherrywood lanes. Greenbelt Metro Drive is just beyond the overpass.

Food and Drink

A short distance west in College Park or on Crescent Road in Greenbelt.

Side Trip

To check out the National Wildlife Visitor Center at the Patuxent Research Refuge, go straight past Springfield Road at mile six and look for a right onto Visitor Center Entrance Road. For Goddard Space Flight Center, turn left to stay on Good Luck Road at mile 10 followed by rights on Greenbelt and Goddard roads. To visit the historic planned community of Greenbelt, use Crescent Road off Edmonston.

Links to 50

Where to Bike Rating 

About...

The area encompassing the Beltsville Agricultural Research Center offers one of the region's classic shorter rides. Classic because it's situated both near enough to D.C. to provide a quick getaway, yet far enough away to thumb its nose at the thicket of traffic and street lights looming just outside its boundaries. As a rural bubble set down in suburbia, it manages to provide a winning combination of easy Metro access with solid natural scenery and unbroken expanses of relatively low-trafficked roads.

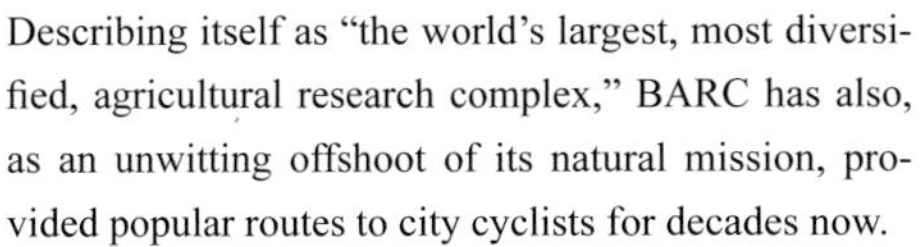

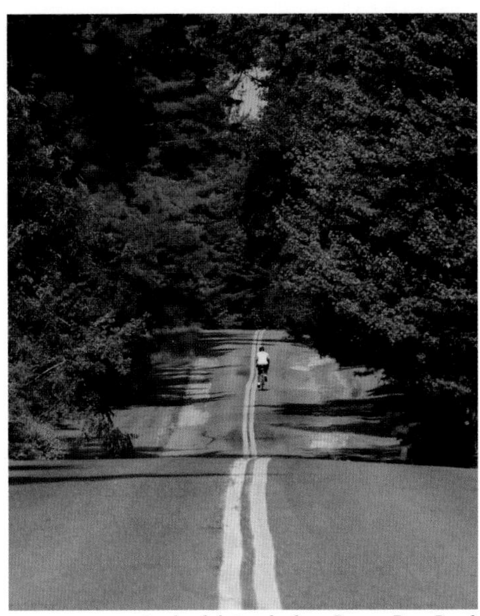

A splendid stretch along Beaver Dam Road.

Describing itself as "the world's largest, most diversified, agricultural research complex," BARC has also, as an unwitting offshoot of its natural mission, provided popular routes to city cyclists for decades now.

Welcome, then, to the land of strange road names (and even stranger plant diseases). This ride finds you traversing Powder Mill, Good Luck, Soil Conservation and Beaver Dam roads, while sadly missing some of the research center's blunter offerings, including: Poultry, Entomology, and Animal Husbandry. How positively pedestrian, then, to begin by linking Greenbelt Metro Drive to Cherrywood and Edmonston.

The latter of which sweeps you into the BARC countryside along with a significant dose of traffic. Thankfully, its shoulders are just wide enough to salvage a stretch which might otherwise be a touch overwhelming for less experienced cyclists.

Soon, too, you're on Powder Mill, still a touch busy and with just enough space to operate safely, but that much closer to this ride's real blessings as well. Expect it to bring you up and down a bit and make sure to look for BARC's impressive main buildings atop hills to the left. There's a visitor center off to the right a ways on, but you'll have to have made an appointment to get inside.

Be careful around the BWI/Washington Parkway before dipping right toward one of this ride's blissful stretches. It's smooth pedaling now, with pleasant views of woods and fields to both sides. Shouldn't be many cars either, and should any lingering city stressors remain, feel them slip off your shoulders like that fleece you just shed.

Peak in the windows of Perkins Chapel around mile eight-and-a-half, then use Good Luck to link to a second great stretch along Soil Conservation Road. It's new and wide and smooth and mighty enjoyable, minus a little too much traffic noise. Beaver Dam, then, turns super-rural once more, and though in need of fresh asphalt, it's a near-perfect undulating roll down among the trees and back up again to fields and livestock. It's nice here, so nice, in fact, that when you hit Edmonston, you just might want to do it again. If not, head safely back to Metro.

Ride Log

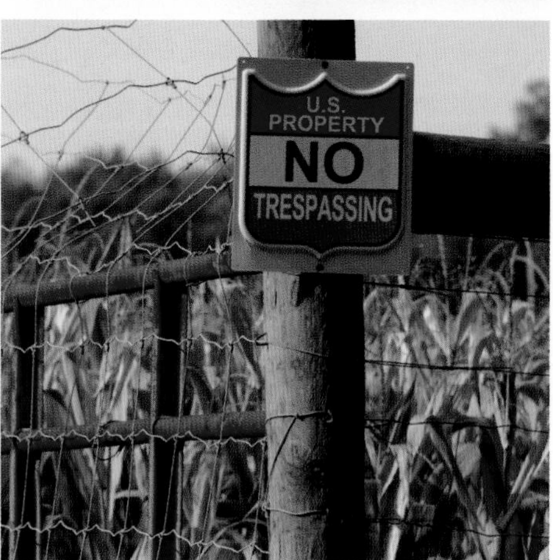

Don't worry, there's plenty more to explore.

0.0 Start at Greenbelt Metro sign near bicycle racks (visible as you exit). Head left past newspaper boxes to take bus drop-off road to Cherrywood Ln exit.
0.6 Left on Cherrywood Ln.
1.25 Left on Edmonston Rd (MD 201).
2.75 Right onto Powder Mill Rd.
5.5 Caution: Cars entering, exiting BWI/Washington Pkwy.
6.1 Right onto Springfield Rd.
8.65 Right on Good Luck Rd.
10.15 Right on Soil Conservation Rd.
12.2 Left on Beaver Dam Rd.
14.0 Straight across Research Rd.
15.3 Left on Edmonston Rd.
16.55 Right on Cherrywood Ln.
17.15 Right to return to Greenbelt Metro.
17.7 Finish at Metro sign near bicycle racks.

This stamp stands for smooth riding.

P

P1 Beltsville Agricultural Research Center
P2 BARC National Visitor Center
P3 National Wildlife Visitor Center
P4 Perkins Chapel
P5 Goddard Space Flight Center
P6 Greenbelt, one of America's first planned communities

B

B1 Proteus Bicycles, 9217 Baltimore Blvd
B2 REI, 9801 Rhode Island Ave Road

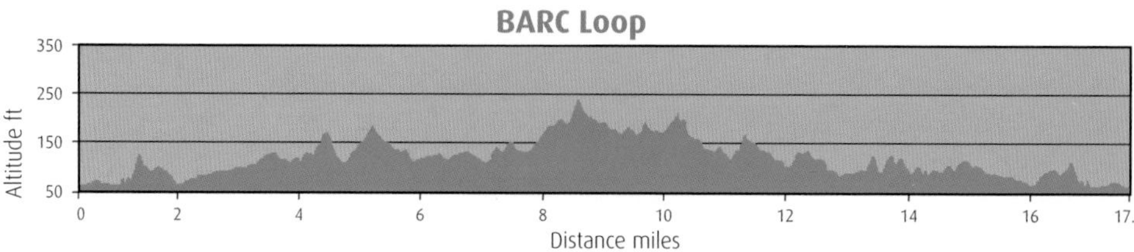

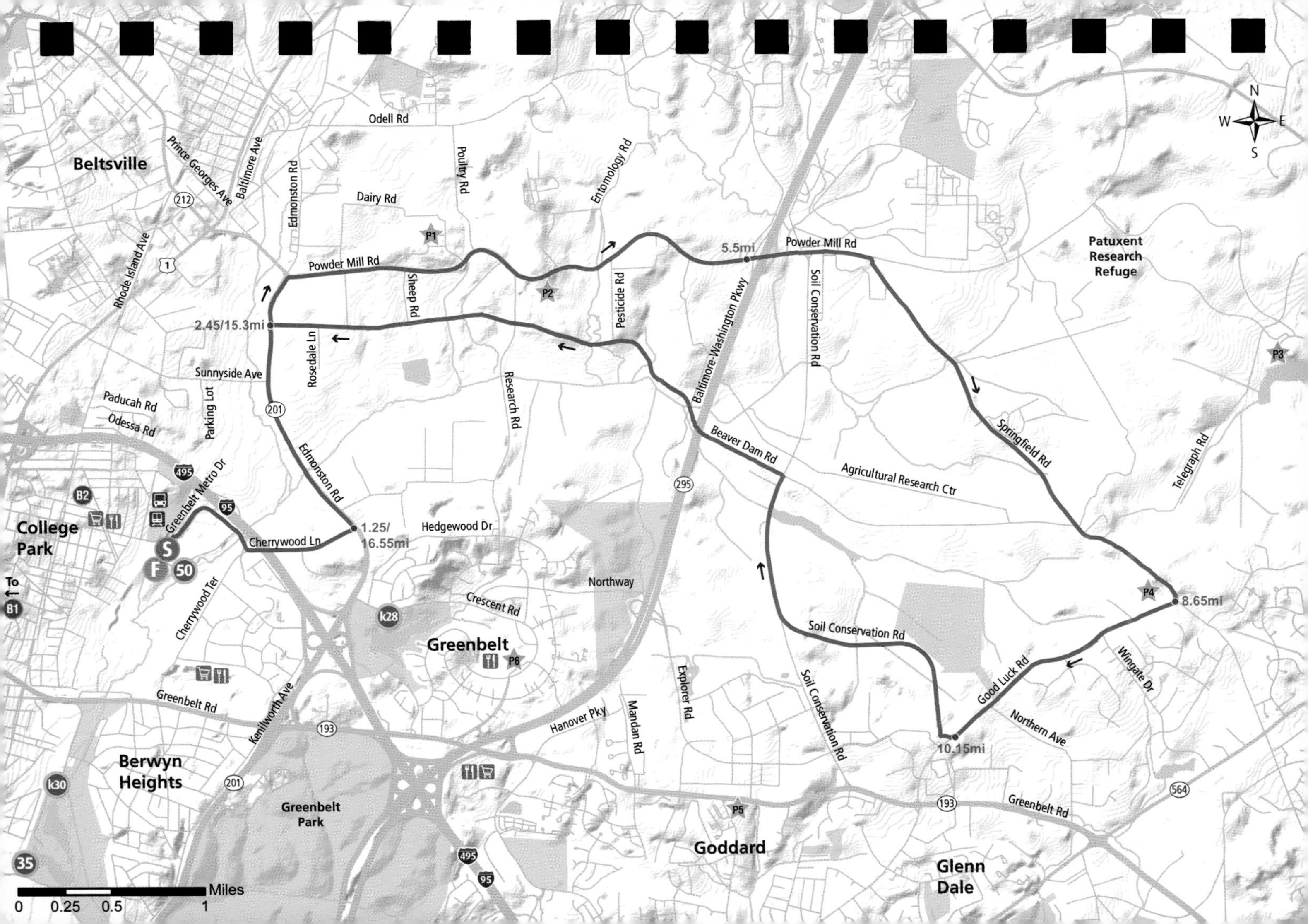
N
W
E
S
Beltsville
Patuxent Research Refuge
College Park
Greenbelt
Berwyn Heights
Greenbelt Park
Goddard
Glenn Dale
Odell Rd
Prince Georges Ave
Baltimore Ave
Edmonston Rd
Poultry Rd
Dairy Rd
Entomology Rd
Rhode Island Ave
Powder Mill Rd
Sheep Rd
Pesticide Rd
Baltimore-Washington Pkwy
Soil Conservation Rd
5.5mi
2.45/15.3mi
Rosedale Ln
Sunnyside Ave
Parking Lot
Paducah Rd
Odessa Rd
Research Rd
Beaver Dam Rd
Springfield Rd
Agricultural Research Ctr
Telegraph Rd
Greenbelt Metro Dr
Edmonston Rd
Hedgewood Dr
1.25/16.55mi
Cherrywood Ln
Northway
Cherrywood Ter
Crescent Rd
Soil Conservation Rd
8.65mi
Good Luck Rd
Wingate Dr
Greenbelt Rd
Kenilworth Ave
Hanover Pky
Mandan Rd
Explorer Rd
Soil Conservation Rd
Northern Ave
10.15mi
Greenbelt Rd
To B1
P1
P2
P3
P4
P5
P6
B2
K28
K30
35
S
F
50
212
1
201
495
95
295
193
564
Miles
0
0.25
0.5
1

The prettiest turn of the day.

At a Glance

Distance 21.6 miles **Total Elevation** 1250 feet

Terrain

Prepare for flat stretches of narrow, tree-lined road interspersed with rolling hills and a handful of steep climbs.

Traffic

Though most definitely out-of-the-way, expect to encounter a few cars and trucks in these parts. Ride with caution as most roads twist and carry blind curves.

How to Get There

Take the Indian Head Highway (MD 210) south off the Beltway all the way to Hawthorn Road (MD 225). Go left, and within two miles, right, onto Chicamuxen Road (MD 224). The entrance to Smallwood State Park is three-and-a-half miles farther along to the right down Sweden Point Road.

Food and Drink

It's a good idea to be prepared down here. Stop along MD 210 on the way in, and don't expect options along the route. There are seasonal concessions at Sweden Point Marina in Smallwood State Park.

Side Trip

For a short detour west to the Potomac and an area wonder, turn right at mile 8.75 onto Wilson Landing Road. Mallows Bay is home since the 1920s to upwards of 200 derelict wooden steamships built to combat German U-boats during WW I. Do some research before you come and be prepared to bushwhack a bit for better visuals. Many of the burned and rotted hulks are still visible, sprouting trees as high as 50 feet tall.

Where to Bike Rating 

About...

Don't put off your introduction to Maryland's Nanjemoy Peninsula much longer. This ramble through one of the area's most rural region's could easily be twice its size. With so many roads to explore down here, consider the mapped course merely a means of getting acquainted and plan on returning time and again. Assuming you begin to cherish the space as much as the locals, there's no reason it won't remain a cycling haven for a long, long time to come.

Follow the bright yellow lines.

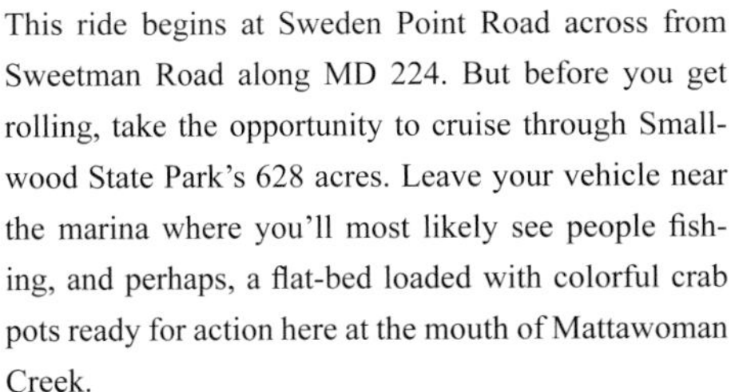

This ride begins at Sweden Point Road across from Sweetman Road along MD 224. But before you get rolling, take the opportunity to cruise through Smallwood State Park's 628 acres. Leave your vehicle near the marina where you'll most likely see people fishing, and perhaps, a flat-bed loaded with colorful crab pots ready for action here at the mouth of Mattawoman Creek.

Now make your way across this former 18th century tidewater plantation to the home of General William Smallwood, the most distinguished Marylander to serve in the Revolutionary War and the state's fourth governor.

The riding is fantastic down here on his peninsula, and MD 224 serves as a fitting introduction to the area's deep woods and rolling byways. After a big climb up from Reeder Run and a swing south on Riverside Road, a feeling of peaceful isolation sets in and you know you've entered one of the region's least populated spots.

The next four-and-a-half miles down toward the turn onto Liverpool Point Road bring options. Perhaps this ride's tantalizing side trip is in order. Or maybe you're feeling strong enough to double your day's distance? Continue straight in that case, tracing the peninsula's tip past Purse State Park to MD 6. Then re-engage with the mapped route in the town of Nanjemoy or at the meeting of MD 425 and Baptist Church Road. Either way ends with a potential mile-long spin east and a well-deserved rest stop along the Potomac.

Soon, you've come to Old Durham Church, the oldest surviving Episcopal church building in Maryland. Originally a log structure built in 1692, it was reconstructed with brick in 1732 and renovated in 1791. Smallwood and colonial Governor William Stone are buried in the adjacent graveyard, and the road the general traveled to arrive here from his plantation is now the curving two-lane you'll use to complete today's loop.

But you shouldn't limit yourself to just one ride in this cycling-rich area. Spend the weekend camping instead, letting the family enjoy Smallwood State Park's playground, nature trails, and nearby arts center while you go explore. Keep your antennae up for periodic craft demonstrations and military exhibitions and plan your visit now.

Ride Log

P1 Smallwood House
P2 The Ghost Fleet of Mallows Bay
P3 Friendship Landing
P4 Old Durham Church

0.0 Set your odometer where Sweden Point Rd/Sweetman Rd meets MD 224.

4.7 Right to stay on Riverside Rd (MD 224).

8.75 Optional side trip right less than a half-mile down Wilson Landing Road.

9.35 Left onto Liverpool Point Rd. Straight to continue larger loop.

11.5 Continue straight across MD 6. Becomes Baptist Church Rd.

13.7 Left at MD 425.

14.0 Right to visit Friendship Park.

15.3 Bear left to stay on MD 425 at Old Durham Church.

16.6 Continue straight across MD 6. Becomes Mason Springs Rd.

16.8 Quick left on Smallwood Church Rd.

21.0 Right onto MD 224 N.

21.6 Finish at MD 224 and Sweden Point.

Stop and stare a while.

Morning, sunshine.

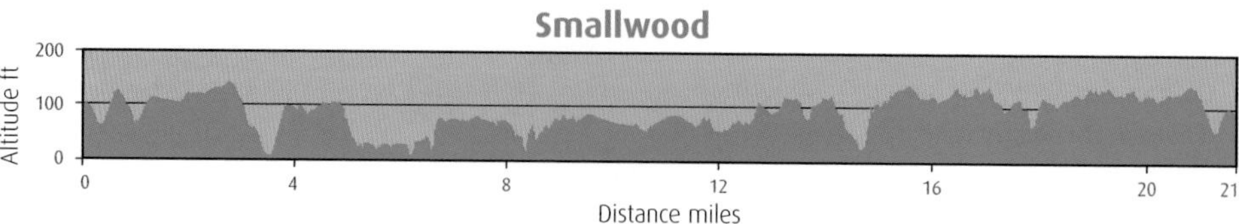

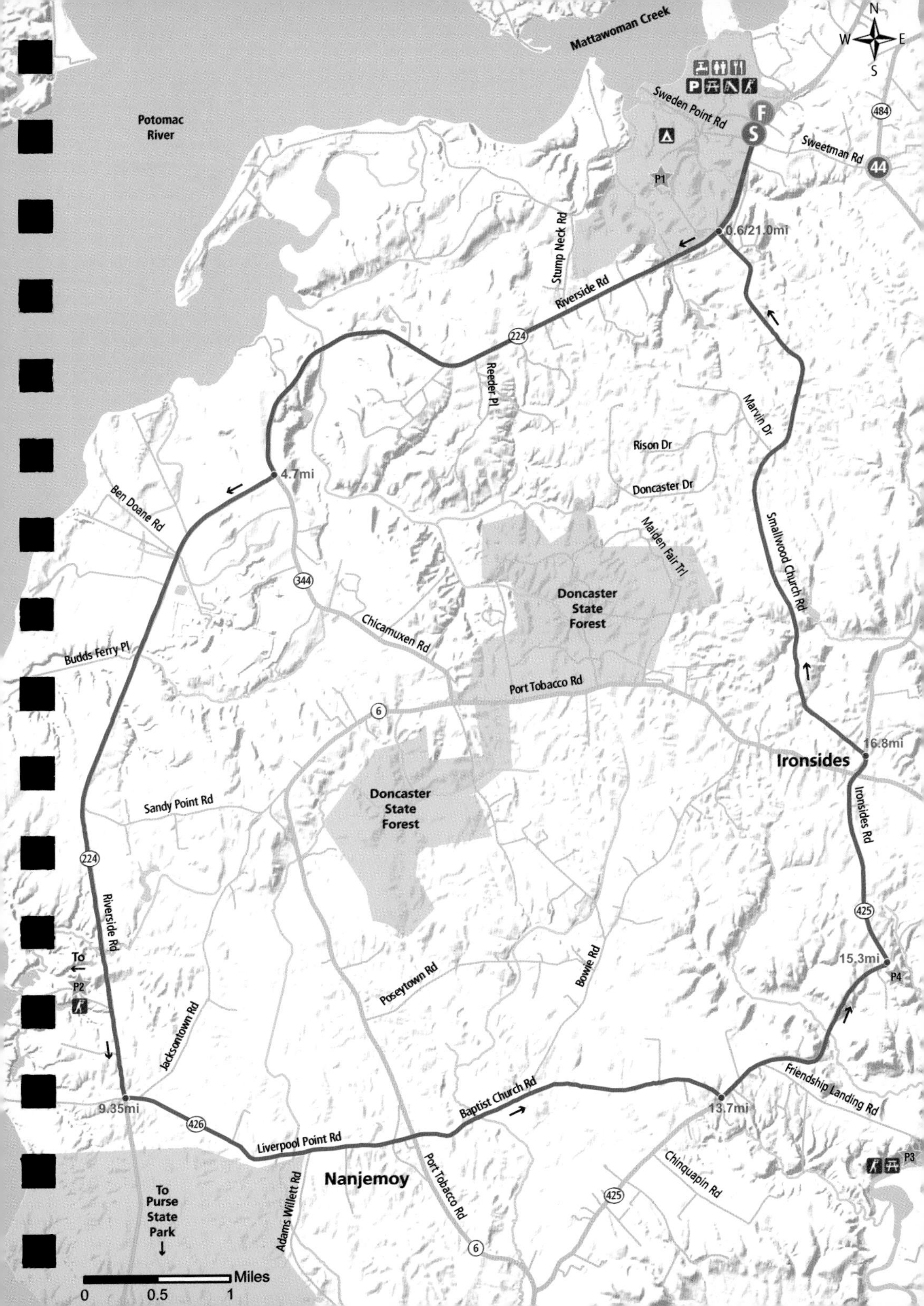
Mattawoman Creek
N
W
E
S
Potomac River
Sweden Point Rd
484
Sweetman Rd
44
P1
Stump Neck Rd
0.6/21.0mi
Riverside Rd
224
Reeder Pl
Marvin Dr
Rison Dr
Doncaster Dr
4.7mi
Ben Doane Rd
Maiden Fair Trl
Smallwood Church Rd
344
Doncaster State Forest
Chicamuxen Rd
Budds Ferry Pl
Port Tobacco Rd
6
16.8mi
Ironsides
Sandy Point Rd
Doncaster State Forest
Ironsides Rd
224
Riverside Rd
425
To
P2
15.3mi
P4
Bowie Rd
Poseytown Rd
Jacksontown Rd
Friendship Landing Rd
9.35mi
426
Baptist Church Rd
13.7mi
Liverpool Point Rd
P3
Nanjemoy
Chinquapin Rd
Adams Willett Rd
Port Tobacco Rd
425
To Purse State Park
6
Miles
0
0.5
1

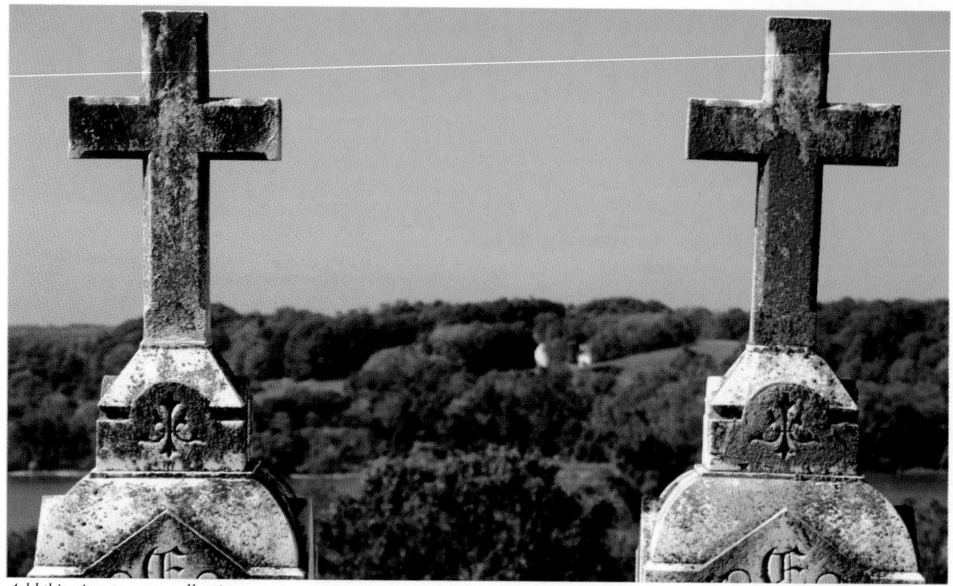

Add this view to your collection.

At a Glance

Distance 37.7 miles **Total Elevation** 1510 feet

Terrain

Long, flat stretches of road punctuated by rolling hills, and a few long and/or steep ascents.

Traffic

Thankfully, the roads with the day's fastest moving traffic—Hawthorn, Chicamuxen, and MD 6 into La Plata—have wide shoulders. Bicknell and Poorhouse are much narrower but less busy. The rest should be good to go.

How to Get There

Use Branch Avenue (MD 5) off the Beltway through its merge with MD 301 to the town of La Plata. Go left onto Charles Street (MD 6) and begin looking for on-street or lot parking.

Food and Drink

Refuel at Pisgah General Store just past mile 27.5, and when the day is done, try The Crossing at Casey Jones in La Plata one block from this ride's start and finish. Not for you? There's all sorts of faster stuff out on MD 301.

Side Trip

Get a preview (or review, as it were) of a portion of John Wilkes Booth's flight from D.C. along Bel Alton Newton Road. Or take the time to dig more thoroughly into the history of Port Tobacco, one of the richest archaeological sites in southern Maryland.

Links to 

Where to Bike Rating 

About...

Only an hour south of Washington, D.C., the rolling farms and forests around La Plata carry the promise of long, flowing stretches of safe, low-traffic roads that towns nearer a big city can't provide. Add to that an amenity-laden hub with a growing list of dining and entertainment options, and nearby historic sites and scenery to rival any in the region, and you've got yourself a combination not too many routes can match. Come see for yourself some of the best cycling southern Maryland has to offer.

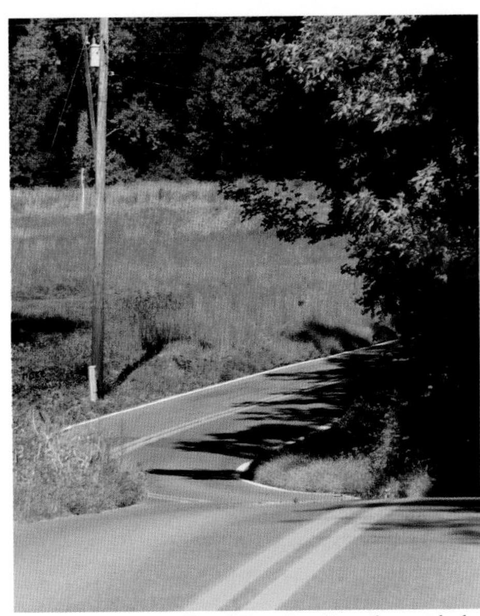

Chapel Point Road is as fun as it looks.

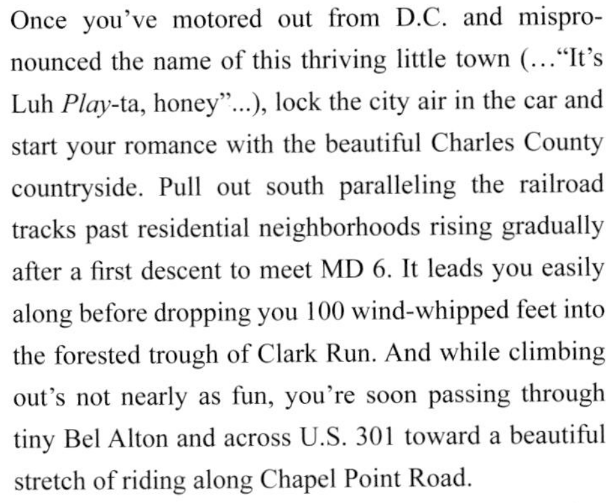

Once you've motored out from D.C. and mispronounced the name of this thriving little town (…"It's Luh *Play*-ta, honey"...), lock the city air in the car and start your romance with the beautiful Charles County countryside. Pull out south paralleling the railroad tracks past residential neighborhoods rising gradually after a first descent to meet MD 6. It leads you easily along before dropping you 100 wind-whipped feet into the forested trough of Clark Run. And while climbing out's not nearly as fun, you're soon passing through tiny Bel Alton and across U.S. 301 toward a beautiful stretch of riding along Chapel Point Road.

You may not have realized your prime position above the Potomac, but its lovely swing around the bend before you leaves no secret as to why the Jesuits chose this spot as one of a select few places to set down their American roots. Don't deny yourself an early break to wander the grounds and have a look inside St. Ignatius Church and St. Thomas Manor. Founded in 1641 by religious freedom-seekers who arrived on the English Ark and Dove, these grounds remain the site of one of the oldest continuously serving Catholic parishes in the United States.

Port Tobacco comes next and though there's not much to it now, an active imagination has the hogsheads rolling again and the port abuzz with the comings and goings of sailing ships. One of the first English-speaking communities on the East Coast, the town grew to become the second largest port in Maryland on the strength of the colonial tobacco trade. And you'll see some evidence of the lavish lifestyle that begat a few miles up the road.

There's a functioning one-room schoolhouse just down the way, before a rise out of the river bottom brings you past two plantation manors, Rose Hill and Thomas Stone National Historic Site. The latter, administered by the National Park Service, hosts ranger-led programs and tours.

Hawthorn Road begins a long stretch of lovely, near hill-free, riding west toward Indian Head before Bicknell and Poorhouse combine to rock and roll and reel you back through the big drop to Port Tobacco River. Then, it's one final, two-mile climb and you're home again in busy La Plata.

Ride Log

 *P1* Booth's Flight—Rich Hall Farm
P2 Booth's Flight—Pine Thicket
P3 St Ignatius Church and Manor
P4 Chapel Point State Park
P5 Port Tobacco Village
P6 One-room schoolhouse
P7 Thomas Stone National Historic Site

 *BR1* Up the Creek Rentals,
108A Mattingly Ave, Indian Head

0.0 Begin at the corner of Charles St (MD 6) and Oak Ave in central La Plata.

0.6 Left at Glen Albin Rd.

2.2 Left on Springhill Newtown Rd.

3.3 Right on Bel Alton Newtown Rd.

7.45 Cross U.S. 301 to continue straight. Becomes Chapel Point Rd.

9.6 Pass St Ignatius Church.

9.85 Pass Chapel Point St Park.

13.25 Pass Port Tobacco to left then look to go left onto Causeway St at one-room schoolhouse.

13.5 Left onto MD 6 before a quick right onto Rose Hill Rd.

15.1 Entrance to Thomas Stone Manor at left.

16.3 Left onto Hawthorne Rd (MD 225).

22.1 Left onto Chicamuxen Rd (MD 224).

24.3 Left onto Bicknell Rd.

27.6 Cross Mason Springs Rd. Bicknell becomes Poorhouse Rd.

33.3 Left onto MD 6 to La Plata.

37.2 Cross MD 301 to continue straight on Charles St (MD 6).

37.7 End at junction of Charles St and Oak Ave.

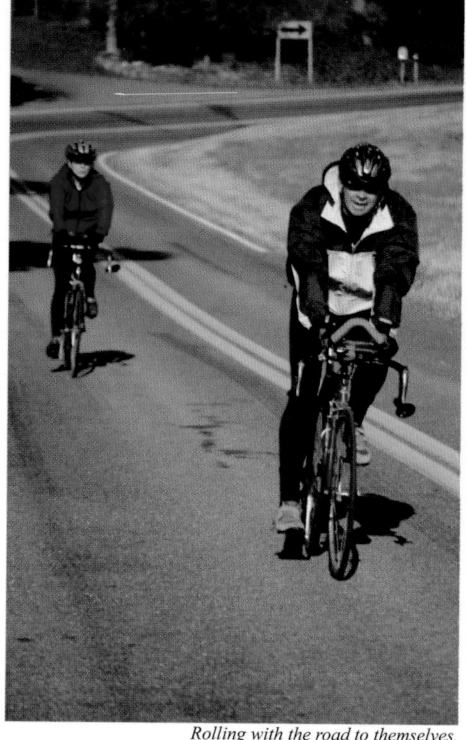

Rolling with the road to themselves.

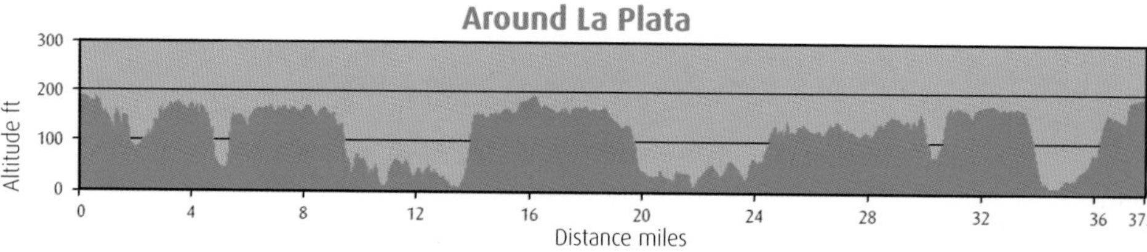

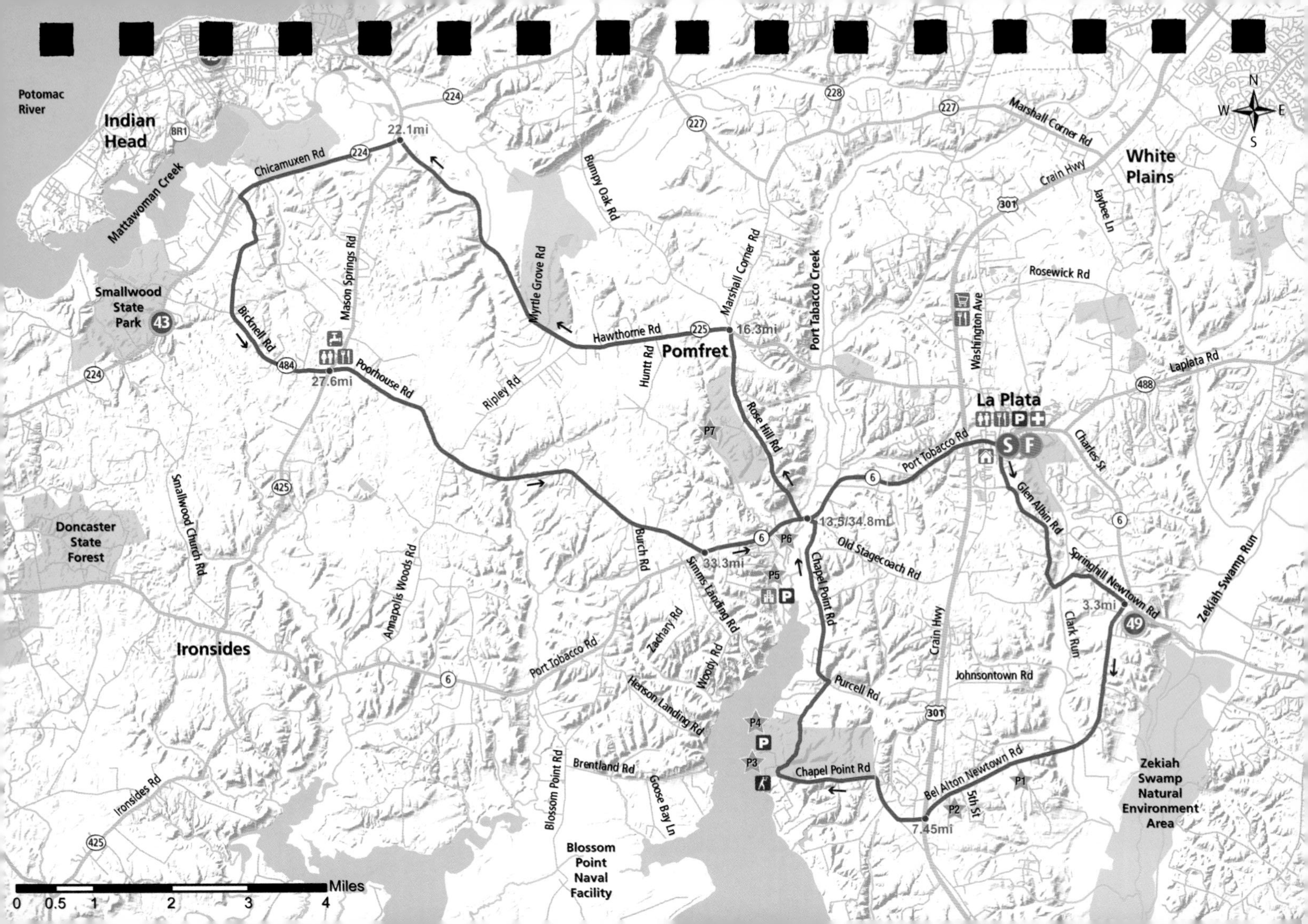
Potomac River
Indian Head
Mattawoman Creek
Smallwood State Park
43
Chicamuxen Rd
22.1mi
Mason Springs Rd
Bicknell Rd
27.6mi
Poorhouse Rd
Ripley Rd
Myrtle Grove Rd
Bumpy Oak Rd
Hawthorne Rd
16.3mi
Pomfret
Hunt Rd
Marshall Corner Rd
Port Tobacco Creek
Rose Hill Rd
P7
Crain Hwy
White Plains
Jaybee Ln
Rosewick Rd
Washington Ave
Laplata Rd
La Plata
Charles St
Port Tobacco Rd
Glen Albin Rd
13.5/34.8mi
Old Stagecoach Rd
Springhill Newtown Rd
3.3mi
49
Zekiah Swamp Run
Clark Run
Johnsontown Rd
Chapel Point Rd
Purcell Rd
Bel Alton Newtown Rd
5th St
P1
P2
7.45mi
Zekiah Swamp Natural Environment Area
P3
P4
P5
P6
33.3mi
Simms Landing Rd
Burch Rd
Zachary Rd
Woody Rd
Henson Landing Rd
Brentland Rd
Goose Bay Ln
Blossom Point Rd
Blossom Point Naval Facility
Port Tobacco Rd
Annapolis Woods Rd
Smallwood Church Rd
Doncaster State Forest
Ironsides
Ironsides Rd
Miles
0 0.5 1 2 3 4

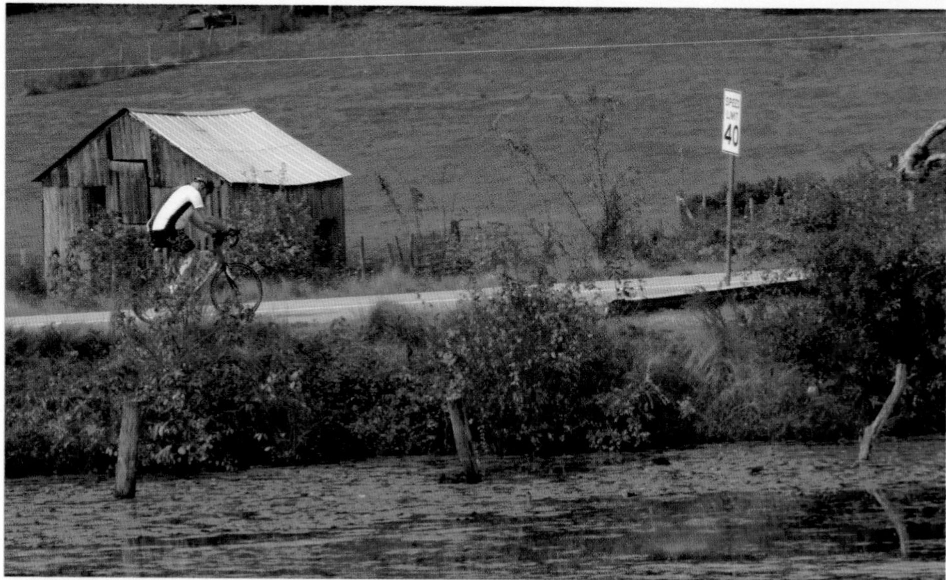

Pedaling off the trail onto Bumpy Oak Road.

At a Glance

Distance 26.0 miles **Total Elevation** 415 feet

Terrain

Wide, bump-free, multi-use path.

Traffic

None except at road crossings.

How to Get There

Take the Indian Head Highway (MD 210) south off the Beltway most of the way through the town of Indian Head. Look right to park at Village Green/Charlie Wright Park then follow signs to the trail's beginning down Mattingly Avenue about a half-mile south. If beginning at the eastern trailhead, use Branch Avenue (MD 5) off the Beltway through its merge with MD 301 to the town of White Plains, just south of Waldorf. Turn onto Theodore Green Boulevard and look to park about three-tenths of a mile on the right.

Food and Drink

Regardless of your arrival point, pick something up nearby along either highway. The intersection of Bryans Road and MD 210 has many options, as do Waldorf and St. Charles on your way in to White Plains. There's also a little weekend spot south down Mattingly Avenue in Indian Head named Up the Creek that rents bikes and kayaks and sells snacks and drinks. Expect only water stops and bathrooms along the trail.

Side Trip

Paddle Mattawoman Creek.

Where to Bike Rating 

About...

The Indian Head Rail Trail rolls 13 miles through the western half of Charles County from the town of Indian Head to White Plains south of Waldorf. A member of the growing list of highly successful area rail-to-trail projects, it moves serenely through largely undeveloped land seemingly far removed from the city. At just 18 miles from the D.C. line though, its accessibility makes it an appealing option, even for those weekday rides your body craves.

Reading up on bald eagles along Mattawoman Creek.

The rail bed on which this trail runs was originally built as a supply route for the military complex located just west of its Mattingly Avenue terminus. Now called the Indian Head Division, Naval Surface Warfare Center, it was established in 1890 and is the longest, continuously operating Naval ordnance facility in the United States. Its rail line was completed in 1918 and last used on a regular basis during the Vietnam War. After the Navy deemed the corridor a surplus property, the land was gifted to Charles County from the National Park Service's Federal Land to Parks Program. Along with state grants and county funds, the 100-foot passageway was transformed into trail using money generated from the recycling of its obsolete steel rails and wooden ties.

The opportunity exists, of course, to begin this ride at either end. Parking is more conveniently located in White Plains, but you might choose to start in Indian Head due to the proximity of its food options. The trail leaves town past backyards and through a few street crossings before coming upon a beautiful overlook within two miles. Be sure to reserve this spot for your sunset return.

It's not long until you're out moving past forests and wetlands through what must be one of the most isolated areas in southern Maryland. There are plenty of benches and rest stops, as well as viewing areas complete with interpretive signs. It's almost a guarantee you'll see families of deer and wading egrets along your way, and don't be surprised if you run across wild turkey, a great blue heron, even your first bald eagle. They're known to nest along Mattawoman Creek.

After mile three the trail begins an extremely gradual rise to mile 11 before leveling and finishing. That little bit of elevation normally makes the way back a touch faster, and you always see things you missed the first time around.

While Ride 45 has not been deemed kid-friendly in its entirety, it does include substantial sections which are entirely safe for family use.

Ride Log

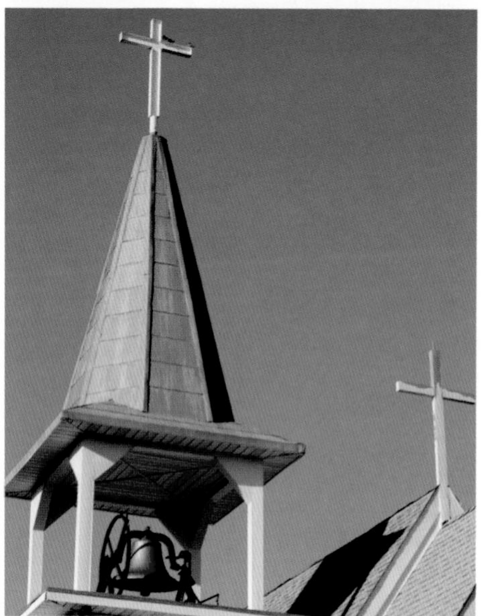
St. Mary's Star of the Sea Church in Indian Head.

0.0 Set your odometer at the Rules of the Trail sign. Water, benches, and racks available.
1.9 Mattawoman Creek overlook.
2.6 Cross MD 225.
3.2 Parking available at MD 224 crossing.
5.5 Cross Bumpy Oak Rd.
9.04 Cross Bensville Rd. A few parking spots available.
11.0 Cross Middletown Rd. Parking available.
12.9 Cross Theodore Green Blvd to finish. Parking, trail news and information, benches, and racks available. Retrace when ready.
26.0 Finish.

P1 Mattawoman Creek Overlook
BR1 Up the Creek Rentals, 108A Mattingly Ave

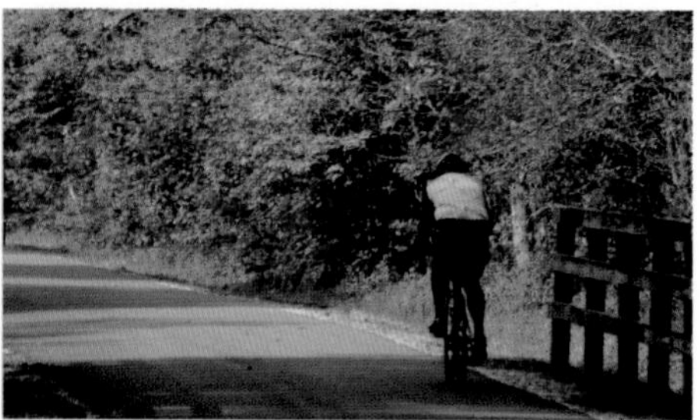
Room to roll west of White Plains.

One of several weathered railroad switch boxes along the way.

The Indian Head Rail Trail

Altitude ft: 0, 100, 200, 300
Distance miles: 0, 4, 8, 12, 16, 20, 24, 26.0

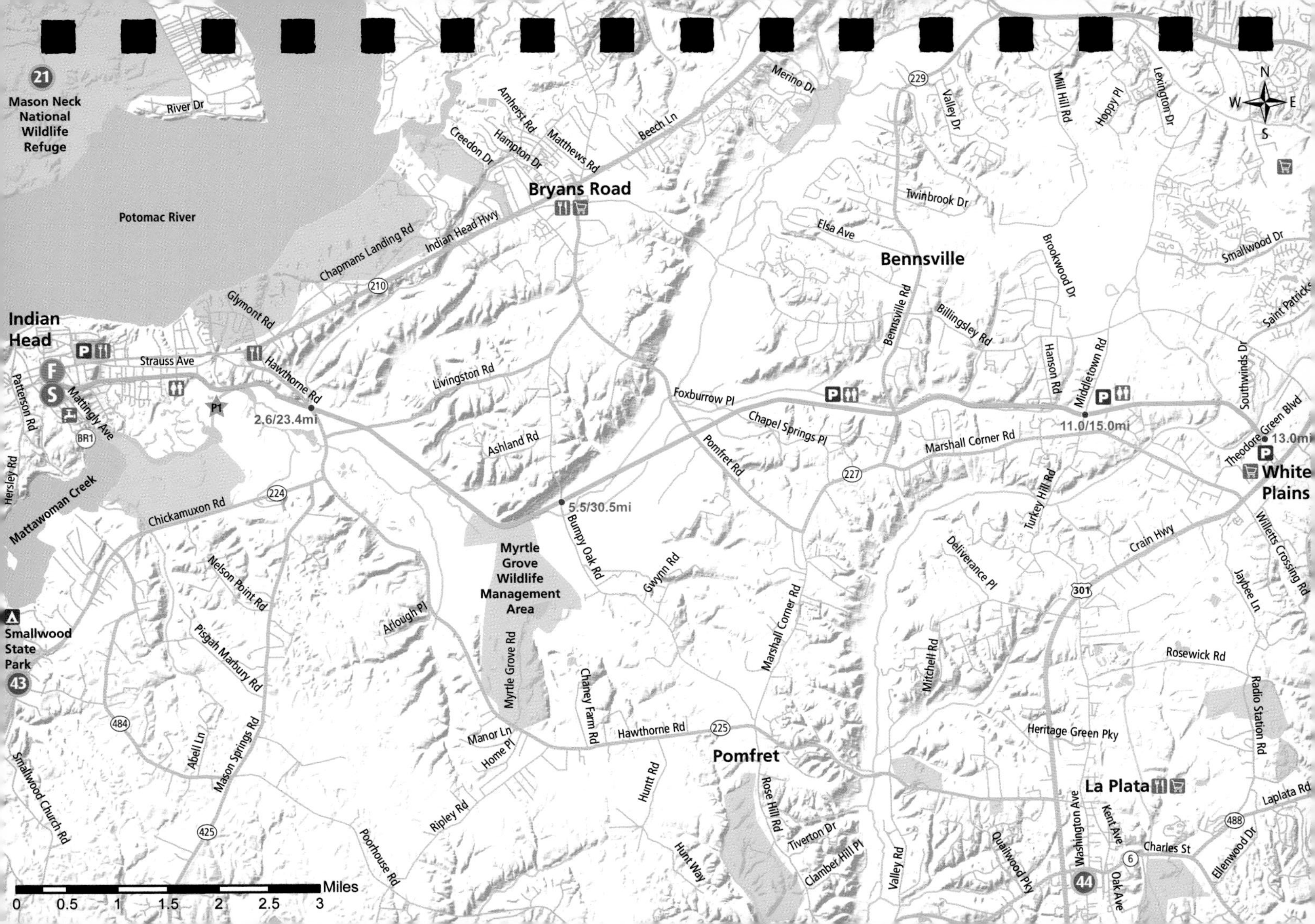

Mason Neck National Wildlife Refuge
21
River Dr
Potomac River
Indian Head
Patterson Rd
Hersley Rd
Mattingly Ave
BR1
Strauss Ave
P1
Glymont Rd
Hawthorne Rd
2.6/23.4mi
Chapmans Landing Rd
Indian Head Hwy
210
Mattawoman Creek
Chickamuxon Rd
224
Smallwood State Park
43
Creedon Dr
Amherst Rd
Hampton Dr
Matthews Rd
Beech Ln
Bryans Road
Merino Dr
Livingston Rd
Ashland Rd
5.5/30.5mi
Bumpy Oak Rd
Myrtle Grove Wildlife Management Area
Myrtle Grove Rd
Nelson Point Rd
Pisgah Marbury Rd
Arlough Pl
484
Abell Ln
Mason Springs Rd
425
Smallwood Church Rd
Manor Ln
Home Pl
Ripley Rd
Poorhouse Rd
Chaney Farm Rd
Hawthorne Rd
225
Huntt Rd
Hunt Way
Gwynn Rd
Pomfret
Rose Hill Rd
Tiverton Dr
Clamber Hill Pl
Marshall Corner Rd
Pomfret Rd
Foxburrow Pl
Chapel Springs Pl
227
Elsa Ave
Twinbrook Dr
Bennsville
Bennsville Rd
Billingsley Rd
229
Valley Dr
Mill Hill Rd
Hoppy Pl
Lexington Dr
Brookwood Dr
Hanson Rd
Middletown Rd
11.0/15.0mi
Marshall Corner Rd
Smallwood Dr
Saint Patricks
Southwinds Dr
Theodore Green Blvd
13.0mi
White Plains
Turkey Hill Rd
Deliverance Pl
Mitchell Rd
Crain Hwy
301
Willetts Crossing Rd
Jaybee Ln
Rosewick Rd
Radio Station Rd
Heritage Green Pky
La Plata
Valley Rd
Qualwood Pky
Washington Ave
Kent Ave
Oak Ave
44
6
Charles St
488
Ellenwood Dr
Laplata Rd
N
W
E
S
0
0.5
1
1.5
2
2.5
3
Miles

Originals, Oddballs and Outliers

Welcome to Triple O, a distinctive WTB D.C. section out to enlighten you a bit, challenge you a lot, strengthen, or in cases, reawaken your love of the area, and take you places in and around it you might never have known existed. These rides live up to their title. Some are freshly sprung, some are a little goofy in the headset, and some take you to the region's edge (with the promise of pushing you further).

The following offerings range from easy sightseers through to greater D.C.'s most difficult routes. Seasonal jaunts exist side-by-side with tours strictly designed for only the most seasoned cyclists. Terrain defines itself broadly. The book's longest natural surface ride lives here beside its hilliest.

All within a few pages, two short routes aim for simple pleasure, while three others appear on a special mission to test the limits of both your legs and your logic. Don't try Booth's Flight unless you're up for an extreme challenge. And it's a good idea to get a bunch of rides under your bib before you bolt out for all Fifty States or attempt to link the area's Civil War Defenses.

Had you heard the nation's capital was ringed by a complex system of forts constructed to defend it from Confederate attack? Have you ridden When the Cherries Blossom and thrown open the city's window to spring? Did you realize biking to Baltimore, or the Bay, isn't nearly as difficult as you might have thought? Were you aware the C&O Canal Towpath is capable of taking you not only to Great Falls, but 170 miles further to Cumberland, Maryland, and then, with the help of another epic path, 150 miles further still, all the way to Pittsburgh?

Greetings again, then, from a section poised where the rubber truly meets the road. For those whose cycling crush has bloomed to true love, time spent with this series of admitted eccentrics is sure to challenge the heartiest among you and enliven the most staid.

Originals, Oddballs and Outliers

Members of the 1st Massachusetts with Parrott Gun, Fort Totten. *Photo courtesy the Library of Congress*

At a Glance

Distance 55.55 miles **Total Elevation** 4900 feet

Terrain

Extremely hilly, this tour incorporates long stretches of road riding with six miles of natural surface trail, numerous bike lanes, and several bridge crossings.

Traffic

Expect miles of mild riding. Intense sections tend to be quarter to half-mile connectors. Take care along Western Avenue, and Military, Bladensburg, Benning, Seminary, and Braddock roads, using sidewalks as necessary.

How to Get There

Take Metro's Orange/Blue Line to Rosslyn. Drivers can park nearby at Teddy Roosevelt Island off the northbound lanes of the George Washington Memorial Parkway. Reach it by way of Interstates 66 and 395, and numerous other roads and highways. If busing, check local schedules and aim to connect to the D.C. Circulator.

Food and Drink

It's a good thing possible stops along this route are too numerous to mention, because a journey of this distance needs fuel. Ride assured. You won't go far here without the chance to eat and drink.

Side Trip

Visit Battleground National Cemetery just north of Fort Stevens on Georgia. Pre-schedule a tour of the Franciscan Monastery, with sight left on 14th NE. Visit Cedar Hill, the home of Frederick Douglass at 1411 W St SE. Or relax at National Harbor.

Links to

Where to Bike Rating 

About...

Here's a route inviting riders to wipe modern Washington from their minds and experience the feeling of being inside capital's boundaries during the war for the nation. Extremely challenging, it approaches one full mile of climbing while aiming to connect the chain of half-buried forts hidden in plain sight across the highest hills of the District. If you enjoy great views, seek new discoveries, crave splendid cycling, and think you're up to an unyielding, day-long adventure; come geared up and dare to endure.

A plaque commemorates Lincoln under fire.

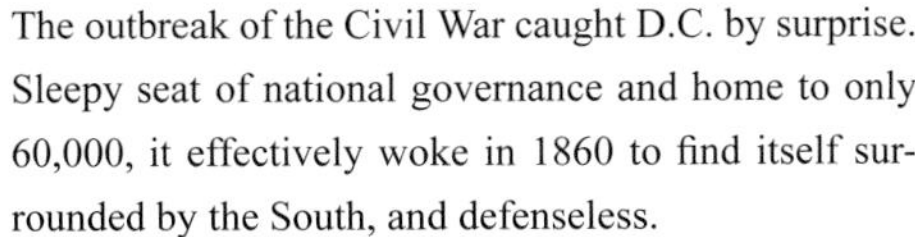

The outbreak of the Civil War caught D.C. by surprise. Sleepy seat of national governance and home to only 60,000, it effectively woke in 1860 to find itself surrounded by the South, and defenseless.

Virginia, capital of the Confederacy, lay seceded to the west, and neutral, yet staunchly slave-owning Maryland spread in all other directions. The clear need to fortify the nation's capital crystallized even further after the Union's sound defeat at Manassas, the first major battle of the war.

Immediately, a team of engineers, soldiers, former slaves, and assorted laborers began building a system of detached forts connected by a continuous trench line. By 1865, 68 earthworks, 93 unarmed batteries, 20 miles of rifle pits, and 32 miles of military roads had transformed the capital into one of the most heavily fortified cities in the world.

Led by General Jubal A. Early, the South mounted only one direct attack upon the system at northernmost Fort Stevens. Repulsed, the battle is just as famous for having been visited by Abraham Lincoln, and stands as only one of two times a sitting American president has come under wartime fire.

Hastily dismantled or abandoned after the assurance of victory, subsequent D.C. park plans have recognized the recreational potential of the forts and efforts periodically arise to promote their legacy and the greenspace they preserve.

With the coverage only cycling provides, this all-access tour has to be considered one of the most effective. It takes in every interpretive sign, turns every corner, and peeks past every tree in tribute to a string of singular treasures forever in jeopardy of being lost to evolving landscape.

Ride Log

Vestiges of some forts' earthworks still remain.

0.0 Begin by going right out of the Orange/Blue Rosslyn Metro elevator. Take another immediate right to join N Moore St.

0.15 Slide right following sign for Custis Trail. Cross Lee Hwy N and S to take Custis left.

0.3 Continue straight until further notice.

1.05 Trail bears right. Follow Custis sign.

1.7 Left down ramp to bottom. Two more lefts bring you through Thrifton Hill Park.

1.9 Left onto Lorcom Ln.

2.25 Right onto Nelly Custis Dr.

4.45 Right onto Old Glebe followed by left on N Randolph St.

4.7 Right on 41st St N downhill toward Chain Bridge.

4.85 Join Chain Bridge sidepath.

5.2 Left onto downramp to join C&O Towpath.

6.2 Left over footbridge then R to diagonally cross Canal to Reservoir.

6.65 Left on MacArthur.

7.25 Right on Chain Bridge.

7.7 Battery Kemble.

8.1 Soft left to Indian, to right on Rockwood, to left on Glenbrook.

8.45 Right on 49th.

9.55 Right on Western.

9.85 Right on Fessenden. Ft Bayard.

10.7 Ft Reno.

11.2 Cross Conn Ave to left on 36th.

11.45 Right on Nevada/Broad Branch.

11.9 Left on 27th.

12.25 Right on Military to left onto Oregon sidepath.

12.55 Right at Ft DeRussy sign.

13.2 Left to cross Beach, to right on Joyce.

13.6 Right on 16th. Left onto Ft Stevens.

14.1 Right on 13th to left on Quackenbos.

14.45 Right on Eighth.

14.65 Left on Oglethorpe.

15.05 Right on Third. Ft Slocum.

15.25 Left on Madison.

15.4 Left on Kansas.

Ride Log continued...

15.5 Right on Nicholson.
15.7 Right on N Capitol.
15.8 Left on Madison to right on Blair/Rock Creek Church.
16.55 Ft Totten.
16.8 Left onto Metro Branch Trail.
17.3 Cross to continue.
17.95 Jog left past Metro and right up road.
18.1 Left on Seventh to left on Monroe.
18.4 Left on 12th.
18.55 Right on Otis.
18.7 Left on 13th. Fort Bunker Hill
18.8 Right on Perry.
18.9 Right on 14th/becomes Montana.
20.4 Left to continue on Montana.
20.6 Right on Bladensburg.
21.25 Left on Mt Olivet to immediate left on M.
21.8 Right on Maryland.
21.95 Left on 22nd.
22.5 Left on Benning.
23.4 Left onto bridge path.
23.95 Right to Ft Circle Trail then jog left to go right up 41st.
27.6 Jog left to right on Park then right to re-engage trail.
28.1 Left on 28th. Re-engage trail right before stop sign (unmarked).
28.4 Cross to resume. Caution: fast merging traffic.
29.3 Left at trailhead. Right on Bruce. Left on Erie. Ft Stanton.
30.0 Left on Pomeroy.
30.7 Use elevated crosswalk to Dunbar then left on MLK. Ft Carroll.
32.7 Left onto S Cap.
32.85 Soft right to resume MLK.
33.45 Fort Greble down Elmira.
33.7 Soft right on Blue Plains.
34.15 Left at D.C. Village then left to Oxon Farm Trail (unmarked).
36.4 Use overpass to go right on Oxon Hill.

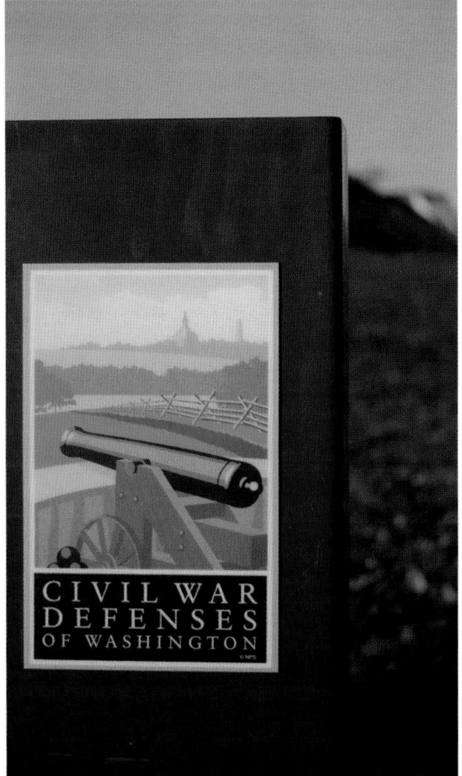

Look for this sign throughout your ride.

36.85 Cross Harborview to go right on sidepath.
37.7 Right over WW Bridge.
39.85 Left twice at end of bridge to go down ramp.
40.1 Left under bridge.
40.25 Right on Green St. Left on S Lee. Battery Rodgers.
40.55 Right at Franklin. Left at S Union.
40.8 Left through Wilkes Tunnel.
41.5 Right on S Payne to successive LRL onto Jamieson sidepath.
41.8 Use crosswalk to right along Hooff's Run then carefully cross Duke to Daingerfield.
42.05 Left to King.
42.3 Left to climb GW Memorial.

Ride Log continued...

42.8 Left on Hilltop to left on S View.

43.45 Left on Janneys Ln.

45.15 Right on N Howard.

45.5 Right on Braddock.

46.0 Left on N Early. Right on Menokin.

46.3 Right on Outer King. Left on S Wakefield.

46.65 Left on 34th.

47.0 Right on 31st.

47.7 Cross S Arlington Mill to right on sidepath.

47.8 Cross to access Four Mile Run Trail toward Mt Vernon.

50.05 Curve left to go north on Mt Vernon Trail.

55.3 Left to Rosslyn Metro.

55.55 Finish at elevator.

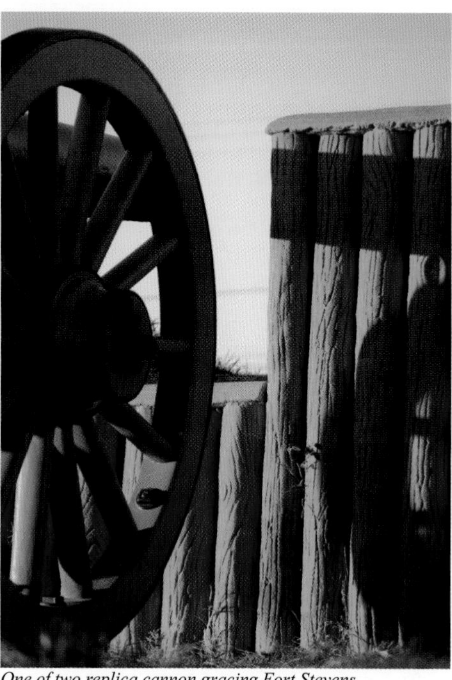

One of two replica cannon gracing Fort Stevens.

P

P1 Battery Kemble
P2 Ft Reno
P3 Ft DeRussy
P4 Ft Stevens
P5 Battlefield National Cemetery
P6 Ft Totten
P7 Franciscan Monastery
P8 Frederick Douglass Home
P9 Battery Rodgers
P10 Alexandria National Cemetery
P11 Matthew Brady Photograph
P12 Ft Ward

B

B1 Revolution Cycles, 3411 M St
B2 Bicycle Pro Shop, 3403 M St
B3 Hudson Trail Outfitters Ltd, 4530 Wisconsin Ave, NW #1
B4 Velocity Bicycle Cooperative, 204 S Union St
B5 Big Wheel Bikes, 2 Prince St
B6 Revolution Cycles, 220 20th St South

BR

BR1 Bike and Roll Alexandria, One Wales Alley

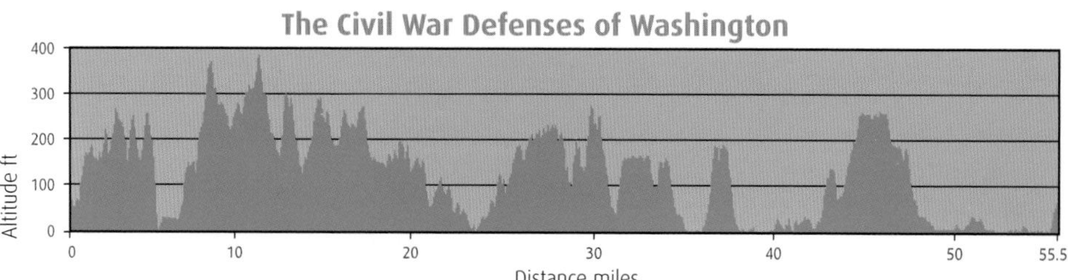

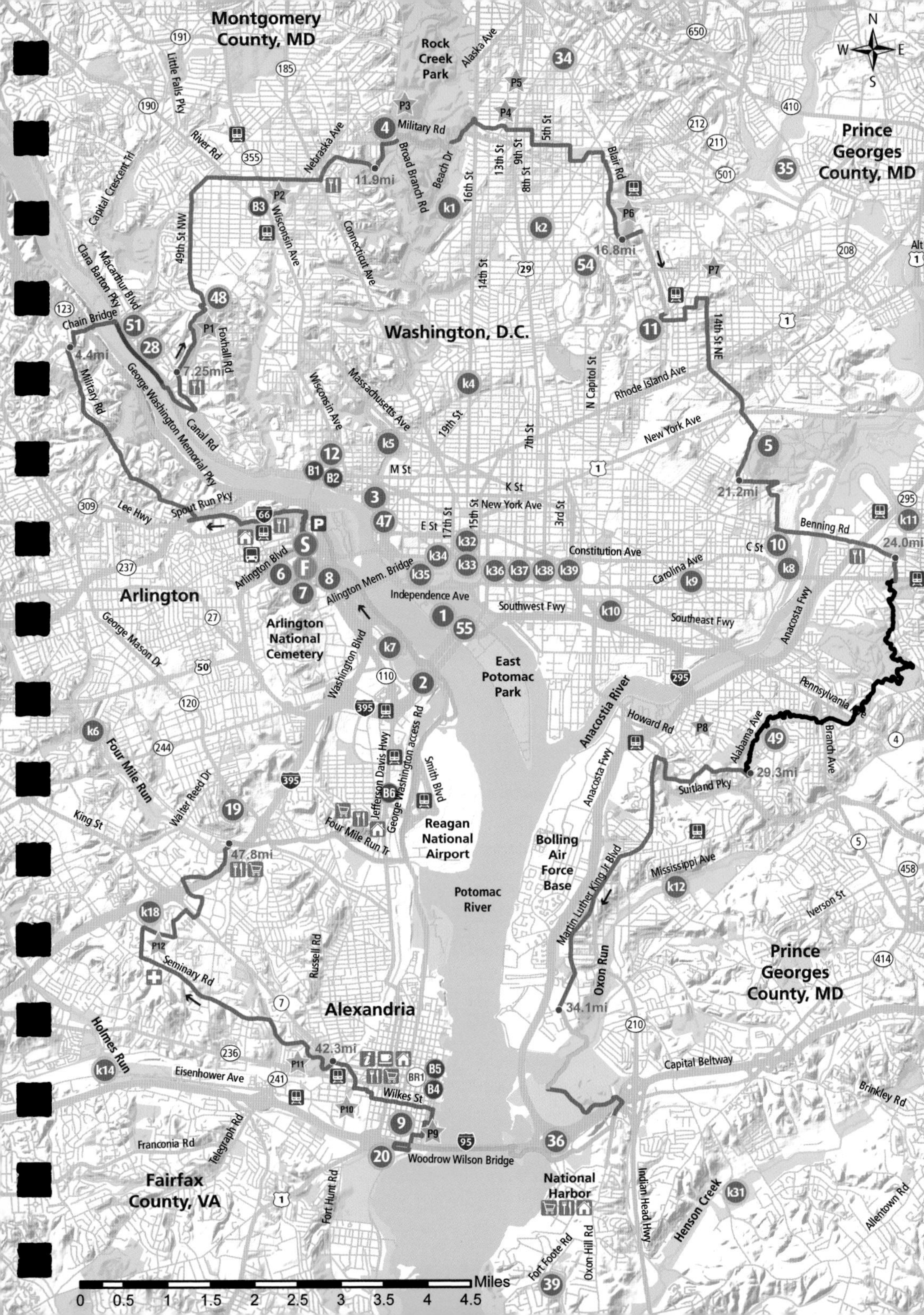

Montgomery County, MD
Rock Creek Park
Prince Georges County, MD
Washington, D.C.
Arlington
Arlington National Cemetery
East Potomac Park
Reagan National Airport
Bolling Air Force Base
Potomac River
Anacostia River
Alexandria
Fairfax County, VA
National Harbor
Four Mile Run
Holmes Run
Oxon Run
Henson Creek
Chain Bridge
Woodrow Wilson Bridge
Arlington Mem. Bridge
Military Rd
Nebraska Ave
Broad Branch Rd
Beach Dr
16th St
13th St
9th St
8th St
5th St
Blair Rd
14th St
14th St NE
Wisconsin Ave
Connecticut Ave
Massachusetts Ave
19th St
N Capitol St
7th St
Rhode Island Ave
New York Ave
M St
K St
E St
17th St
15th St
3rd St
Constitution Ave
Independence Ave
Southwest Fwy
Southeast Fwy
Carolina Ave
C St
Benning Rd
Anacostia Fwy
Pennsylvania
Branch Ave
Alabama Ave
Howard Rd
Suitland Pky
Mississippi Ave
Iverson St
Martin Luther King Jr Blvd
Capital Beltway
Brinkley Rd
Indian Head Hwy
Allentown Rd
Oxon Hill Rd
Fort Foote Rd
Fort Hunt Rd
Little Falls Pky
River Rd
Capital Crescent Trl
Clara Barton Pky
Macarthur Blvd
49th St NW
Foxhall Rd
Canal Rd
George Washington Memorial Pky
Spout Run Pky
Lee Hwy
Arlington Blvd
George Mason Dr
Washington Blvd
Jefferson Davis Hwy
George Washington access Rd
Smith Blvd
Four Mile Run Tr
Walter Reed Dr
King St
Seminary Rd
Russell Rd
Eisenhower Ave
Wilkes St
Franconia Rd
Telegraph Rd
Alaska Ave
4.4mi
7.25mi
11.9mi
16.8mi
21.2mi
24.0mi
29.3mi
34.1mi
42.3mi
47.8mi
Miles
0 0.5 1 1.5 2 2.5 3 3.5 4 4.5
N W E S

DDOT's comprehensive D.C. bike map helps move you about the city.

At a Glance

Distance 15.6 miles **Total Elevation** 595 feet

Terrain

This route combines unlaned on-road sections with stretches of segregated bike lane. Expect climbs up to the Capitol Building, on Sixth Street coming off Pennsylvania Avenue, and on the hills of its last quarter back toward Kalorama Park.

Traffic

Covering a busy section of D.C., many of this ride's streets are oftentimes thick with cars and trucks.

How to Get There

Take Metro to the Red Line's Adams Morgan/Woodley Park stop, exit onto Connecticut Avenue and turn left onto Calvert Street to cross the Duke Ellington Bridge. Then go left onto Columbia Avenue. The park appears soon to your right. Drivers should look to access Columbia Road from Connecticut Avenue or from 16th and 18th streets NW. Parking can be limited.

Food and Drink

You won't travel much more than a mile here without the chance to stop and refuel. And when it's all over, jump across the street to The Grill from Ipanema, or try other nearby options in the restaurant and bar-blessed Adams Morgan neighborhood.

Side Trip

Houses of government, museums, parks, embassies, churches, shops, the choices are yours, and virtually unlimited.

Links to 1 2 3 6 10 11 12 48 49 51 54

Where to Bike Rating 

About...

This route is the shorter of two singular urban rides hosted jointly each year by the Washington Area Bicyclist Association. It connects each D.C. avenue which bears the name of an original American colony by traveling the gridded streets and grand diagonals of Pierre L'Enfant's famed city plan. Moving through much of the District's core while exploring several of its most distinctive neighborhoods, it functions as a rolling celebration of the nation's capital and a reminder of advocacy's on-going push for national cycling equality.

Ready to roll.

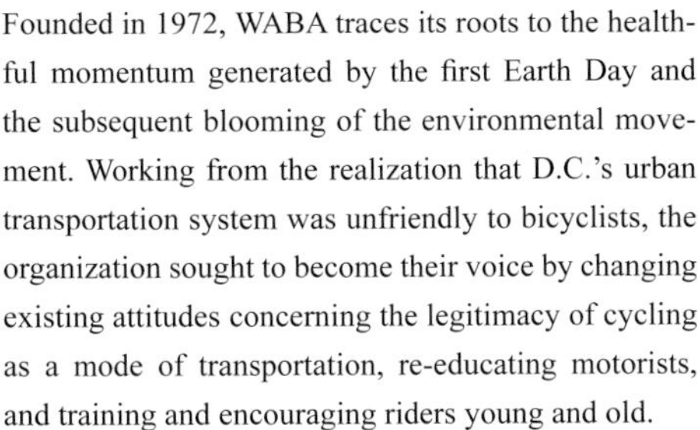

Founded in 1972, WABA traces its roots to the healthful momentum generated by the first Earth Day and the subsequent blooming of the environmental movement. Working from the realization that D.C.'s urban transportation system was unfriendly to bicyclists, the organization sought to become their voice by changing existing attitudes concerning the legitimacy of cycling as a mode of transportation, re-educating motorists, and training and encouraging riders young and old.

These days WABA is an area institution with the mission of "creating a healthy, more livable region by promoting bicycling for fun, fitness, and affordable transportation; advocating for better bicycling conditions and transportation choices for a healthier environment; and educating children and adults about safe bicycling." Stronger than ever, it has now expanded its service to the entire national capital region including the District of Columbia, the City of Alexandria, the Virginia counties of Arlington and Fairfax, and Montgomery and Prince George's counties in Maryland.

Among the many teaching, service-oriented, fundraising and out-and-out fun events the non-profit sponsors each year, none are more enjoyable than its two tours of the avenues. Promoted by WABA as part of its on-going effort to get more people on bikes, look to join the hundreds who cycle these gems each fall by getting out now and practicing for the big day all by your lonesome, remembering to always ride responsibly.

The 13 Colonies takes off through the heart of the Adams Morgan neighborhood and moves beyond WABA headquarters straight toward Howard University. Busy Georgia and Florida then lead through a quiet connecting stretch to heavily trafficked Rhode Island. A turn past the historic Shaw neighborhood brings both late 19th century row houses and shiny examples of urban renewal, and soon, D.C.'s grand Union Station.

Intimate, bike-friendly Capitol Hill follows and grants a great midway rest stop at Reconstruction-era Eastern Market's ever-thriving cluster of shops and restaurants. Pennsylvania then begins a stretch back around the United States Capitol Building, through Judiciary Square, onto New York Avenue, and past the White House. Foggy Bottom appears next before graciously giving way to Dupont Circle, and after a spin down Embassy Row, busy Connecticut turns to Calvert. Once there, the Duke Ellington Bridge brings you over the Rock Creek gorge and back home.

Ride Log

0.0 Begin at Kalorama Park exiting left where Columbia Rd meets Belmont.

0.2 Bear right onto Euclid after crossing 18th St.

1.3 Right onto Georgia Ave.

1.8 Right onto Florida Ave.

2.0 Left onto Vermont Ave.

2.2 Bear left onto 11th St.

2.45 Slide left onto Q St to go left onto Rhode Island Ave.

3.0 Right onto New Jersey Ave.

3.5 Bear right onto Third St, a quick right onto M St, and a left onto Fourth St.

4.3 Left onto E St.

4.55 Turn right onto New Jersey Ave.

4.7 Left onto Louisiana Ave.

4.95 Right at Columbus Circle.

5.0 Right onto Delaware Ave to a quick left onto D St.

6.1 Right onto 13th St.

6.25 Bear right onto Tennessee Ave.

6.4 Turn right to go around Lincoln Park.

6.7 Right onto Kentucky Ave.

6.95 Right onto South Carolina Ave.

7.25 Right onto 10th St.

7.5 Left onto North Carolina Ave.

7.85 Bear right onto Seward then again onto Pennsylvania Ave.

8.15 Right on Second St.

8.45 Left onto Constitution Ave.

9.15 Bear right as Constitution merges with Pennsylvania Ave.

9.25 Right onto Sixth St.

9.9 Left onto Massachusetts Ave.

10.1 Go straight past Mount Vernon Square on K St before joining New York Ave.

P

P1 WABA headquarters
P2 Union Station
P3 Eastern Market
P4 Library of Congress
P5 U.S. Supreme Court Building
P6 U.S. Capitol Building
P7 White House
P8 Watergate Complex
P9 Kennedy Center
P10 Embassy Row
P11 Rock Creek gorge

B

B1 City Bikes, 2501 Champlain St, NW
B2 BicycleSPACE, 459 I St, NW
B3 District Hardware—The Bike Shop, 1108 24th St, NW

BR

BR1 Bike and Roll Union Station, 50 Massachusetts Ave, NE

10.7 Cross 15th St to pass in front of White House.

11.1 Cross 17th St to continue on Pennsylvania Ave.

11.5 Left onto 21st St.

11.9 Right onto E St before quickly bearing right onto Virginia Ave.

12.3 Right onto New Hampshire Ave.

12.6 Travel halfway round Washington Circle to continue on New Hampshire Ave.

13.1 Left onto 20th St to a left onto Massachusetts Ave.

13.6 Use Sheridan Circle to continue along Massachusetts Ave.

14.1 Right onto Belmont St to a quick right onto Tracy Place (unmarked) to a left on Kalorama Rd.

14.6 Left onto Connecticut Ave.

15.0 Right onto Calvert St.

15.5 Right onto Columbia Rd.

15.6 Right to finish at Kalorama Park.

WABA's 13 Colonies

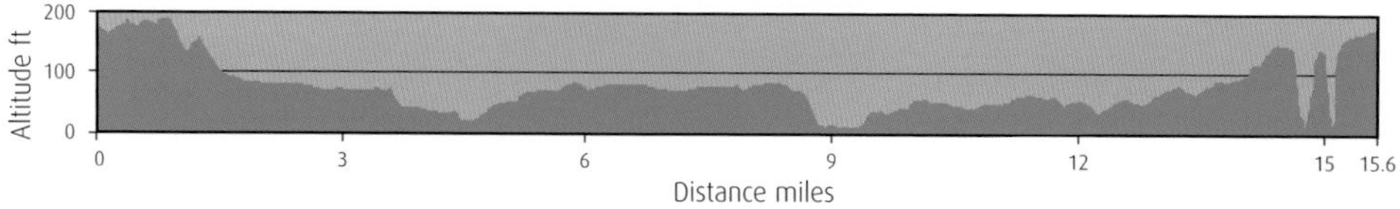

Altitude ft: 200, 100, 0

Distance miles: 0, 3, 6, 9, 12, 15, 15.6

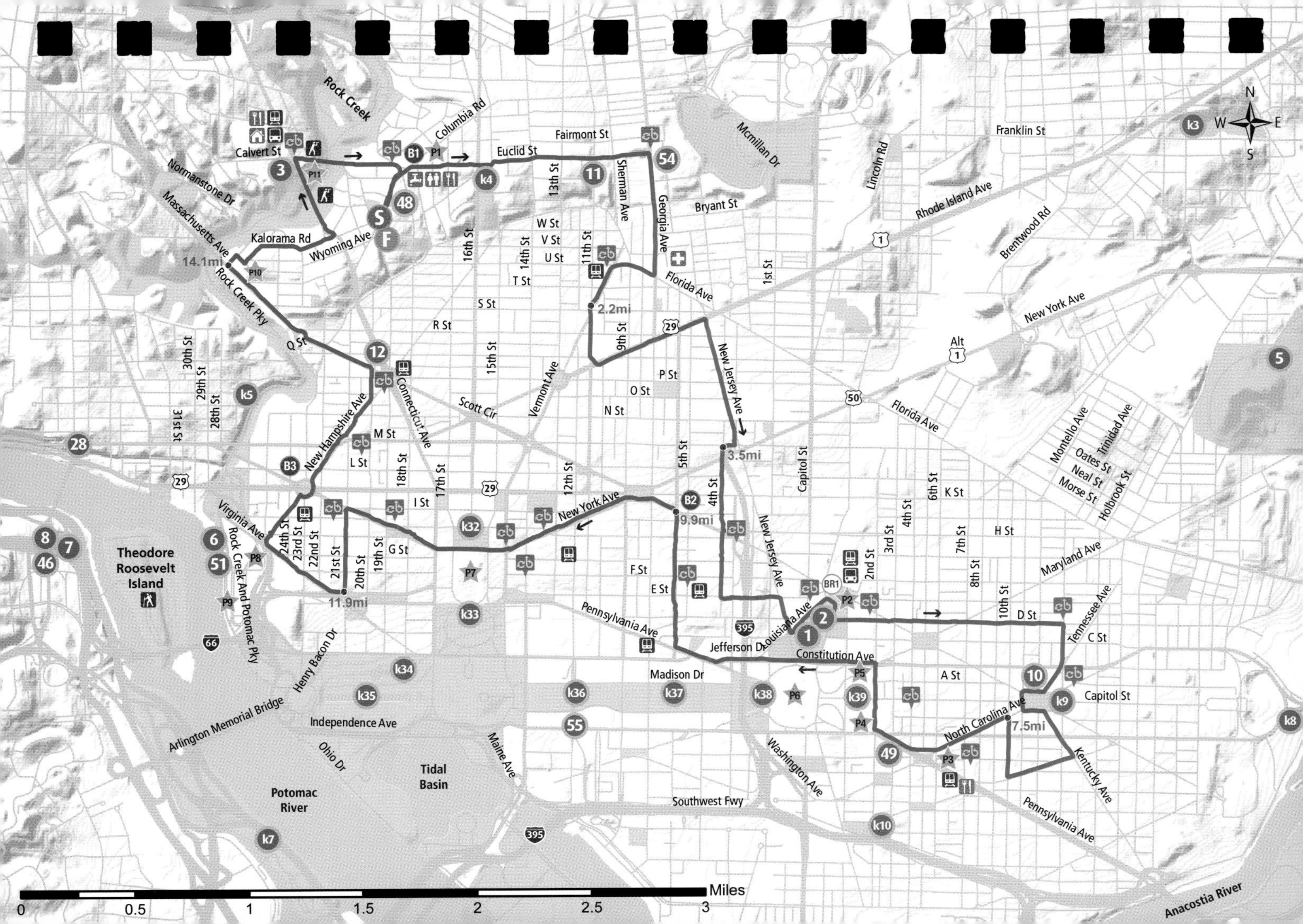

N
W
E
S
Rock Creek
Calvert St
Normanstone Dr
Massachusetts Ave
14.1mi
Kalorama Rd
Wyoming Ave
Columbia Rd
Euclid St
Fairmont St
Sherman Ave
Georgia Ave
Mcmillan Dr
Bryant St
Lincoln Rd
Franklin St
Rhode Island Ave
Brentwood Rd
Rock Creek Pky
Q St
16th St
13th St
14th St
W St
V St
U St
T St
11th St
S St
R St
15th St
2.2mi
Florida Ave
1st St
9th St
New York Ave
Alt 1
New Jersey Ave
P St
O St
N St
Vermont Ave
Scott Cir
Connecticut Ave
New Hampshire Ave
M St
L St
18th St
17th St
12th St
5th St
3.5mi
Capitol St
Florida Ave
Montello Ave
Trinidad Ave
Oates St
Neal St
Morse St
Holbrook St
30th St
29th St
28th St
31st St
I St
New York Ave
B2
9.9mi
4th St
6th St
K St
3rd St
4th St
7th St
H St
Maryland Ave
8th St
2nd St
Virginia Ave
24th St
23rd St
22nd St
21st St
20th St
19th St
G St
F St
E St
11.9mi
Theodore Roosevelt Island
Rock Creek And Potomac Pky
Pennsylvania Ave
New Jersey Ave
Louisiana Ave
Jefferson Dr
Constitution Ave
10th St
D St
Tennessee Ave
C St
A St
Capitol St
Madison Dr
Henry Bacon Dr
Arlington Memorial Bridge
Independence Ave
Ohio Dr
Maine Ave
Tidal Basin
Potomac River
Washington Ave
North Carolina Ave
7.5mi
Kentucky Ave
Southwest Fwy
Pennsylvania Ave
Anacostia River
Miles
0
0.5
1
1.5
2
2.5
3

The (not a) race is on.

At a Glance

Distance 65.5 miles **Total Elevation** 3940 feet

Terrain

This ride is all on-road and incorporates bike lanes and bridge sidepaths. Expect lots of hills in parts, especially southeast and northwest D.C.

Traffic

Most of this route is only mildly to moderately busy, but it's wise to approach stretches along these narrow, high-volume, high-speed avenues with extra caution: Independence, Montana, South Dakota, Michigan, Oregon, Wisconsin, Nebraska, and Connecticut.

How to Get There

Take Metro to the Red Line's Adams Morgan/Woodley Park stop, exit onto Connecticut Avenue and turn left onto Calvert Street to cross the Duke Ellington Bridge. Then go left onto Columbia Avenue. The park appears soon to your right. Drivers should look to access Columbia Road from Connecticut Avenue or from 16th and 18th streets NW. Parking can be limited.

Food and Drink

You won't go more than a few miles, at most, without the opportunity to stop and refuel today, though it's still a good idea on long rides such as this to keep water bottles filled and calories on hand.

Side Trip

Feel free to split this monster in two, and when you're finally finished, however long it takes, treat yourself to a cold beer somewhere...anywhere. Or try the Grill from Ipanema across Columbia Avenue from Kalorama Park.

Links to 1 2 3 4 6 10 11 12 46 47 49 54 55

Where to Bike Rating 

About...

Without doubt one of the most unique and challenging rides within any American city, this long, legendary tour instituted by the Washington Area Bicyclist Association connects all 50 D.C. state avenues and leaves no neighborhood unexplored. It's designed for experienced cyclists comfortable with intense urban riding as well as those with a penchant for pushing envelopes. At turns, 'brutal', 'beautiful', 'engrossing', and 'exhausting', after completing this epic there's one thing on which all will agree. They've only just met the true nation's capital.

Worked but happy.

Ride Log

0.0 Begin by exiting right out of Kalorama Park along Columbia Rd across from Belmont Rd.

0.1 Left 19th, immediate left Wyoming.

0.3 Right 18th, left California, right Florida.

0.65 Left 19th.

0.9 Left Corcoran, left New Hampshire.

1.35 Right T, left 16th.

1.65 Right W.

2.3 Right Sherman, right Vermont.

2.65 Bear left 11th.

2.9 Right Rhode Island, then bisect Logan Circle ahead to continue on R.I.

3.5 Round Scott Circle halfway to continue on R.I. (becomes M past Conn Ave).

4.1 Left 21st.

4.4 Left Pennsylvania Ave (follow past White House).

5.15 Right 15th, left to rejoin Penn (toward Capitol).

6.0 Left Seventh, immediate right Indiana.

6.25 Left Fifth (before courthouse).

6.8 Left K, right Seventh, immediate right New York.

7.3 Right Fourth.

7.9 Left E.

8.15 Right New Jersey.

8.3 Left Louisiana.

8.5 Right Columbus Circle, immediate right Delaware, left D St.

8.9 Straight across Massachusetts Ave to remain on D.

9.2 Sharp right Maryland, then round Stanton Park halfway to re-engage it.

9.6 Left Second.

10.1 Right D.

10.3 Left New Jersey, right Ivy.

10.5 Right Canal, immediate right Washington Ave (toward Capitol, bikes ok through barriers).

10.7 Left Independence.

11.7 Left L'Enfant Plaza.

12.1 Right Banneker Circle, immediate right over Case Bridge sidepath (watch curb).

12.5 Continue straight along sidewalk instead of curling left to ramp.

12.7 Right Buckeye Dr, right Ohio (jogging left ahead over Tidal Basin bridge).

Originals, Oddballs and Outliers

Ride Log continued...

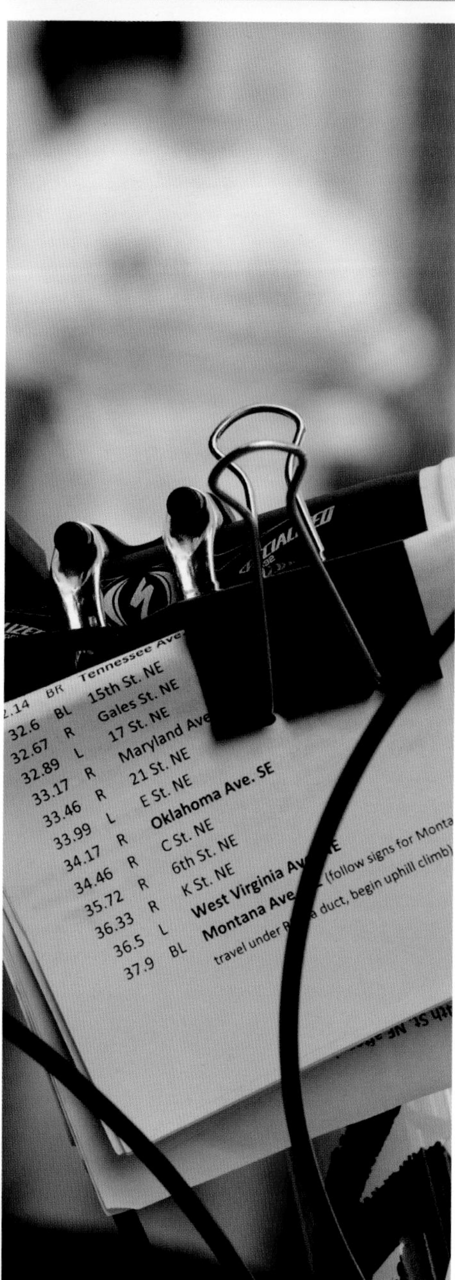

Copy and clip this cuesheet to keep it hands-free.

14.1 Right Independence, bear right beyond Kutz Bridge.

15.1 Stay straight to go under freeway (busy, use sidewalk if necessary).

15.2 Bear right Maine.

16.0 Road curves, becomes M.

17.0 Left Third.

17.3 Right Virginia (continue along freeway).

17.7 Right Eighth, left M.

18.0 Left 11th, right K.

18.5 Right 15th, immediate left in alleyway (Sousa Bridge access).

18.7 Right on sidewalk to cross bridge.

19.1 Exit bridge right, left Anacostia Park Rd at bottom (watch curb, keep river to right).

20.0 Left Good Hope Rd.

20.2 Right MLK Ave.

21.9 Left Malcolm X.

22.1 Right Eighth, left Alabama, right Wheeler.

22.6 Left Mississippi.

23.4 Left Stanton.

23.7 Right Alabama.

24.7 Stay right Alabama (as 25th splits off).

25.9 Left 38th, left Penn Ave, right Texas.

26.6 Right Nash, right Carpenter, left 38th.

27.2 Left Pennsylvania Ave, immediate left Ft Davis Dr (sidewalk available).

27.8 Left Massachusetts Ave.

28.5 Right three-quarters around Randle Circle to right on Minnesota.

29.2 Bear right to cross Pennsylvania Ave and angle left back to Minnesota (signposted).

29.4 Right Nicholson.

29.7 Right Anacostia Park Rd, under Sousa Bridge, then curl right up ramp to cross it.

30.3 Bear left as sidewalk splits, use curb cut to access Kentucky right.

31.0 Left South Carolina.

31.3 Left 10th, right Pennsylvania Ave.

31.7 Right Sixth, right North Carolina.

Ride Log continued...

32.2 Straight E Capitol, (past Lincoln Park).

32.4 Left 13th.

32.6 Bear right Tennessee.

33.0 Left on 15th.

33.2 Zigzag across Benning to a right on Maryland.

33.8 Right 21st (to recross Benning ahead).

34.3 Left E.

34.5 Right Oklahoma.

34.8 Right C, (stay right on C ahead at split).

36.0 Right Sixth.

36.7 Right K, bear left W Virginia.

38.1 Circle right to join Montana to north and go right under railroad viaducts (signposted).

38.9 Straight across R.I (becomes 14th).

39.5 Right Newton.

40.2 Left S Dakota (narrow, fast traffic, sidewalk available).

40.9 Left Michigan (narrow, sidewalk and bridge sidepath available).

41.9 Right John McCormack Rd (just after bridge).

42.5 Left to Taylor (after going under overpass), immediate right Hawaii.

43.1 Left to Allison, then bear left at light to go uphill on Rock Creek Church.

43.9 Right Randolph, immediate right Illinois (continuing around Grant, Sherman circles).

44.9 Left Farragut, right Georgia.

45.5 Right Longfellow.

45.7 Left Eighth.

45.9 Left Missouri, right Ninth, left Peabody, left 13th.

46.5 Right Colorado.

46.9 Left 14th.

47.3 Left Farragut, right Arkansas.

47.8 Left Iowa (easy to miss).

48.2 Cross Georgia, bear left Kansas (continuing past Sherman Circle).

49.5 Left Longfellow, right Third.

49.8 Right Oglethorpe, left Second.

50.0 Left North Dakota, right Third.

50.6 Left Whittier, right Fourth, left Aspen.

51.1 Right Eighth (bikes ok).

51.6 Left Geranium.

52.0 Left Alaska.

52.4 Left 16th, right Sherrill Dr (into RC Park).

Pre-ride research.

Post-ride refreshment.

Originals, Oddballs and Outliers

Ride Log continued...

52.9 Left Beach.
53.3 Right Bingham.
53.8 Right Oregon.
54.3 Left Beech (easy to miss, at bottom of hill).
54.8 Left Western.
55.2 Left Pinehurst Circle (at second entrance), immediate right Utah.
55.6 Right Rittenhouse.
56.2 Left Nevada.
56.7 Right Livingston, (continuing across Connecticut Ave).
57.3 Left 41st, (continuing across Military).
58.0 Right Ellicott, left Wisconsin.
58.6 Bear right at Tenley Circle to Nebraska.
59.2 Use interior lanes to remain on Nebraska (busy, becomes Loughboro).
60.1 Left Arizona.
60.4 Left Garfield, left University Terrace.
61.0 Right Loughboro.
61.4 Right Newark, right New Mexico.
61.9 Left Cathedral.
62.2 Left 39th, (cross Massachusetts Ave), bear right Idaho.
62.7 Left Newark, right 38th, right Porter.
63.0 Left Idaho.
63.2 Right Rodman, (cross Reno, fast traffic).
63.7 Right Conn Ave.
64.9 Left Calvert, over Ellington Bridge.
65.3 Right Columbia,
65.5 Finish Kalorama Park.

P1 WABA headquarters

B1 City Bikes, 2501 Champlain St, NW
B2 BicycleSPACE, 459 I St, NW
B3 City Bikes-Capitol Hill, 709 8th St, SE
B4 Hudson Trail Outfitters Ltd, 4530 Wisconsin Ave, NW #1
BR1 Bike and Roll Downtown, 1100 Pennsylvania Ave, NW
BR2 Bike and Roll Union Station, 50 Massachusetts Ave, NE

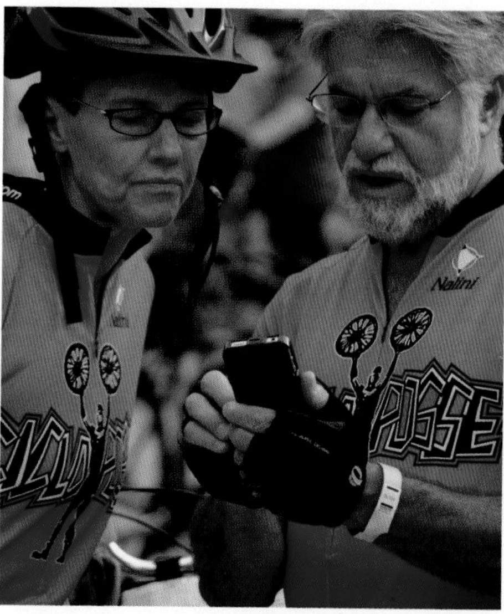

A couple fixes its coordinates.

Please note: WABA's 50 States map contains numerous links to Kids' Rides. These links have been intentionally left off the map to improve readability.

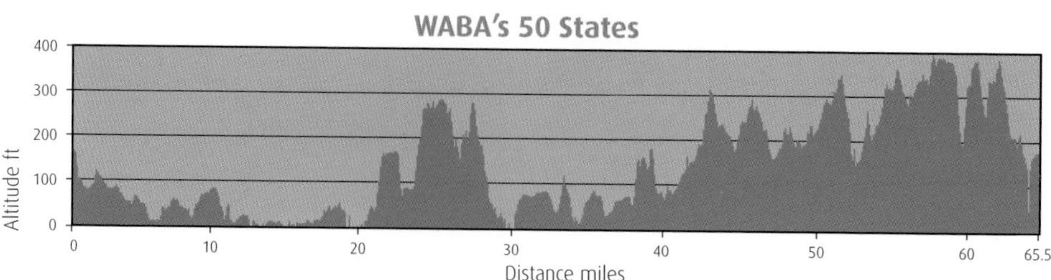

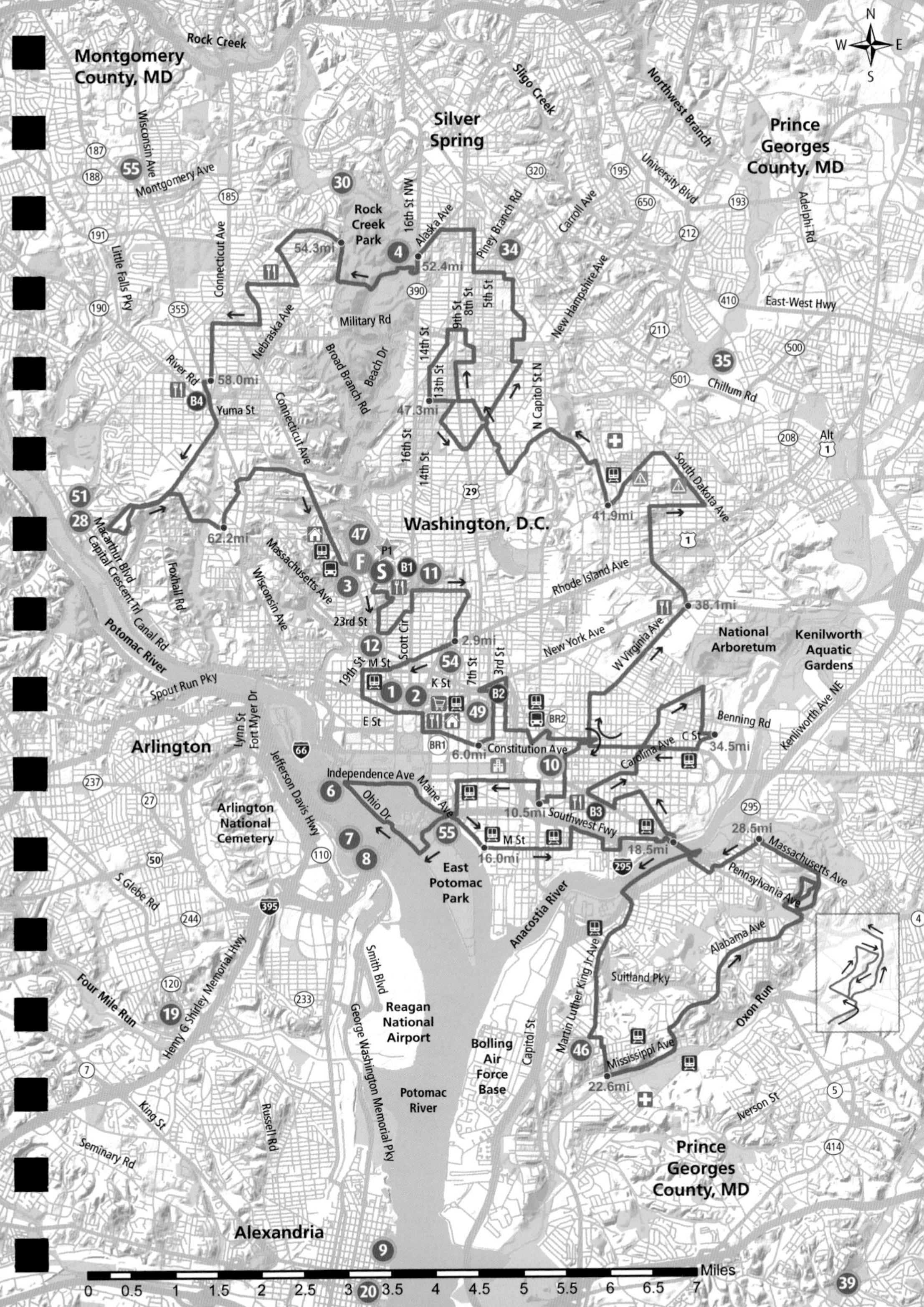

Montgomery County, MD
Rock Creek
Silver Spring
Sligo Creek
Northwest Branch
Prince Georges County, MD
Wisconsin Ave
Montgomery Ave
Connecticut Ave
Rock Creek Park
16th St NW
Alaska Ave
Piney Branch Rd
Carroll Ave
University Blvd
Adelphi Rd
Little Falls Pky
Nebraska Ave
Military Rd
Broad Branch Rd
Beach Dr
14th St
9th St
8th St
5th St
New Hampshire Ave
East-West Hwy
Chillum Rd
River Rd
Yuma St
13th St
N Capitol St N
Connecticut Ave
16th St
14th St
South Dakota Ave
Macarthur Blvd
Capital Crescent Trl
Foxhall Rd
Massachusetts Ave
Wisconsin Ave
Washington, D.C.
Rhode Island Ave
Canal Rd
Potomac River
23rd St
Scott Cir
New York Ave
W Virginia Ave
National Arboretum
Kenilworth Aquatic Gardens
Spout Run Pky
19th St
M St
K St
7th St
3rd St
E St
Benning Rd
Kenilworth Ave NE
Arlington
Lynn St
Fort Myer Dr
Jefferson Davis Hwy
Constitution Ave
Carolina Ave
C St
Independence Ave
Maine Ave
Ohio Dr
Southwest Fwy
M St
Arlington National Cemetery
East Potomac Park
Massachusetts Ave
Pennsylvania Ave
S Glebe Rd
Anacostia River
Alabama Ave
Smith Blvd
Martin Luther King Jr Ave
Suitland Pky
Four Mile Run
Henry G Shirley Memorial Hwy
Reagan National Airport
George Washington Memorial Pky
Bolling Air Force Base
Capitol St
Mississippi Ave
Oxon Run
Potomac River
Iverson St
King St
Russell Rd
Seminary Rd
Prince Georges County, MD
Alexandria
54.3mi
52.4mi
58.0mi
47.3mi
62.2mi
41.9mi
38.1mi
2.9mi
6.0mi
34.5mi
10.5mi
16.0mi
18.5mi
28.5mi
22.6mi
Miles
0 0.5 1 1.5 2 2.5 3 3.5 4 4.5 5 5.5 6 6.5 7

Washington or Wild West? Ford's Theater around the time of the assassination. *Photo courtesy the Library of Congress.*

At a Glance

Distance 51.1 miles **Total Elevation** 2160 feet

Terrain

Expect the usual D.C.-area dips into and out of Potomac tributaries. Piscataway Creek brings one south of Clinton, Zekiah Swamp Run shows up three times mid-ride, and Clark Run cuts through near Bel Alton.

Traffic

Can be very heavy, lessening only inside the last 15 miles.

How to Get There

Take the Orange, Blue or Red Lines to Metro Center, exiting on the SE corner of 11th and G streets. Head towards Ford's Theater at 10th and F. You want an alleyway halfway to the right down F Street. Another right brings you to the back of the theater. If driving, aim for the middle of the triangle formed by Interstate 395, New York Avenue, and Pennsylvania Avenue in downtown D.C. If busing, link to the Circulator.

Food and Drink

There are plenty of opportunities to snack and fill water bottles along the way, with an ultimate reward at Billy's Crab House in Pope's Creek.

Side Trip

Explore Booth lore by touring Ford's Theater in downtown D.C., Surratt House Museum in Clinton, and Dr. Samuel A. Mudd House Museum outside Waldorf. And be sure to catch the roadside markers at Samuel Cox's Place on Rich Hill near mile 44.5, in the thick pine woods at mile 45.5, along Pope's Creek Road, and at ride's end.

Links to 1 2 10 11 39 44 46 47 48

Where to Bike Rating 

About...

It is well-known that accomplished actor, and rabid Southern sympathizer, John Wilkes Booth, shot President Abraham Lincoln at Ford's Theater in Washington, D.C. on the evening of April 14th, 1865. What is less well-known is Booth's escape and the 12-day manhunt it produced. This tour attempts to follow that route through SE D.C. and into southern Maryland to Pope's Creek along the Potomac. Traversing high traffic roads for much of its distance, ride at your own risk and beware; the way is tinged with a touch of madness.

Light pours down into Clark Run.

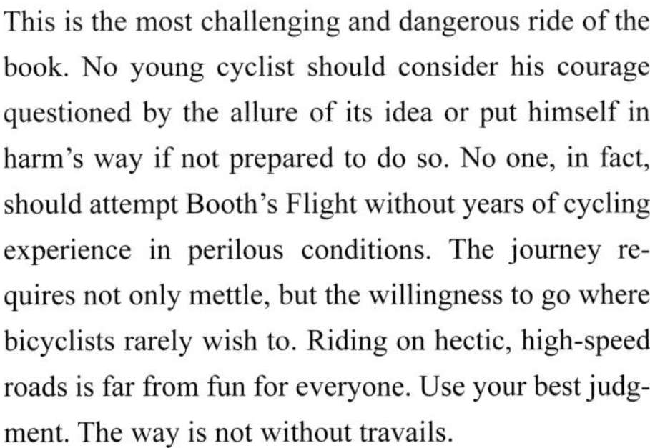

This is the most challenging and dangerous ride of the book. No young cyclist should consider his courage questioned by the allure of its idea or put himself in harm's way if not prepared to do so. No one, in fact, should attempt Booth's Flight without years of cycling experience in perilous conditions. The journey requires not only mettle, but the willingness to go where bicyclists rarely wish to. Riding on hectic, high-speed roads is far from fun for everyone. Use your best judgment. The way is not without travails.

Designed to trace Booth's gallop as it appears on maps today, this tour uses the roads closest to those he is known to have traveled. It's not the mileage that makes this ride as tough as it is. And it's not the terrain it travels. Its chief difficulty is its path, and more specifically, the few short miles along Branch Avenue (MD 5) that require cyclists to ford traffic merging onto the Beltway. All other rides in this book avoid that situation. This one doesn't.

It's understandable, then, that some will choose to link to this route after taking the Green Line Metro to Branch Avenue. Still others will opt to drive to Dr. Mudd's House, where the course improves dramatically, turning downright pleasant toward Bel Alton and again across U.S. 301 to the ride's finale.

To those that go the distance, Godspeed and have a blast. Booth didn't. With an ankle broken from his jump to the stage at Ford's Theater, he rode in great pain across the 11th Street bridge. Stopping to rest and recover arms at Mary Surratt's boardinghouse, moving onward toward medical attention at Dr. Mudd's, and receiving food and shelter at Samuel Cox's on Rich Hill, he ended up spending five miserable days and nights hidden in pine woods awaiting the chance to cross the Potomac into Virginia and everlasting glory. That wasn't to be the case.

Do some research, stop at the locations detailed in this ride's side trip, and take proper care. Hopefully, you won't feel the way the assassin felt only half way through his ordeal. "After being hunted like a dog through swamps," he wrote in his diary, "I am here in despair."

Ride Log

0.0 Begin with your back wheel touching the far-right-as-you-face-it back door of Ford's Theater. Proceed down Baptist Alley (so named because theater used to be church), going left down first available alley. Turn right at F St. Food.

0.45 Just before Judiciary Square Metro sign cut right down driveway alongside the National Law Enforcement Officer's Memorial.

0.55 Now quickly turn right into pathway through grounds of D.C. Courthouse cutting a diagonal left to a left on opposite side of grounds at Fourth and D streets.

0.7 Merge right onto Third St NW.

1.0 Left down Pennsylvania toward the Capitol Building.

1.15 Follow traffic pattern halfway round Peace Memorial to continue up Capitol Hill on its left (north) side.

1.7 Left on Independence to slight right onto Pennsylvania. Food.

2.4 Right onto Eighth St SE.

2.9 Left onto M St.

3.1 Right to go one block along 11th St SE to join sidepath over Anacostia River.

3.7 Turn left at bottom of path's exit ramp.

3.8 Go straight at light onto Good Hope. Food.

5.15 Right onto Naylor Rd. (At top of big hill.) Food.

6.15 Bear left to continue on Naylor then continue half-way around next traffic circle before merging with Branch Avenue (MD 5). Food.

7.8 Extreme caution. Merging traffic next one-and-a-half to two miles.

9.75 Merge right off MD 5 onto Linda Ln to immediate left onto Old Branch Rd. Food.

Booth's flight through Maryland ended near Pope's Creek.

13.4 Continue straight. Becomes Brandywine Rd. Surratt House to left. Food.

17.9 Left on Floral Park Rd.

18.3 Merge right onto MD 5, 301 to Mattawoman.

21.7 Left onto Mattawoman Beantown Rd then right at next light to remain on it. Food.

24.4 Left onto Poplar Hill Dr.

27.2 Bear right on Dr Mudd Rd.

27.6 Mudd House to right.

29.2 Right on Bryantown Rd.

32.0 Go straight. Bryantown becomes Olivers Shop. Food.

37.8 Right on MD 6.

42.2 Left onto Bel Alton-Newtown Rd.

45.6 Left onto MD 301 S. Food.

48.1 Right onto Pope's Creek Rd.

51.1 End at Pope's Creek, even with entrance to Captain Billy's Crab House.

Please note: Booth's Flight map contains numerous links to Kids' Rides. These links have been intentionally left off the map to improve readability.

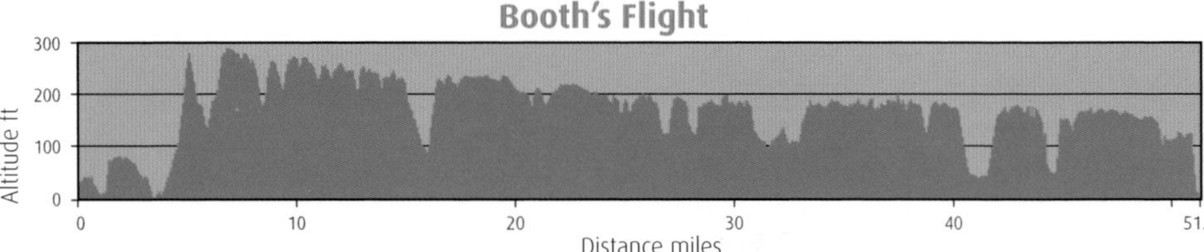

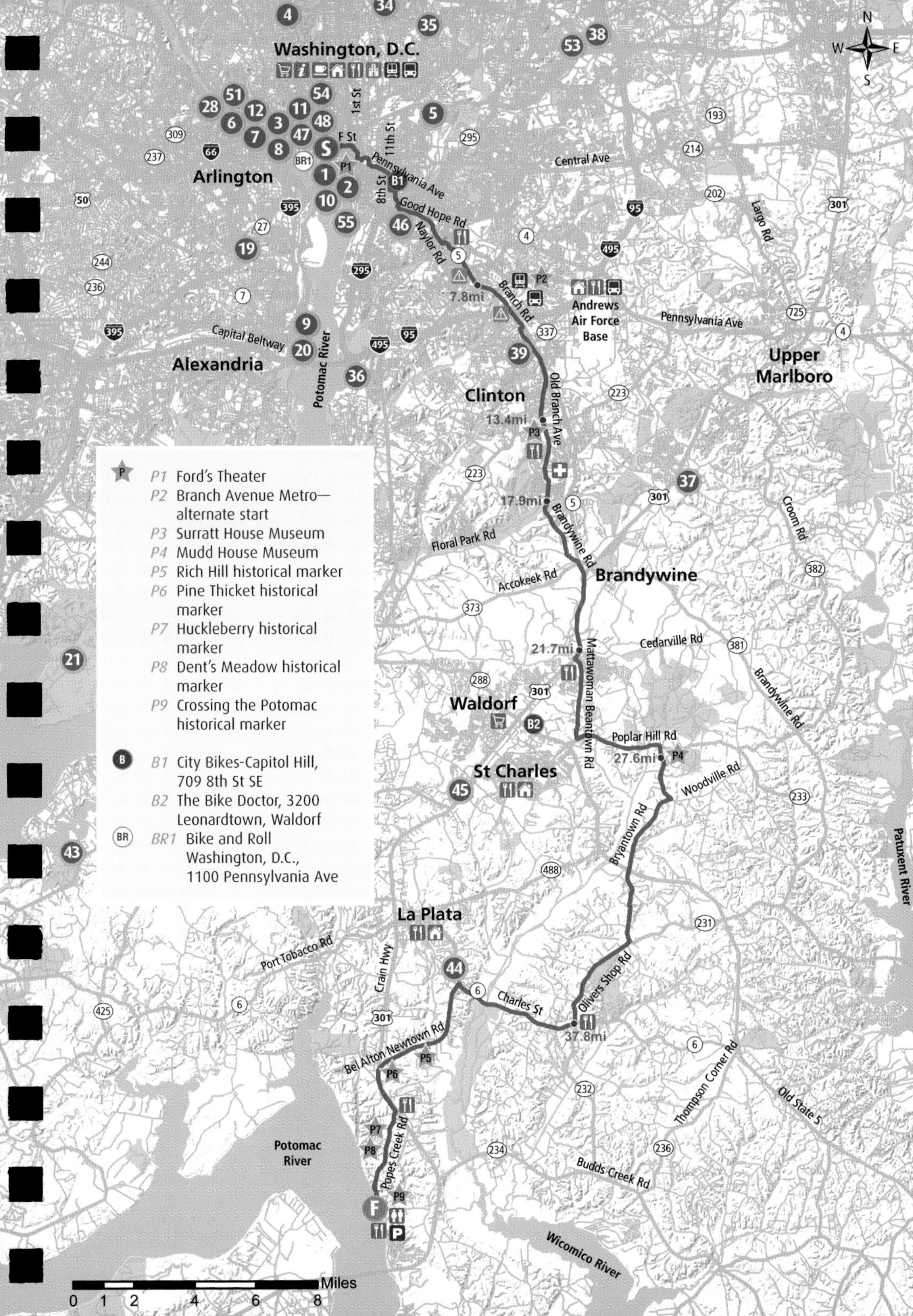

Washington, D.C.
Arlington
Alexandria
Potomac River
Capital Beltway
Clinton
Andrews Air Force Base
Upper Marlboro
Brandywine
Waldorf
St Charles
La Plata
Patuxent River
Wicomico River
F St
1st St
11th St
8th St
Pennsylvania Ave
Good Hope Rd
Naylor Rd
Branch Rd
Central Ave
Largo Rd
Pennsylvania Ave
Old Branch Ave
Brandywine Rd
Floral Park Rd
Accokeek Rd
Croom Rd
Cedarville Rd
Mattawoman Beantown Rd
Poplar Hill Rd
Woodville Rd
Bryantown Rd
Brandywine Rd
Port Tobacco Rd
Crain Hwy
Charles St
Olivers Shop Rd
Bel Alton Newtown Rd
Popes Creek Rd
Thompson Corner Rd
Old State 5
Budds Creek Rd
7.8mi
13.4mi
17.9mi
21.7mi
27.6mi
37.8mi
P1 Ford's Theater
P2 Branch Avenue Metro—alternate start
P3 Surratt House Museum
P4 Mudd House Museum
P5 Rich Hill historical marker
P6 Pine Thicket historical marker
P7 Huckleberry historical marker
P8 Dent's Meadow historical marker
P9 Crossing the Potomac historical marker
B1 City Bikes-Capitol Hill, 709 8th St SE
B2 The Bike Doctor, 3200 Leonardtown, Waldorf
BR1 Bike and Roll Washington, D.C., 1100 Pennsylvania Ave
Miles
0 1 2 4 6 8
N
S
E
W

Rolling toward a mess of Chesapeake Bay blue crab is reason enough to enjoy this ride.

At a Glance

Distance 35.8 miles **Total Elevation** 1550 feet

Terrain

Expect mild to moderate hills with plenty of easy pedaling over roads, highways, and trails.

Traffic

Vehicular congestion is surprisingly light on many roads throughout this route, and when present, plenty of cycling space most often remains. It can be nerve-racking crossing the Baltimore-Washington Parkway along MD 198 at mile 11 and again as Telegraph Road widens to merge with MD 32 at mile 18.

How to Get There

Take the Green Line Metro to its last stop at Greenbelt Metro Station. Use the Beltway if arriving by car. Traveling clockwise? Use exit 24. It will bring you directly into Metro's parking lot. Counter-clockwise? Use exit 23 to MD 201, followed by lefts onto Ivy and Cherrywood lanes. Greenbelt Metro Drive is just beyond the overpass.

Food and Drink

Multiple options exist at the turn onto MD 198 just shy of mile 11, along Hammonds Ferry and Hollins Ferry roads, and in downtown Baltimore and its Inner Harbor.

Side Trip

Explore Baltimore. And Pull into the North Tract of the Patuxent Research Station right at mile 13. Sign in at the visitor's center at the end of Bald Eagle Drive, grab a map, and bike away. Though not extensive, the refuge offers both natural surface trails and road riding opportunities.

Links to 

Where to Bike Rating 

About...

Consider an inter-urban spin too dangerous? What if safety weren't an issue? Home to Poe, Fort McHenry, and an authentic dialect all her own, birthplace of the National Anthem, Babe Ruth and The Wire; gritty Charm City just might have more on tap than you previously thought. And getting here by way of this surprisingly easy, Google-generated route will also leave you impressed. For those times when D.C. gets a bit big for its britches, remember this one. It leads to a dose of real.

Lock up and walk the Inner Harbor.

This ride begins spaciously from Greenbelt Metro, rises gradually along the wooded backside of the Beltsville Agricultural Research Center, and flows downhill through residential Montpelier onto lightly-trafficked Brock Bridge Road and over the Patuxent River. A few hump hills within Maryland City's suburban cluster then usher in the day's first patch of tighter riding at the turn onto MD 198.

The danger inherent in crossing above a parkway lies in underestimating the speed of merging traffic. Pick a point at the far edge of the shoulder straight across the curving lane, make sure the way is clear, and pedal straight to it, from point A directly to point B. That accomplished, do it again a little further downhill before enjoying a doubly-good descent past this ride's possible side trip and a brief rise to MD 32.

What makes the shot down the Patuxent Freeway so exciting is the natural speed riders tend to build in the presence of all that hurtling nearby steel. And what makes the feeling particularly satisfying here seems to be due not only to the state's radical notion of putting cyclists where many would not think to put themselves, but also by giving them jurisdiction over a well-signed, shoulder's worth of play space.

Buoyed by such subsidized passage, continue onward now beyond the narrower roads of Odenton, cautiously through another set of merges, past a dip to the Severn River, and onto the WB&A Road's steady, quiet line to the BWI Trail. That path carries you forward four more easy miles onto Hammonds Ferry, and after a short spin in the pleasant suburb of Linthicum, a descent brings you safely by three superhighways to the bottomlands along the Patapsco River. Initiated by a nice climb, Hollins Ferry then leads you deeper into greater Baltimore toward Mount Auburn, the city's historic, African-American cemetery.

Waterview Road delivers just that as a rise brings a vista of the bay-like Patapsco River straight ahead as well as a clean look north over downtown. After catching the Gwynns Falls Trail under Interstate 95, stay patient through its twists and turns toward Inner Harbor, and once there, a whole new city awaits your wheels. Pop into the visitor's center to begin your tour.

Ride Log

P1 Patuxent Research Refuge, North Tract
P2 Dixon Aircraft Observation Park
P3 National Aquarium, Baltimore, 501 E Pratt
P4 National Visionary Art Museum, 800 Key Highway
P5 Babe Ruth Birthplace and Museum, 216 Emory St
P6 Poe House and Museum, 203 N Amity St

B1 Proteus Bicycles, 9217 Baltimore Ave
B2 REI, 9801 Rhode Island Ave
B3 Bike Doctor of Linthicum, 507 S Camp Meade Rd
B4 Light Street Bicycles, 1124 Light Street

0.0 Begin at Greenbelt Metro sign (near bicycle racks) visible upon exiting station. Start left, passing left bank of newspaper boxes to curl right on access road curving out of Metro drop-off area.

0.6 Left onto Cherrywood Ln.

1.2 Left onto Edmonston Rd (MD 201).

3.4 Right at Old Baltimore Pike.

3.65 Continue straight/bear slightly right to join Odell Rd.

4.9 Stay right on Odell.

5.6 Stay left on Odell.

6.2 Left onto Muirkirk to immediate right onto Cedarbrook Ln.

7.1 Right at Montpelier (MD 197).

7.5 Continue straight through light. Becomes Brockbridge Rd.

8.15 Parallel path begins to right in Maryland City Park.

9.5 Right at N Sudlersville Rd. Parallel path ends at Brockbridge Elementary School.

9.8 Left at Chaptico to right on Old Line Ave.

10.4 Right at Greensboro S to right on Old Annapolis Rd.

10.6 Left at Red Clay Rd to right onto MD 198. Food.

11.2 Caution: Merging traffic.

13.0 Patuxent Research Refuge North Tract at right.

13.8 Continue straight along MD 32 E. Wide shoulder.

15.8 Take exit 6 to merge right onto MD 175 E.

17.1 Left at Telegraph Rd.

18.0 Caution: Merging traffic.

18.3 Cross stream, turn right to go through the Church at Severn Run's parking lot, and exit on its far side.

18.7 Go left onto WB&A Rd.

23.0 Turn right to join BWI Airport Trail. Soon come to snacks, rest area, planes landing.

24.5 Left at Stewart Ave and Newport Rd to continue on BWI Trail. Opposite B&A Trail direction.

27.3 Right onto Hammonds Ferry Rd soon after crossing Camp Meade Rd.

29.4 Cross Nursery Rd. Food.

30.3 Right on Hollins Ferry Rd. Food.

32.6 Right on Waterview.

33.0 Left at Annapolis.

33.5 Slide right to join Gwynns Falls Trail alongside Annapolis.

34.4 Right onto Warner.

34.5 Right at Stockholm. Becomes S Sharp after curving left.

35.0 Pass through Solo Gibbs Park and cross W Hamburg St.

35.1 Right on W Henrietta.

35.4 Right at Light St.

35.8 Right toward Inner Harbor, Baltimore visitor's center.

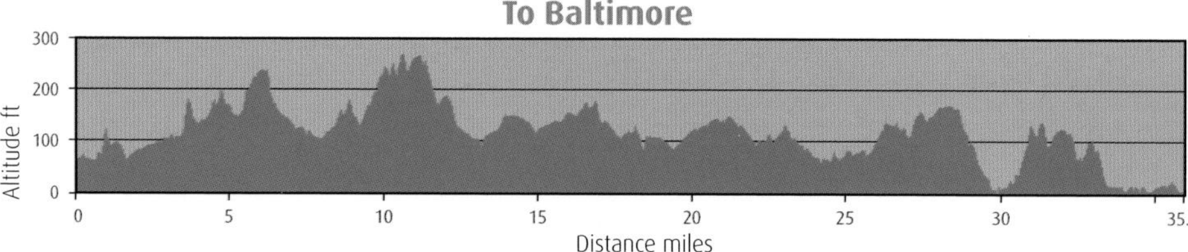

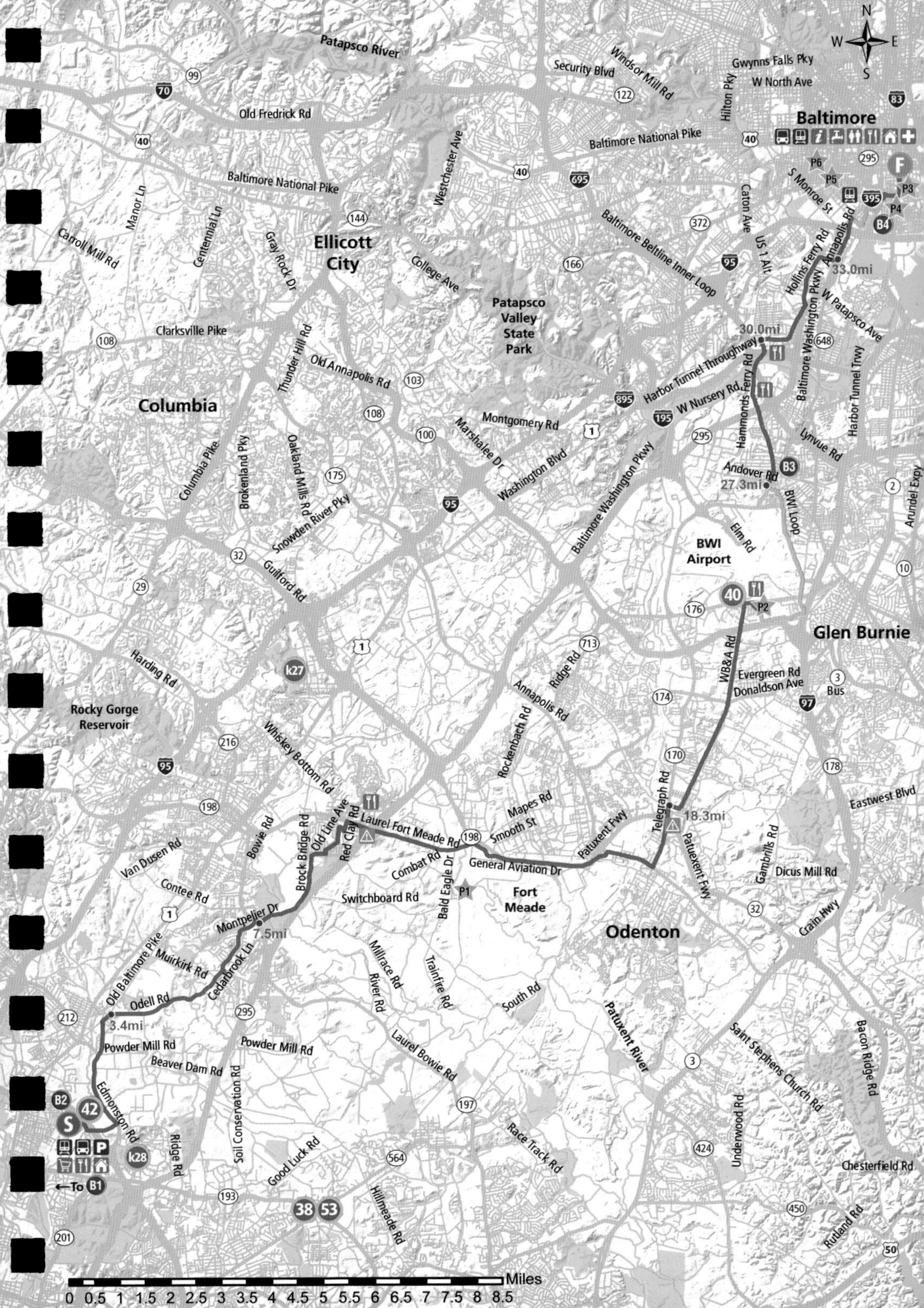

Patapsco River
Security Blvd
Windsor Mill Rd
Gwynns Falls Pky
W North Ave
Old Fredrick Rd
Baltimore
Baltimore National Pike
Baltimore National Pike
Hilton Pky
Westchester Ave
S Monroe St
Caton Ave
Manor Ln
Carroll Mill Rd
Centennial Ln
Gray Rock Dr
Ellicott City
College Ave
Baltimore Beltline Inner Loop
US 1 Alt
Annapolis Rd
Hollins Ferry Rd
33.0mi
Patapsco Valley State Park
Clarksville Pike
Thunder Hill Rd
Old Annapolis Rd
W Patapsco Ave
Baltimore Washington Pkwy
30.0mi
Harbor Tunnel Throughway
Harbor Tunnel Trwy
Columbia
Montgomery Rd
W Nursery Rd
Hammonds Ferry Rd
Marshalee Dr
Washington Blvd
Lynvue Rd
Columbia Pike
Brokenland Pky
Oakland Mills Rd
Snowden River Pky
Andover Rd
27.3mi
BWI Loop
Arundel Expy
Elm Rd
BWI Airport
Guilford Rd
Glen Burnie
Harding Rd
Ridge Rd
Annapolis Rd
WB&A Rd
Evergreen Rd
Donaldson Ave
Bus
Rocky Gorge Reservoir
Whiskey Bottom Rd
Rockenbach Rd
Telegraph Rd
18.3mi
Eastwest Blvd
Mapes Rd
Smooth St
Patuxent Fwy
Bowie Rd
Brock Bridge Rd
Old Line Ave
Red Clay Rd
Laurel Fort Meade Rd
Combat Rd
Bald Eagle Dr
General Aviation Dr
Patuxent Fwy
Gambrills Rd
Dicus Mill Rd
Van Dusen Rd
Contee Rd
Switchboard Rd
Fort Meade
Crain Hwy
Montpelier Dr
7.5mi
Odenton
Old Baltimore Pike
Muirkirk Rd
Cedarbrook Ln
Millrace Rd
River Rd
Trainfire Rd
South Rd
Odell Rd
3.4mi
Patuxent River
Powder Mill Rd
Powder Mill Rd
Beaver Dam Rd
Laurel Bowie Rd
Saint Stephens Church Rd
Bacon Ridge Rd
Edmonston Rd
Soil Conservation Rd
Underwood Rd
Ridge Rd
Race Track Rd
Good Luck Rd
Chesterfield Rd
←To
Hillmeade Rd
Rutland Rd
Miles
0 0.5 1 1.5 2 2.5 3 3.5 4 4.5 5 5.5 6 6.5 7 7.5 8 8.5

Lori and Ed, just pulling in from Pittsburgh.

At a Glance

Distance 29.0 miles **Total Elevation** 250 feet

Terrain

Natural surface trail, quite bumpy in parts, over flat to near-flat ground.

Traffic

Zero cars. Zero road crossings. You'll only have to contend with other non-motorized folk, sometimes thick near D.C. and Great Falls but more often few and far between.

How to Get There

The Orange/Blue Foggy Bottom Metro is nearest. Exit the elevator west down I Street to a left on New Hampshire. Swing right onto Virginia Avenue and cross the parkway to the ride's beginning. If driving, use Interstate 66 and the George Washington Memorial Parkway to get you near here from Virginia and the RCPP and K Street/Whitehurst Freeway if coming from the District. Of course, there are numerous other options, including the D.C. Circulator.

Food and Drink

Along the waterfront, and on K and M streets in Georgetown. At Old Angler's Inn on Macarthur Boulevard. And seasonally at Fletcher's Cove and Great Falls.

Side Trip

Take a mule drawn canal boat ride in Georgetown or Great Falls. Hike the Billy Goat Trail. Spend the night in Lockhouse Six. Or complete the C&O's full 184.5 mile course to Cumberland, Maryland. And when even that proves pedestrian, pedal to Pittsburgh by way of the Great Alleghany Passage, passing nary a car the full 335 miles from D.C.

About...

Tracing the north bank of the Potomac River from Georgetown to Cumberland, Maryland, the Chesapeake & Ohio Towpath is the longest trail originating in the District. This tree-lined route between grand old waterways introduces you to what could be a week's journey on an afternoon's jaunt to Great Falls. One of the region's most spectacular natural sights and a favored area destination for centuries, cycle in style to where the river drops steeply and plunges past a mass of jagged rock through narrow Mather Gorge.

Losing yourself here is much easier than losing the way.

George Washington dreamed of a water route connecting mid-Atlantic seaports to the Ohio Valley, but didn't see it happen in his lifetime. The C&O Canal Company inherited his vision and dug from 1828-1850, but was beaten by the rise of the railroads. Though both accomplished much, perhaps the most lasting features of what was once called America's "Great National Project" are the humble towpath built for boat-pulling mules beside its banks and the historic structures standing along its course.

Though 500 boats did ply the canal during the 1870s, it officially closed in 1924, and might have been paved to parkway if not for U.S. Supreme Court Justice William O. Douglas. An avid outdoorsman, he led a celebrated eight-day hike along the towpath in 1954 which eventuated the creation of the Chesapeake and Ohio National Historical Park.

Slip to the river side of Thompson Boat Center before your spin to see the surviving wooden watergate where the canal meets the Potomac at this ride's very beginning. Then, having begun back around front, an option exists at this ride's first crossing to utilize the first three smooth miles of the Capital Crescent Trail from here. Connect to it along K Street past the Georgetown Waterfront. It meets the towpath at Fletcher's Cove.

The mapped route brings you beyond the canal's first lock and visitor center, widens its way past Key Bridge, and faithfully hugs the basin from there onward. A total of 74 locks were needed to bring the C&O 605 feet up to Cumberland, and you'll pass a handful of them today. Families lived in the adjoining brick houses, many of which are named after their last owner. Lockkeepers were diligent souls and might be summoned by a bugling pilot at any hour of the day or night.

The towpath makes for a nice, if sometimes bumpy ride, and with the canopy and its reflection to your right and the river and its islands to your left, you might find yourself spirited away on occasion. Don't miss the 220-foot stone arch of Cabin John Bridge just past Lock Seven or the beautiful scenery through Widewater Lagoon. Lock up and walk to impressive Great Falls Overlook when you arrive. And check out the historic tavern. Built as a hostelry in 1831, it now houses the park's visitor center.

Ride Log

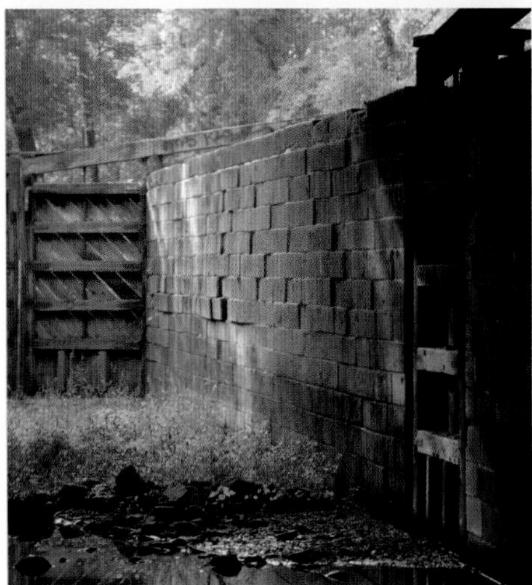

A grand old lock along the C&O.

P1 Georgetown C&O visitor center
P2 Abner Cloud House—circa 1802
P3 Lockhouse Six
P4 River Center at Lockhouse Eight
P5 Carderock—rock climbing
P6 Angler's Inn
P7 Widewater Lagoon
P8 Great Falls Overlook
P9 Great Falls Tavern C&O visitor center

B1 Revolution Cycles, 3411 M St, NW
B2 Bicycle Pro Shop, 3403 M St, NW
B3 Big Wheel Bikes, 1034 33rd St, NW
B4 Cycle Life USA, 3255 K St, NW
B5 District Hardware—The Bike Shop, 1108 24th St, NW

BR1 Thompson Boat Center
BR2 Fletcher's Boathouse

0.0 Begin at Thompson Boat Center sign adjacent to parking lot along Rock Creek Trail.

0.2 Turn left onto beginnings of C&O Canal Towpath through Georgetown.

0.4 Pass C&O Canal visitor center.

0.85 Curl right up ramp, cross bridge, and continue on other side of canal.

1.05 Stairs to parking below Key Bridge. Capital Crescent access.

3.2 Fletcher's Boathouse. Bicycle, boat rental. Capital Crescent access ends.

4.2 Chain Bridge.

5.0 Inlet Locks. Bathrooms.

5.35 Lockhouse Six.

8.35 Lockhouse Eight. River Center.

12.5 Access to Old Angler's Inn, dining along Macarthur Blvd.

14.3 Great Falls Overlook.

14.5 End even with access ramp to Great Falls Tavern. Retrace.

29.0 Finish at Thompson Boat Center.

Widewater Lagoon near Great Falls.

The C&O Towpath to Great Falls

Altitude ft: 0, 100, 200
Distance miles: 0, 5, 10, 15, 20, 25, 29.0

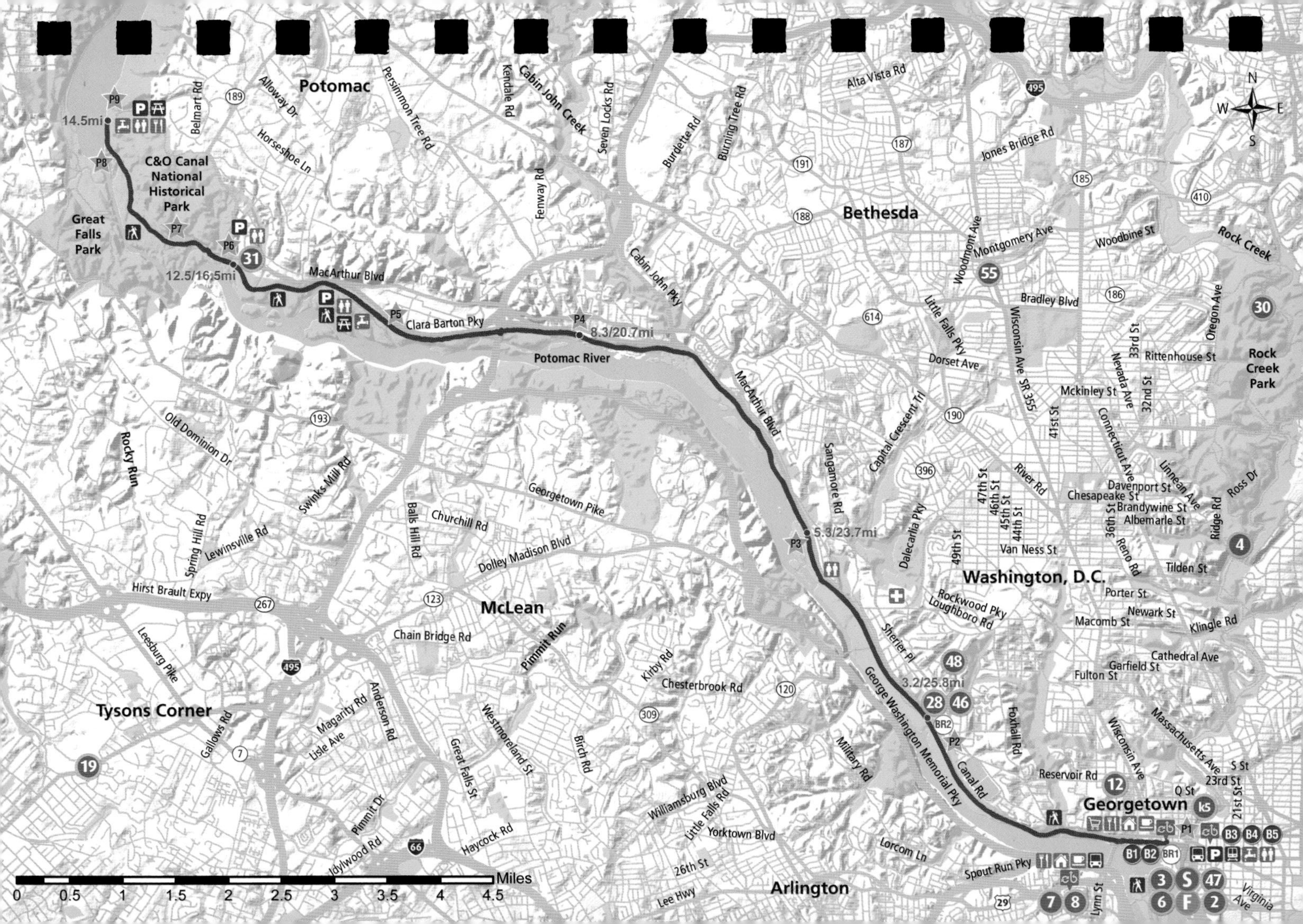

Potomac
Great Falls Park
C&O Canal National Historical Park
14.5mi
12.5/16.5mi
8.3/20.7mi
5.3/23.7mi
3.2/25.8mi
Potomac River
Bethesda
Washington, D.C.
Georgetown
McLean
Tysons Corner
Arlington
Rock Creek
Rock Creek Park
Cabin John Creek
Pimmit Run
Rocky Run
MacArthur Blvd
Clara Barton Pky
George Washington Memorial Pky
Canal Rd
Cabin John Pky
Persimmon Tree Rd
Kendale Rd
Seven Locks Rd
Burdette Rd
Burning Tree Rd
Alta Vista Rd
Jones Bridge Rd
Belmart Rd
Alloway Dr
Horseshoe Ln
Fenway Rd
Woodmont Ave
Montgomery Ave
Woodbine St
Bradley Blvd
Little Falls Pky
Dorset Ave
Wisconsin Ave SR 355
Capital Crescent Trl
Sangamore Rd
Dalecarlia Pky
Oregon Ave
Rittenhouse St
33rd St
32nd St
Nevada Ave
Mckinley St
41st St
Connecticut Ave
Linnean Ave
Ross Dr
Ridge Rd
Davenport St
Chesapeake St
Brandywine St
Albemarle St
36th St
Reno Rd
River Rd
47th St
46th St
45th St
44th St
49th St
Van Ness St
Tilden St
Porter St
Newark St
Macomb St
Klingle Rd
Rockwood Pky
Loughboro Rd
Sherier Pl
Cathedral Ave
Garfield St
Fulton St
Foxhall Rd
Wisconsin Ave
Massachusetts Ave
S St
23rd St
21st St
Q St
Reservoir Rd
Lynn St
Spout Run Pky
Virginia Ave
Lorcom Ln
Military Rd
Old Dominion Dr
Swinks Mill Rd
Spring Hill Rd
Lewinsville Rd
Georgetown Pike
Churchill Rd
Balls Hill Rd
Dolley Madison Blvd
Hirst Brault Expy
Chain Bridge Rd
Kirby Rd
Chesterbrook Rd
Leesburg Pike
Gallows Rd
Magarity Rd
Lisle Ave
Anderson Rd
Great Falls St
Westmoreland St
Birch Rd
Williamsburg Blvd
Little Falls Rd
Yorktown Blvd
Pimmit Dr
Idylwood Rd
Haycock Rd
26th St
Lee Hwy
N
S
E
W
Miles
0
0.5
1
1.5
2
2.5
3
3.5
4
4.5

Layers of color off Loyalty Road.

At a Glance

Distance 41.1 miles **Total Elevation** 3035 feet

Terrain

Expect hills, a cool car ferry, more hills, a narrow bridge (with walkway), and yet more hills over good, two-lane country roads. And prepare for four miles of hard-packed gravel riding on Old Waterford Road.

Traffic

A little more than usual—and a little faster—on Elgin Road (MD 109) out of Poolesville, and parts of MD 28.

How to Get There

Exit 45 off the Beltway brings you to Dulles Toll Road (VA 267). Stay off its airport access section continuing on the Dulles Greenway to a left on the Leesburg Bypass (U.S. 15, VA 7). Then go right on South King through Leesburg to the entrance to Ida Lee Park. Look to park near its recreation center. Leesburg Pike (VA 7) will also get you to the bypass.

Food and Drink

Take a break on the Maryland side of White's Ferry, at Dickerson Market, or in Point of Rocks.

Side Trip

Visit the Monocacy Aqueduct left down Mouth of Monocacy Road just past Dickerson, and take a break in Waterford by going straight (not left) before sliding right downhill on Water Street at mile 35.

Links to 13 24 29 32

Where to Bike Rating 

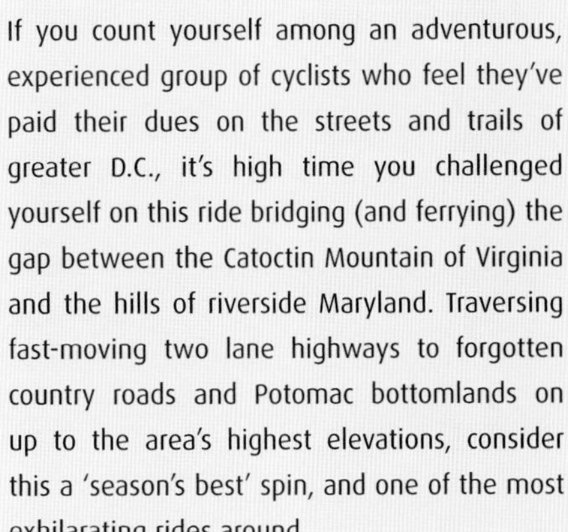

About...

If you count yourself among an adventurous, experienced group of cyclists who feel they've paid their dues on the streets and trails of greater D.C., it's high time you challenged yourself on this ride bridging (and ferrying) the gap between the Catoctin Mountain of Virginia and the hills of riverside Maryland. Traversing fast-moving two lane highways to forgotten country roads and Potomac bottomlands on up to the area's highest elevations, consider this a 'season's best' spin, and one of the most exhilarating rides around.

Crossing the Potomac on the Jubal A.

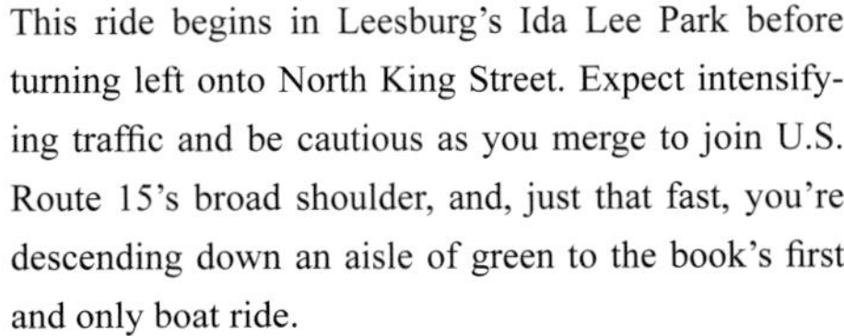

This ride begins in Leesburg's Ida Lee Park before turning left onto North King Street. Expect intensifying traffic and be cautious as you merge to join U.S. Route 15's broad shoulder, and, just that fast, you're descending down an aisle of green to the book's first and only boat ride.

White's Ferry is the sole remaining ferry of dozens that used to operate at points up and down the Potomac River. One dollar will get you and your bike across on board the 24-car General Jubal A. Early.

The ensuing stretch through bottomlands begins benignly enough but a strenuous mile-long climb awaits, as does Poolesville further along another four moderate miles.

Perhaps you've been here before. It's the hub of a regional cycling sweet spot with explorable roads galore. Today, head north to Beallsville as you prepare for a tussle with the faster cars and bigger trucks of MD 28. There are hills here, to be sure, but each climb promptly repays you in kind as Dickerson gives way to the Monocacy River and blue sky views beyond Tuscarora.

A turn there brings more open, rolling expanse as well as a preview of what's to come in the hills of Virginia. Point of Rocks arrives quickly and offers the chance to rest, refresh, and admire its Gothic Revival train station. There, walk along the left path of the two-lane bridge is highly recommended and allows you to gaze upward at the formation from which the town derived its name. Then, it's up onto the Catoctin Mountain after a two mile, 270 foot ascent, for the beginning of a length of riding to rival the best.

After descending to Taylorstown, pick up Loyalty Road as it drops you past an impressive estate toward a series of short, demanding climbs. Soon, as the beginnings of the Blue Ridge spread before you, you're off past deep, green fields and rolling, plank-fenced, horse pasture.

At Waterford, consider the saner option of continuing on VA 665 and returning to Leesburg via Clarke's Gap Road and the W&OD Trail. Otherwise, hit the hard-packed gravel of VA 698 for yet more rugged climbing, thrilling descents and a sudden, sneaky approach back to Ida Lee.

Ride Log

0.0 Begin by going left out of Ida Lee Park's recreation center parking lot (across from Rust Library) then immediately right toward park's exit.

0.3 Turn left onto Hwy 15. (Sidepath available for short while.)

1.55 Be cautious. Merging traffic.

2.8 Turn right onto White's Ferry Rd (VA 665).

4.05 Cross Potomac at White's Ferry.

10.5 Left onto (109) Elgin Rd (MD 109).

10.9 Stay left on Beallsville.

12.9 Left onto Darnestown Rd (MD 28).

15.1 Right to continue on MD 28.

16.6 Mouth of Monocacy Rd provides access to C&O Canal Towpath at left.

18.1 Cross Monocacy River.

20.0 Left onto MD 28 to Point of Rocks, MD.

24.3 Point of Rocks (MARC Station) at left.

24.8 Left to remain on road's left side to access bridge's left (and only) walkway. Take care.

25.2 Cross carefully to join Lovettsville Rd (VA 672).

27.9 Left onto Taylorstown Rd (VA 668).

29.9 Right onto Loyalty Rd (VA 665) to Waterford.

35.1 Left onto (VA 698) Old Waterford Rd.

37.0 Bear left to remain on Old Waterford.

38.7 Turn right to stay on Old Waterford.

39.9 Concrete resumes.

40.5 Turn left onto Ida Lee Park Trail.

41.1 Use trail to curl past Rust Library and left toward recreation center's bicycle racks.

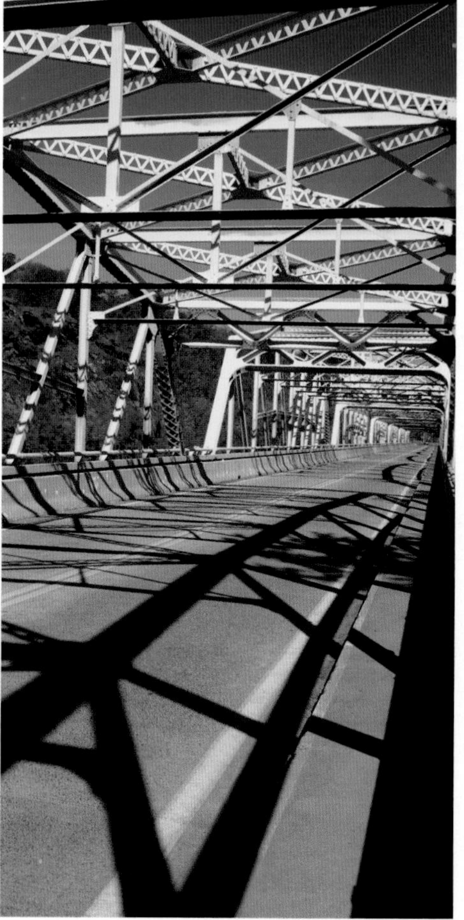

The bridge at Point of Rocks.

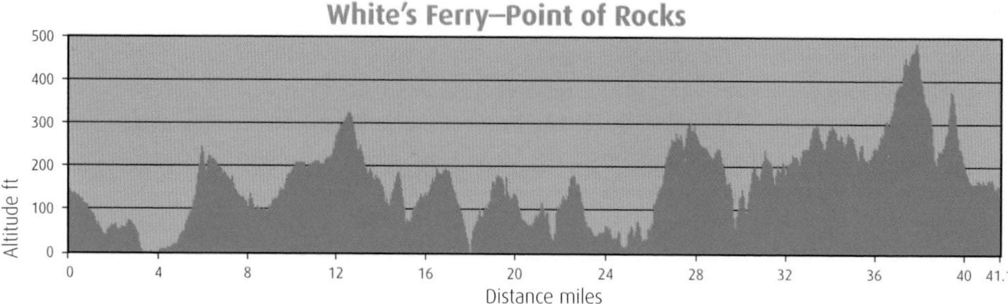

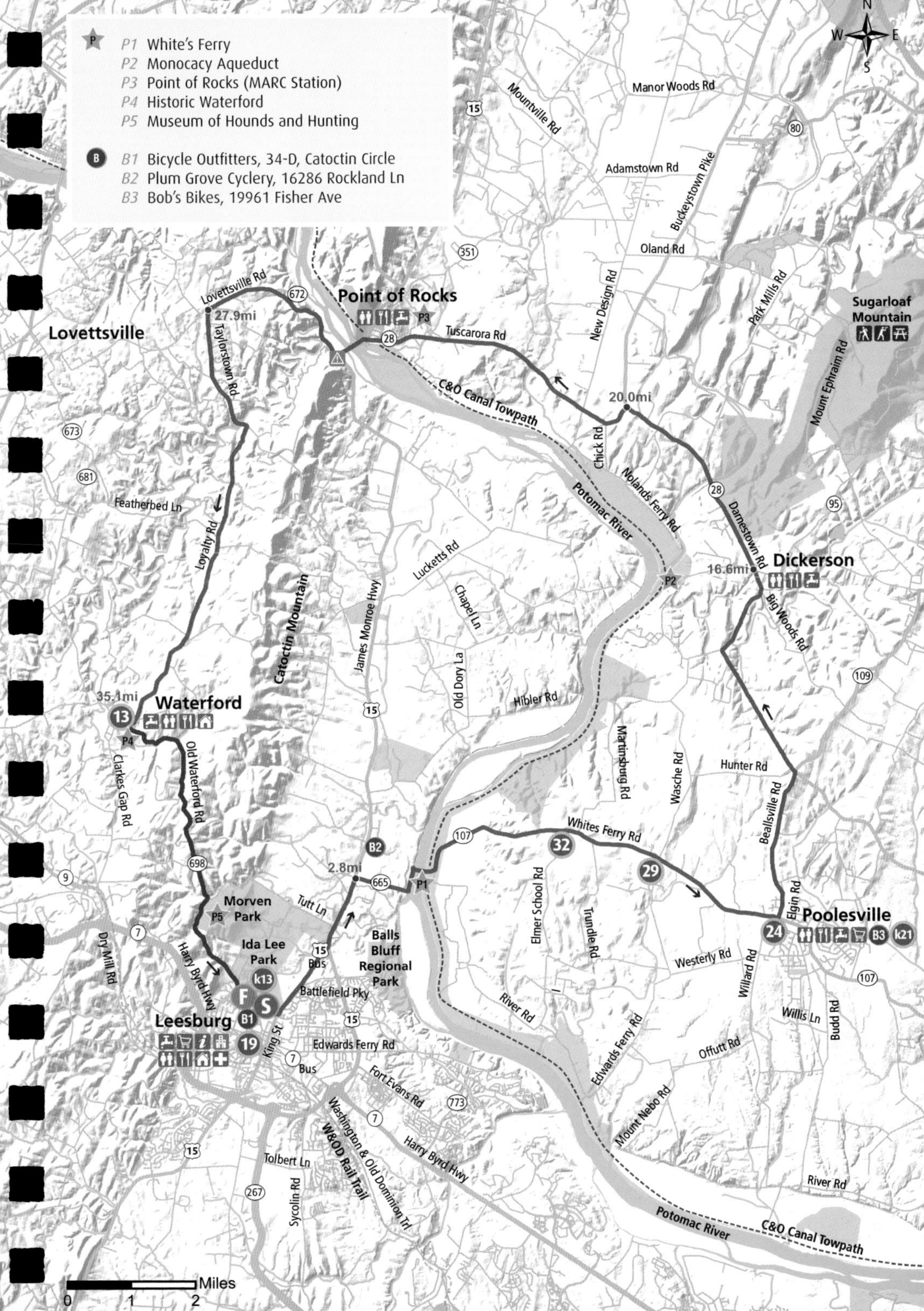
P1 White's Ferry
P2 Monocacy Aqueduct
P3 Point of Rocks (MARC Station)
P4 Historic Waterford
P5 Museum of Hounds and Hunting
B1 Bicycle Outfitters, 34-D, Catoctin Circle
B2 Plum Grove Cyclery, 16286 Rockland Ln
B3 Bob's Bikes, 19961 Fisher Ave
Point of Rocks
Lovettsville
Waterford
Leesburg
Dickerson
Poolesville
Sugarloaf Mountain
Catoctin Mountain
Morven Park
Ida Lee Park
Balls Bluff Regional Park
Potomac River
C&O Canal Towpath
W&OD Rail Trail
27.9mi
20.0mi
16.6mi
35.1mi
2.8mi
Lovettsville Rd
Taylorstown Rd
Loyalty Rd
Featherbed Ln
Old Waterford Rd
Clarkes Gap Rd
Harry Byrd Hwy
Dry Mill Rd
Tuscarora Rd
Chick Rd
Nolands Ferry Rd
Darnestown Rd
Big Woods Rd
Bealsville Rd
Hunter Rd
Whites Ferry Rd
Elgin Rd
James Monroe Hwy
Lucketts Rd
Chapel Ln
Old Dory La
Hibler Rd
Martinsburg Rd
Wasche Rd
Elmer School Rd
Trundle Rd
Westerly Rd
Willard Rd
Willis Ln
Budd Rd
Offutt Rd
River Rd
Edwards Ferry Rd
Mount Nebo Rd
Tutt Ln
Battlefield Pky
King St
Edwards Ferry Rd
Fort Evans Rd
Washington & Old Dominion Trl
Tolbert Ln
Sycolin Rd
Mountville Rd
Manor Woods Rd
Adamstown Rd
Buckeystown Pike
Oland Rd
New Design Rd
Park Mills Rd
Mount Ephraim Rd
Miles
0
1
2

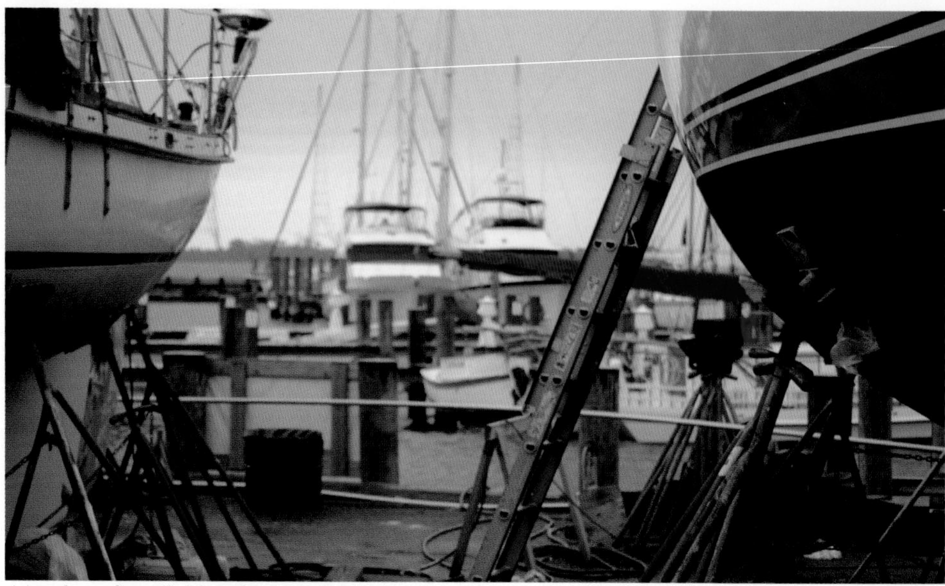

Annapolis is often called the sailing capital of the United States.

At a Glance

Distance 28.0 miles **Total Elevation** 1050 feet

Terrain

Patches of moderate hilliness punctuate long stretches of easy, nearly flat, riding.

Traffic

Take extra caution the opening 3.5 miles beyond Metro, and again through the conglomerations around Bowie and the outskirts of Annapolis.

How to Get There

Take the Orange Line Metro to its eastern terminal stop at New Carrollton. If arriving by car, use exit 19 off the Beltway or exit seven off U.S. Highway 50. They will bring you to parking off Garden City Drive.

Food and Drink

Concentrations of possible stops exist just prior to joining the WB&A Trail, along Laurel Bowie Road, at the MD 301 crossing in Bowie, and, with increasing frequency, along Riva Road on the way into Annapolis.

Side Trip

Visit the Banneker-Douglas Museum and the harborside Kunte Kinte-Alex Haley Memorial, both of which document the history of African-Americans in Maryland. Additionally, cruise the grounds of historic St. John's College, or lock your bike and take a walking tour around the campus of the U.S. Naval Academy.

Links to 

Where to Bike Rating 

About...

A singular American city, Annapolis offers many reasons for visiting, and barring an arrival by boat, biking just might be the best option for making your way here. Situated along Chesapeake Bay, this home to the U.S. Naval Academy has, throughout its storied history, operated as temporary capital of the United States and hosted a Middle East peace conference. The ride itself is one of this book's two-Google-generated routes and succeeds in linking existing trails and avoiding major highways to the fullest extent possible.

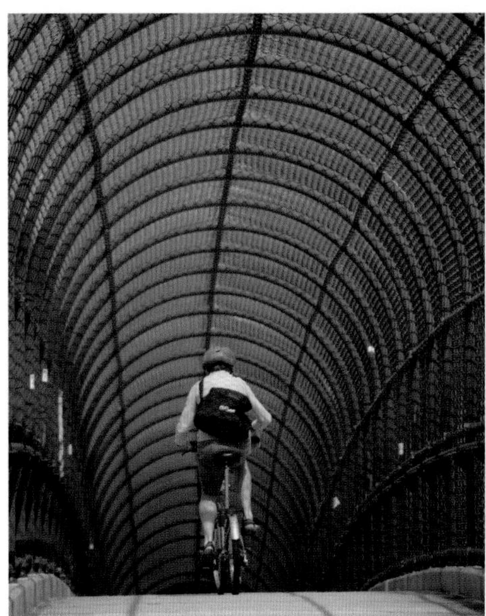

Pedaling to the vanishing point over U.S. 50.

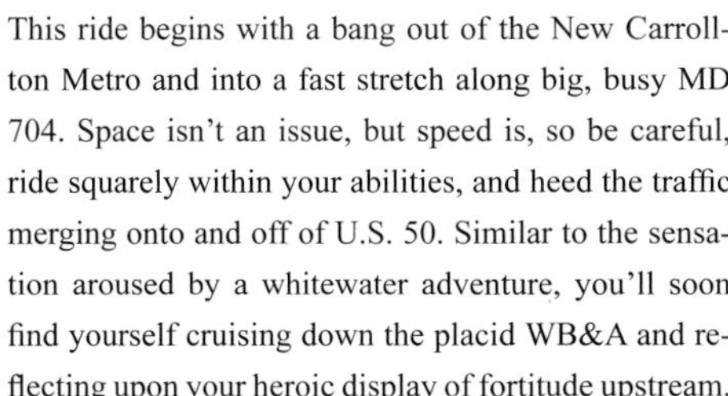

This ride begins with a bang out of the New Carrollton Metro and into a fast stretch along big, busy MD 704. Space isn't an issue, but speed is, so be careful, ride squarely within your abilities, and heed the traffic merging onto and off of U.S. 50. Similar to the sensation aroused by a whitewater adventure, you'll soon find yourself cruising down the placid WB&A and reflecting upon your heroic display of fortitude upstream.

A series of roads and an additional trail through suburbia follow. Be sure to mind the ride log as the way depends on its precision to keep you rolling pleasantly past bustling Bowie and into a hugely satisfying stretch which ultimately makes this route both practical and worthwhile.

Essentially performing the same function as U.S. 50, but with a fraction of the traffic, Governor Bridge Road is one of those safe, scenic, almost secret country byways that find you writing letters in your head asking state officials to close its way now and forever to all future vehicular traffic. Roads reaching obsolescence given over to permanent bike highways, now wouldn't that be nice?

A turn onto Riva Road brings you back to reality, and after crossing the wide South River, it's easy to see why this lovely area has been such a strong magnet for recent development. Once through the increasingly thick traffic on the outskirts of Annapolis, the route introduces you to the ease of the Poplar Trail and ushers you past a national cemetery into the first of three circles, each of which brings you nearer the city's nationally registered historic district.

Finish by curving to the front of the domed Maryland State House, the oldest state capitol building still in legislative use in the country. Perched upon a hilltop overlooking City Dock and protectively ringed by numerous colonial-era brick buildings, it briefly served as the U.S. capitol in 1783-84 and is further distinguished as the place George Washington resigned his commission as commander and chief before the Continental Congress in 1783. After peaking through the gates of Government House, home of the Maryland governor, explore the bayside city's oddly angled streets and alleys as the feeling strikes you.

Ride Log

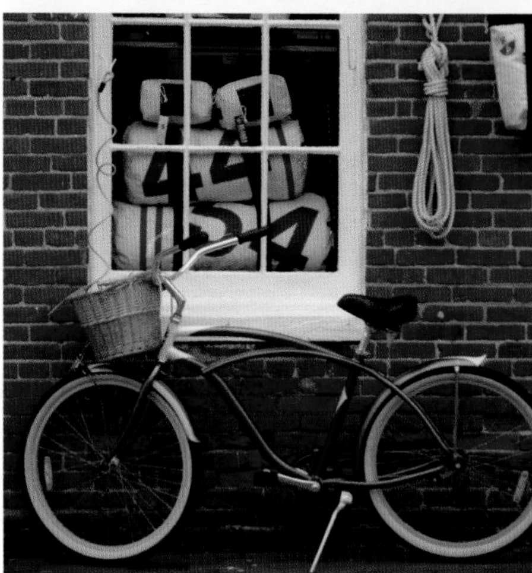

Re-sails on Randall sells goods made from recycled sails.

P1 Hammond-Harwood House, 19 Maryland Ave
P2 United State Naval Academy, 52 King George St
P3 City Dock

B1 A & M Cycle, 1300 9th St, Bowie
B2 Eastern Mountain Sports, 200 Harker Place, Ste 105
B3 Hudson Trail Outfitters Ltd, 1079 Annapolis Mall
B4 Bike Doctor of Annapolis, 160-C Jennifer Rd
B5 Capital Bicycle Inc, 436 Chinquapin Round Rd

0.0 Curl right from Metro turnstiles past newspaper boxes to bus shelter. Begin at crosswalk.

0.15 Turn right, then bear left toward U.S. 50 E to Annapolis and Ardwick-Ardmore Rd.

0.35 Stay right at fork. This is Ardwick-Ardmore.

1.2 Turn left onto MLK, Jr Hwy (MD 704).

2.0 Caution: Prepare for merging traffic (next .5) and high speeds (next 1.5).

3.6 Turn left onto Annapolis Rd using crosswalks if necessary.

3.8 Take a right on WB&A Trail.

7.4 Trail goes over High Bridge Rd before bridging rail tracks.

7.6 Take unassuming trail to right to go right again on Old Chapel Rd then left at Arrowwood Ln.

7.9 Right at Old Chapel Dr.

8.2 Left at Old Chapel Rd.

8.7 Right onto Laurel Bowie Rd.

9.55 Cross Laurel Bowie at Annapolis Rd to continue on sidewalk along opposite side. Use crosswalks if necessary. Bike/ped trail then quickly slides left.

11.7 Cross Northview Dr to join Old Collington Rd or remain on path.

12.15 Cross Holiday Ln to remain on trail.

12.50 Turn left onto Mitchellville Rd.

12.8 Turn right at Harbour Way to cross U.S. 301 and join Governor Bridge Rd.

20.4 Left onto Riva Rd.

24.6 Stay right at fork to continue straight along West St.

25.9 A left at Admiral Dr to a right onto Poplar Tr.

26.8 Turn right to curve briefly downhill.

27.0 Take third exit (on West again) after entering traffic circle.

27.7 Go right at Church Circle to School St then right again to circle Maryland State House.

28.0 Circling three-quarters brings you to the building's front steps. Now go explore.

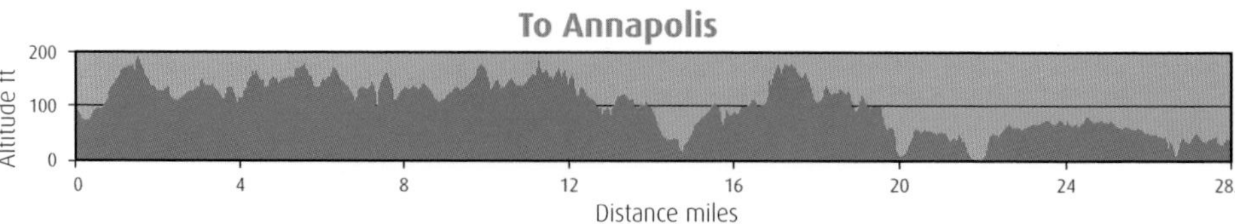

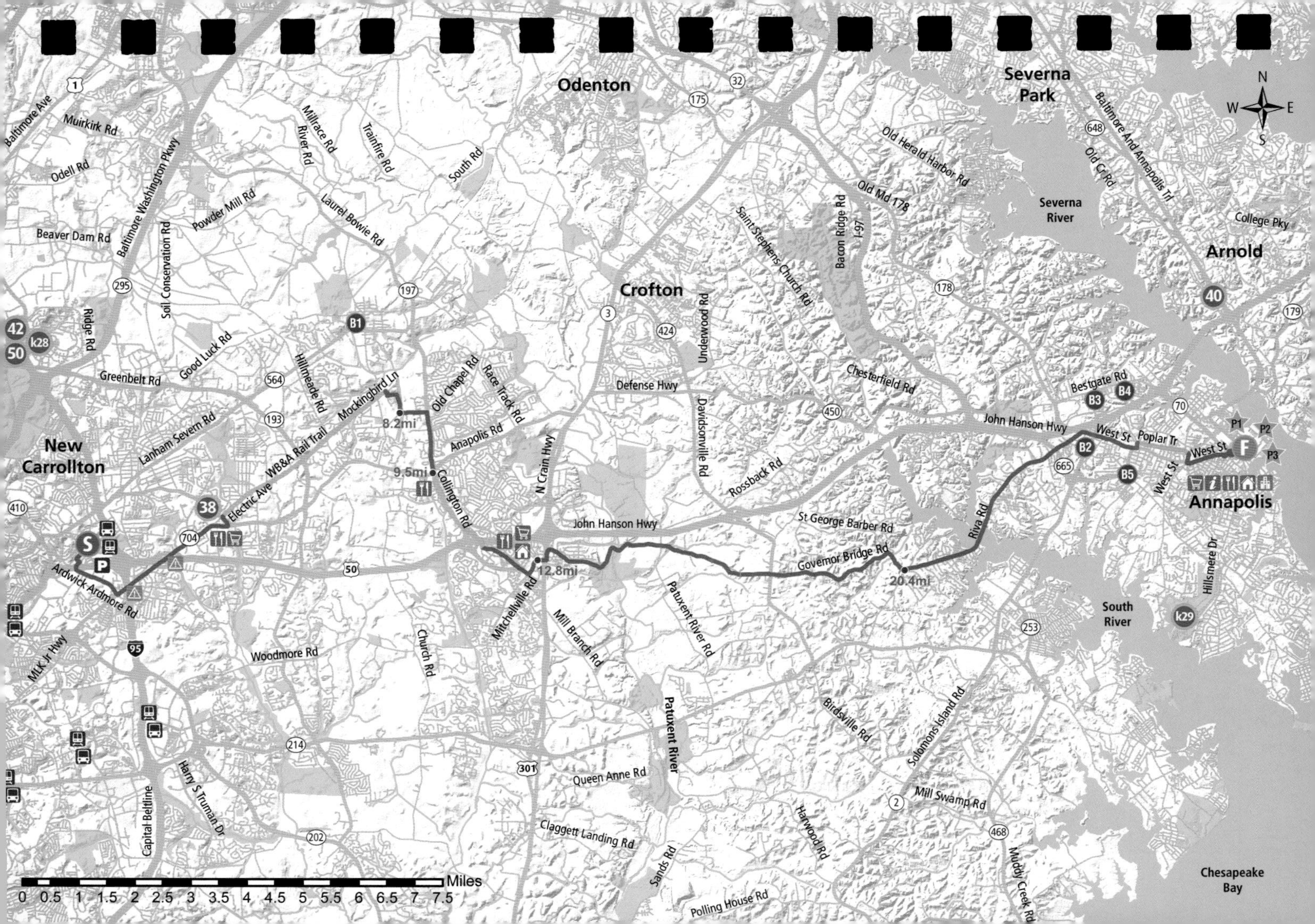

Odenton
Severna Park
Crofton
Arnold
New Carrollton
Annapolis
Severna River
South River
Patuxent River
Chesapeake Bay
Baltimore Ave
Muirkirk Rd
Odell Rd
Beaver Dam Rd
Baltimore Washington Pkwy
Powder Mill Rd
Soil Conservation Rd
Millrace Rd
River Rd
Trainfire Rd
South Rd
Laurel Bowie Rd
Ridge Rd
Good Luck Rd
Greenbelt Rd
Hillmeade Rd
Mockingbird Ln
Lanham Severn Rd
WB&A Rail Trail
Electric Ave
Old Chapel Rd
Race Track Rd
Anapolis Rd
Collington Rd
N Crain Hwy
Defense Hwy
Underwood Rd
Davidsonville Rd
Rossback Rd
John Hanson Hwy
Saint Stephens Church Rd
Bacon Ridge Rd
I-97
Old Md 178
Old Herald Harbor Rd
Chesterfield Rd
Baltimore And Annapolis Trl
Old Cr Rd
College Pky
Bestgate Rd
West St
Poplar Tr
St George Barber Rd
Governor Bridge Rd
Riva Rd
Hillsmere Dr
Ardwick Ardmore Rd
MLK Jr Hwy
Woodmore Rd
Church Rd
Mitchellville Rd
Mill Branch Rd
Patuxent River Rd
Birdsville Rd
Solomons Island Rd
Mill Swamp Rd
Muddy Creek Rd
Harwood Rd
Sands Rd
Polling House Rd
Claggett Landing Rd
Queen Anne Rd
Harry S Truman Dr
Capital Beltline
8.2mi
9.5mi
12.8mi
20.4mi
Miles
0 0.5 1 1.5 2 2.5 3 3.5 4 4.5 5 5.5 6 6.5 7 7.5

McPherson Square at Vermont and K.

At a Glance

Distance 8.0 miles **Total Elevation** 275 feet

Terrain

Effectively uphill toward Lincoln's Cottage and downhill to the White House, this ride incorporates on-road sections with bike lanes, plazas, and some sidewalk. Expect a big climb along Georgia and another up Rock Creek Church Road.

Traffic

Much of this route is car-heavy and commercial and a touch hectic. Expect lots of action along Georgia Avenue, Rhode Island, lower Vermont below Scott Circle, and K Street.

How to Get There

The Metro stops nearest this ride's dual destinations are the Green/Yellow Georgia/Petworth Station or the Orange/Blue McPherson Square Station. If driving to the cottage, make your way to Georgia Avenue. For the White House, use K as a guide.

Food and Drink

Stay on the hilltop for some of the finest southern food in the city at the Hitching Post across Rock Creek Church Road from Lincoln's Cottage. Otherwise, there are lots of neighborhood options along Georgia, and a heap of hip choices near Vermont and K and around the White House.

Side Trip

Tour either the cottage, the president's house, or both, take some time at each statued open space the ride passes, and explore Georgia north of Rhode Island Avenue. Distinguished home of Howard University since 1867, it's one of D.C.'s liveliest, most authentic streets.

Links to

Where to Bike Rating

About...

Sitting stifling hot beside a disease-ridden swamp and beset day and night with the noise of drilling soldiers, there were clearly more peaceful places than the wartime White House during summer. So despite a round-trip horseback ride of about an hour, Abraham Lincoln chose to spend a quarter of his presidency in a country cottage high in the hills of northwest D.C. Here, then, is the chance to join him in spirit, duplicating the route he rode each working morning from June to November 1862-64.

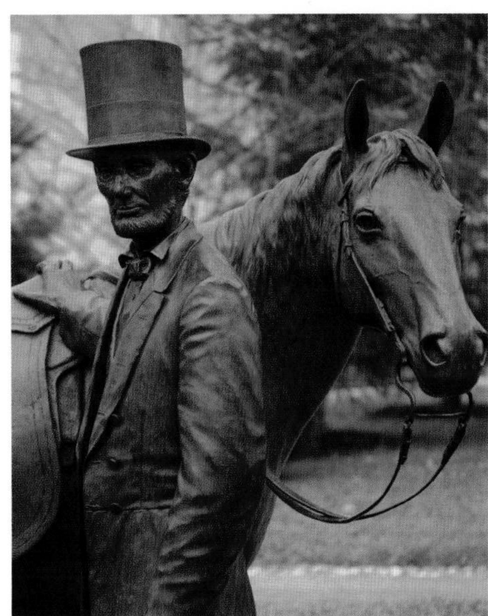

A likeness of Lincoln outside his cottage.

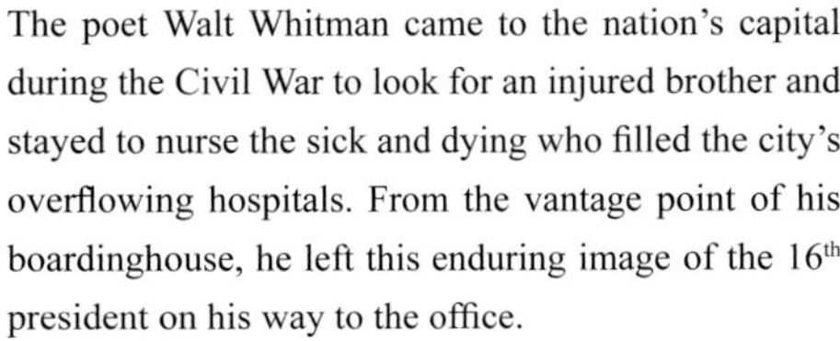

The poet Walt Whitman came to the nation's capital during the Civil War to look for an injured brother and stayed to nurse the sick and dying who filled the city's overflowing hospitals. From the vantage point of his boardinghouse, he left this enduring image of the 16th president on his way to the office.

"I saw him this morning about 8:30 coming in to business, riding on Vermont Avenue, near L Street. He always has a company of 25 or 30 cavalry, with sabres drawn and held upright over their shoulders. They say this guard was against his personal wish, but he let his counselors have their way. The party makes no great show in uniform or horses. Mr. Lincoln on the saddle generally rides a good-sized, easy-going gray horse, is dressed in plain black, somewhat rusty and dusty, wears a black stiff hat, and looks about as ordinary in attire as the commonest man."

Lincoln's four miles are now, of course, markedly changed, and this route bears little resemblance to his. The cottage on the grounds of what was formerly called the Old Soldiers' Home then stood squarely in the countryside, Georgia Avenue was but a muddy road known as the Seventh Street Turnpike, and the city proper only began at its junction with today's Florida Avenue, then known as Boundary Street. Though the plan was drawn up for the circles and squares you'll pass along your way, but it took the war to bring the nation's attention to Washington and it would take the last quarter of the 19th century to bring the city toward any semblance of the D.C. we know today.

Feel free, of course, to start this ride at whichever end you choose. Both of its destinations are near Metro stations and serviced by buses. The mapped route itself begins at the cottage in an effort to focus your attention there. Take the guided tour before you set off and relax over a cooked-to-order meal across the street at the Hitching Post afterwards. The fried chicken would have brought Lincoln back to his Kentucky youth, and a post-commute beer would have helped calm his fraying nerves. Marvin Gaye on the jukebox? Bet he would have liked that too.

Ride Log

0.0 Begin across the street from Lincoln's Cottage where the walkway leading to the entrance of the Robert H. Smith Visitor Education Center meets the road. Take a left just beyond Eagle Gate onto Rock Creek Church Rd.

0.45 Right onto Quincy St.

0.8 Left onto Georgia Ave.

2.55 Right onto Rhode Island Ave.

3.0 Zigzag left then right to enter and bisect Logan Square.

3.1 Left onto Logan Circle, then right onto Vermont Ave.

3.35 Begin heading left halfway around Scott Circle.

3.45 Go right to re-engage Vermont Ave.

3.65 Right onto 14th to first left into 15th St bikeway.

3.9 Jog left to ride between barriers beside Lafayette Square.

3.95 Right to White House.

4.05 Finish directly in front of White House, heading back right when ready to retrace.

4.1 Turn left to ride beside Lafayette Square.

4.2 Jog left across H St crosswalk to access 15th St bikeway.

4.4 Right on K St to next left onto Vermont Ave.

4.65 Begin going left halfway around Scott Circle.

4.75 Right onto Vermont Ave.

5.0 Left onto 13th Ave.

5.1 Right onto Rhode Island Ave.

5.5 Left onto Georgia Ave.

7.2 Right onto Rock Creek Church Rd.

7.9 Right onto Upshur/Lincoln Rd to enter grounds of Armed Forces Retirement Home.

8.0 Meet walkway left past gate. A bike rack sits behind the visitor center.

Balancing act on the 15th Street Bikeway.

P

P1 Lincoln's Cottage
P2 Hitching Post Restaurant
P3 Howard University
P4 Carter G. Woodson Home
P5 Logan Circle
P6 Mary McLeod Bethune Council House
P7 Thomas Circle
P8 Former location of Whitman residence
P9 McPherson Circle
P10 White House

B1 Rollin' Cycles, 1314-A 14th St, NW
B2 The Bike Rack, 1412 Q St, NW
B3 BicycleSPACE, 459 I St, NW
B4 City Bikes, 2501 Champlain St, NW

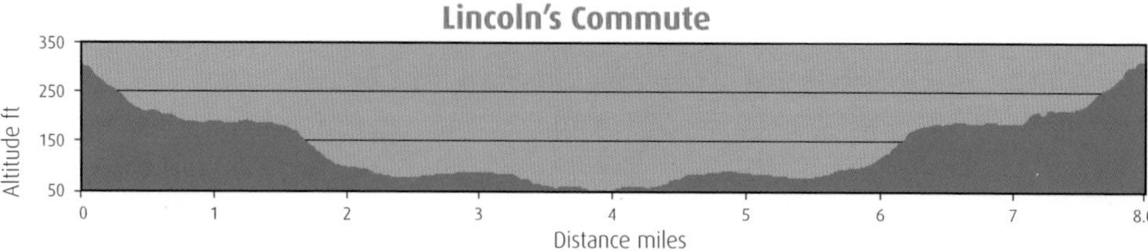

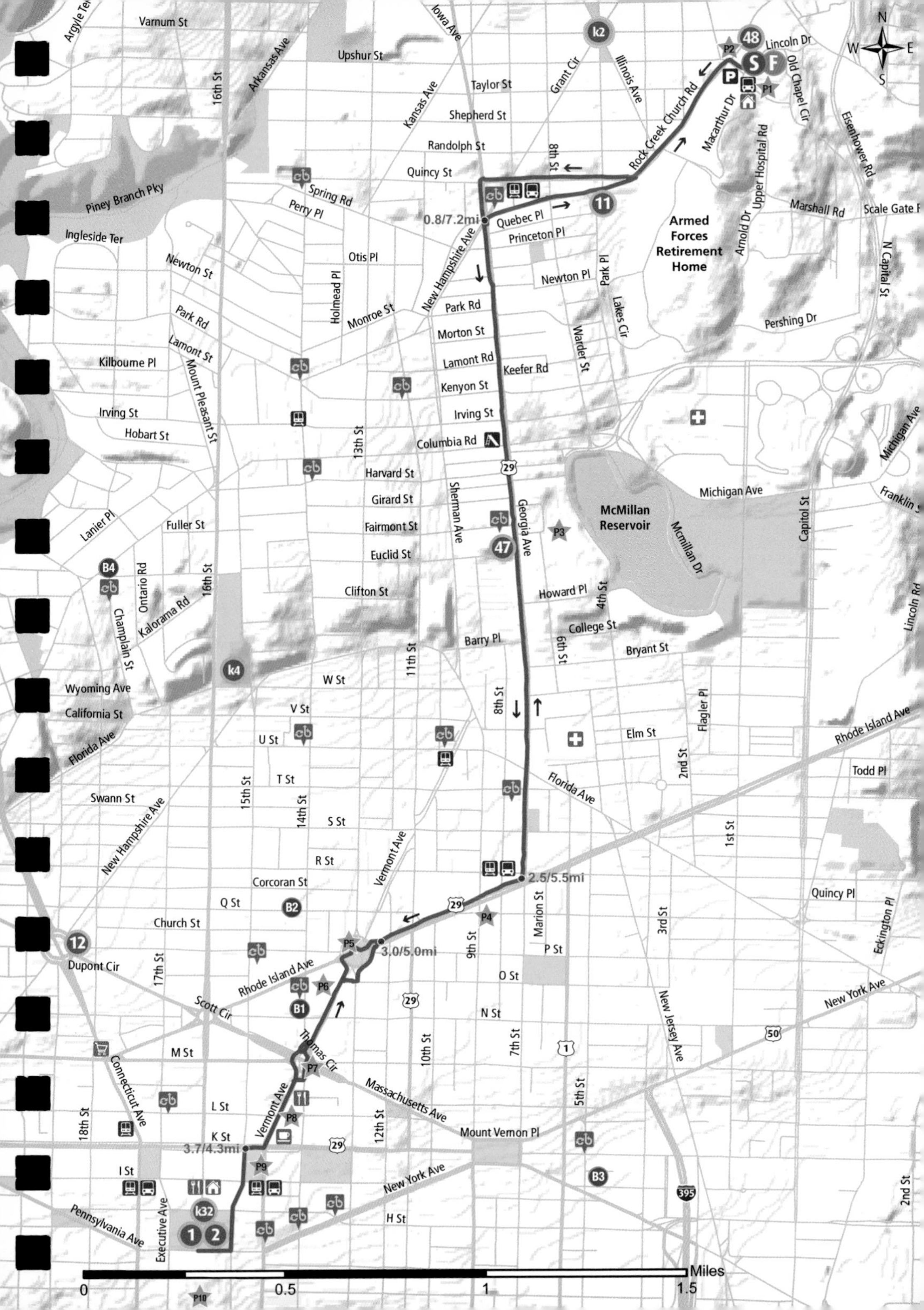

Armed Forces Retirement Home
McMillan Reservoir
Georgia Ave
New Hampshire Ave
Rock Creek Church Rd
Vermont Ave
Rhode Island Ave
Florida Ave
Massachusetts Ave
New York Ave
Pennsylvania Ave
Connecticut Ave
Michigan Ave
0.8/7.2mi
2.5/5.5mi
3.0/5.0mi
3.7/4.3mi
Thomas Cir
Scott Cir
Dupont Cir
Mount Vernon Pl
Miles
0
0.5
1
1.5

Five-petaled Yoshino blossoms backed by the Jefferson Memorial.

At a Glance

Distance Tidal Basin/East Potomac 6.45 miles
Bethesda/Kenwood 4.1 miles

Total Elevation 225 feet / 275 feet

Terrain

The first ride is flat and includes sidewalks, roads, and pea gravel pathway. The second consists of roads, bike lanes, and paved paths, with one or two modest climbs.

Traffic

Expect lots of cars and an abundance of blossom-seekers around the Tidal Basin. The Kenwood neighborhood is also a happening place during peak flowering weekends.

How to Get There

Metroing is highly encouraged during the National Cherry Blossom Festival, especially on weekends. Use the Orange/Blue Smithsonian Station and try to avoid peak times. Or pull a sneak attack at any time from the Yellow/Blue Crystal City Metro across the Potomac. If driving, parking will be hotly contested. Try spaces along Ohio Drive first.

Though use of the Bethesda Red Line Metro is also a sound option, drivers should aim south off the Beltway using MD 355 to its junction with MD 187.

Food and Drink

Look for kiosks around the Tidal Basin and on the National Mall. Patronize a lemonade stand in Kenwood and dine up the trail in Bethesda.

Side Trip

The National Mall is your oyster. Shop Bethesda Row.

Links to Tidal Basin    1 2 6 10 48
Bethesda  28

Where to Bike Rating

About...

You only get around three weeks for this one, but they're some of the three best D.C. offers. Granted good weather, the National Cherry Blossom Festival upholds its status as the nation's premier springtime celebration. Saddled with bad, its thinner crowds grant intrepid blossom lovers an even more intimate experience with what is surely the capital's most fleetingly beautiful annual sight. The Tidal Basin has been the occasion's epicenter for a century now, but this offering's second route might suit your viewing needs just as well.

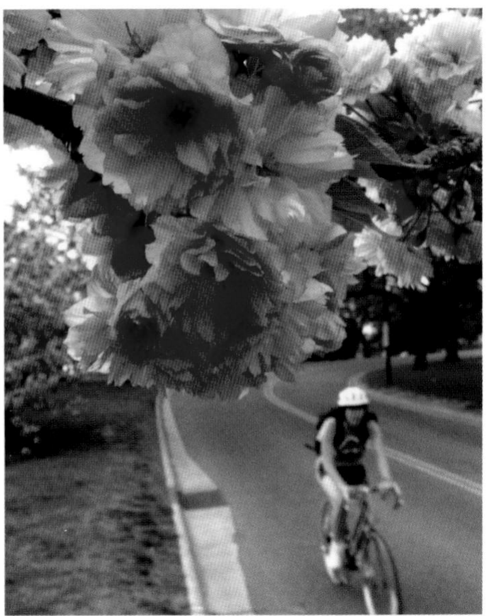

The pink pom-pons of a Kwanzan Cherry enliven Ohio Drive.

The National Cherry Blossom Festival was officially instituted during the Great Depression in 1935, but the origins of Washington, D.C.'s most famous trees trace themselves back to the early 20th century, and beyond.

The area now home to the celebratory proceedings each late March and early April was once foul-smelling marshland. It wasn't until the early 1890s when a monumental, decade-long effort led by U.S. Army Engineer Peter Conover Hains drained the space south of the National Mall by way of dredging the Washington Channel, constructing the Tidal Basin, and creating what is now East Potomac Park and Hains Point.

Plans to beautify the newly reclaimed Potomac waterfront began with the introduction of Japanese flowering cherry trees and were led by Ms. Eliza Scidmore, a National Geographic writer, photographer, and geographer, in conjunction with USDA official Dr. David Fairchild. The initial batch gifted by Japan in 1909 was discovered to be diseased however, and it wasn't until three years later that the first successful shipment of 3,020 cuttings arrived and was planted.

A bronze plaque now marks the spot near Independence Avenue between Kutz Bridge and the Martin Luther King, Jr. Memorial where the first two trees of that second offering were dedicated in a small ceremony presided over by First Lady Helen Herron Taft and Viscountess Chinda, wife of the Japanese Ambassador. Though the average cherry lives around 40 years, those two Yoshino varietals remain remarkably alive today.

The timing of the National Cherry Blossom Festival is weather-specific, varies slightly year to year, and is based on the average peak bloom date of April 4. Events range among a long-standing parade to informational talks, art shows, Potomac sightseeing cruises, and a youth kite-making competition. Each season hosts upwards of a million visitors as admirers the world over come to stroll amid, picnic beneath, and cycle among the cherries' stunning display.

If possible, pick a time less trod for your ride, perhaps a weekday morning, or as an alternative, make your way to this selection's other highlighted route near D.C.'s northwest boundary in Kenwood, Maryland. A short way south of Bethesda off the Capital Crescent Trail, it is also overwhelmed with blossoms each early spring, and the blooms are the pride of the neighborhood.

Ride Log

Tidal Basin/East Potomac Park

0.0 Exit Smithsonian Metro elevator left to go immediately left along 12th St toward National Mall.

0.1 Use crosswalk to enter mall and go left along inner pea gravel path toward Washington Monument.

0.3 Turn left as path ends then right at corner using sidewalks and crosswalks to cross 14th and 15th streets. After crossing 15th go left along sidewalk.

0.75 Cross roads (Maine Ave N & S) to continue left along outer Tidal Basin sidewalk.

0.95 Use sidewalk ramp to join Ohio Dr and immediately bear left under overpass toward East Potomac Park. Jefferson Memorial straight.

1.65 Jog left to continue straight toward Hains Point.

2.85 Bottom of the point.

4.15 Continue straight at stop sign.

4.65 Stay straight to go over bridge. Jefferson Memorial, WABA Bike Valet to right.

5.1 Turn right onto W Basin Dr. FDR Memorial. MLK, Jr Memorial.

5.35 Turn right onto Independence Ave then quickly use crosswalk left to go right along sidewalk past white-domed D.C. War Memorial.

5.7 Cross road (Homefront Dr) to jog right and cross 17th St toward Washington Monument.

5.85 Begin looping monument on lower (outer) path past bandstand.

6.05 Angle right and safely join Jefferson Dr to cross 15th and 14th streets continuing straight.

6.35 Turn right to join 12th St then right toward Metro elevator.

6.45 Finish.

Bethesda/Kenwood

0.0 Begin by exiting the Bethesda Metro elevator at the corner of Wisconsin Ave and Montgomery Ln. Use sidewalk to go right along Wisconsin one short block to Hampden. Turn right.

0.15 Turn left onto Woodmont Ave.

0.3 Jog right then left onto Capital Crescent Trail.

1.25 Turn right onto Dorset Ave.

1.5 Turn right onto Highland Dr.

1.85 Bear right onto Chamberlin Ave.

1.95 Bear left to stay on Chamberlin.

2.15 Turn right onto Kennedy Dr.

2.25 Bear right onto Woodlawn Ave.

2.4 Turn left onto Brookside Dr.

2.55 Use traffic circle to access Parkway Dr. (4th right).

2.65 Turn right onto Kennedy Dr.

2.85 Turn left on Dorset and immediate left to return to trail.

3.8 Use crosswalks to go left on Woodmont.

3.95 Right onto Hampden, then left one short block using sidewalk along Wisconsin Ave.

4.1 Finish at Metro elevator.

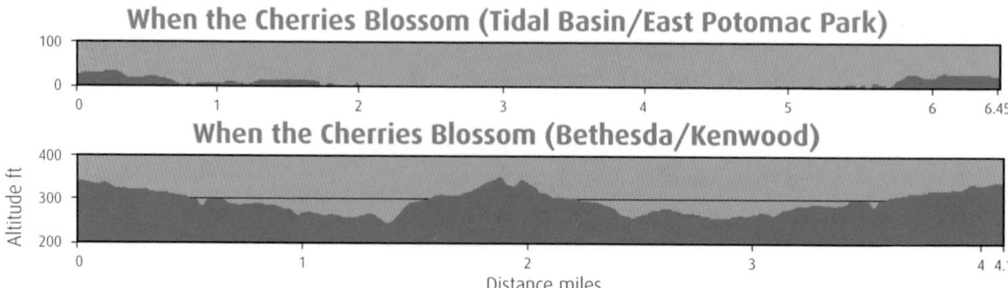

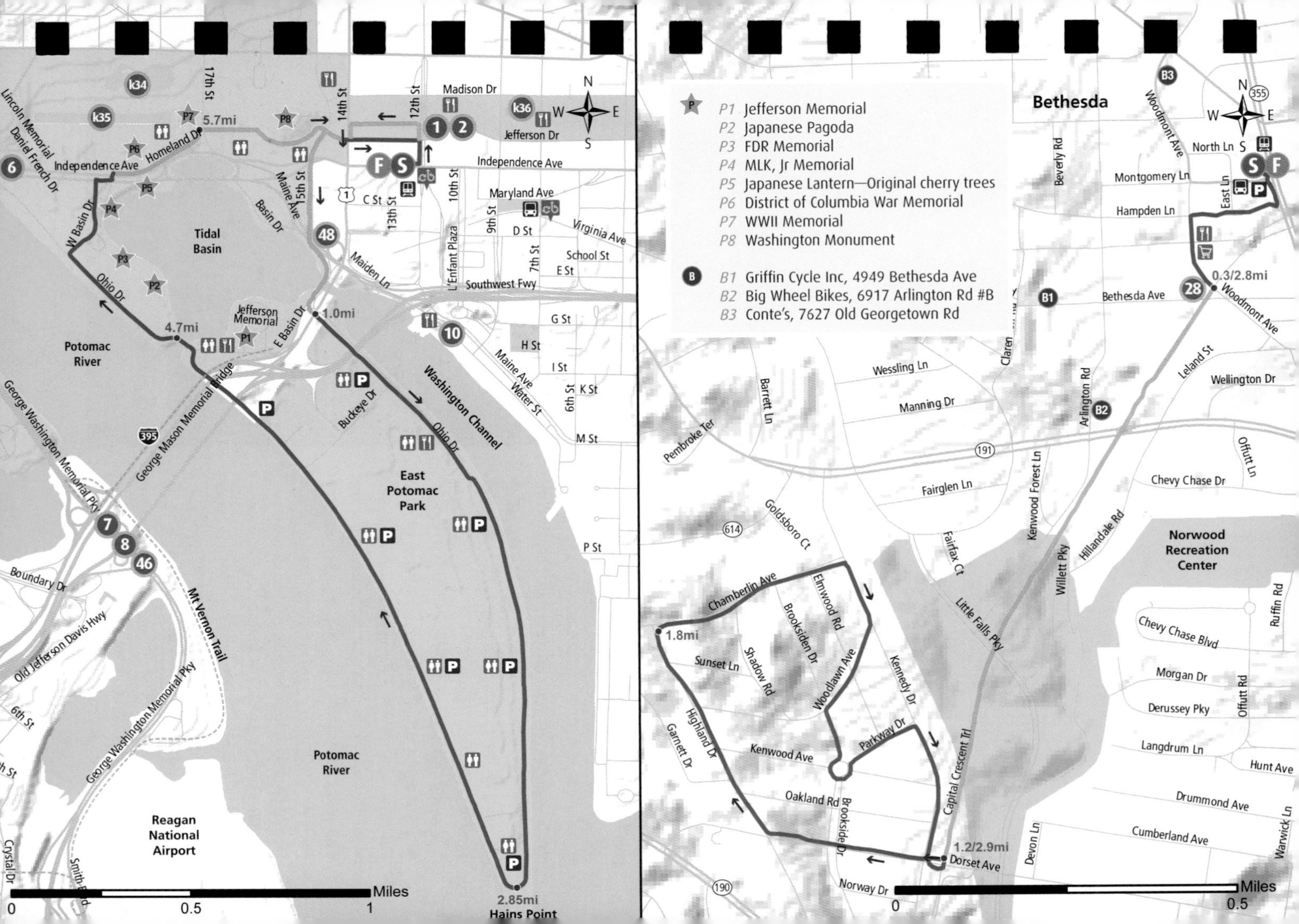

P1 Jefferson Memorial
P2 Japanese Pagoda
P3 FDR Memorial
P4 MLK, Jr Memorial
P5 Japanese Lantern—Original cherry trees
P6 District of Columbia War Memorial
P7 WWII Memorial
P8 Washington Monument
B1 Griffin Cycle Inc, 4949 Bethesda Ave
B2 Big Wheel Bikes, 6917 Arlington Rd #B
B3 Conte's, 7627 Old Georgetown Rd
Bethesda
Tidal Basin
Potomac River
East Potomac Park
Washington Channel
Hains Point
Reagan National Airport
Mt Vernon Trail
Norwood Recreation Center
5.7mi
4.7mi
1.0mi
2.85mi
0.3/2.8mi
1.8mi
1.2/2.9mi
Lincoln Memorial
Daniel French Dr
Independence Ave
Homeland Dr
W Basin Dr
Ohio Dr
Basin Dr
Maine Ave
15th St
14th St
17th St
12th St
13th St
10th St
9th St
7th St
6th St
Madison Dr
Jefferson Dr
Maryland Ave
C St
D St
E St
G St
H St
I St
K St
M St
P St
Virginia Ave
School St
Maiden Ln
L'Enfant Plaza
Southwest Fwy
E Basin Dr
Buckeye Dr
Water St
Jefferson Memorial
George Mason Memorial Bridge
George Washington Memorial Pky
Boundary Dr
Old Jefferson Davis Hwy
Crystal Dr
Smith Blvd
Woodmont Ave
North Ln
Montgomery Ln
Hampden Ln
East Ln
Beverly Rd
Bethesda Ave
Arlington Rd
Leland St
Wellington Dr
Offutt Ln
Chevy Chase Dr
Kenwood Forest Ln
Hillandale Rd
Willett Pky
Little Falls Pky
Capital Crescent Trl
Wessling Ln
Manning Dr
Fairglen Ln
Fairfax Ct
Barrett Ln
Pembroke Ter
Goldsboro Ct
Chamberlin Ave
Elmwood Rd
Brooksiden Dr
Shadow Rd
Sunset Ln
Woodlawn Ave
Kennedy Dr
Parkway Dr
Kenwood Ave
Highland Dr
Garnett Dr
Oakland Rd
Brookside Dr
Dorset Ave
Norway Dr
Devon Ln
Ruffin Rd
Chevy Chase Blvd
Morgan Dr
Derussey Pky
Offutt Rd
Langdrum Ln
Hunt Ave
Drummond Ave
Cumberland Ave
Warwick Ln
Miles
0
0.5
1

Kids' Rides

Because your children need safe places to ride even more than you do; because driveways, alleyways, and busy streets no longer suffice; because ducking between parked cars and battling bustling street crossings are things you did but hope your little ones can avoid, along comes WTB D.C.'s groundbreaking Kids' Rides. With junior routes in each of its five adult sections, families now have the necessary information to utilize the metro area's parks, trails and open spaces securely, in style, and squarely focused on training riders of the next generation.

Remember that first sensation of pulling your feet up, beginning to pedal, and cycling forward under your own power? One of the earliest personal freedoms, it's the moment you went from being merely along for the ride, to actually in charge of it. And when the time comes to pass that feeling on to your children, finding urban spaces suited to the task can be difficult. Available choices often appear too hectic, unsuitably small, or seemingly designed for some other activity altogether. To that end, the following learner's routes help parents reimagine the greater D.C. metropolitan area as a haven for young cyclists by detailing nearly 40 fun, safe riding spots throughout the region.

Ranging from ultra-short beginner's loops, to balancing acts of a mile or more, to family spins of up to five miles, most of these offerings are completely free of all vehicular traffic and only require sharing space with other cyclists, walkers, and joggers. The former are flat, have absolutely no road crossings, and are meant for those with little to no biking experience whatsoever. Middling length rides require a higher level of mastery and the accompanying confidence it instills. While the latter exist specifically for those young riders old enough, strong enough, and skilled enough to keep up with Mom and Dad for short distances and perhaps even handle a touch of traffic in the form of a minor road crossing or two. Whatever the level, you'll find it here.

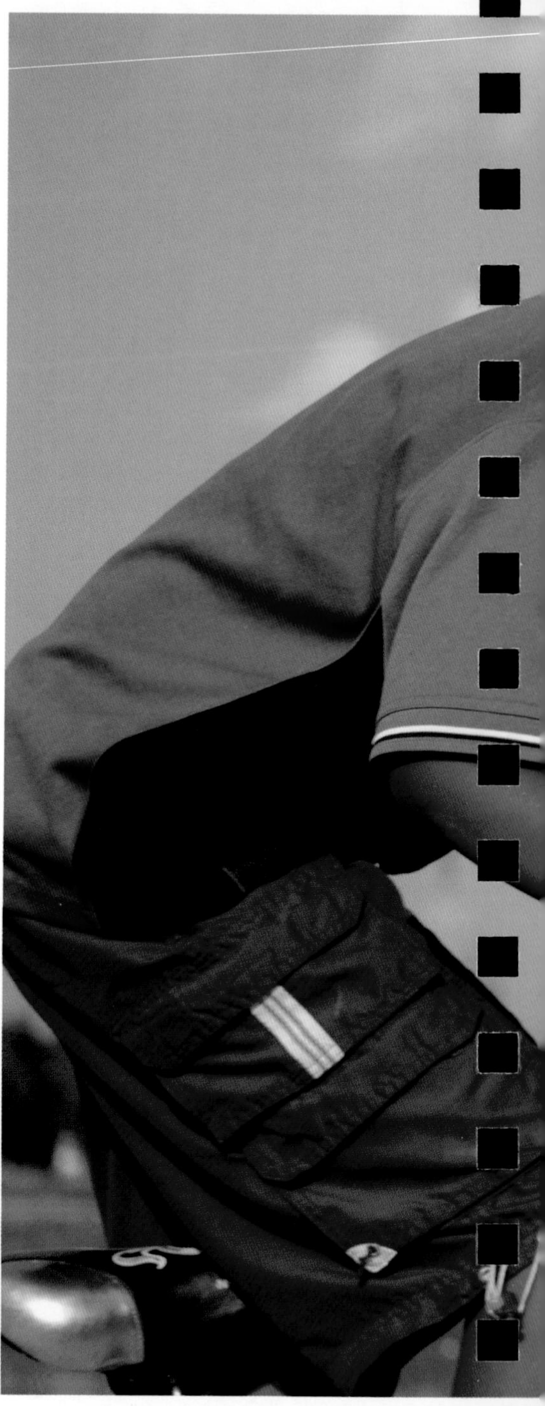

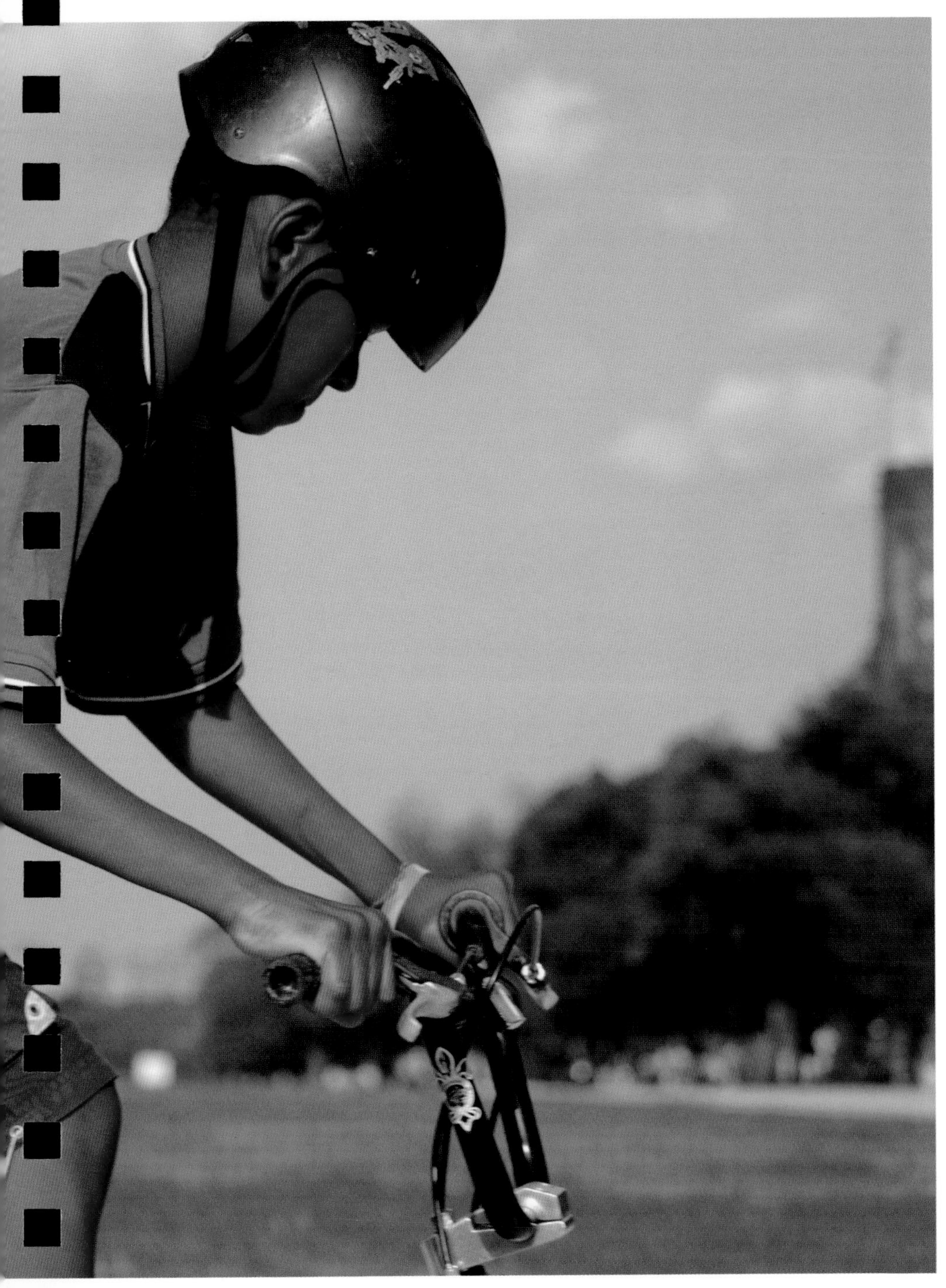

Ride K1 - Rock Creek Park Tennis Center (NW)

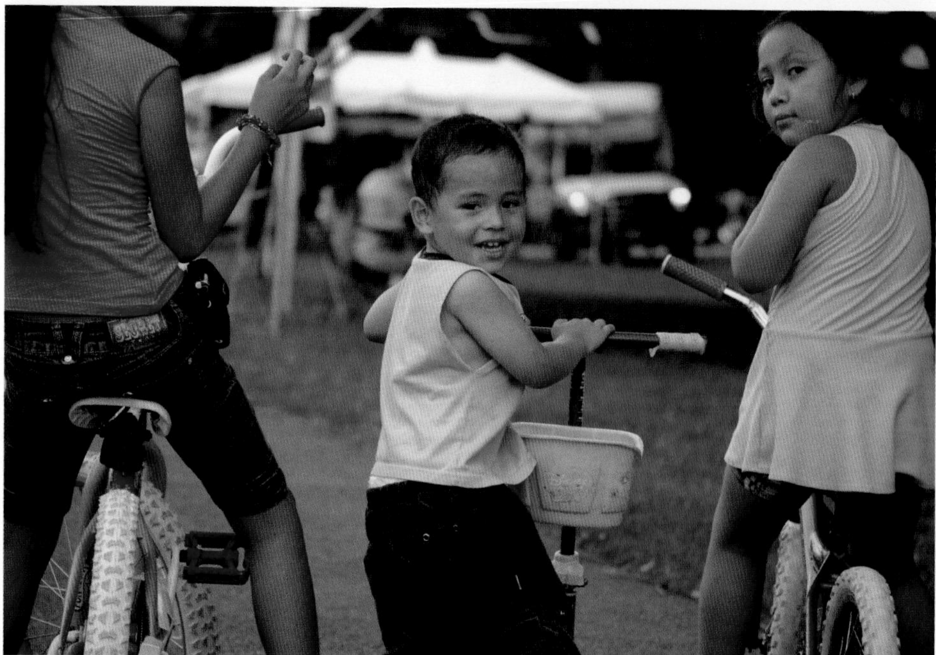

Little guy with big sisters.

Distance
0.45 miles

Terrain

Flat, narrow asphalt footpath connecting work-out stations makes a big near-square around a huge playing field.

How to Get There

Metro isn't a viable option here. Use 16th Street buses or drive to arrive at Kennedy Street Northwest. Parking shouldn't be a problem.

Amenities and Things to Do

Snacks and restrooms can be found inside the tennis center complex on its south side. More restrooms, a pavilion, a swing set, a jungle gym and fire pits are located across the entrance driveway. Tennis courts are by reservation only.

About

This open lawn adjacent to Rock Creek Park is amenable to all sorts of activities (bring a kite on windy days) and an ideal place for an afternoon idle.

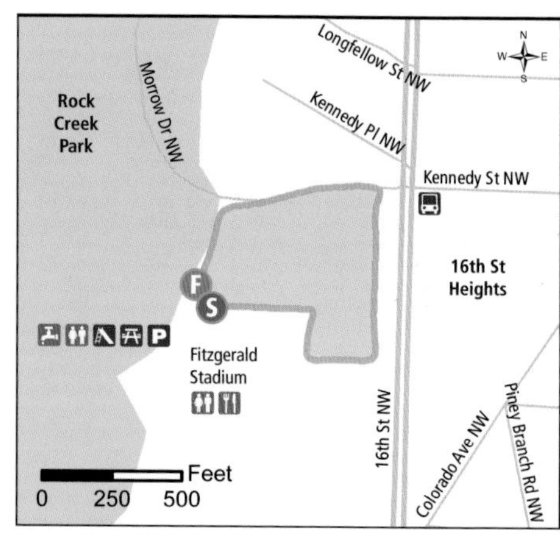

Ride K2 - The Circles - Sherman and Grant (NW)

Maurice, late summer at Grant Circle.

The Circles—Sherman

Distance 0.2 miles

Terrain

Flat concrete sidewalk.

How to Get There

Set your car's course for the confluence of Illinois, Kansas, Seventh, and Crittenden Northwest. Free parking is available along side streets. Buses possible too. Check schedules.

Amenities and Things to Do

You're in the heart of residential D.C., nothing to do here but ride. Bring a cooler, throw down a blanket, and relax as the kids go safely round and round.

About

This statue-free traffic circle in the Petworth neighborhood is just as scorched-earth-scourge-of-the-south General William Tecumseh Sherman would have liked it. Just be happy it's shaded.

The Circles—Grant

Distance 0.2 miles

Terrain

Sidewalk set on a slight hillside.

How to Get There

Just three blocks southeast from Sherman Circle on Illinois, New Hampshire, Fifth, and Varnum Northwest. Free side street parking available. Check bus schedules.

Amenities and Things to Do

Much like its circular sibling, don't expect much but the chance for the kids to ride free and easy. There are benches here though, along with pockets of shade under pines and water fountains that usually work. Corner markets are within walking distance but bringing your own is the cooler choice.

About

If you're thinking that including these two is a bit of a stretch, maybe you'll reconsider when you or your children need just that.

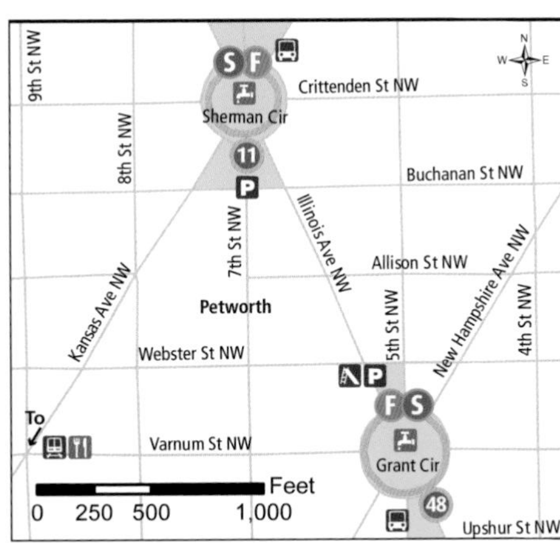

Ride K3 - Langdon Park (NE)

Sunshine, mother and sons.

Distance 0.55 miles

Terrain

Smooth asphalt path loops down, through, and back up around the kids' play area in the middle of the western section of this hilly space.

How to Get There

Use New York, Rhode Island and South Dakota Avenues NE to get near to 20th and Franklin or Hamlin streets. Parking is available all around the park's perimeter. Check bus schedules too. There are several routes that will get you in the vicinity.

Amenities and Things to Do

There's a community center here and outdoor pool, both with restrooms, as well as a small amphitheater which hosts mostly weekend events. Be sure to check hours. Families also picnic, barbeque, and use the fields and courts. Teens can skateboard, and children enjoy two next-generation jungle gyms at the park's center. Find plentiful food and drink along Rhode Island Avenue.

About

Think of this course as one lap, with the possibility of many more. What makes it unique, and fun, is its dips and dives and one short, challenging, uphill. The action really heats up here in the summer. This is the place where former Mayor Anthony Williams first began signaling the traditional opening of D.C. city pools by cannonballing off the high dive.

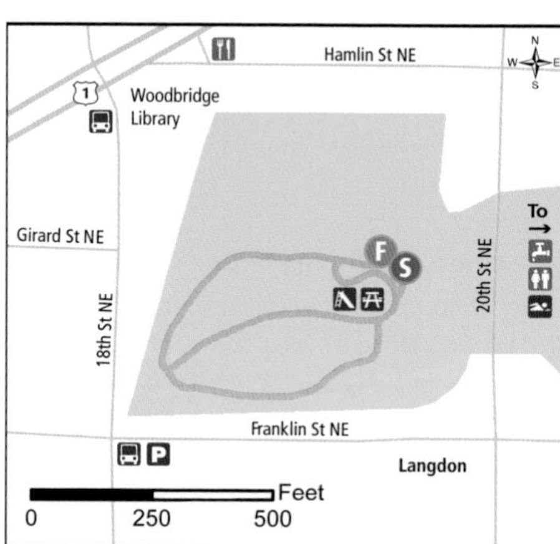

Ride K4 - Meridian Hill Park (NW)

Distance 0.35 miles

Terrain

Slightly sloping pebbled concrete footpath makes a giant rectangle within this park's upper section.

How to Get There

Set your compass for Euclid, W, 15th, and 16th NW. Many bus routes bisect the area. The nearest Metro is the Yellow/Green Columbia Heights Station several blocks northwest. Metered on-street parking is available, but spots are highly prized.

Amenities and Things to Do

Take in the views, the fresh mix of people and pastimes, the Joan of Arc sculpture, and the unmatched 13-basin cascade fountain before plopping down with a newspaper on one of numerous benches. Bathrooms are located on both the park's upper and lower levels. Food and drink are within blocks in every direction.

About

Located due north of the White House on its meridian, this is a cool spot sequestered above the downtown fray. Its hip, urban feel (and unofficial nickname, Malcolm X Park) stand in contrast to the Neoclassical Renaissance villa landscape. The Sunday evening drum circles are a pulse-quickening pleasure.

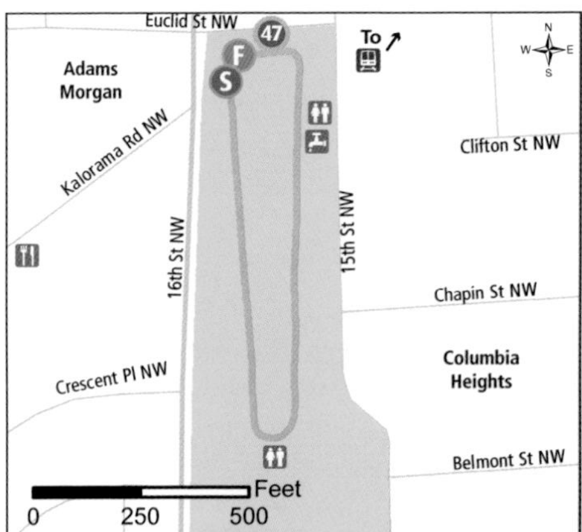

Looking north through upper Meridian Hill Park.

Ride K5 - Rose Park (NW)

Ride Rose and play the day away.

Distance 0.8 miles

Terrain

Mostly flat path makes a nice spin when connected to sidewalks at either end.

How to Get There

It's not a long walk down P Street from Dupont Metro. If driving, make your way just west of Rock Creek Parkway and the P Street Bridge.

Amenities and Things to Do

Two popular play areas, three tennis courts, a hoops court, a baseball diamond, plenty of open space, a summer farmer's market, bathrooms, and water fountains are all available. Food and drink available within blocks in all directions.

About

This Mom's, Dad's, tot's and dog walker's kind of place sits on a slice of land on Georgetown's eastern edge.

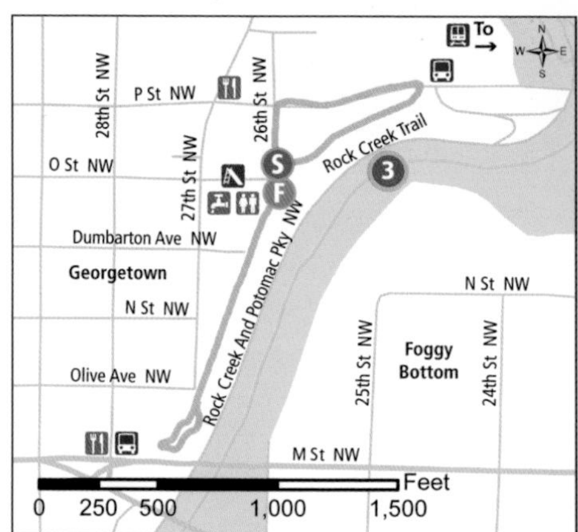

Ride K6 - Glencarlyn Park - Arlington (SW)

Distance 0.45 miles

Terrain

This path incorporates one hefty hill and crosses two footbridges while linking two parking lots. Parents should use their best judgment.

How to Get There

It is imminently possible to take either the W&OD or Four Mile Run trails to arrive here by bicycle. Drivers should use Arlington Boulevard (U.S. 50) to South Carlin Springs Road before going left on Third Street South to South Harrison Street. There are two parking areas.

Amenities and Things to Do

Come here for an old-fashioned, family-day in the park. Have a cook-out. Skip rocks. Fish for trout. Throw the football around. Play on the jungle gym. Utilize the community canine area. And ride the paved path off the southern parking lot to nearby Long Branch Nature Center. Bathrooms and water are on-site.

About

South Arlington is blessed. It offers several children's options within a short distance of one another off its signature trails, the W&OD and Four Mile Run. If the hill and parking lots of Glencarlyn turn you off, be sure to check out the straighter, flatter (though less amenity-laden) out-and-backs of Lubber's Run and Bluemont Junction. And there's yet another loop opportunity at Bon Air Park. Grab a Fairfax County Bicycle Route Map for even more detailed information.

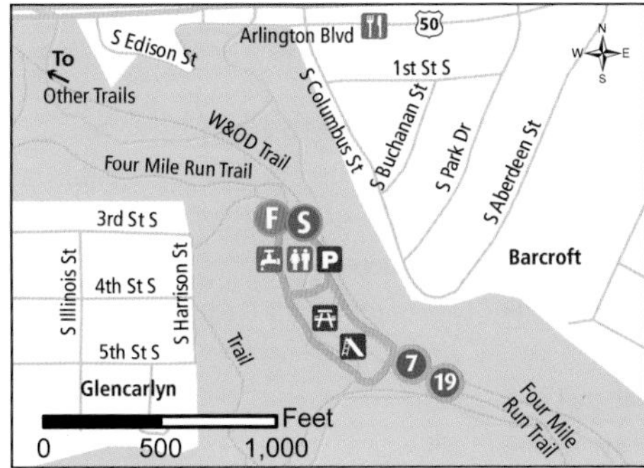

Don't forget your helmet!

Ride K7 - The LBJ Memorial Grove (SW)

Distance 0.55 miles

Terrain
Well-maintained flagstone/crushed stone path.

How to Get There
Use North Boundary Drive off the Jefferson Davis Highway to park and walk over the boardwalk bridge or take the Columbia Island Marina exit off the George Washington Parkway South (just north of I-395 and the 14th Street Bridge). I-66 and the Beltway will get you in the vicinity.

Amenities and Things to Do
Choose to picnic or enjoy the offerings at the Columbia Island Café. Hike Lady Bird Johnson Park and, if so inclined, bring a paddleboat to explore its surrounding waters. Public bathrooms are off the parking lot.

About
This site on Columbia Island was chosen by Lady Bird herself as the spot for her husband's memorial. It's said the couple often stopped here to look across the Potomac and admire Washington, D.C. Begin at the big, pink-granite monolith dedicated to the 36th president. Set down in a peaceful grove of white pines with unobstructed views of West Potomac Park and the Washington Monument, it's located on the opposite end of the long parking lot from the café and marina.

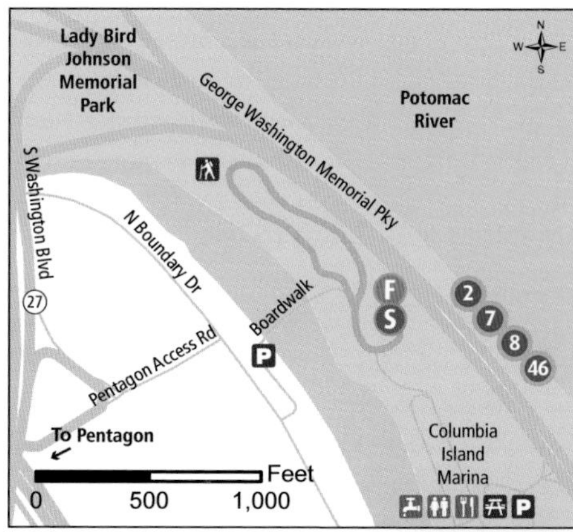

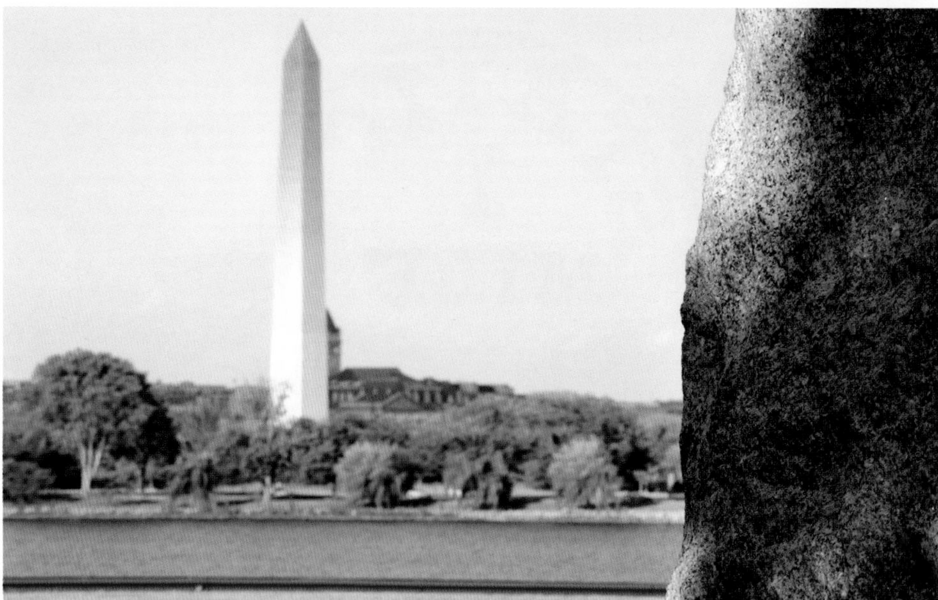

A view across the Potomac from the LBJ Memorial Grove.

Ride K8 - RFK/Kingman Island (NE)

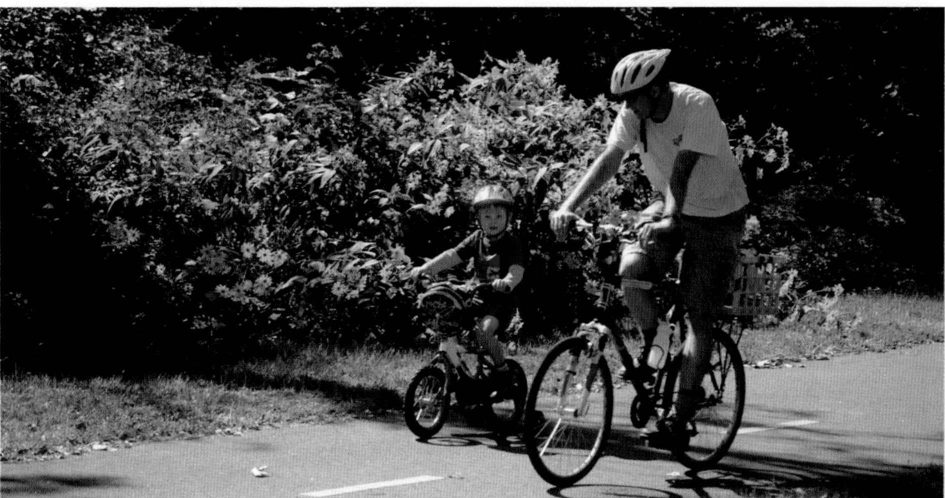

A father and son along the Anacostia Riverwalk Trail.

Distance 1.6 miles

Terrain

Nice and smooth aside from a short rougher stretch alongside Oklahoma Avenue.

How to Get There

Steer toward Benning Road, Oklahoma Avenue, and C Street/North Capital in northeast D.C. Use Interstate 295 if coming from farther afield.

Amenities and Things to Do

Enjoy lovely water views, wetlands, and riverfront trails while riding, picnicking, bird watching, and honing your photographic skills. Visit the anticipated Kingman Island Environmental Education Center and the memorial tree grove dedicated to D.C.'s schoolchildren killed on 9/11.

In addition to the mapped loop, cycling is permitted along the bridge boardwalk and Kingman Island's main trail. Bathrooms are available on the island as well. For a playground, basketball, and tennis, take the Benning Bridge bike/ped path across the Anacostia to River Terrace Park.

About

Though on first glance this may recall the place Dad took you to learn to drive, don't be put off. The area as a whole, and its remarkable battle back from neglect, is one of the District's recent success stories. The spin begins where the northernmost stretch of the Anacostia Riverwalk Trail meets the entrance to the boardwalk bridge over to Kingman Island. Circling as it does RFK Stadium's enormous north lot, parking will pose no problem.

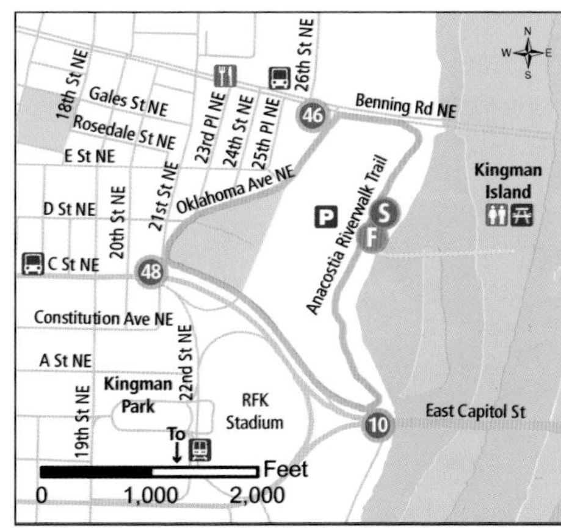

D.C. Diamond
Kids' Rides

Ride K9 - Lincoln Park (NE,SE)

Distance 0.45 miles

Terrain

An old-fashioned brick sidewalk framing a long rectangular 'square'.

How to Get There

Exit the Orange/Blue Eastern Market Metro and cross Pennsylvania to go north on Eighth. Two blocks and a right on North Carolina will set you three short blocks straight away. The park is one mile west of the U.S. Capitol on the quadrant line separating northeast from southeast D.C. Parking shouldn't pose a big problem.

Amenities and Things to Do

This park boasts two kids' play areas and plenty of shade surrounding open space. There's a market across 11th on its west side.

About

The poet Walt Whitman was a frequent visitor to a soldier's hospital located at this site during the Civil War. Now there are two compelling sculptures here. One, the Emancipation Memorial, is controversial in its depiction of Lincoln standing over a kneeling, shackled slave (presumably in the act of being freed). The other is of educator and civil rights leader Mary McLeod Bethune, founder of the National Council of Negro Women.

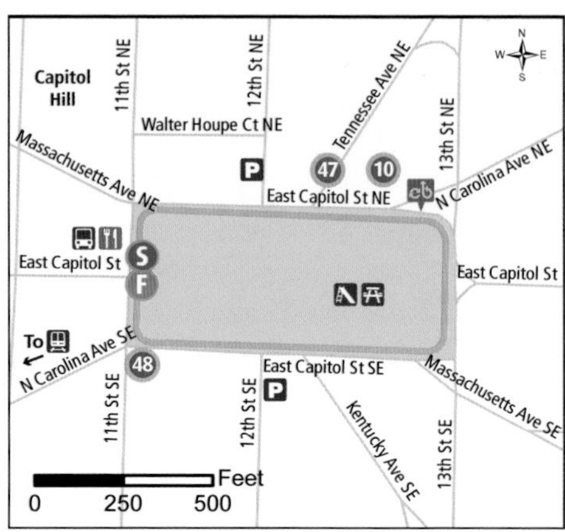

Positively wide-eyed with excitement.

Ride K10 - Capitol Hill Parks: Garfield and Folger (SE)

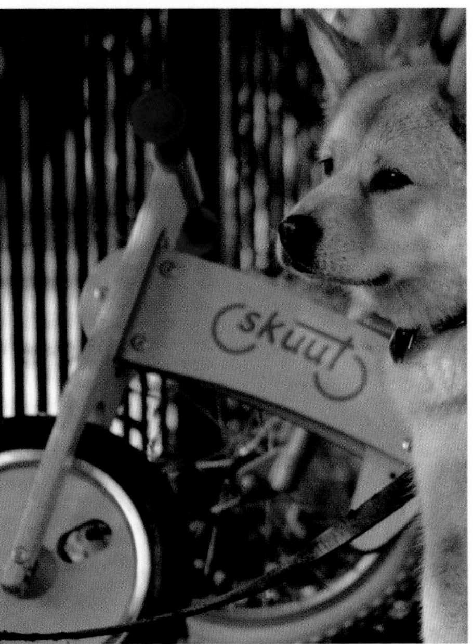

Two of a kids' best friends.

Capitol Hill Parks - Garfield

Distance 0.55 miles

Terrain

Footpaths meander up and around a slight hillside.

How to Get There

Turn right exiting the Orange/Blue Capitol South Metro Station and walk a few minutes to F Street Southeast. There are pay parking spots, but spaces are at a premium.

Amenities and Things to Do

Bocce ball anyone? Tennis, volleyball, basketball, swings, slides, skateboarding? This park has a little bit of everything, including a nice play area for tiny tots aside another with a huge rope-climbing contraption fit for adults and kids alike. Food, drink, and restrooms are available near the Metro.

About

This slice of sloping land in Capitol Hill, partially tucked under Interstate 395, is a neighborhood gem/gym. Expect nannies, mommies, doggies, daddies, and strollers galore.

Capitol Hill Parks - Folger

Distance 0.3 miles

Terrain

Good old-fashioned sidewalk over flat ground.

How to Get There

The Orange/Blue Capitol South Metro Station is two short blocks away down Second off D Street. Parking is again at a premium.

Amenities and Things to Do

This is a spartan spot ideal for lounging and cracking a good read. Bring food and drinks purchased near the Metro or try the sixth-floor cafeteria at the Madison Memorial Building of the nearby Library of Congress.

About

The official Folger Park across D Street has benches but isn't pleasurably bikeable. Instead, try this bare-bones former site of Providence Hospital.

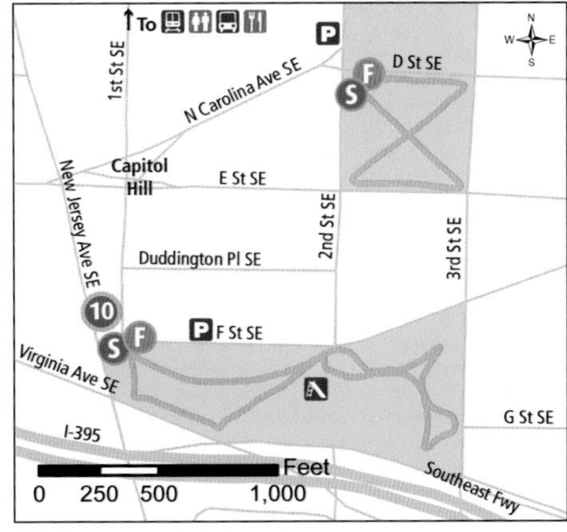

Ride K11 - The Marvin Gaye Trail (NE)

Distance 3.8 miles

Terrain

Smooth, flat asphalt and sidewalk.

How to Get There

Exit the Blue Line Metro at Capitol Heights, cross East Capitol Street to 61st Street, and travel a block to Banks Place NE. The trail begins to your left, opposite the Marvin Gaye Recreation Center. If driving, Highway 295 to East Capitol Street or the Beltway to Central Avenue will get you to this, the far eastern corner of the District. Buses available as well.

Amenities and Things to Do

Use the workout equipment along the fitness trail, stop at the state-of-the-art playground, visit the Lederer Environmental Education Center, and don't forget your high-tops. Check out the Riverside Center too, a burgeoning hub of fresh food, arts, and culture at 5200 Foote Street. Bathrooms and snacks available there, the M.G. Recreation Center, or McDonald's at the turnaround.

About

This ride is intended for young cyclists who are ready for longer distances and low-traffic road crossings. It's also for you adventurous parents willing to give formerly off-limits areas of D.C. a fresh chance. After a concentrated effort by non-profit Washington People & Parks in conjunction with local government, this once-blighted area has transformed back into cherished community ground. And, so far, it's offering solid proof parks bring pride. Come see for yourself!

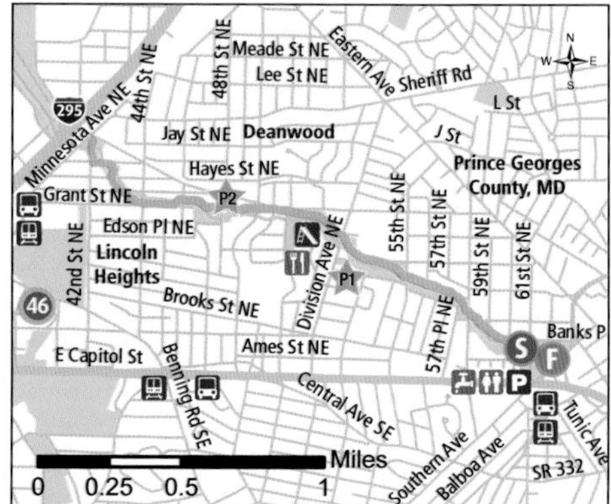

Mosaic of legendary soul singer, and neighborhood export, Marvin Gaye by D.C. artist G. Byron Peck.

Ride K12 - Oxon Run (SE)

Distance 0.7 miles

Terrain

Asphalt, sidewalk, and footbridges over flat ground.

How to Get There

Exit the Green Line Congress Heights Metro, cross Alabama Avenue, and follow 13th Street three blocks down to the stream. Depending on direction of travel, drivers can use exit 4B off the Beltway to MD 414, then connect to Wheeler Road and Mississippi. South Capitol and Southern Avenue will also bring you near. Look to park on Valley Avenue along the south side of Oxon Run. Buses are available too.

Amenities and Things to Do

There's a big playground here along with a pavilion and at least two more miles of intertwined trail and stream. A public pool isn't far either. And be sure to venture down the road to the impressive community space at 1901 Mississippi as well. Called THEARC, it's home to 10 cultural and social service agencies and boasts the only theater in Anacostia dedicated to music, drama, and dance. Bring your own snacks, but stop here for restrooms and water.

About

Flanked on both sides by plentiful green space, the Oxon Run cuts a shallow path through southeast D.C. to the Potomac. This area nestled below the tall, straight trees between 13th and Wheeler is particularly well-suited to recreation and relaxation. All it needs is pioneers.

Beneath the tall trees at Oxon Run.

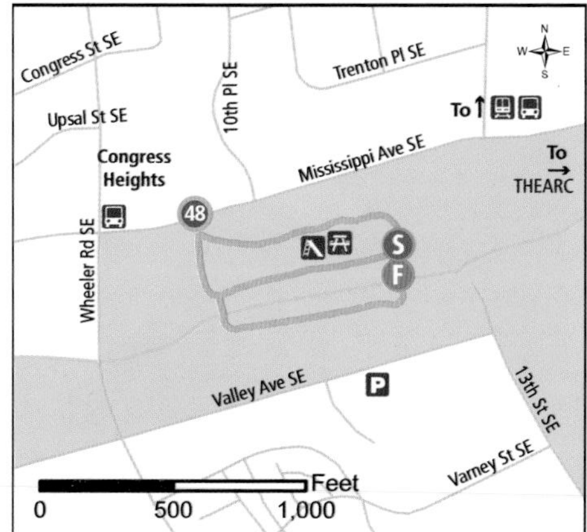

Ride K13 - Ida Lee Park - Leesburg

Distance 1.6 miles

Terrain

This smooth course moves through open, rolling parkland.

How to Get There

Exit 45 off the Beltway brings you to Dulles Airport and Access Toll Road. Take it to a left on the Leesburg Bypass (U.S. 15, VA 7). Then go right on South King through Leesburg to the park's entrance. Leesburg Pike (VA 7) will also get you to the bypass.

Amenities and Things to Do

There shouldn't be any post-ride boredom at this first-class place. Choose among indoor or outdoor aquatic opportunities, a recreation and fitness center, tennis courts, and a beautiful library. There are over 370 acres for the outdoor adventurer as well, and nearby Morven Park hosts equestrian events on land adjacent to former Virginia governor Westmoreland Davis's mansion. Bathrooms and water are readily available.

About

Ida Lee was a "Virginia gentlewoman" par excellence, and the park nestled against the Catoctin Mountains on the former grounds of her estate is the crown jewel of the Leesburg system. Your mapped ride starts in front of Rust Library and goes west toward the hills, u-turns just before .45, crosses library drive entranceway (caution) at .85, and u-turns once again at Highway 15 around mile 1.25. That's one way to ride this double out-and-back. What's yours?

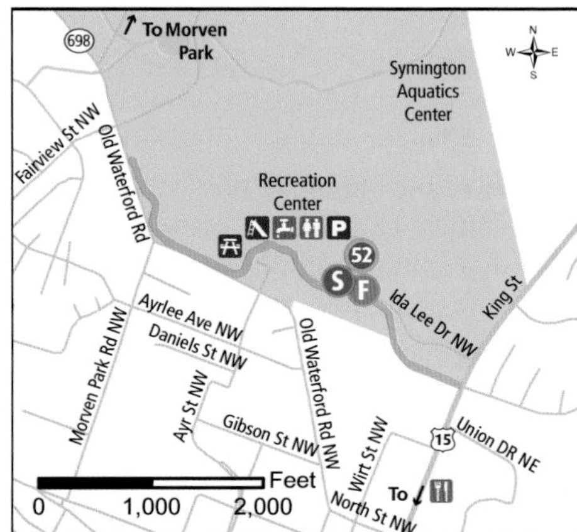

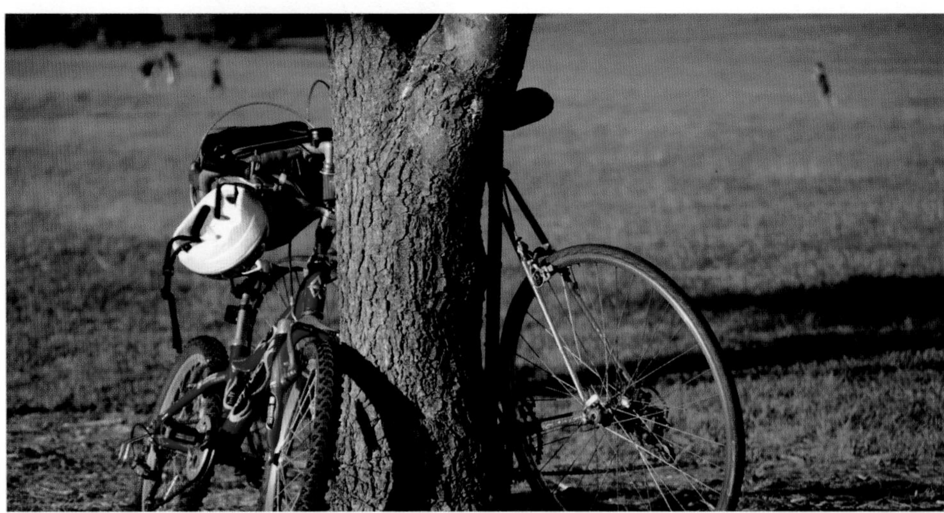
Ride, park and play.

Ride K14 - Ben Brenman Park - Alexandria

Distance 1.5 miles

Terrain

A nice path meanders all over this flat, well-designed space.

How to Get There

The park is located at 5000 Duke Street off Interstate 395.

Amenities and Things to Do

This is a great place to explore, with a lagoon, a baseball diamond, running routes, a soccer field, one small jungle gym and the possibility of a little off-roading for your bigger kids. Grander yet, peddle east on the Holmes Run Trail for a dip in the wave pool or a spot of miniature golf down at nearby Cameron Run Regional Park.

About

The City of Alexandria's done well along Holmes Run. There are numerous green spaces scattered along its length. Cameron Station is a pleasant, diverse, planned community that plays together.

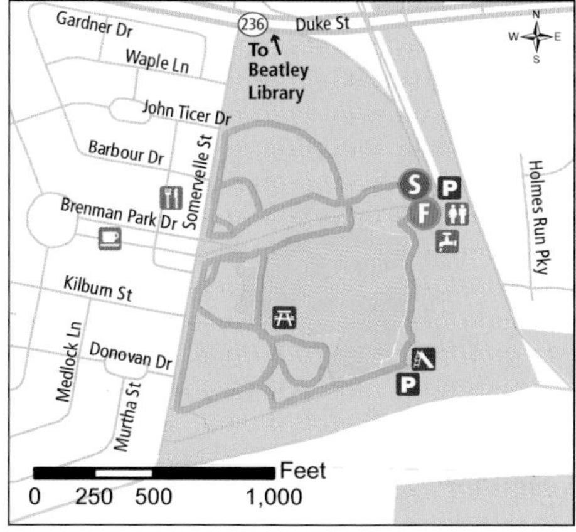

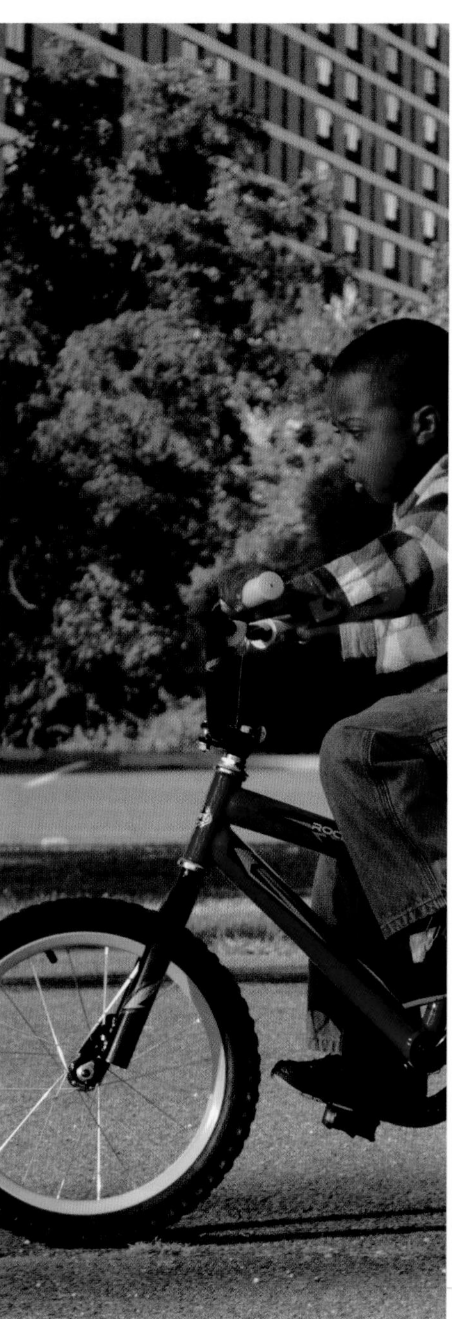

Saturday afternoon.

Ride K15 - Nottoway Park - Vienna

Picture your child here.

Distance 0.65 miles

Terrain

Expect a touch of uphill as this path skirts two parking areas and loops two ball fields.

How to Get There

Arriving here by way of the Orange/Blue Vienna/Fairfax-GMU Metro is a definite option if you don't mind a few easily managed road crossings. Curl left out of its exit turnstiles and take the path alongside the parking structure to Vaden Drive. Then head right, cross Virginia Center Boulevard, and take the signed City of Fairfax Connector Trail straight here. If driving, take Beltway exit 49 left (west) onto Route 66 before exiting onto Route 243/Nutley Street right (north). Turn left on Courthouse Road, and look for the park entrance to your left.

Amenities and Things to Do

This neighborhood park boasts a fitness trail, gardens, and a wooded nature path along with the standard issue courts and playing fields. Bring snacks. Bathrooms and a water fountain are centrally located.

About

Until the littlest ones get a few months more experience, this near figure-eight just might remain your Nottoway staple. Have a spin around and you'll find other short satisfying ride options here, but nothing equal to this contained circuit. Some of the acreage you're exploring is the former vineyard at Hunter House, the park's turn-of-the-century historic mansion.

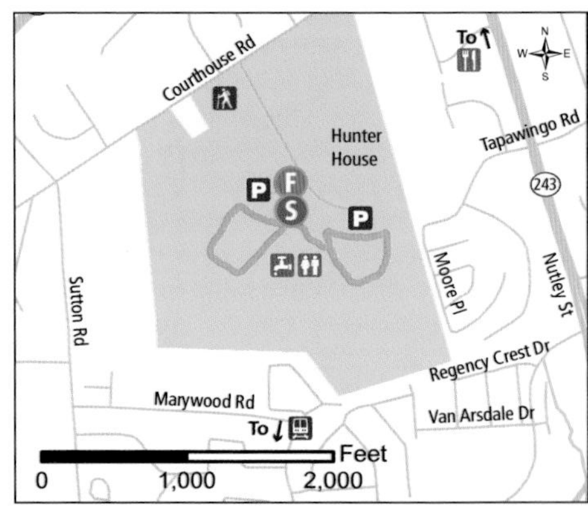

Ride K16 - Wakefield Park - Annandale

Distance 0.3 miles

Terrain

This smooth, flat path loops a playing field and skirts basketball courts.

How to Get There

Use the Beltway to access exit 54 onto Braddock Road (VA 620). Then go west briefly to West Braddock Road and the park's entrance.

Amenities and Things to Do

Outside, along with the usual hoops, nets, and backstops, use the BMX-ready skate park and frequent the May to November farmer's market. Inside the Audrey Moore RECenter, combine all your fitness needs with a dance room, a pottery lab, and a cycling studio. Then hit the expansive sundeck for some well-deserved downtime.

About

This simple little oval is a great spot to get your children the laps they need to quickly become proficient cyclists. And, once that's done, up the difficulty by accessing the Cross County Trail and its natural surface connection south to Lake Accotink Park. Additionally, popular mountain bike trails intersect the CCT as it heads north through the woods directly beyond this park.

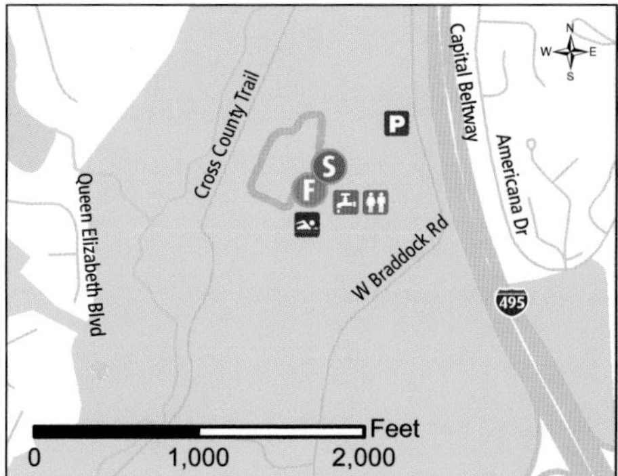

Still life with bike lock.

Ride K17 - Lake Accotink - Springfield

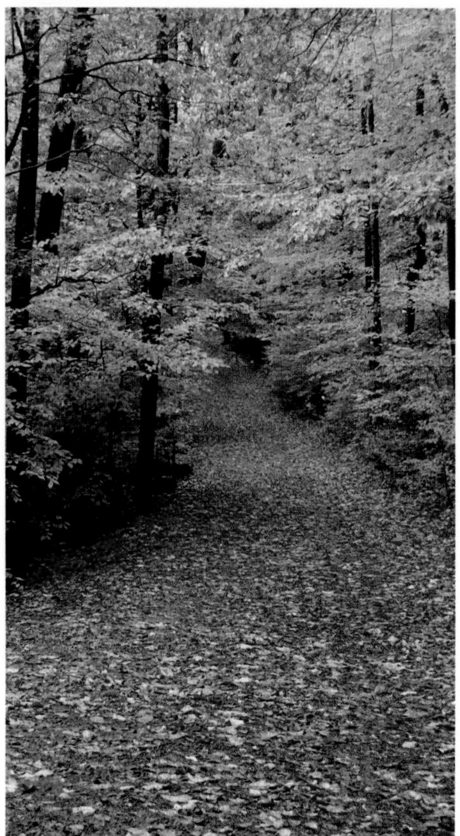

It's hard to top Accotink in fall.

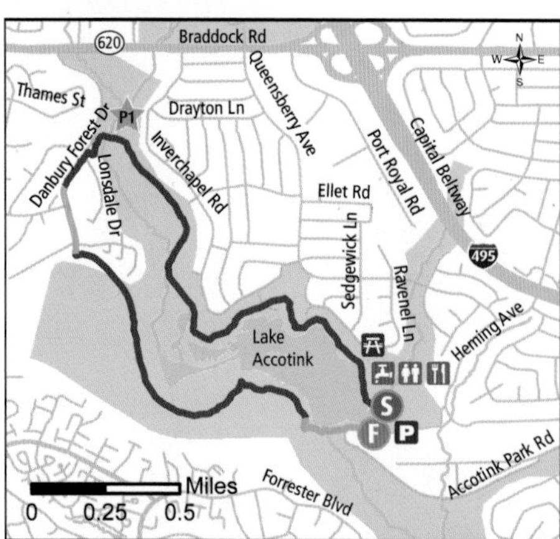

Distance 3.75 miles

Terrain

This challenging, wooded loop traverses natural lakeside surface, concrete path, and neighborhood sidewalk.

How to Get There

Exit the Beltway and go briefly west on Braddock Road (VA 620). After a left (south) onto Queensbury Avenue, take it to a T-intersection with Heming Avenue. Go right to the park's entrance.

Amenities and Things to Do

Go boating, fish, experience the old carousel, play mini-golf, or picnic at this suburban hideaway. Explore here all year long, but facility hours, including a snack bar and bathrooms, vary with the season. A section of this route incorporates Fairfax's ambitious Cross County Trail. Head north on its natural surface to Wakefield Park or go south beyond the railroad tracks on a paved section stretching to Hunter Village Drive.

About

The back portion of this ride is tough. Turn around at the kiosk (mile 1.7) for a much easier return trip. If electing the mapped loop, go left at the kiosk, cross a footbridge, then left over another to climb to Lonsdale Drive. Now head along the Danbury Forest Drive sidewalk past King's Glen School, re-engage the trail at the cul-de-sac (mile 2.2), climb, and turn left again. Please accompany your child and consider dismounting on the ensuing steep descent to the dam.

P1 Kiosk turnaround

Ride K18 - Fort Ward - Alexandria

Distance 0.6 miles

Terrain

Lovely loop path with a nice climb through a pleasant, shaded atmosphere.

How to Get There

Take Interstate 395 and access the King Street or Seminary Road exits. Van Dorn Street then brings you to West Braddock Road.

Amenities and Things to Do

Come to experience a period reenactment, visit the museum, and amble on well-manicured grounds. Interpretive signs enable self-guided tours of the historical gate, bastions, and trenches. There are picnic tables, an amphitheater, pavilions, a natural area and jungle gyms. Restrooms are both behind the museum and near the amphitheater. No food or vending machines are available on site. Shopping centers, supermarkets, and gas stations are near however.

About

This is the fifth biggest, and best preserved, of the 161 Civil War forts commissioned by Lincoln to defend D.C. from the Confederacy. It's situated on a big hill which overlooked both the Leesburg and Little River Turnpikes in the Civil War era. The very popular path you're taking occasionally doubles as an access road and has speed bumps, but pedestrians and bicycles rule the roost most often.

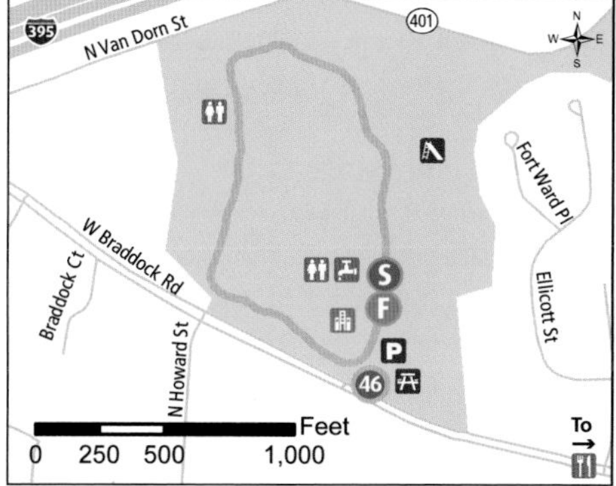

Riding's just the beginning to a great day at Fort Ward.

Ride K19 - The South Germantown Park Trail - Boyds

Distance
2.1 miles

Terrain
A rolling perimeter path winds its way around well-manicured parkland.

How to Get There
Take the Beltway to Interstate 270. After exiting west onto West Montgomery/Key West Avenue (MD 28) take a right on Great Seneca Highway (MD 119), then go left on Richter Farm Road, left on Schaeffer Road and right on Central Park Circle.

Amenities and Things to Do
There's some cool stuff here besides the playground equipment, ball fields, courts, picnic shelters, and community garden. Play a round of miniature golf or practice your swing at the driving range, enjoy the splash and adventure playgrounds, take a dip at the state-of-the-art indoor swim facility, discover archery, fish the pond, or visit the King Farm Dairy Mooseum. Water and restrooms are available in most facility buildings. And there's a café inside the Discovery Sports Center, but be sure to check hours.

About
Most of this modern mega-park's nearly 700 acres were once part of a working dairy farm. They're now home to gobs of open space alongside one of the premier soccer facilities in the country. Able to accommodate multiple sports, the Maryland SoccerPlex comprises dozens of synthetic and natural turf fields both indoors and out and hosts numerous high-profile matches and tournaments year-round.

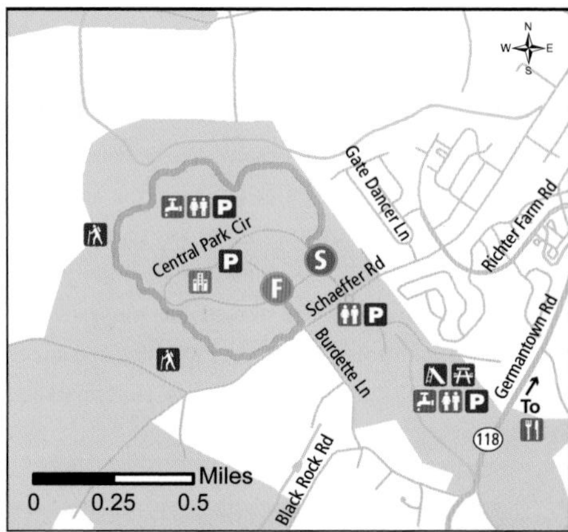

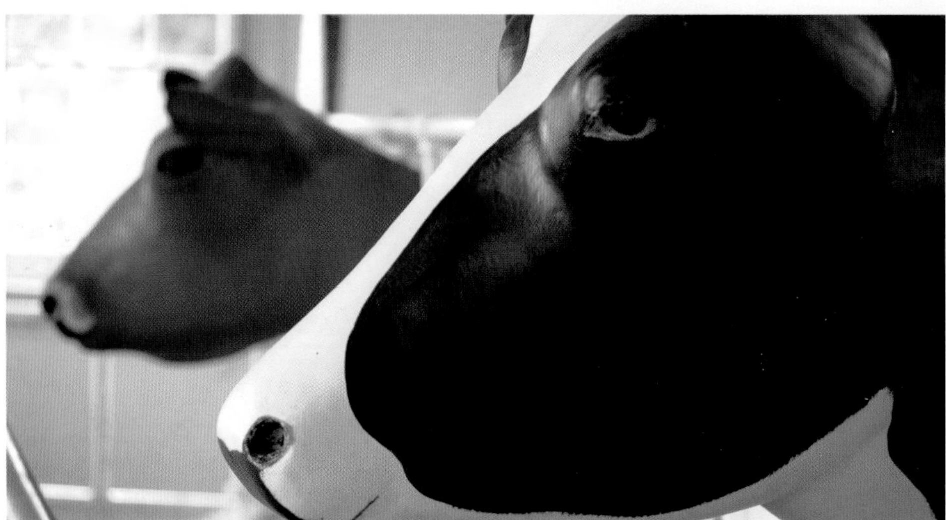
Life-size cows in the Mooseum.

Ride K20 - Bohrer Park - Gaithersburg

Distance 1.1 miles

Terrain

This hard surface path throws a broad, gently-graded loop around two ponds.

How to Get There

Use Interstate 270 north off the Beltway, exiting right onto Shady Grove Road, left onto South Frederick Avenue (MD 355), then left again onto Education Boulevard. Your ride starts down the hill from the parking area nearest the big white barn.

Amenities and Things to Do

Adjacent as it is to the headquarters of Gaithersburg Parks and Recreation, your post-ride activities here could include time spent hitting the courts, enjoying the water and skate parks, playing miniature golf, pitching horseshoes, or simply picnicking and admiring the greenery. Have a peek, too, at the old smokehouse, thought to be the oldest building in town. Water and restrooms are on-site. The café is seasonal and potentially subject to water park fees.

About

The rich history of this 58-acre portion of old Summit Hill Farm stretches back to Montgomery County's earliest days, while its present incarnation plays host to all types of community activities and family outings. Be prepared to share the popular trail with after-work and weekend walkers and joggers. Ride-wise, there's just enough uphill here to challenge young riders and enough downhills to keep them coming back.

A teachable moment.

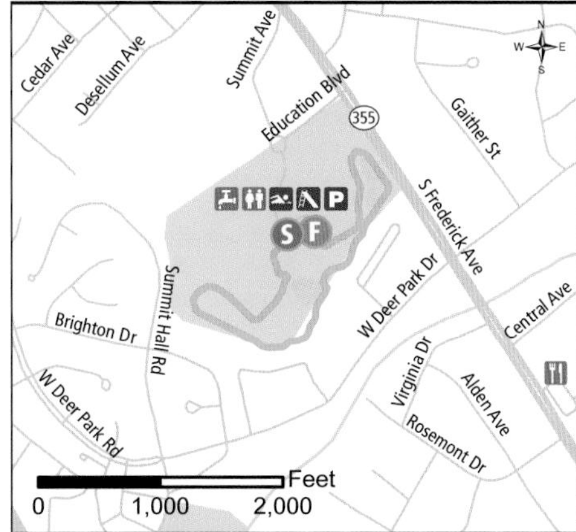

Ride K21 - Whalen Commons - Poolesville

The Maryland State Flag backed by blue sky.

Distance 0.2 miles

Terrain

A flat, painted-brick perimeter path rings the town's bright green lawn.

How to Get There

Take Interstate 270 north off the Beltway. Use exit 6A to go left onto West Montgomery Avenue and, soon, left again on Darnestown Road (MD 28). Look for White's Ferry Road (MD 107) bearing left toward Poolesville at the unincorporated crossroads of Dawsonville. It will roll you straight to your destination.

Amenities and Things to Do

The idea behind this super-short selection is to give the kids a chance to model what Mom and Dad just did out on the back roads. So grab a bite (within sight) after your ride, and let the children take over while you sit the bench, recuperate, and instruct. Then, in lieu of action at the amphitheater, explore the area's Civil War history. You'll have to pop inside a local business for a bathroom break.

About

Though this inclusion is admittedly a touch eccentric, being so slight and situated as it is so far out on the region's fringe, it is unquestionably safe, and offers the space the youngest ones need to get their wheels under them. That, and Poolesville's just country enough to convince you you've managed to escape the bonds of the city, however briefly.

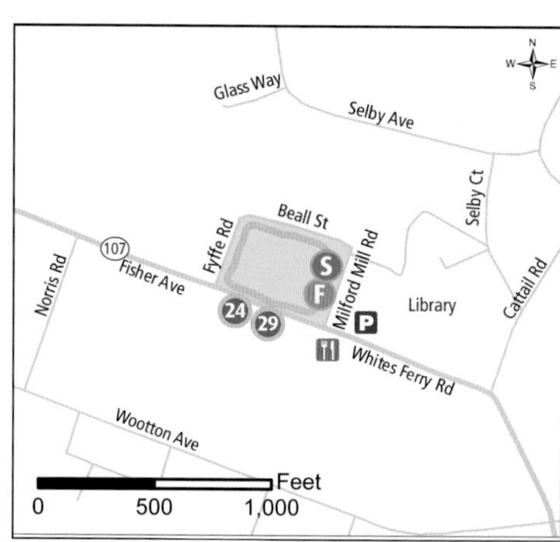

Ride K22 - Fallsgrove Park - Rockville

Distance 0.5 miles

Terrain

New asphalt trail and a sidewalk, smooth as can be.

How to Get There

Using Interstate 270 north off the Beltway, take exit 6A left onto West Montgomery Avenue (MD 28). Then look for a left onto Fallsgrove Drive. The park is on your left just beyond the Thomas Farm Community Center.

Amenities and Things to Do

Among the attractions here are four barbeque pits, numerous picnic tables, two tennis courts, three pieces of new-fangled playground equipment, swings, a pavilion, benches, and a community (members-only) garden. The adjacent community center offers tons of activities too, as well as bathrooms, drinking fountains, and vending machines. For more substantial food and beverage, continue away from West Montgomery a few hundred yards on Fallsgrove.

About

The prescribed half-mile is pretty much a perimeter loop, though your kids will surely find other little zigs and zags to occupy them. This clean, attractive space is newly dedicated, and also accessible by way of the Rockville Millennium Trail.

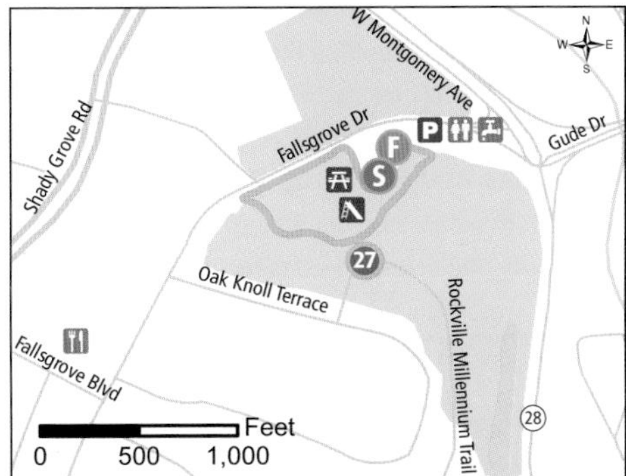

This is a white picket fence kind of place.

Ride K23 - Fairland Recreational Park - Fairland

Distance 3.25 miles

Terrain

Hard surface path drops and rises twice into and out of a wooded stream valley.

How to Get There

Use 95 north off the Beltway to exit briefly right on Powder Mill Road (MD 212). Go left at Old Gunpowder Road and follow it to the park. Alternatively, use Colesville Road/Columbia Pike (MD 29) off the Beltway to a right on Greencastle Road.

Amenities and Things to Do

Get back to nature here by way of a close encounter with nearly 300 undeveloped acres. When you're significantly reacquainted, utilize the area's playgrounds, courts, and ball fields, then have a look around the Fairland Sports and Aquatics Complex and The Gardens Ice House. Those two first-class facilities are stacked with opportunities for numerous indoor recreational activities, plus food, drinks, and restrooms.

About

This, the only bi-county park in the Maryland-National Capital system, also combines geographical elements of both the Piedmont and Coastal Plain. Start your exploration in either Montgomery or Prince George's. The mapped trail begins near the northernmost parking lot off Greencastle (though you could access the route using Old Gunpowder), enters woods, and drops down along Little Paint Branch before curving, rising, skirting fields, and circling a duck pond to retrace its path back.

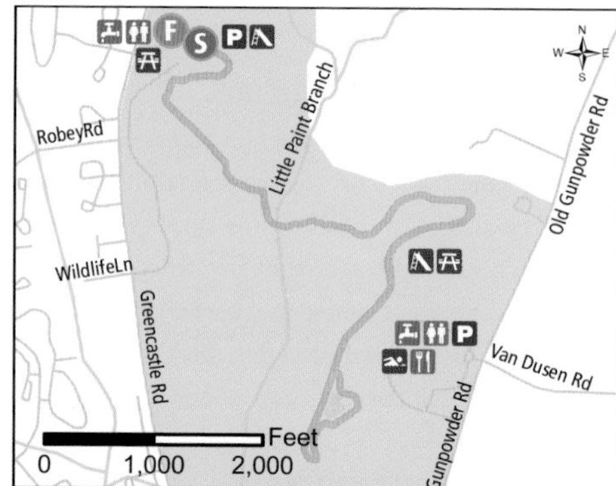

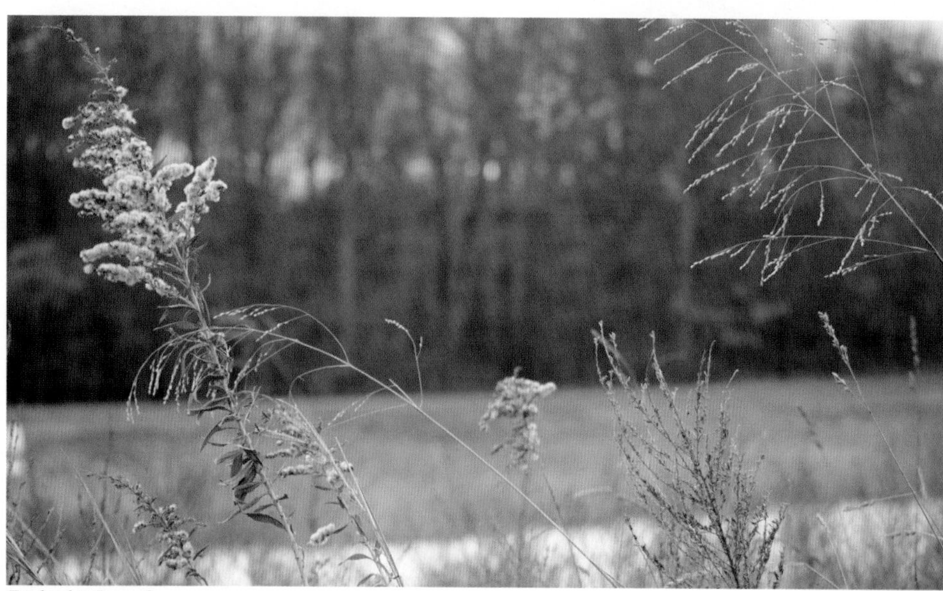

Fairland in December.

Ride K24 - Wheaton Loops - Wheaton

Distance 2.7 miles

Terrain

Nice asphalt trail twisting through hilly woods.

How to Get There

Take Georgia Avenue (MD 97) north off the Beltway past the Wheaton Metro and through University Boulevard. One of three park entrances is right down Shorefield Road. Veirs Mill Road and Randolph Road also provide proximate access.

Amenities and Things to Do

Merry-make on an old-fashioned carousel, ride on a miniature train, horseback ride, fish, ice skate, play tennis, basketball, baseball, or handball, enjoy a nature walk, picnic, or visit the renowned Brookside Gardens. That's all above and beyond the playgrounds and trails. Vending machines, water fountains, and bathrooms are readily available.

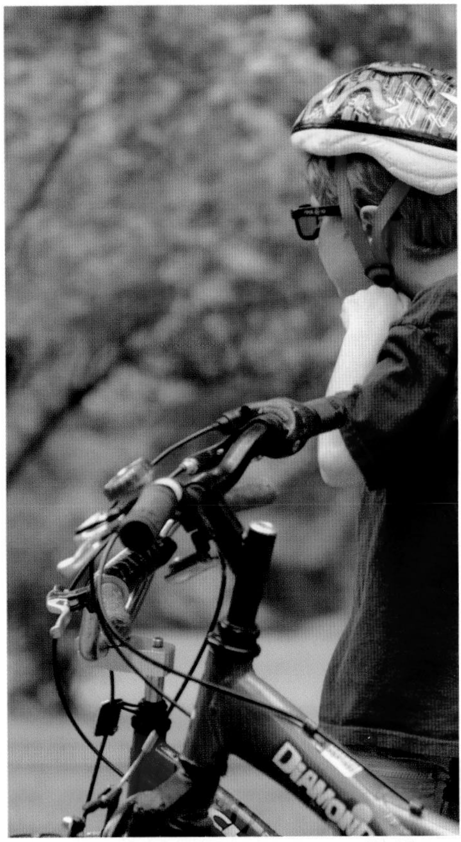

Buckling up.

About

This has to be one of the best parks in the entire region. Your littlest ones will be content around the play areas. Your bigger, more advanced bikers will love the prescribed loops. And your most adventurous and best riders will more than likely explore their way to the wide, gravel trail around Pine Lake.

Ride Log

0.0 Start at the Sligo Creek Trail sign on the path closest to the train's final swing into the station. Proceed over a bridge and into the woods before forking left.
0.3 Left again.
0.9 Cross road carefully to access second loop.
1.0 Go right to begin second loop.
1.7 Right to finish second loop.
1.8 Cross road.
2.35 Stay straight.
2.65 Left on bridge to finish near train station at SC Trail sign.

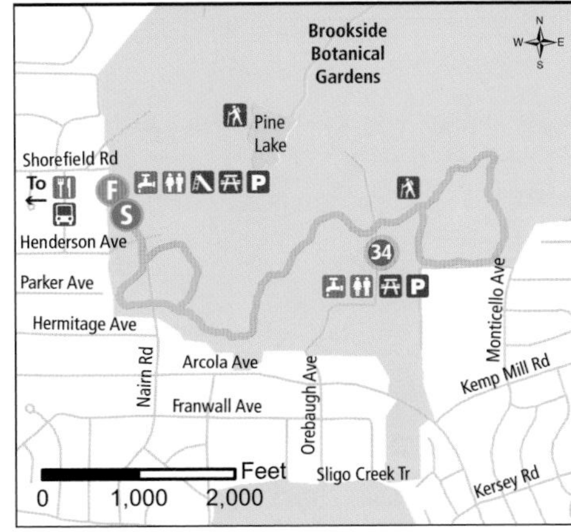

Ride K25 - MLK Jr. Park - Paint Branch - Silver Spring

"Have fun... and be careful."

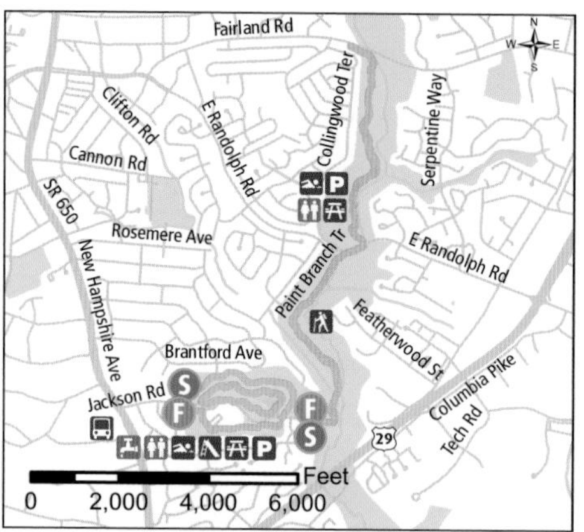

Distance 0.8, 1.2, 4.1

Terrain

Well-maintained, hard surface paths trace gently graded fields and a stream valley.

How to Get There

Take exit 28 north off the Beltway onto New Hampshire Avenue (MD 650). Continue under Columbia Pike (MD 29) then look to turn right onto Jackson Road.

Amenities and Things to Do

This open space and adjacent woodland is ideal for an afternoon outing. Hike and bike at your leisure, then picnic, fish the pond, swim indoors or out, and use the playground, courts and ball fields. Drinking water and bathrooms are on site. Pick up food near the New Hampshire/ Columbia Pike junction on your way in or out.

About

These three discreet routes could all be connected quite easily. Two move through a familiar park setting. The first circles the pond while the second loops more widely, crossing Jackson Road and skirting some parking lots in the process. The third wends its way alongside the Paint Branch, passing two mill sites that, dating back to the 1700s, are some of the oldest in Montgomery County.

Ride K26 - Jesup Blair Park - Takoma

It's all yours.

Distance
0.5 miles

Terrain
A nice, gently rolling, asphalt path.

How to Get There
Georgia Avenue (MD 29) brings you to Eastern Avenue. Buses are frequent. If driving, leave your car near the Jesup Blair House via a short access road on the park's north side. The Metro's Red Line Silver Spring Station is three-quarters of a mile north.

Amenities and Things to Do
After dipping and diving along the trail and its offshoots, play tennis, basketball, or soccer. There's a pavilion and playground as well. Duck across Georgia or into the Art Center of Montgomery County Community College for food, drinks, and restrooms.

About
Tucked between Metro tracks and the D.C./Maryland border, these 14.5 acres have much to recommend them. The Jesup Blair House, dating to the 1850s, is their centerpiece.

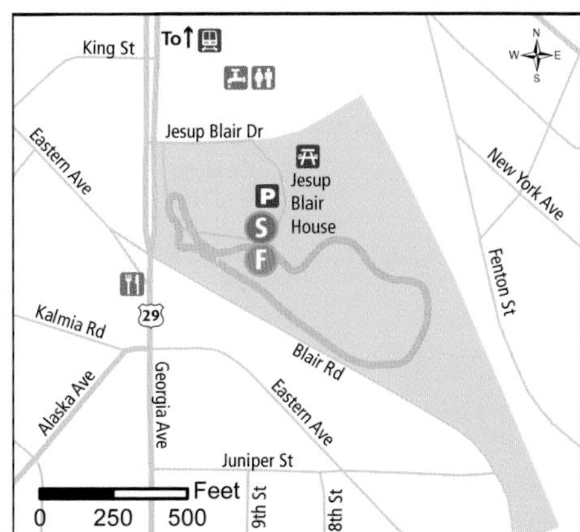

Ride K27 - The Savage Mill Trail - Savage

Distance 1.45 miles

Terrain

Wide, flat, natural surface trail runs through a lovely setting above the Little Patuxent River.

How to Get There

From Interstate 95, go right (east) on MD 32, then right (south) onto Route 1 (Washington Boulevard). Turn right again at Howard Street or Gorman Road and you'll begin to see directional signs for Savage Mill. Look to park on Foundry Street down near the bridge.

Amenities and Things to Do

Be sure to examine the Bollman Railroad Bridge up close. The woven geometry of its rust-red iron trusses is a compelling sight. Go inside to eat and shop then return outdoors refreshed to the challenge of the ropes and cables of Terrapin Adventures. If craving a longer bike ride, head down Fair Street two blocks to Savage Park and take the portion of the Patuxent Branch Trail running to Lake Elkhorn.

About

View this selection as a chance to get your littlest one her first mini-mountain biking experience. The way isn't difficult, just less smooth. Chances are she'll love it! There's history here too, of course. The river-powered, brick textile mill operated from 1822-1947. Canvas, its primary product, was fashioned into sails for clipper ships, helped multiple war efforts, and became painted backdrops for some of America's first silent movies.

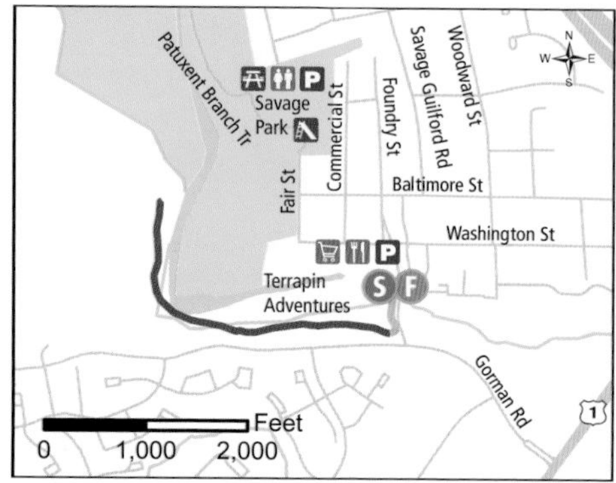

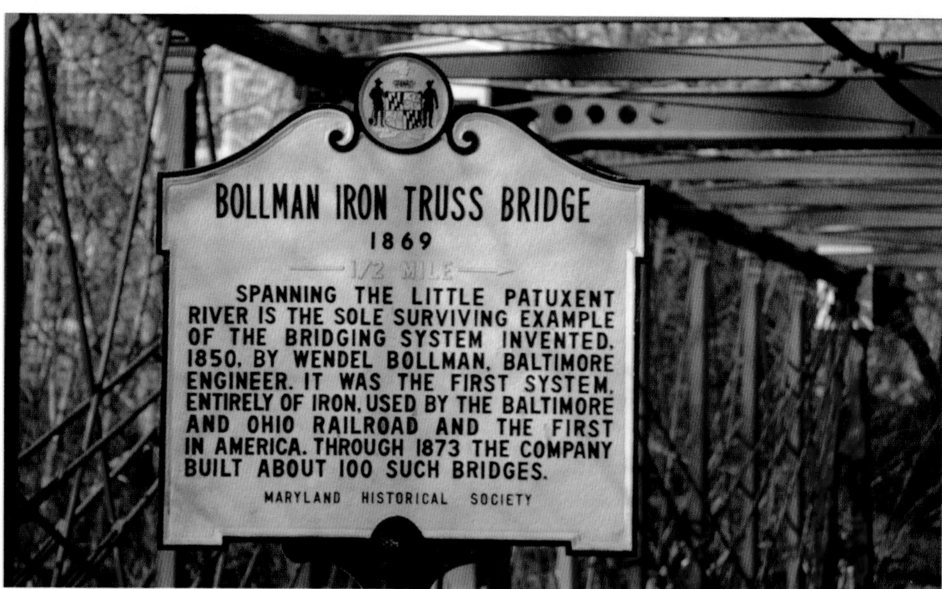

Begin your ride on this National Historic Landmark.

Ride K28 - Greenbelt Lake - Greenbelt

New Deal-era bas relief in Greenbelt.

Distance 1.3 miles

Terrain

Wide, crushed-stone path with a few minor twists and inclines.

How to Get There

Go to the Green Line Metro's last stop at Greenbelt. Exit the parking area left onto Cherrywood Lane to go over the Beltway. Follow that with rights on Ivy Lane and Kenilworth/Edmonston Avenue (MD 201) and a left on Crescent Road. The lake will be on your right beyond Albert "Buddy" Attick Park. If driving, take MD 201, exit 23, off the Beltway to Crescent.

Amenities and Things to Do

There are shelters here, with tables, benches and BBQ grills on an open hillside or down near the lake. Bathrooms, a basketball court, playground equipment, and a water fountain sit near the parking lot. Fishing and picnicking are popular. Go further down Crescent into greater Greenbelt for a convenience store and restaurant or two.

About

The historic city of Greenbelt was one of three "green" towns planned by the FDR Administration during the Great Depression. Construction on the project began with Greenbelt Lake on October 12, 1935, and the dig took one year and over 200 men to complete.

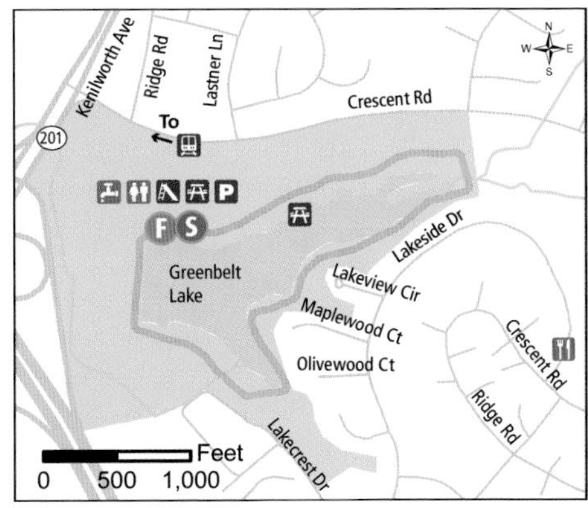

Ride K29 - Quiet Waters - Annapolis

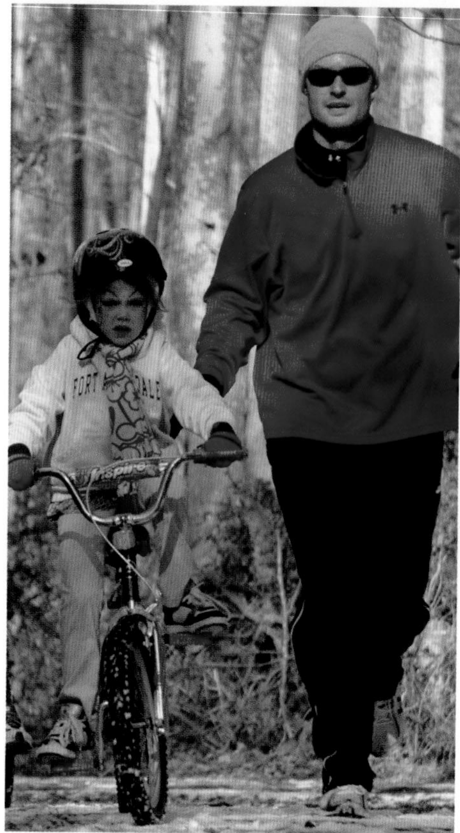
Sunday morning on the move.

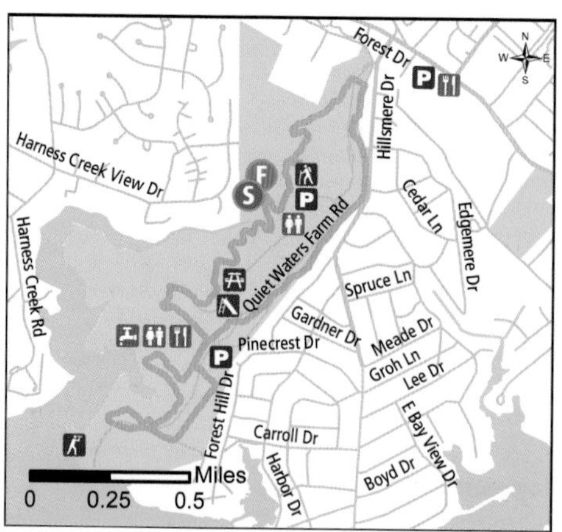

Distance 4.3 miles

Terrain

A well-paved path twists through woods and fields around this bayside jewel. Be mindful of a few low-traffic road crossings.

How to Get There

Take U.S. 50 east off the Beltway. Nearing Annapolis head southeast on MD 655/ Forest Drive. Go right briefly on Hillsmere Drive for park access.

Amenities and Things to Do

Use The Friends of Quiet Waters webpage for specifics on this park's annual Earth Day activities, Arts and Music Festival, summer concert series, rotating gallery exhibitions, and winter ice skating hours. Other amenities include food, drink, restrooms, pavilions, gardens, a playground, a dog park, and the Blue Heron event center. The seasonal Paddle or Pedal located down Harness Creek Trail rents watercraft of all kinds, as well as bicycles.

About

Though there's a $6 car fee here, cyclists have the option of parking across Hillsmere and spinning in. Access this ride's beginning by taking the first right after the entrance kiosk toward the Sassafras Pavilion. A path off the parking lot will connect you with the greater loop trail. Dog leg left at the Dogwood pavilion just past mile one then right at the Holly Pavilion just before a-mile-and-a-half to continue circling. And don't forget the scenic overlook just beyond mile two!

Ride K30 - Lake Artemesia - College Park

Distance 1.4 miles

Terrain

Flat, perfectly paved path wide enough to contain all comers.

How to Get There

Although College Park Metro is near, directions from its exit to the lake are a touch convoluted. In a nutshell, use sidewalks going right (east) along the Paint Branch Parkway to access the NE Branch Trail left (north). Driving instructions are equally involved. Use exit 22 off the Beltway to access Greenbelt Road (MD 193) toward College Park. After a slew of food and beverage options, look to jog right onto Branchville Road/55th Avenue. It will take you to a parking area near the lake at Berwyn Road.

Amenities and Things to Do

Along with aquatic gardens, fishing piers, the Luther Goldman Birding Trail, and ranger-led canoe and kayak programs, there are benches and shade by the score. Restrooms, water, and more information are available on the land "between" the lakes. The College Park Aviation Museum isn't far either.

About

Though this lake was famously created by Metrorail's need for earth to complete its Green Line, the resulting natural recreation area was a boon. The lily pad-filled pond offers sweet retreat, and its path has proven extremely popular for walkers, joggers, cyclists, and families alike.

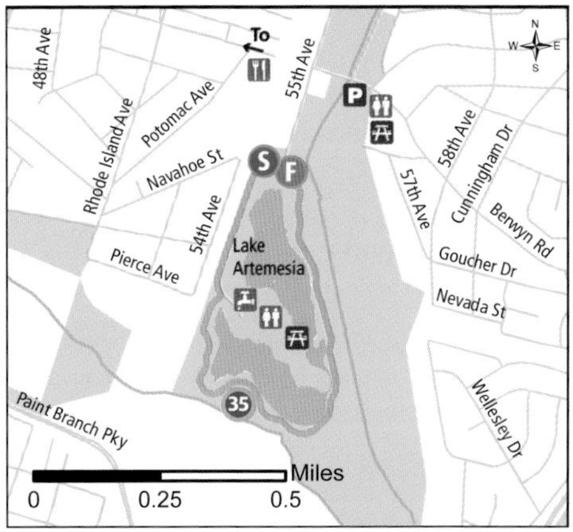

Looping the lake's aquatic gardens.

Ride K31 - Tucker Road Athletic Complex - Fort Washington

Distance 0.8 miles

Terrain

This perfectly flat path curves amongst woods, playing fields, and a pretty little pond.

How to Get There

Using exit 4 off the Beltway, go west on Saint Barnabas Road before merging right onto Oxon Hill Road. At the first light turn left onto John Hanson Lane then right back onto St. Barnabas at the second light. Continue through Bock Road intersection to a left onto Tucker Road. The athletic complex is on your left.

Amenities and Things to Do

After the bikes get locked up and you've exhausted the ball fields, the basketball and tennis courts, and the fitness and play equipment, try your hand at fishing the pond, skating the rink, or swinging the clubs. There are indoor possibilities too, not to mention vending machines, bathrooms, and showers.

About

Hanging in the middle of the linear Henson Creek Stream Valley Park, this community gem in southern Prince George's County is a popular piece of real estate for active folks who run the gamut. If you like to move, chances are you can do it here.

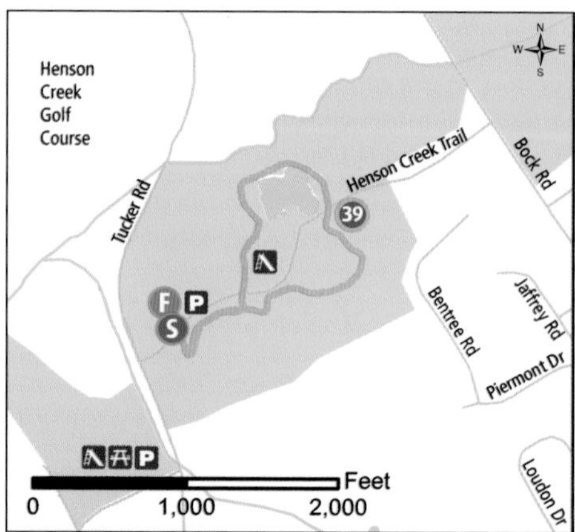

Not an uncommon sight along Henson Creek.

Ride K32 - President's Park - Lafayette Square

Distance 0.45 miles

Terrain

Smooth brick sidewalk over mostly flat ground traverses the heart of historic D.C.

How to Get There

Take the west exit of the Orange and Blue McPherson Square Metro. Go south one block on Vermont Avenue. Polish freedom fighter Tadeusz Kosciusko awaits you. On-street parking possible but could be patience-testing and time-limiting. Buses might be better options. Check schedules.

Amenities and Things to Do

Spin by the statues of Revolutionary War heroes in each of the park's four corners. Tune in to news crews and political protests. Get as up close and personal as possible with one of the most famous houses on earth. Dip into a restaurant or hotel north across H Street for food and restrooms.

About

Planned as part of the pleasure grounds surrounding the Executive Mansion, these seven, shaded acres have, instead, hosted a racetrack, a graveyard, a zoo, a slave market, and an Army encampment during the War of 1812. Today's incarnation is supposedly home to one of the densest squirrel populations known to science (as well as nuclear arms protestor Concepcion Picciotto, who has allegedly lived here continuously since August 1st, 1981).

Relaxing with friends in Lafayette Square.

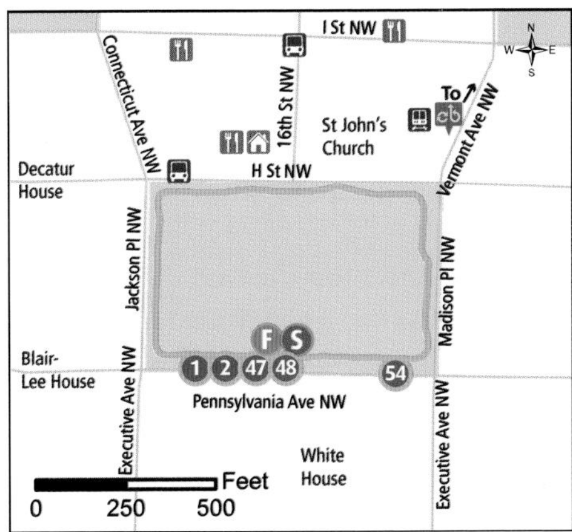

Ride K33 - President's Park - The Ellipse

"Is that me in front of the White House when I was little, Dad?"

Distance 0.55 miles

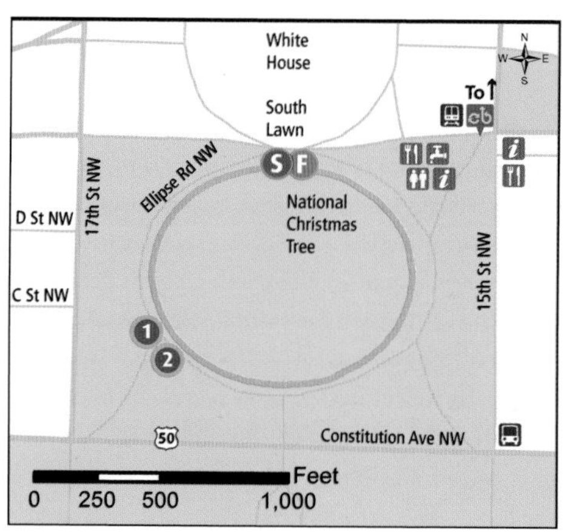

Terrain

Smooth, gently sloping, concrete footpath brings you joyously round and round.

How to Get There

The west exit of the McPherson Square Metro is also your safest bet here. Your destination now, though, is the White House's south side. Head through Lafayette Square to go left onto the car-free area of Pennsylvania Avenue (another unique place for riding). At 15th Street head right past the Treasury Department to E Street. Another right brings you in sight of your destination.

Amenities and Things to Do

The north-south view is refreshment in and of itself, but during warm weather months snack and drink trucks can be found to the east on 15th. Bring a Frisbee to toss, a ball to kick around, and a picnic to dig into. For more substantial fare head northwest to E or F streets. Restrooms are open weekdays at the visitor's center near the Sherman Memorial.

About

This beautiful expanse of lawn has bivouacked Civil War soldiers, witnessed religious revivals, and hosted the first-ever Boy Scout Jamboree. It's now home to games of all sorts, the White House Christmas Tree, the Zero Milestone, and other obscure to unknown statues and memorials.

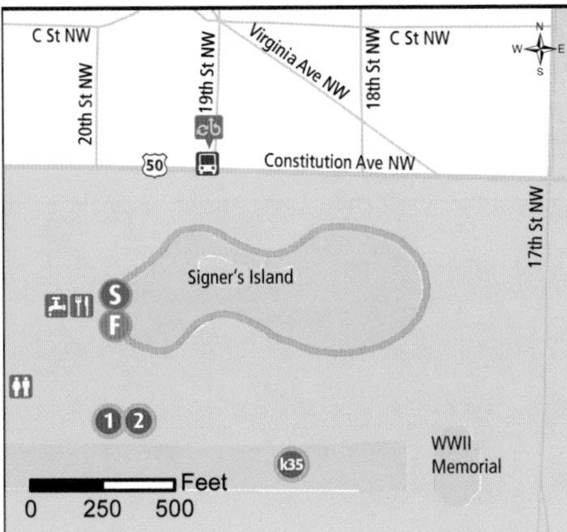

Distance 0.5 miles

Terrain

Wide footpath over gently sloping ground.

How to Get There

This ride is a bit farther from Metro. It remains advisable, though, as parking is a burden worth avoiding. The Orange/Blue Federal Triangle Station and the Smithsonian Station are a nice walk or a safe, sidewalk spin away.

Amenities and Things to Do

Ride, relax, and repeat. A snack shack and restrooms are right here.

About

This pleasant, contemplative lagoon and surrounding area has, at its heart, a monument to the 56 signers of the Constitution.

The coolest way to see the sites.

Ride K35 - The Memorial Mall - The Reflecting Pool

The Memorial Mall - Outer Reflecting Pool

Distance 0.95 miles

Terrain

Nice, smooth shaded footpath.

How to Get There

The Orange/Blue Federal Triangle, Smithsonian, and Foggy Bottom Metro stations are pretty much equidistant. Check bus schedules.

Amenities and Things to Do

Tell your kids about Dr. King's dream. There's a snack stand within sight. Restrooms are under Lincoln, over at Constitution Gardens, or better (and cleaner) yet, down near the WWII Memorial.

About

As well as connecting the WWII Memorial with memorials to Lincoln, Korea and Vietnam, this path connects Americans to their history. Millions have gathered here. Act like a tourist (but get up earlier or stay later) to soak it in.

The Memorial Mall - Inner Reflecting Pool

Distance 0.85 miles

Terrain

Wide footpath over flat ground.

How to Get There

Metro first, bus second, drive if you must. Parking is available by meter on surrounding streets and in local paid parking garages.

Amenities and Things to Do

Take in the view. Take in the view. Take in the view. You might want to pack a picnic as prices here can be steep. Bathrooms are free, thankfully. The one at the WWII Memorial is the newest.

About

You're just a bit below the tourist thicket here, and may find this a lesser-trafficked option. The ones nearest the WWII Memorial are best.

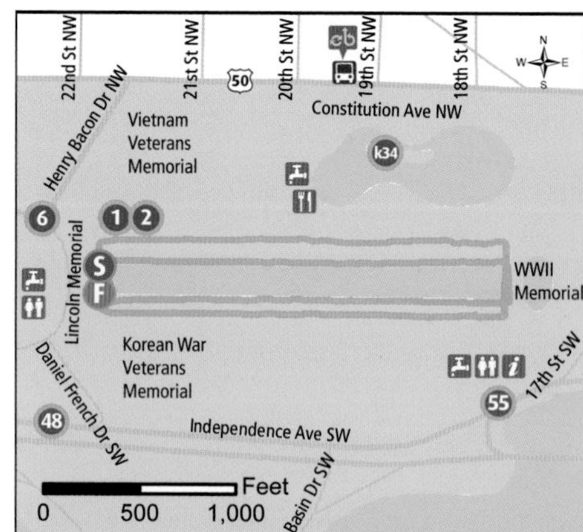

Riding along the Reflecting Pool.

Ride K36 - The National Mall - West

A cyclist waves to his child on the old carousel.

Distance 1.15 miles

Terrain

Wide, multi-purpose, pea gravel path over flat ground. Loose in parts.

How to Get There

Use the northern Mall exit of the Orange /Blue Smithsonian Metro Station. Parking is available by meter on surrounding streets and in local paid parking garages. The area is bordered by Madison and Jefferson drives and 14th and Seventh streets northwest.

Amenities and Things to Do

The red sandstone Smithsonian Castle, the institution's original building, is quite an architectural sight. There are restrooms, a café and public wifi inside. Outdoors you'll find an historic wooden carousel, room to roam and people (watching) aplenty.

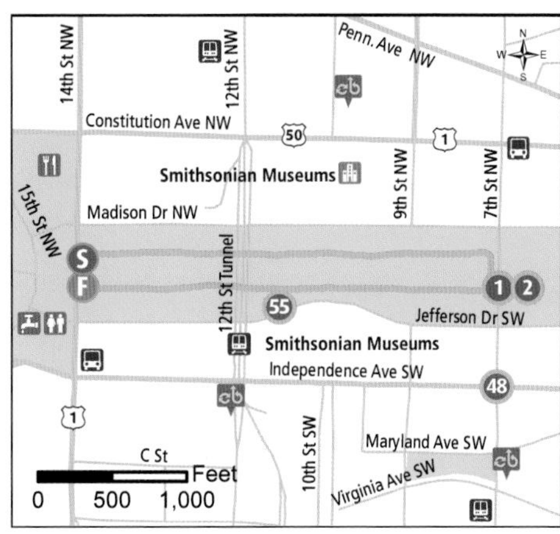

About

This ride is split from the following two National Mall rides for one simple reason, absolute traffic avoidance.

Ride K37 - The National Mall - Middle & East

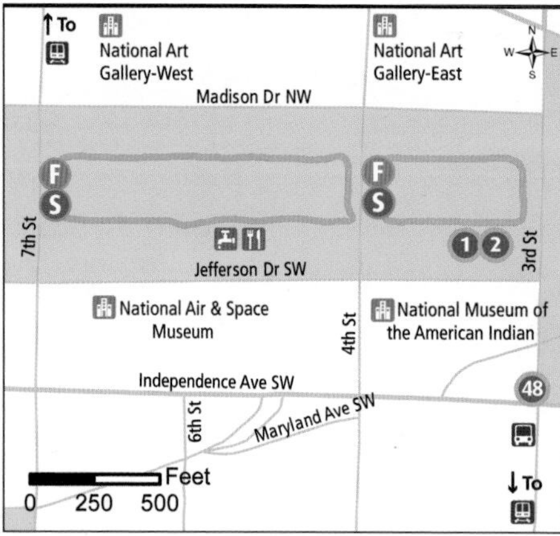

The National Mall - Middle

Distance 0.5 miles

Terrain

Wide, multi-purpose, pea gravel path over flat ground. Loose in parts.

How to Get There

The Smithsonian Metro is still there for you, but Yellow/Green/Orange/Blue L'Enfant Plaza's Maryland exit is closer to the south, as is Yellow/Green Archives Station to the north. Parking is available by meter on surrounding streets and in local paid parking garages. This space is bordered on the west by Seventh and the east by Fourth.

Amenities and Things to Do

Art, history, space, it's all yours. Bathrooms also free.

About

This huge space is the modern incarnation (reflecting the Mitchell Plan of 1901) of D.C. designer Pierre L'Enfant's 1791 vision of a grand avenue extending west of the National Capitol Building.

The National Mall - East

Distance 0.30 miles

Terrain

Wide, multi-purpose, pea gravel path over flat ground. Loose in parts.

How to Get There

L'Enfant Plaza's Maryland/Smithsonian Museum exit is still near, as is the Orange/Blue Federal SW Station. Parking remains available by meter on surrounding streets and in local paid garages. This section is bordered by Third and Fourth.

Amenities and Things to Do

You're surrounded by Smithsonians and lots and lots of space. (All free if you hadn't known.) Lock up and take advantage after your ride.

About

There's almost always something big going on here, be it a party, a protest, or those pervasive groups of middle-schoolers. The National Museum of the Native American, the 16th and newest Smithsonian Museum has restrooms and the Mitsitam Café, which features traditionally-inspired native food.

Space enough to make you smile.

Ride K38 - The Capitol Complex - Reflecting Pool

The incredibly life-like, artillery group section of the Ulysees S. Grant Memorial.

Distance 0.4 miles

Terrain

Concrete walkway over flat ground.

How to Get There

It's a quarter-mile walk from the Orange/Blue Federal Center SW Metro. Buses and on-street metered parking available as well.

Amenities and Things to Do

You'll be cycling under the U.S. Grant Memorial so be sure to look up, though you'll probably be doing that already as the U.S. Capitol Building looms above you in all its unrivalled glory.

About

This reflecting pool isn't as well-known as its skinnier big brother on the other end of the National Mall, but the area affords an equally great all-American view. You're actually riding over Interstate 395 here as it makes its brief drop belowground.

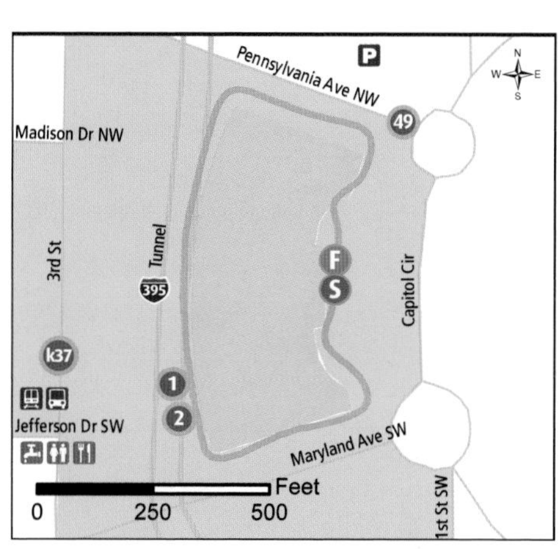

D.C. Originals Kids' Rides

Ride K39 - The Capitol Complex - East Loop d'Loop

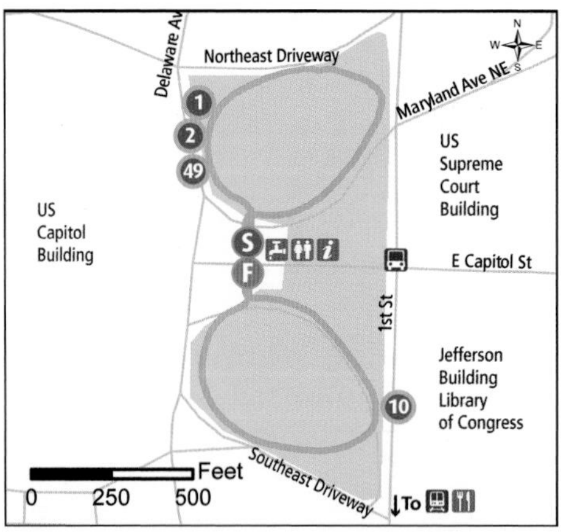

Don't overlook the Capitol grounds come blossom time.

Distance

0.7 miles

Terrain

Flat, smooth concrete footpaths join a new stone plaza.

How to Get There

The Orange/Blue Capitol South Metro will drop you a block-and-a-half away. Buses are legitimate options too. Drivers should be able to find metered spaces nearby.

Amenities and Things to Do

Take in the view. There's often a lovely breeze around sundown. Bathrooms are below ground in the visitor's center, which is new and of interest. Give yourself a minute in the Jefferson Building of the Library of Congress across First Street as well. It is without doubt one of D.C.'s most beautiful interiors. The Supreme Court isn't far either. Eateries near the Metro.

About

It's hard to disagree with D.C. designer L'Enfant's placement of the U.S. Capitol on this surprisingly high hill above what would one day become the National Mall. From its truly humble beginnings as the (much smaller) house of not only the nation's legislature but also its Supreme Court, Library of Congress, and sundry district courts, the U.S. Capitol Complex you are now wheeling freely through includes about a dozen buildings.

Also in this Series!

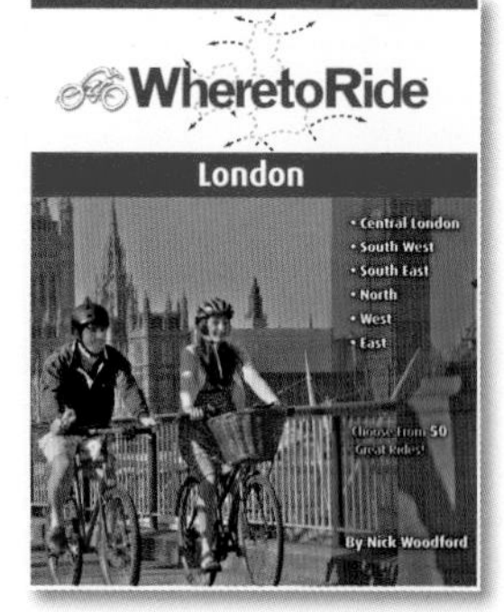

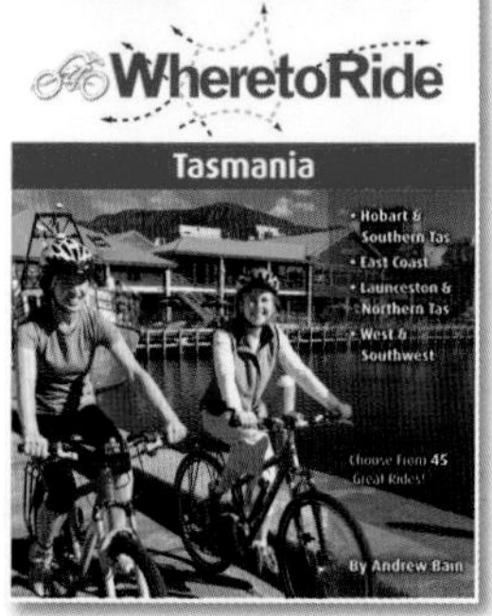

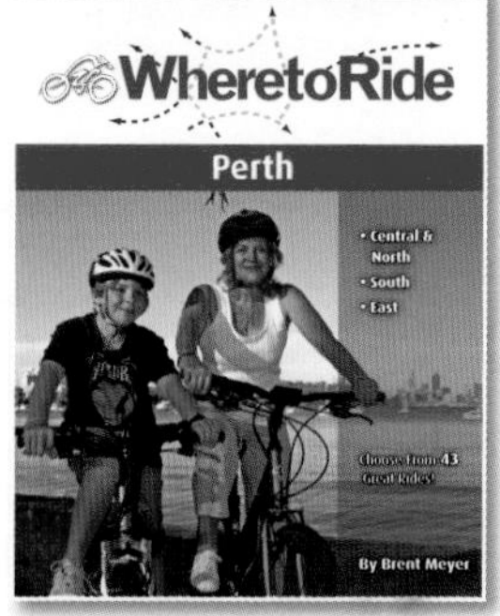

www.WheretoBikeGuides.com

Also in this Series!

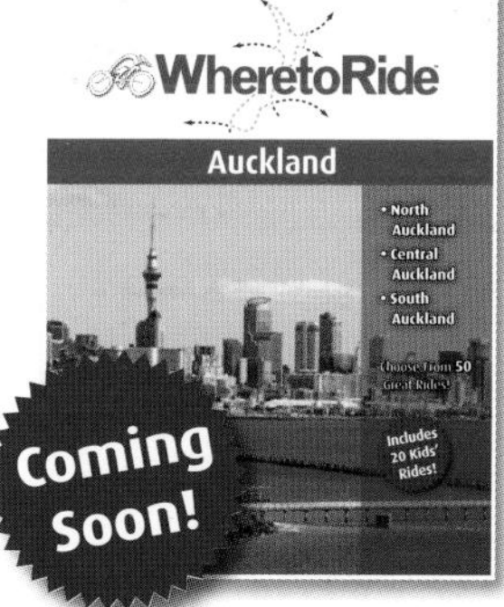

Notes

12/20/11